TOWARDS POSITIVE SYSTEMS OF CHILD AND FAMILY WELFARE

Edited by Nancy Freymond and Gary Cameron

The need for services that respond to the maltreatment of children and to the struggles of families is at the core of social service systems in all developed nations. While these child and family welfare systems confront similar problems and incorporate common elements, there are substantial differences in philosophy, organization, and operation across international settings and models.

In this new collection of essays, Nancy Freymond and Gary Cameron have brought together some of the finest international minds to provide an original and integrated discussion of child protection, family service, and community caring models of child and family welfare. The volume not only examines child protection and family service approaches within Western nations – including Canada, the United States, England, the Netherlands, France, and Sweden – it is also the first comparative study to give equal attention to Aboriginal community caring models in Canada and New Zealand.

The comparisons made by the essays in this volume allow for a consideration of constructive and feasible innovations in child and family welfare and contribute to an enriched debate around each system. This book will be of great benefit to the field for many years to come.

NANCY FREYMOND is a PhD candidate in the Faculty of Social Work at Wilfrid Laurier University.

GARY CAMERON is the Lyle S. Hallman Chair in Child and Family Welfare in the Faculty of Social Work at Wilfrid Laurier University.

EDITED BY NANCY FREYMOND
AND GARY CAMERON

Towards Positive Systems of Child and Family Welfare:

International Comparisons of Child Protection, Family Service, and Community Caring Systems

UNIVERSITY OF TORONTO PRESS
Toronto Buffalo London

© University of Toronto Press Incorporated 2006
Toronto Buffalo London
Printed in Canada

ISBN 10: 0-8020-9028-1 (cloth)
ISBN 13: 978-0-8020-9028-7 (cloth)

ISBN 10: 0-8020-9371-X (paper)
ISBN 13: 978-0-8020-9371-4 (paper)

Printed on acid-free paper

Library and Archives Canada Cataloguing in Publication

Towards positive systems of child and family welfare : international
comparisons of child protection, family service and community caring
systems / edited by Nancy Freymond and Gary Cameron.

Includes bibliographical references.
ISBN 13: 978-0-8020-9028-7 (bound)
ISBN 13: 978-0-8020-9371-4 (pbk.)
ISBN 10: 0-8020-9028-1 (bound)
ISBN 10: 0-8020-9371-X (pbk.)

1. Child welfare.   2. Family services.   I. Freymond, Nancy, 1962–
II. Cameron, Gary

HV713.T67 2006   362.7   C2005-905914-1

This book has been published with the help of a grant from the Canadian
Federation for the Humanities and Social Sciences, through the Aid to
Scholarly Publications Programme, using funds provided by the Social
Sciences and Humanities Research Council of Canada.

University of Toronto Press acknowledges the financial assistance to its
publishing program of the Canada Council for the Arts and the Ontario
Arts Council.

University of Toronto Press acknowledges the financial support for its
publishing activities of the Government of Canada through the Book
Publishing Industry Development Program (BPIDP).

Contents

PART ONE

Overview

1 Understanding International Comparisons of Child Protection, Family Service, and Community Caring Systems of Child and Family Welfare[1]

GARY CAMERON and NANCY FREYMOND

The policy and practice of protecting children living in unsafe environments and facilitating their proper development have limited common ground across international settings. There is no necessary line of reasoning that leads from the circumstances confronting children and their families to any one country's particular configuration of community, service, and legal responses. The creation of the 'problem of child maltreatment,' and how we deal with it, are best understood as particular discourses, or frameworks for understanding, which grow out of specific histories and social configurations. Neutral determinations about best responses to child maltreatment and superior systems of child and family welfare are not possible. Such determinations inevitably are shaped by the social and value contexts in which they arise (Marneffe & Broos, 1997).

Particular systems of child and family welfare are social configurations rooted in specific visions for children, families, community, and society. Various societies have constructed quite different responses reflecting their own priorities and desired outcomes. Building on this premise, a basic rationale for the international comparisons in this book is the conviction that 'to realize that elsewhere things are done differently expands one's confidence in the belief that "different" things can be done' (Hetherington, Cooper, Smith, & Wilford, 1997, p. 124). This realization allows us to step outside of what we take for granted in our own systems of child and family welfare, and to consider whether a value or procedure used elsewhere might improve what we are doing. It helps us to imagine and to believe in the possibility of more satisfying arrangements.

A basic tenet in this book is that every child and family welfare configuration is created out of a need to balance a common set of system design requirements. All systems must come to terms with similar challenges and choices. It is the nature of the choices made, and the balance struck among competing priorities, that give each approach to child and family welfare its unique profile. This chapter provides a brief overview of these common system design requirements and a sampling of the range of choices available. It provides a framework within which to understand the different countries' systems of child and family welfare presented in the following chapters.

All child and family welfare systems have their strengths and limitations, and their own cadres of proponents and critics. The discussions in this volume do not assume that any particular orientation is superior. There are, however, different priorities and choices reflected in the design of these systems. These are choices with consequences. Most importantly, as the analyses in this volume will indicate, the reported consequences of these choices for children and families, as well as for service providers working in these systems, differ in significant ways.

Child and family welfare systems mirror the cultural and institutional contexts in which they have evolved. These local cultural and institutional environments impose strong constraints on the choices any child and family welfare project will be allowed to try (O'Hara, 1998). Nonetheless, despite such barriers, looking at our own realities in light of experiences elsewhere highlights a range of possibilities, and underscores the fact that our current arrangements are neither inevitable nor universal. Both to generate hope as well as to stimulate creativity, it is worthwhile to examine our existing systems of child and family welfare in the light of a continuum of existing and suggested alternatives.

Three Generic Systems of Child and Family Welfare

The chapters in this book illustrate three generic systems of child and family welfare in 'developed' (relatively affluent) countries: child protection, family service, and community caring. These categories are heuristic. Like all 'ideal' constructions, these divisions do not neatly categorize all systems of child and family welfare. There is a good deal of diversity among settings falling within any of these generic categories of child and family welfare. In addition, some child and family welfare orientations may most appropriately be situated in a space between two categories.

The following chapters discussing different international approaches to child and family welfare are grouped under these three generic categories. They illustrate the commonalities and the variations that exist within each broad orientation to child and family welfare. They also provide an understanding of existing arrangements, discuss current controversies, and identify directions for reforms.

Child Protection Systems

The state is a regulator of social and moral arrangements, with an emphasis on individual rights and responsibilities. There is a clear division between private and public domains that protects the privacy of the family. Intrusion into families by child protection authorities is permitted only when parents violate minimum standards for the care of children. The primary focus of child protection is to protect children from harm in their own homes. Child protection service providers increasingly rely on adversarial judicial systems to confer authority on their work (Freymond, 2003). Reliance on state care of children has increased in recent years in many jurisdictions, and providing support for parent-child relationships is a secondary consideration. The child protection mandate is conferred on a stand-alone authority with minimal formal involvement by other service sectors or the broader community. The chapters on child protection in this volume focus on England, Canada, and the United States.

Family Service Systems

The state supports child and family welfare systems that reflect communal ideals about children, family, and community. Principles of social solidarity and, in some settings, of subsidarity (local responsibility) are emphasized. Fostering the proper care of children is seen as a shared responsibility. Providing support for parent-child relationships and the care of children are primary focuses. Demonstrating risks of harming children is not a necessary precursor for families or children to receive assistance. Some child and family welfare services are not separate from services to the general population. Legal systems are inquisitorial, and mediating dialogues with specialized judges and mandated officials are common in many settings. Ideally, there is an emphasis on reaching consensual agreements with families. The chapters in this volume examine family service orientations in France, the Netherlands, and Sweden.

Community Care Systems

Community care models are unfolding in many Aboriginal communities in various parts of the world. Ties to extended family, community, place, history, and spirit are considered integral to healthy individual identities. Ideally, community caring relies on consultations with parents, extended family, and the local community about the protection and care of children. Because of the devastating effects on Indigenous Peoples of colonialism, residential care, and child protection systems, a strong connection is made between caring for children and fostering a healing process for whole communities. A strong value is given to keeping children within their families and communities. Respect for traditional Aboriginal values and procedures is integral to community care processes. Two chapters in this volume assess First Nation community caring orientations in Canada, and another focuses on the Maori experience in Aotearoa/New Zealand.

Why Do Families Experience Difficulties?

At the root of every child and family welfare system are ideas about the nature of child maltreatment and the reasons why families have difficulty providing adequate care for their children. There is no single set of explanations of child maltreatment and family difficulties common to all child and family welfare systems. In addition, there is near unanimity in the literature that child maltreatment is a complex problem with many contributing elements (Ammerman & Hersen, 1990; Cameron, Vanderwoerd, & Peirson, 1997; National Research Council, 1993; Peirson, Laurendeau, & Chamberland, 2001).

The rationale for every child and family welfare system acknowledges the contributions that challenges with parental history, parental functioning, emotional and physical illness, substance abuse, lack of knowledge, social isolation, lack of child development opportunities, violence, economic distress, and community disintegration make to child maltreatment and family breakdown. Nonetheless, no child and family welfare system is organized with this full range of contributing factors all carrying equal weight. Likewise, no system is solely influenced by only one explanatory model. Each child and family welfare system places greater emphases on some of these challenges, and the particular combination of explanatory perspectives emphasized influences the ways help is given to distressed children and families.

Table 1.1 summarizes a selected range of explanations about why children are maltreated and why families experience difficulties caring for their children. Some of these perspectives exert great influence on existing child and family welfare systems, while others have achieved recognition only within smaller demonstration projects or have been highlighted by outside commentators. This selection of explanations provides an initial framework within which the various systems of child and family welfare discussed in this volume can be considered.

Parental Deficiency

A common perspective holds parents responsible for providing adequate care for their families. This is the de facto dominant emphasis in child protection systems. In child protection systems, parents are both entitled, and expected, to provide proper care for their children. If minimal norms for child care are violated, it is because the parents will not or cannot take proper care of their children (Marneffe & Broos, 1997; Martin, 1985; Schene, 1998; Swift, 1995a; Tunstill, 1997).

Within this perspective, parents have personality characteristics which prevent them from adequately providing and caring for their children. As a result, interventions focus predominantly on producing change in individual parents (usually the mother), rather than in the environments in which they live (Martin, 1985; Tunstill, 1997). Also, there is an implicit assumption that families do not normally need assistance with their child care. Consequently, the majority of families coming into contact with child protection systems do so through agency investigations and third-party reports of suspected child maltreatment. Furthermore, because parental behaviours often are considered harmful to their children, there is an insistence that parents carry out their child-care responsibilities or the children can be moved to another home where they can be adequately protected (Schene, 1998).

Family Breakdown

In some continental European systems, child maltreatment is primarily understood as a symptom of family dysfunction or breakdown. Within this frame of reference, the concern is with the health of the families as basic units of socialization and child development, and with the help families need to function properly. Family and parenting problems are

TABLE 1.1: Why Do Families Experience Difficulties?

Explanations	Implications of This Model
Parental Deficiency • Parents who maltreat their children often have problematic personality characteristics which are the root of the problem. • Parents are solely responsible for the care and well-being of their children.	• State, community, and extended family members are not expected to contribute to child well-being. • Parents will not come forward voluntarily for assistance. • Parents are generally assumed to be the major source of risk to children. Thus, children should be removed from parents, if it is thought to be in the child's best interest. • If families have problems, parents are responsible.
Family Breakdown • Child maltreatment occurs when the family is not functioning as a healthy unit. • Poverty, environmental stress, and lack of appropriate supports contribute to family dysfunction and child-care problems.	• Emphasis is placed on supporting families and maintaining child-family connections. • Children will be removed from the family's home without the parents' permission only in extreme cases. • Parents are expected to seek help voluntarily if they need assistance. • Emphasis is placed on providing support and social provisions for families.
Societal Breakdown • Child maltreatment results from inadequate support and resources. • Child care and development are shared responsibilities of society. • Family breakdown is as much a failure of society as individuals.	• Emphasis is placed on providing support and social provisions for families. • Greater involvement of the community in the functioning of families is expected. • Parents are expected to seek help voluntarily if they need assistance. • Children are removed from home as a last resort, usually only temporarily.
Continuum of Normal Behaviour • Child maltreatment is an exaggeration of normal behaviour in society. • At some point in their lives, most families will receive some sort of assistance.	• Emphasis placed on providing support and social provisions for families. • Children will be removed from the family's home without the parents' permission only in extreme cases. • Parents are expected to seek help voluntarily if they need assistance.

TABLE 1.1 (*concluded*)

Explanations	Implications of This Model
Risk and Protective Factors	
• There are risk and protective factors that contribute to the likelihood that families will experience difficulties. • Families with several risk factors are likely to experience more problems than others.	• To be effective, treatment and prevention programs should address many of these risk and protective factors. • Programs may need to cross service jurisdictional boundaries, and may need to be intensive and long-term.
Economic Distress and Community Disintegration	
• Family difficulties result from economic distress and community disintegration. • Most consistent predictor of child welfare involvement is living in extreme poverty and deteriorating neighbour-hoods.	• Focus on placing child and family healing within the context of the healing process for the whole community. • Emphasis placed on providing support and social provisions for families. • Focus on maintaining children within their communities and/or extended families
Systems of Oppression	
• Child maltreatment issues are rooted in economic, class, gender, and racial oppression. • Child welfare/ protection agencies are seen as reinforcing these oppressive relationships and being destructive of the ways of living of the people they 'target.'	• Agencies need to reform relations with oppressed groups. • Emphasis placed on providing support and social provisions for families. • Focus on collective, participatory responses to empower communities. • Calls for child welfare/ protection workers to advocate for social change based on their knowledge of their clients' lives.

perceived as being exacerbated by external circumstances such as poverty and environmental stress (Fox Harding, 1991). This view of family difficulties leads to an emphasis on supporting families and maintaining child-family connections. For example, this perspective has been influential in Belgium:

> Both the abuser and the child are perceived as victims influenced by broad sociological and psychological factors beyond their control ... Protection of the child is a priority, but the child is more often maintained in the child's family together with the provision of services to support the parents and help them cope. (Marneffe & Broos, 1997, p. 181)

Ideally, only in exceptional cases, where a child is in severe danger, should a child be removed from the family home without the family's permission. Within this approach, it is assumed that families often will seek out help with their children voluntarily (Olsson Hort, 1997; Marneffe & Broos, 1997; Roelofs & Baartman, 1997).

Societal Breakdown

A different perspective is emphasized by many First Nations and, to a lesser extent, by some more collective European societies, who view child development as a shared responsibility of the society. First Nations caring systems place a heavy emphasis on understanding the persistent negative impacts of colonialism, systemic racism, and economic and social disintegration in their communities as central to comprehending the plight of children, adults, and families. As evidenced by the community caring papers in this volume, the well-being of children, adults, families, and community are seen as indivisible and requiring attention in a respectful healing process. This perspective also leads to an emphasis on social provisions to support families and children. For example, in Denmark, the 'social infrastructure reflects a cohesive national concept of what constitutes quality of life for the individual and a belief that society has a collective responsibility to ensure that individuals have equal access to attaining quality of life' (Pires, 1993, p. 47).

Continuum of Normal Behaviour

Another influential perspective in continental Europe on child maltreatment was developed in the Berlin Child Protection Centres. This perspective views child maltreatment as a continuation or exaggeration of patterns to be found in most families and in society as a whole. In fact, from this point of view, child abuse does not differ significantly from patterns of oppression and violence that are both obvious and even praised elsewhere in society (Marneffe & Broos, 1997). Accordingly, no stigma should be attached to families seeking help and no implication made that they are somehow abnormal.

In child and family welfare systems influenced by this perspective, child abuse would not be separated out as a specific problem and would not be a necessary or even typical precursor for families' involvement. For example, Finland has a child and family welfare system 'in which child abuse as such is seldom reported or diagnosed as a specific problem for treatment ... From this perspective, it is difficult to identify child abuse as a separate problem requiring special treatment' (Poso, 1997, p. 160). Within the continuum of normal behaviour perspective, it is assumed that, at some point in their lives, most families will receive social welfare assistance (Marneffe & Broos, 1997; Olsson Hort, 1997; Poso, 1997).

Risk and Protective Factors

Another explanatory perspective has evolved from research on risk and protective factors for various social problems, including child maltreatment. This research concludes that child maltreatment and family breakdown are complex difficulties influenced by multiple factors. Families involved with child and family welfare agencies often have difficulties in many areas of living, including family functioning, addictions, individual physical and mental health, finances, social integration, and access to community resources. As well, this research shows that many of these difficulties tend to 'cluster' together into common profiles for many distressed parents and children (Cameron, O'Reilly, Laurendeau, & Chamberland, 2001; Nelson, Laurendeau, Chamberland, & Peirson, 2001; Peirson, Laurendeau, & Chamberland, 2001). From this point of view, there is no clear theoretical or empirical way to isolate one or more problems as the key points for intervention. To be effective, a range of risk and protective factors for both parents and children needs to be addressed simultaneously and sequentially.

Economic Distress and Community Disintegration

Another position views family breakdown and child maltreatment as being substantially influenced by economic distress and community disintegration. Proponents of this explanatory model point out that the most consistent and strongest statistical predictors of having an open child protection case, in Anglo-American child protection systems at least, are living in extreme conditions of poverty and neighbourhood dissolution; this relationship is even stronger for families with children in out-of-home care (Costin, Karger, & Stoesz, 1996; Courtney, 1998; English, 1998; Lawrence-Karski, 1997; Peirson, Laurendeau, & Chamberland, 2001). In addition, during economic hard times, the number of families experiencing difficulty caring for their children increases, as does involvement with the child and family welfare system (Hughes, 1995). This perspective emphasizes the need to bring more helpful social and economic resources to struggling families, individually as well as through local community capacity building and more equitable social and economic policies.

Systems of Oppression

Some authors see family breakdown and child maltreatment rooted in economic, class, gender, and racial oppression. Child protection systems, in particular, have been described as reinforcing these oppressive relations and as destructive of people and traditional ways of living (Armstrong, 1995; Swift, 1998; Thorpe, 1994). For example,

> because the foundation of patriarchal public policies is based on the traditional beliefs about women and their place in society, these policies become self-fulfilling ... stingy services are provided by ill-paid women to women and their children, selected because of their inability to provide for themselves. The status quo is maintained. (Callahan, 1993, p. 196)

Such a perspective prescribes a radical shift in existing relations. Proponents favour more generous social provisions and, in particular, they propose collective and participatory responses which respect and empower families and communities (Maidman & Connors, 2001; McKenzie, 1989; 1997; Morrissette, McKenzie, & Morrisette, 1993; Swift, 1995a; Wharf, 1992).

To improve outcomes for children and families, it is essential to realize that there are various ways of understanding the reasons why families experience difficulties. Perspectives on the causes of child maltreatment and family breakdown dramatically influence the approaches taken to assist children and families. Because culture and values play such an important role in how our world is understood, it is easy to forget that there are alternatives to our particular ways of seeing children, families, and communities. Awareness of a range of perspectives on these complex and controversial issues has the potential to expand the boundaries constraining our particular notions of proper ways to help children and families.

Choices in Child and Family Welfare System Design

All child and family welfare systems have a set of common design dimensions along which they may be compared. This section of the book identifies these dimensions and briefly discusses the different choices associated with each dimension. The purpose is to identify a spectrum of possibilities in child and family welfare system design. In addition, this overview provides a supplementary framework for considering the various systems of child and family welfare examined in subsequent chapters.

Managing Dual Mandates

Each of the three generic systems of child and family welfare operates within a dual mandate, incorporating only partially compatible requirements to provide care or assistance to children and families, and to exert control over their behaviour. However, there are important differences in how various child and family welfare orientations manage these mandates.

Child protection systems increasingly are focused on monitoring and controlling the behaviour of parents in high-risk families. The typical initial response of child protection systems is one of a mandatory legal investigation of an allegation of child maltreatment, with any care responses coming later in the process if at all. It is the formal authority of the law and the courts that provides the primary legitimacy for intervening in families. Formal and contested court proceedings to stipulate supervision conditions for children in the family home, or to remove children from the home, are common within this control emphasis.

At the same time, family service systems strive to emphasize the provision of service to maintain the family and the parent-child bond as an initial response. Except in extreme situations, family service systems focus on finding ways to support family functioning. As an illustration, in Finland, preventive, nonstigmatizing, and supportive measures and services encourage and support the maintenance of children in their own homes:

> Maternity and child health clinics have expanded and diversified family training, and intensified co-operation with families. In day care, various forms of co-operation supporting parental participation were developed.

Also home help services have been developed to support child rearing by
parents (Tuomisto & Vuori-Karvia, 1997, p. 92).

In these family service systems, the use of formal coercion and contested court involvements is considered a last resort and avoided, if
possible. Some family service systems (for example, those in France and
Belgium) make frequent use of the authority of specialized family
judges in a relatively informal fashion to negotiate intervention plans
with families and service providers. Other countries, such as Finland,
Germany, and Denmark, also have legislated informal negotiations
with families to try to resolve child care concerns (Bering Pruzan, 1997;
Wolff, 1997).

First Nations' visions for community caring systems prioritize providing support to families and maintaining children in their own community as initial responses. They place the highest emphasis of the
three generic systems on the involvement of relatives and others in the
local community in the process. The approach taken by the Cham-
pagne/Aishihik Band illustrates these principles by working with parents, extended family, and community members to develop a plan of
action and to identify resources for the family within the community.
Ideally, parents' hardships are acknowledged, and although they should
not be blamed for these problems, there is an insistence that parents
take ownership of the difficulties and take an active role in problem-
solving. The involvement of the community is intended to connect
parents and children with helping resources and to provide support for
the family (Wharf, 1992). However, as discussed in the community
caring chapters, community caring systems function within the broader
context of countries with dominant child protection systems. Consequently, they are heavily constrained by the investigative and legal
orientations of these larger systems.

Child and family welfare systems also differ in the extent to which
they house the care and control dimensions of their mandates within
one agency. Child protection systems usually invest their child protection mandate in a single public or parapublic agency. These systems
operate under specific legal guidelines and have close connections with
the courts, and increasingly with the police. Other social service and
community organizations (unless under contract to supply specific types
of child protection services such as foster care or in-home supports)
have a comparatively minimal and unclear involvement in the protection mandate.

Many family service systems formally involve their broader social service networks, as well as specialized child and family welfare support agencies, in their mandates. In addition, family service systems typically have separate jurisdictions where child abuse specialists are housed and where formal legal actions and child placements are managed. Belgium exemplifies this approach by having two separate functional areas for its care and control operations (Hetherington, Cooper, Smith, & Wilford, 1997).

The community caring chapters in this volume stress that First Nations strive to involve all relevant local organizations in the provision of child and family services. As mentioned, they place a very high priority on involving all relevant family and community members, sometimes through local self-government institutions. Because of a paucity of formal services in many First Nation communities, securing culturally appropriate assistance from non-Indigenous agencies is an ongoing challenge. These efforts take place within an evolving context of negotiating a place for respectful community caring within the expectations of larger child protection environments.

Relationship with the Legal System

One of the central choices in constructing child and family welfare is defining the role of the legal system (judges, courts, police). Formal legal authority plays an important part in every child and family welfare system; however, the point at which formal legal authority is used and the use of the legal system varies widely across settings.

In child protection systems, families have a right to privacy and the state, represented by the child protection agency, becomes involved only if there is a suspicion that the minimum legal standards of child care have been violated. From the beginning, in mandatory investigations of reports of child maltreatment, the child protection agent must be conscious of gathering evidence to ascertain (and, if necessary, to prove in court) that a transgression has taken place, in order to justify the agency's continued intervention with the family.

During investigations, child protection workers typically complete standardized recording forms. This formal record is structured to satisfy the requirements of gathering evidence that can be used in court. Child protection systems work within adversarial legal systems in which the role of the judge is to decide between formal arguments presented by lawyers representing each party to the dispute (often the parents, the

children, as well as the child protection agency). Due process considerations are paramount and have led to 'new training programs, new
legislation and procedures designed to increase specificity and "objectivity" in the evidence gathering procedure' (Swift, 1997, p. 52).

The intention in family service systems is that the first responses to
most reports of child maltreatment be an assessment of the family's
situation and an offer of help to the family. How this help is given is
guided substantially by professional judgment and local interactions,
rather than by prescribed procedures or the requirements of gathering
evidence for possible legal proceedings. Usually, there is a stated intention to avoid involvement with the formal legal system as much as
possible.

As indicated, some family service systems have created intermediate
structures where negotiations between the family members, the service
workers, and the mediator or judge can take place. Inquisitorial legal
systems allow judges in some family service systems to take a more
active and informal role in asking questions and gathering information
than is permitted in adversarial legal systems common in English-
speaking countries. In inquisitorial systems, fewer child and family
welfare cases reportedly go to contested court hearings, and most
service decisions – even those involving the placement of a child – are
made with parental agreement.

For example, the Belgian approach to child and family welfare has
separated supportive services to families from interventions ordered by
the legal system. This separation is described as allowing 'social workers, doctors, and other professionals concerned about children to consult with the VAC teams (a specialized child and family welfare service)
without reporting to the judicial system ... The VAC ... (also) provide an
intensive therapeutic service to [self] referred families' (Luckock, Vogler,
& Keating, 1997, p. 109). The Belgian system also attempts to avoid
unnecessary court involvement through a lay mediation procedure.
Only when all of these voluntary involvements cannot be made to work
should the power of the formal legal system be invoked, except in
emergencies (Luckock et al.). Reportedly, self-referrals by maltreating
parents rose from 2% to 38% under these arrangements; the risk of a child
being reinjured was reduced; and, between 1986 and 1994, 81% of children in care were returned to their families (Marneffe & Broos, 1997).

Similarly, the inquisitorial courts in Germany provide an intermediary space for negotiations with families involved in the child and
family welfare system:

Parties can be represented and witnesses can be heard but the judge holds sole responsibility for the investigation ... Judges have a mediating as well as an investigative function and will frequently conduct 'round table' discussions which take into consideration all the provisions available under the KJHG ['Kinder und Jugendhilfegesetz' – Children and Youth Services Act] to help a child and its family. (Wilford, Hetherington, & Piquardt, 1997, pp. 18–19)

German families are expected to be involved in all decisions concerning their welfare, especially when developing a plan of action in cases of crisis or need (Wilford, Hetherington, & Piquandt, 1997). However in cases of extreme severity, or when agreements cannot be reached, interventions for families are legally mandated (Wolff, 1997).

Ideally the legal system does not play a central role in First Nations' visions of community caring systems of child and family welfare. The adversarial and authoritarian nature of contested court procedures run counter to the importance First Nations place on self-determination and community empowerment. For example, in 1980, the Spallumcheen Band in British Columbia passed a by-law in which they assumed full control of child welfare services. Under this by-law 'apprehending authority and final decision-making reside with the ... Chief and members of the Band Council, [and] placement and review decisions are made by means of a vote at Band Council meetings following lengthy informal discussion by all who wish to speak' (McKenzie, 1989, p. 9). However, it is important to highlight once again that most efforts to create community caring systems by Aboriginal peoples take place within the broader contexts of child protection systems in English-speaking countries. This creates a constant tension for these initiatives as proponents try to negotiate the child protection expectations of the broader society as well as pursue their own preferences for models congruent with Indigenous experiences and values.

The Nature of Authority

Some parents will resist intrusions into their homes, regardless of how they are approached. Eventually each child and family welfare system must be able to use formal authority to compel family compliance or to remove children from a home. However, systems differ in the extent to which they use authority other than the coercive power of the law to engage families. A core decision in the design of child and family welfare systems is the relative balance desired among the primary bases of authority or legitimacy to be used in engaging families.

As indicated, in child protection systems, where individual rights and family privacy are central values, the legal power of the state is the prime mode of ensuring access to families. In more communal societies, including some continental European countries and First Nations, the well-being of children and families is understood to be a collective responsibility. Ideally this perspective leads to more ready acceptance of community norms of helping by families as reasons for their engagements with professional or community helpers. The flip side of this social contract is that families also have expectations of assistance from the collectivity with the responsibilities of child care.

A related consideration is the extent to which lay people and civic groupings have an active role to play in child and family welfare systems. In child protection systems, for all practical purposes, child protection is the purview of service and legal professionals. In contrast, nonprofessional involvement is most dramatic in some First Nations communities, where child and family welfare services are directed and delivered through self-government institutions and community networks. In addition, consulting with nonprofessionals is heavily emphasized in some Innu and Inuit communities. When a decision must be made about the removal of a child from his/her family, ideally the judge will ask 'everyone involved in the child's life, from distant aunts to family friends, to come talk at the hearing ... He understands that here people are not individuals, that [they] are a part of a very extended family' (Toughill, 2001).

To a lesser extent, involvement of civil society in child and family welfare is evident in some European systems, reflecting their concepts of social solidarity and subsidarity. For example, in Denmark, the power to authorize involuntary, out-of-home placements is vested in local elected Children's Boards (Bering Pruzan, 1997). Belgium also exemplifies this involvement of lay helpers in its child and family welfare system: 'Each Committee [Special Youth Assistance] consists of a council of 12 volunteers active in child welfare and each carries responsibility for an administrative district' (Luckock, Vogler, & Keating, 1997, p. 104).

Systems also differ in whether they require by law community professionals and the general public to report to child and family authorities any suspicions that they have about children being maltreated. Both child protection and family service systems are found in societies which have mandatory child maltreatment reporting requirements (for example, Canada and Finland). Likewise, both types of systems are found in societies without mandatory reporting laws (for example, England and Germany).

The argument for mandatory reporting is the belief that more vulnerable children will receive protection from harm. The danger is that parental fear of the intrusions of designated authorities, in child protection systems at least, will attach itself to other service organizations. As a result, parents needing help may be less willing to come forward. Mandatory reporting may have different meanings for families where the system's first response is an offer of assistance than where formal investigations are required by law.

In addition, there is no evidence from our review clarifying whether or not finding and providing assistance to children at risk of maltreatment is more effective in systems with mandatory reporting. There also is no evidence that child protection systems with or without mandatory reporting legislation are superior to other child and family welfare paradigms at preventing child maltreatment deaths. For example, a recent report for the United Nations Children's Fund (Innocenti Research Centre, 2003) about child maltreatment deaths in rich countries found that the United States had a rate of child deaths from abuse of 22 per million population, while Spain, Greece, France, Poland, and Holland reported much lower rates (1, 2, 5, 5, and 5 per million, respectively). Canada had a rate of 7 child abuse deaths per million population.

Separate or Embedded Child Welfare Organization

One of the basic decisions in child and family welfare system design is whether child protection functions are to be allocated uniquely to a specialized unit or shared across several social welfare and/or justice units. Child protection systems in England, the United States, and Canada have invested their child protection mandate in stand-alone public or parapublic agencies. The rest of the social welfare delivery system has no clear role in carrying out the protection mandate, although other agencies are often involved with the same families.

In family service systems, the child and family welfare mandate typically is shared across multiple partners in the social welfare and youth justice systems. It is common for local general service organizations to provide assistance to distressed families and to be the first contact with many families suspected of maltreatment. Some of these service organizations may have formal mandates within the child and family welfare system. Other elements of the social welfare systems in these countries, such as day care and community nursing, are frequently used to enrich child protection and family support:

> [In Finland] the child welfare legislation reforms of 1990 emphasise preventive, non-stigmatising, and supportive measures and services. One of the central objectives of the reform was to shift the emphasis of child welfare from extra familial care to measures that encourage and support the maintenance of children in their own home. As a result, work methods of all welfare services were adapted toward strengthening child rearing by carers. Maternity and child health clinics have expanded and diversified family training, and intensified co-operation with families. In day care, various forms of co-operation supporting parental participation were developed. Also home help services have been developed to support child rearing by parents. (Tuomisto & Vuori-Karvia, 1997, p. 92)

Family service systems often have specialized units, usually within the youth justice system, which focus on investigation and enforcement. The boundaries between the care and control components of these family service systems have been described as fluid, with information flowing informally both ways. For Luckock, Vogler, and Keating (1997), this raises concerns about confidentiality of information about families. Also, as discussed in the family service chapters in this volume, cooperation across the care and control sectors in family service systems can be challenging.

A related choice in child and family welfare system design is how families may enter the system. Child protection systems have single access points, as well as the narrowest criteria for entering the child protection system. As mentioned, most involvements come on the basis of third-party reports of suspected child maltreatment which are then substantiated or dismissed in the process of a formal investigation. To enter the formal child protection system, families must be proven to be abusive or neglectful of their children, or likely to become so in the near future; increasingly fewer engagements are on the basis of mutual consent.

Many continental European family service systems have several access points, including social welfare agencies serving the general population or serving a broad range of families in difficulty. Many families reportedly become involved when either a parent or a child requests assistance, or on the basis of an offer of service from the agency following up on a report of suspected child maltreatment. There is usually no specific requirement that assessment criteria indicate a risk of child maltreatment in order for someone to receive assistance. For example: '[in Sweden] child abuse or neglect is not a necessary or even typical precondition for beginning child welfare services. It is part of the normal course of life that children receive child health and welfare services' (Olsson Hort, 1997, p. 107).

Maintaining Families and Protecting Children

All child and family welfare systems balance the goals of maintaining the family as a viable social unit for child development and protecting the child's right not to be harmed physically, sexually, or emotionally in his or her home. All systems have the capacity to remove children from their parents' home; likewise, all have some capacity to assist families with their child-rearing responsibilities. However, the differences in relative emphasis across systems are striking.

In some family service systems, the connection between children and their parents is rarely severed completely or permanently. In addition, all family service systems place greater importance than child protection systems upon attaining parental agreement with intervention plans (sexual abuse is an exception in some settings, leading to quick involvement with the justice system). As well, all family service systems go to greater lengths to provide supportive services to families than child protection systems are able or disposed to do. In family service systems, healthy families are viewed as fundamental for social cohesion and properly educating children. In these more communal cultures, the well-being of families is not secondary to protecting individual rights.

The priority placed on family support is exemplified in Germany's Child and Youth Service Act (1990), which emphasizes providing extensive 'preventive and supportive measures to help with the care and education of children in their families' (Hetherington, Cooper, Smith, & Wilford, 1997, p. 68). This approach also is evident in Denmark where policy is designed to 'facilitate a voluntary, family-oriented approach to the problem of child abuse' (Bering Pruzan, 1997, p. 126).

Similarly, in First Nations' visions of community caring systems, a great emphasis is placed on keeping children in their families and communities, and other forms of care are considered less satisfactory:

Placement priorities, in order of preference, are the extended family, families within First Nations communities in the tribal council area, other First Nations families, and non-First Nations caregivers ... extended family placements outside the community and family foster homes within the community were given relatively equal weight. This indicates the importance attached to community as well as family connections. (McKenzie, 1995, p. 644)

The discussions in this volume indicate that, in First Nations' conceptions of child and family welfare, the well-being of children, parents, families, and community are parts of an indivisible whole.

In contrast, in child protection systems, the child's right to be protected from harm takes precedence by law over any consideration of the family's need for assistance to care for the child. Child protection systems primarily intervene in order to protect children from harm in their homes. Consequently, much less emphasis is placed on the importance of maintaining children's connections with family and community than in other orientations to child and family welfare.

A related choice in systems design is whether to use the concept of child maltreatment as the central organizing concept for the child and family welfare system, or to operate within a broader framework of child, family, and community welfare. Beginning with the 'discovery' of child abuse in the 1960s in America, the focus of child protection systems has narrowed from an already limited conception of child welfare to a concentration on physical, sexual, and emotional child abuse (Swift, 1995a). Conversely, family service systems typically are incorporated into a broader philosophy of societal, family, and child welfare. In family service systems, a more collective ideology is reflected in higher levels of social provisions and, in theory, less blaming of families experiencing difficulties. For example:

[In Finland] from the multi-problem perspective, physical violence or child abuse in the family is seen as too narrow a category that emphasizes the symptoms of the problem more than the basic causes and stigmatizes or blames the perpetrators too easily. (Poso, 1997, p. 153)

As is evident in the community caring chapters in this volume, First Nations in Canada as well as the Maori in Aotearoa / New Zealand envision child and family welfare systems incorporating holistic concepts of healing for individuals, families, and whole communities.

Discretion and Control

A fundamental system design choice is whether to place confidence in decisions made based on the judgment and training of local service providers, or to rely on the standard prescriptions and controls characteristic of formal bureaucracies. Continental European and First Nations' community caring systems generally prefer to use more discretion, rather than relying on detailed rules and regulations to guide assessments and interventions, as the child protection systems in England, the United States, and Canada do.

Many family service and community caring systems do not use a formal standard risk assessment procedure with families, as is common in the Anglo-American systems. However, some family service systems, such as that in the Netherlands, are introducing more formality into their processes; in addition, there has recently been a move in the Dutch system towards increasing requirements for social workers to provide judges with evidence of child abuse (Hetherington, Cooper, Smith & Wilford, 1997). Nonetheless, family service systems generally put more faith in the discretion and judgments of service providers, endorsing welfare and social work principles as their preferences in working with families (Hetherington et al., 1997; Olsson Hort, 1997; Poso, 1997).

While published information is limited, in one study, social workers in a First Nation community caring system were seen as having greater discretion in their work, as well as more input into child welfare policies, than their mainstream counterparts:

> In a ministry often characterized by low morale and frequent staff turnover, staff of the Native unit are enthusiastic about and committed to their work ... They went on to talk about the mission – to work with and provide services to a group of people who have rarely received satisfactory services from the ministry. Thus there is an identification with a cause, a sense of being different and distinctive. The distinctiveness is revealed in part by the way clients are treated – as friends, rather than people with problems. Second, staff see themselves as innovators and creators. Rather than simply and only implementing established policy, the Native unit is helping the ministry develop policy for Native child welfare. (Wharf, 1992, pp. 108–9)

At the same time, child protection systems have become increasingly reluctant to trust local professional and community decision making about maltreating families. For example, in Ontario, Canada, where we live, over the past decade, reliance on standardized information record-ing and prescribed service time lines and people processing procedures has increased substantially. These bureaucratic procedures have been married to a standard child abuse risk assessment instrument intended to increase the accuracy and objectivity of making decisions about families. As a result, front-line service provider and local community discretion has been substantially reduced in deciding how to interact with families, and time spent fulfilling formal recording requirements has greatly increased.

Concluding Comments

The arguments in this chapter were developed as part of the program of research for the Partnerships for Children and Families Project, a Com-munity University Research Alliance funded by the Social Sciences and Humanities Research Council of Canada. This work provided the basis for identifying the child protection, family service, and community caring systems examined in this volume, and for choosing the illustra-tive child and family welfare systems discussed in subsequent chapters. The chapters in this volume served as the foundation for the interna-tional Positive Systems of Child and Family Welfare conference hosted at Wilfrid Laurier University in June 2002. They also provided the initiative for the development of the international comparative child and family welfare research project, Towards Positive Systems of Child and Family Welfare, through the Partnerships for Children and Fami-lies Project.[2]

Our motivation for looking for ideas internationally was our increas-ing conviction that the child protection paradigm was in urgent need of new ideas and renewed hope for a better future. We became convinced that substantial progress could not be made if we restrict our thinking to protecting children from a narrow range of dangers within their homes. We needed to move beyond what was already familiar to un-cover a range of new possibilities. Our intentions in this international comparative project are twofold: (1) to free us to imagine alternatives – to disturb conventional certainties about the inevitability or the superi-ority of current child and family welfare arrangements; and (2) to identify possible niches for reform and perhaps more basic shifts in system design as signposts for future explorations.

If we are not to be frozen into believing in the inevitability and immutability of our current child and family welfare arrangements, we require both a vision of what might be more satisfactory and achievable, and some steps with which we can begin our journey. This chapter highlights a number of choices that can be explored in reconsidering how we conduct the business of child and family welfare.

One of the overarching ambitions of the Partnerships for Children and Families Project is to articulate the principles and procedures that might characterize a positive and inclusive paradigm for child and family welfare. In a very general fashion, from our perspective, the operating principles potentially characterizing such a positive and inclusive system could include the following:

1 Providing assistance in ways that are welcomed by the parents and children involved
2 Taking advantage of up-to-date information about promising programming for disadvantaged children, parents, and families
3 Having holistic concepts of well-being for children, parents, families, and communities central to their frame of reference
4 Placing a priority on keeping children safe from harm and understanding this as a complement to the previous principles rather than a competing priority
5 Ensuring that service providers find their work worthwhile and feasible
6 Accommodating variations in the ways of living and service requirements of particular families and communities
7 Enhancing the motivation, talent, and judgment of both service providers and family members in providing help

These are preliminary principles and may not reflect the thinking which emerges at the end of the Partnerships for Children and Families program of research. But, coupled with the explanations of family difficulties and the system design choices discussed in this chapter, they provide useful frameworks for considering the discussions of specific systems of child and family welfare in this book. The concluding chapter returns to these general principles in examining what we can learn from the international comparisons in this book and how we can move ahead with positive reforms.

NOTES

1 This overview chapter draws substantially upon arguments developed in Cameron, Freymond, Cornfield, and Palmer (2001).
2 For more information about the Partnerships for Children and Families Project's program of research, review papers, and research reports go to the web site, www.wlu.ca/pcfproject, or call 1-519-884-0710, ext 3636, or email partnerships@wlu.ca.

2 Learning from Difference: Comparing Child Welfare Systems

RACHAEL HETHERINGTON

Introduction

Learning from difference is a complex process. This paper describes that process and considers the problems and benefits of working with intercountry comparisons. The author's interest stemmed from the work of the Centre for Comparative Social Work Studies (CCSWS) at Brunel University in London.[1] Initial attempts to describe another child protection system led us, through the exploration of difference and similarity, to a new understanding of our child welfare system in England, and to a consideration of the role of the wider culture in determining these systems. Social workers and social work academics are familiar with working across the boundaries that define the disciplines of psychology, sociology, and social policy. Working with cross-country comparisons adds a whole range of linguistic, social, and historical considerations to the relevant disciplines. What we found might be obvious to experts in those fields, but it is new for us, and has provided us with a new slant on old problems.

This chapter is in two parts. The first part describes the process of making comparisons. Following a brief account of the context of comparative studies relating to child welfare, the methodology of the research projects on which this chapter is based is described. The process of learning from difference is analysed and three stages of the process are outlined. The second part of the chapter uses comparative studies to analyse the factors that determine the functioning of child welfare systems, and raises questions about the relationship between child welfare systems and the wider socioeconomic systems within which they function. The implications for creating change in child welfare systems are discussed.

For simplicity, the systems we studied will be referred to throughout as child welfare systems, on the grounds that both child protection and family welfare are always an aspect of child welfare. Where the term 'child protection' is used, this is done with the narrow meaning of services or systems that focus on child rescue. References throughout this chapter are to England rather than the United Kingdom because the child welfare systems of England, Scotland, and Northern Ireland are not the same. Wales shares the same system as England, but our research was conducted in England, and can only be taken as relating to England.

The Context in Comparative Studies

Comparative research as a means of studying social welfare systems is well established, and there is a considerable body of work comparing the welfare benefits and health service systems of European countries.[2] However, using comparison to study social welfare structures has many problems because of the difficulty of establishing what is truly the same or different. Jones (1985) singled out social work as a particularly intractable area of study, calling it 'a messy area for research' (p. 172). In the field of child welfare, there are some single country studies where there is no comparative element either in the authorship or the editing (for example, Hellinckx, Colton & Williams [1997]). These studies provide useful source material from which comparisons can be developed. There are a few studies that are overtly comparative such as Millar and Warman (1996), Gilbert (1997), and Pringle (1998). However, although there has been a considerable increase in descriptions of other systems, particularly in the European context, there is still a shortage of information that is directly based on practice and also takes into account the structural context in which the work takes place.[3]

Two comparative studies are described here in more detail, as there will be later reference to them. In 1990, Esping-Andersen published a seminal study of welfare regimes, in which he suggested a categorization according to the underlying socio-economic philosophy of the state. Welfare regimes were typified as social-democratic, conservative, or liberal. The Scandinavian countries were grouped as social-democratic, the continental European countries as conservative, and the English-speaking countries as liberal. Subsequent studies of welfare regimes have challenged or modified some of his conclusions, but the main outline remains intact.

In the social work field, Gilbert (1997) brought together studies of child abuse reporting systems in nine countries. Comparing them, he differentiated between those that had a 'family service' orientation and those that had a 'child protection' orientation. The countries with a family service orientation did more preventive work and offered more family support more readily and at an earlier stage. The countries with a child protection orientation delayed intervention and were less optimistic about the effectiveness of intervention. Their response to situations was more legalistic. The three English-speaking countries in his sample, the United States, Canada, and England, had a child protection orientation. The other countries, Sweden, Denmark, Finland, Belgium, Germany, and the Netherlands, all had a family service orientation. Gilbert also described a further divide within the family service group between the Nordic countries, which had laws requiring the reporting of child abuse, and the other European countries in his sample, which did not. Gilbert's work suggests that the major divide lies between the countries that focus on child protection and those that work preventively to support the family.

The Cross-Country Projects of the CCSWS

The starting point for the comparative studies of the CCSWS was a wish to find out how other countries in Europe responded to the problems of child abuse. In the late 1980s, following a series of child death inquiries, there was a great deal of dissatisfaction with the English system. A new act (the Children Act 1989) was being debated and preparations were being made for its implementation. There may have been some optimism about a fresh beginning, but nevertheless arguments seemed to follow a well-worn track without advancing the discussion. To find a way of opening up this debate, we turned outwards to look for other ideas. As it is well established that child abuse is a problem in all developed countries, we assumed that other European countries have systems in place for child protection. We wanted to learn more about other approaches because we hoped to learn about new ways of responding to common problems. We wanted to know about the laws and the formal structures for child protection, and we wanted to understand what actually happens 'on the ground'; that is, how the systems work in reality.

The fulcrum of our comparisons was the problem to which the task of social work was a response, the abusive or dysfunctional family situation that raises the issue of possible intervention. The focus of comparison was to determine 'what happens for this family.' As soon as there is any official intervention with a family, the system used affects the development of the case so powerfully that comparison becomes very difficult. To overcome this concern, we invented an initial hypothetical case situation that posed a potential child protection problem. The same case vignette could be presented in each country, providing a basis for comparison of the actions that would, or would not, be taken and the expectations, structures, laws, and resources that might be involved in the process.

The Methodology of the Research

There were three sets of studies using slightly different methodologies, but all sharing certain features. All focused on the practical functioning of child welfare systems. People closely involved with the operation of the system, including social workers, other professionals, and parents became the sources of information. All the studies introduced, or attempted to introduce, an element of reflective comment from the participants.

The main studies used a case vignette to elicit information about the functioning of a child welfare system and to collect an expert opinion on the comparisons between that system and another. In each participating country, a group (or groups) of social workers and other relevant professionals was established. Each group heard the same story, which was developed over several stages. The group decided what would be most likely to happen to the family in their locality. This provided a picture of the system in action.

The group then heard about the discussion and decisions made by a group in another country working on the same case material. They identified similarities and differences between the way the systems worked, as well as the anxieties and preoccupations of the social workers within these systems. In making these comparisons, they reflected on their own system as well as on the other system.

Four sets of data could be derived from this material. The first data set was a description of the functioning of the system made by experts – the people who work in it. The second data set was information about the preoccupations and concerns of the workers who operate the system, as demonstrated by the process of their discussions (this was based on a content analysis of the verbatim transcript). The third data set was the practitioners' view of the differences and similarities between the systems. The fourth data set contained the reflections of the practitioners on these differences. This material was supported by information about the formal structures and resources of the involved countries that was provided by the researchers.

The role of the international group of researchers was to create the case vignette, to provide information about the structures of child welfare of their own country and to work as an international team on the analysis of the material. The team sought to establish the aspects of child welfare systems that were common to the countries participating and those that appeared to be specific to one country or a group of countries. In addition, the researchers in each country drew their own conclusions about the particular relevance of the comparisons for their own system.

More detailed descriptions of the methodology of the two main projects that used the vignette technique can be found in *Protecting Children: Messages from Europe* (Hetherington, Cooper, Smith, & Wilford, 1997) and *The Welfare of Children with Mentally Ill Parents: Learning from Inter-country Comparisons* (Hetherington, Baistow, Katz, Mesie, & Trowell, 2002).

The examples used in this chapter are drawn mainly from the studies using the vignette technique. Other examples are taken from a project where social workers in France and England were paired and followed each other's work over a ten-month period. During this period, they visited each other five times. After each visit, they discussed what they had learned about the other system with a member of the research team. The research data derived from the transcriptions of these discussions and from the discussions at a final meeting of all the participants and researchers at the end of the project. Details about this project are given in *Positive Child Protection: A View from Abroad* (Cooper, Hetherington, Baistow, Pitts, & Spriggs, 1995).

This chapter also draws on comparative biographical work undertaken with parents who had been involved with their child welfare system. The researchers interviewed parents, who gave an unstructured account of their experience of the system. The researchers analysed these transcripts and attempted to compare in meaningful ways the experiences of parents in one country with experiences of parents in another country, given the substantial service and socioeconomic contextual differences among settings. The analysis offered a view of the possible alternative experiences of parents involved with the systems of the countries concerned. It was possible in only a few instances to have a further interview with the parent to ask for their reflections on the suggested alternatives. The biographical material that was collected in the initial interviews provided a rich source of data, and added another dimension to the picture of the differences between the systems, confirming the findings of the previous projects undertaken with social workers. The work with parents is discussed in Baistow and Hetherington (1998), Baistow and Wilford (2000), and Hetherington and Piquardt (2001).

The Value of Using Comparisons

The aim of using comparison and learning from difference is to identify possible improvements in child welfare systems. When we undertook our studies of child protection systems in six European countries, we were amazed to discover that aspects of the English system we had assumed to be necessary and normal might not exist at all in other countries. Other countries had no child protection register, no formal child protection conference, and did not involve the police in child protection investigations. We found countries that had different grounds from ours for court action, and countries where a court hearing would happen within a fortnight of referral and last for forty minutes. We found countries where decisions about compulsory placement in care were undertaken by a single judge, and others where elected local government members would share in this decision making. We found countries where 'child protection' was understood to include the full range of protective measures including, for example, the employment rights of children and the prevention of exploitation rather than exclusively the protection from abuse within the family. There was no way to prove that one way of doing things was more successful than another. The information on outcomes was not available, and there was no way of arriving at a shared definition of success. Nevertheless, our ideas and the ideas of the participating social workers about what was possible and what was necessary underwent a radical change. This gave us new perspectives on the problems that we saw in the English system.

The Process of Learning from Difference

Three elements are involved in the process of learning from difference. They are description, comparison, and reflection. Comparison requires knowledge about two things, one of which is familiar or known, and the 'other,' which is not familiar. These two things may have some attributes that are alike and some that are not.

Comparisons, therefore, have to start with learning about and describing an 'other.' But all descriptions of an 'other' are based on knowledge of something that is 'like' the object you are describing. In the Middle Ages, people who had travelled to Africa or India tried to describe elephants when they got home. The pictures they drew from memory frequently showed the elephant with hind legs like a horse or a cow that bend backwards at the knee. Their attempt to describe the elephant was taken over by their assumptions about how a four-legged animal would look. In order to give an accurate description of something new, it is necessary to notice difference from something known. Trying to give a truthful and accurate description of the 'other' is a fundamental part of making comparisons. It is not easy or straightforward.

Comparing goes hand in hand with describing, but there is an inherent paradox. I have to describe the 'other' before I can know whether there are enough similarities and differences to provide a starting point for making comparisons. I cannot give an accurate description of the 'other' until I have identified the aspects of the 'other' that are the same as, or different from, the familiar. The resolution of this paradox lies in accepting that the process is circular, not linear. You make a comparison and say, 'This is like, that is not.' You attempt a description on this basis, and realise that you have not understood something. You look again at the things that are 'like,' and discover that some of them are not alike after all (and vice versa). Reflection follows from comparison, and leads to an increase in understanding, and to a more detailed and complex description. Then the description takes a step forward. However, the process has to start with a first attempt at a straight description of the 'other' system.

Describing

For the purpose of describing a child welfare system, the factors that influence its functioning can be categorized under three headings: structures, professional ideology, and culture. Describing a child welfare system may start with an account of the formal structures, but it must also describe how the system works on a day-to-day basis, which involves a complex interaction of various structures, including the important element of resources. The professional ideology of the workers – the theories, concepts, and values of the professionals who operate the system – influence how the structures are employed. The expectations, values, and social philosophies of the surrounding community form the culture within which the system works. The families, their friends and neighbours, the professionals, and the policy makers share this culture. It exists simultaneously at local, regional, and national levels.

Structures, professional ideology, and culture are interconnected. Any aspect of functioning may have its origins in all three. Generally, there are many reasons why a system functions as it does. For example, resources can be seen as part of the structure of a system, but the extent and allocation of resources, although forming part of the structure, may express the philosophy of the culture and the value it attaches to different processes. Resources will also be responsive to the professional ideologies of the people who are deploying them, to a greater or lesser extent.

Structures

Structures are the mechanisms through which child welfare services are delivered. They include the way in which government is organized locally and centrally, the place of nongovernmental organizations, and how central and local governments relate to health and social welfare structures and to resources. The law relating to child welfare and family support is clearly important, but other areas of the law are relevant, for example, the laws concerning confidentiality. The structure and process of the courts play a part. Information is also needed about the structures and resources of other welfare and health services, and the specific child welfare resources available locally and nationally.

Therefore, many structures play a part in the working of a child welfare system. Studying the child welfare system of another country requires extensive background knowledge. In one's own country, most of this knowledge is taken for granted, and not regarded as integral to understanding the child welfare system, but in practice it forms a part of what determines the social workers' response to a situation. Child welfare and the welfare of the family are indivisible, and families at some stage include adults, children, infants, women, men, the employed and the unemployed, the well and the ill. Most aspects of civil society affect families. Families may be involved with the full range of services, including health, welfare, the courts and legal services, income support, housing, employment, education, and leisure. The organization and resourcing of each of these services are important. Child welfare can be seen as a meeting point for many aspects of the organization of the state. The structures of child welfare systems demonstrate how the state chooses to organize the interconnections between its different parts and the balance among different priorities.

Professional Ideology

Structures are not the only factors that have a profound effect on the way services function. The professional ideology of social work, the information on which the social workers base their decisions, and the theories that guide the selection and interpretation of this information are all important. Structures (organizational structures, resources, and the law) provide the framework within which decisions are made and set boundaries for the range of choices available, but final choices are made often on the basis of social work theory and knowledge.

Information about the professional ideology of the social workers (and other professionals) can be gained from a study of professional training courses and from the discussions of social workers about a particular case situation. Within the groups of social workers participating in our research, the language in which discussions took place, the assumptions made about relationships, or cause and effect, demonstrated the underlying theories and conceptualizations that informed decision making. Our research suggests that there is a great deal of shared ground among social workers in different European countries, and the functioning of the system is influenced by the social workers' acquaintance with, and use of, theories of human growth and development (e.g., psycho-dynamic, behavioural, systemic). Their use of theories of social work intervention (e.g., ecological, systemic, psychosocial, crisis intervention, task-centred), and conceptualizations of the social work task and the role of specialization also play a part in the decision making process and the intervention options considered. However, the amount of discretionary space that a system allocates to professional judgment varies considerably from one country to another. Heavily proceduralized systems are likely to allow less space for the use of professional knowledge.

Culture

Child welfare decisions are not only framed by systemic structures and influenced by the theories and information that guide professional judgment. They are also constrained and directed by the culture of the society in which the service systems exist.

By culture, we mean the nexus of views, understanding, habits of mind, patterns of living, and use of language that are built up in a community, nation, or state by the shared history, language, and social circumstances in which people grow up and live. The culture of a society is pervasive. It is expressed in part through the structures of the society, but also through the use that society makes of those structures. Culture is influenced strongly by history, but some aspects of a culture may persist unchanged over long periods. Moreover, culture is variable between different sectors of society and different geographical areas.

It was apparent from our comparative research that there were important inter-country differences between child welfare systems that were not explained by the structures of the system or the professional ideology of the workers. Child welfare highlights relationships among individuals, families, and the state, some of the fundamental building blocks of a culture. Problems relating to the well-being of children are caught up in the complex network of interests among parents, children, the community, and the state. Culture influences and expresses expectations of the various roles that should be played by the state, the family, and the community in relation to the child. These expectations find expression in the functioning of child welfare systems. It is in this context that the social worker represents the state. The aspects of culture that are important for describing a child welfare system are about the relationship between the citizen and the state, and the reciprocal expectations of parents and the state about each other's role in assuring the welfare of children.

Social workers, at the same time as they represent the state, are part of society, and share the society's expectations and assumptions about social behaviour. Like the users of their services, they think in ways integral to their culture. These expectations and assumptions affect the way that professional theory and knowledge are understood and used. At times social workers may differ as a group or individually from the general expectations of the culture within which they are working, but in the main they must accept the boundaries of that culture.

Comparing

The central problem in making comparisons is the difficulty of establishing whether two things that appear the same are really the same, and whether two things that seem different are really different. There are problems of definition. Statistics may not be compiled using the same criteria. Unidentified differences in the division of spheres of influence between central and local government may mask the 'unlikeness' of apparently similar structures and responsibilities. There are problems related to the use of words. The same word may include or exclude a range of functions. Words may have wide ranges of shared meaning but differences in the implications and valuation that they carry. Semantic similarities can mask differences, and the obvious and apparently exact translation of a word may be quite misleading. The following examples from our research experience illustrate some of the pitfalls.

- *'Administratif'* is used in France to describe the structures of that part of the child welfare system that does not directly involve the law on child protection and is run by the local authority. The word 'administrative' in England would probably refer to the paperwork, not the structure, and there is no one word with an equivalent usage.[4]
- In some countries, residential care for children and young people may be delivered partly through the education system or through employment training institutions for young adults. In other countries these institutions are part of completely different service structures. How will this be reflected in statistics?
- Is the care of children in small group homes called foster care or residential care? And how is it conceptualized?
- 'Voluntary organizations' (the usual English designation) may not be run by volunteers nor do they necessarily only work with users on a voluntary basis. The use of the term 'voluntary organizations' is therefore best avoided.
- In England 'volunteer' has a generally positive connotation – to work as a volunteer is generally a 'good' thing to do. Elsewhere, the volunteer may be seen, more critically, as someone who takes employment from a paid worker.
- 'Education' in English is tied to academic learning. *'Education'* in French is a much broader concept and includes what in English we might call 'socialization' or 'upbringing.' It is interesting that English lacks a single word with which to translate the concept embodied in the French word.
- The term 'pedagogy,' which has a positive meaning in both French

and German related to helping children to learn, in English is usually pejorative, implying an over-directive and pedantic approach. In many European countries, there is a social work profession of social pedagogy that does not appear to exist in the United Kingdom.

- In English, the word 'foster' (fostering, foster child/parent) has a long history and a specific meaning, to care for a child from another family. In French there is no similar word. The translation of 'foster family' is *'famille d'accueil,'* a family that 'welcomes' the child. Does this mean that 'fostering' has a different meaning, or carries different implications in these countries? Is fostering used differently?

Reflecting

Reflective learning uses new knowledge about another system to enhance our knowledge of our own system. Such learning develops from self-questioning, and it requires the ability to be both reflective and critical. The questions have to move on from *what* is done and *how* is it done, to *why* is it done and why is it done *that way*.

Being reflective requires self-awareness. I need to be aware of what I bring to the situation or subject. Where you stand affects your point of view. Where do I stand – as a woman or man, as a white person or a black person, as old or young? How may that affect my perceptions? It also requires an acceptance that subjectivity is inevitable: I cannot cease to be who I am.

I have to use this knowledge actively when thinking about a different system or way of working. The different system becomes a mirror in which I can glimpse new facets of the system within which I work, and of the way I work within that system. The examples given below illustrate how reflecting on comparisons with another system can lead to a new perspective and make visible what has been assumed or taken for granted.

Reflection also requires us to be critical, in the original sense of the word, which is not to find fault but to question, to interrogate the material. Why does it work like that, why do you do it that way, why do we do it differently? Why does that system use the law so readily when we would rate the problems as relatively minor? Why do we put off using the law till things are really bad? Is their experience of using the law different from ours? Why is it such a different experience? Are we seeing the problems differently or are we thinking about the law differently? What would happen if we acted differently? What risks would we take, what would we fear? Pursuing these lines of thought leads to reflection on what we take for granted and creates the opportunity to question whether we wish to continue to make the same assumptions. It is not necessarily about *changing* our assumptions; it is about *making it possible* to change them.

The following examples from our research show reflective thinking in action and illustrate the kind of reflections that this approach generates.

- An English social worker discussed one of her cases with her French colleague, and pondered his response. The case involved a teenager, a refugee and recent immigrant, who wanted to leave her residential placement to live in a situation that the social worker thought was very risky. She described to her French colleague the steps that she might take to use the law to prevent the girl from leaving care. They both agreed on her assessment of the situation, but he was puzzled by her emphasis on the legal arrangements – in France the legal situation would not have been an issue. The English social worker reflected that her approach now seemed to her 'devious' and manipulative, whereas before she had viewed it simply as a practical solution. She began to think about the English legal system, and how it might affect practice.
- A group of English practitioners saw a video of a French group discussing a child protection case. One of them commented: 'Their discussion was more philosophical than ours was. They didn't talk about evidence at all. We talked about it all the time. I wonder what that says about them. And I wonder what it says about us.' The social workers in the group began to reflect on their prioritization of evidence, which they had previously taken for granted.
- An English social worker heard about the response of German social workers to the situation of a family with a mentally ill mother. She thought the German social workers had many more resources than the English did. Reflecting on the English responses to the same situation, she noted that a lack of resources began to affect how you thought about a case. You stopped trying to understand all the complexities of the situation if you couldn't do anything to follow up. Your way of thinking about cases changed and became more limited.
- An English parent who had struggled, with the support of her

Health Visitor, to get help from the social services department heard about a system where the social workers and health visitors worked on the same team. She thought that this would have been helpful for her. She had highly valued the confidentiality of the English system, but decided that the relative loss of confidentiality would have mattered less to her than the gain in communication.

In these examples, the participants were taking a critical view of their own system and finding negatives. It also happened that participants began to value more highly, or become conscious of valuing highly, aspects of their own system that they had previously taken for granted. For example, the English valued the transparency of the English system and the efforts to make clear to families their rights and the procedures of the child protection process. They began to feel more positive about their own practice in this respect. They identified a major difference between themselves and their French colleagues in their approach to work with ethnic minority families, and decided that their own position reflected strongly held values. In thinking about other systems, we may often be most interested in the negative points because of the wish to improve our own system, but the positive values that we establish are important. The things that we value set the parameters of possible change. A change that might seem helpful, but which conflicts with deeply held values, is unlikely to be successful or effective.

Comparison leads readily to ranking and the building of hierarchies. We tend to think competitively, in terms of which system is 'best at' this or that function. In itself, this is essentially unproductive, although difficult to avoid. But it can be productive to look at why we rank things and what we choose to rank. For example, at one international seminar, the participants from continental Europe noted that the English were interested in ranking countries according to how successful they were at preventing child deaths. This led to an exploration of the reasons why child deaths might be a greater preoccupation for workers in some countries than others. The ranking was not useful (or realistic – the statistical information base was not there), but it was informative to question why there was a felt need to make such a ranking.

The description of another system is likely to introduce some things that are new to us, and thus lead to a search for things that we can copy or borrow. We hope to be able to learn from the experience of others, and we may learn about useful structures or new ways of doing things. We may get ideas about new services that we could copy or adapt.

However, there are problems in transplanting ideas or structures from one country to another. The soil or the climate may not be congenial. If these problems are recognized, it may be possible to overcome them, and to compensate for differences in context. But this depends on becoming aware of and acknowledging the assumptions that are implicit in both systems. For example, a group of Belgian social workers from the Flemish community attended a seminar introducing the new guidelines published in the UK by the Department of Health (Department of Health 2000), the *Framework for the Assessment of Children in Need and Their Families*. This publication describes an assessment model to be used by social workers. It includes a theoretical exposition of the model and detailed guidelines for its implementation, including a time scale for undertaking the work and a lengthy form to be completed that covers all the elements of the assessment. The Belgian workers were interested in the theoretical approach, which was congenial to them, and they found the formulation of the guidelines useful. However, they did not feel that the procedures, the time scales for undertaking the work, and the forms would be appropriate or relevant for them. The Belgian group identified a similarity in the use of theory and a difference in the attitude to management and professionalism. This led to reflections on the nature of the difference between the Belgian and the English systems. Their own very flat management style, which they had previously taken for granted, became more visible to them. The difference in their management style indicated that they would need to be selective in their borrowing, making use of the theory but not the method of operation.

The Interaction of Culture, Structure, and Professional Ideology

The structure, the professional ideology of social work, and the culture of the setting influence child welfare systems and are subject to change. Structures are constantly evolving. Social work has its fashions in theory and its knowledge base steadily develops. Culture is both highly resistant to change and continually changing. These three factors – structure, professional ideology, and culture – may interact in a variety of ways, and any one may overcome the impact of the others. The following example demonstrates how culture can affect the interpretation of theory, and therefore the action taken.

A group of German social workers and a similar English group considered the same case, and debated whether, at one point, a child should come into care. Both groups based their response on family systems theory, and used the same framework of argument. However, they came to different conclusions because they had different expectations of the family: not of that particular family, but of 'the family' as a social entity. The German group thought of the family as cohesive, and that to take the child out of her family for a while would be helpful. It would disrupt the system and make it more open to change. The English group had a less robust view of the family. They thought that if the child were taken out of her family, the system would close up. The child would be excluded, and it would be difficult to get her back into her family. It appeared that cultural expectations about the family determined how theory was interpreted and used.

Another example demonstrates the impact of structure on professional ideology. Some English social workers showed a high level of anxiety when they discussed a case situation in which they wanted to take a child into care, but child protection law and procedures would not support this intervention. Discussing the same case, French social workers who wanted to take the child into care had no problems, because their legal framework did support their professional view of the best intervention. Here differences in structures were leading to different outcomes, even though the choice suggested by social work knowledge was the same. The differences in structures (the law) may also be considered to have derived from (and reflect) differences in cultures and in the expectations about the relationship between the child, the family, and the state.

The examples above also illustrate the potential for conflict among the three elements of structure, professional ideology, and culture. Dilemmas that may arise from collisions between culture, professional knowledge, and the structures within which social workers operate are reflected in the anxieties of social workers. The greatest area of similarity among the systems studied was noted in the professional ideology of the workers. There were some differences in theoretical approach (broadly between the English-speaking countries, which were more likely to use approaches derived from learning theory than the others), but many more similarities. However, in some of the systems, the international theoretical basis of social work (and other health and welfare professions) was exposed to contrary pressures from the national or local culture within which it operated. Where there was a conflict between professional values and the culture of their society, the participating social workers felt anxious and impotent. The position of

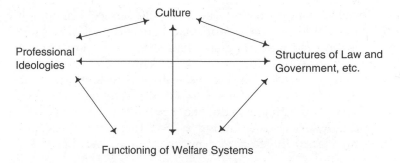

Figure 2.1: The interplay between culture, structure, professional ideology, and the functioning of child welfare systems

social workers in countries that Esping-Andersen (1990) defined as liberal seemed to be particularly conflicted (Hetherington, Baistow, Katz, Mesie, & Trowell, 2002).

There are interactions among local and national cultures, structures, and professional knowledge and ideologies. This interaction determines the functioning of child welfare systems, and ensures that no two systems will ever be identical. As figure 2.1 illustrates, not only do structures, culture, and professional ideology collectively determine functioning, each is also affected by and may be modified by the way the system functions.

The Dominance of Culture

Although culture, structures, and professional ideology all interact to shape the functioning of child welfare systems, their effects are not necessarily equally powerful. There is some evidence from the comparative studies cited earlier in this chapter that culture may be the most powerful factor. Esping-Andersen linked welfare regimes and political philosophies. Gilbert similarly supports the view that there is a cultural divide between child welfare systems focused on family support, and those focused on child protection, and that this divide is related to the social philosophy of the country.

Gilbert (1997) compared descriptions of nine European and North American child abuse reporting systems. One focus of his comparisons was the use of laws concerning the mandatory reporting of child abuse. He divided the countries he compared between those with a 'child protection' orientation and those with a 'family service' orientation. Two of the three 'child protection'–oriented countries had mandatory reporting laws, and the third, England, had strict professional guidelines that amount to something very similar. Three of the six 'family service'–oriented countries also had mandatory reporting laws. Surveying the systems at the end of his book, Gilbert observed: 'The presence of mandatory reporting laws does not appear to be linked to child protective or family service orientations' (p. 234). These structures (mandatory reporting laws) therefore did not determine how the system worked.

Gilbert (1997) also considered the kind of intervention and treatment approaches that were used in various systems:

> Although mandatory reporting operates in both child protection and family service-oriented systems, the filing of a report in each of these two systems has somewhat different implications. Reports filed in systems with a protective orientation prompt investigations that are more legalistic and vested with the coercive powers of the state than those filed in systems with a service orientation, which emphasises therapeutic and voluntary measures. (p. 235)

This suggests that neither structure nor professional ideology determined the response of the system. The way that the laws were used did not appear to be the result of the application of the professional ideology of social work, because, as has been previously noted, the professional ideologies of social work are very similar cross-nationally (Hetherington et al., 2002). It can be argued that both structures and professional ideologies were less significant for the overall functioning of child welfare systems than the culture within which they operated. Gilbert's work suggests that culture may be the most powerful factor in determining overall functioning in child welfare systems.

If culture has the lead role in determining functioning, then the political philosophy that the state embodies will directly affect the experience of families in need of support. The culture of a society is expressed both through the structures of the society and through the use that society makes of those structures. The allocation of resources and delivery of services can be seen as a facet of culture, expressing both the means by which it is culturally acceptable for services to be delivered and the value that society places on different kinds of support. Countries that have similar values in relation to child welfare may thus have different ways of providing these services.

Sweden and Germany are both countries that have a 'family service' orientation (Gilbert, 1997) to child welfare. However, Sweden has mandatory reporting, while Germany does not. Information generated from the discussions with practitioners from these countries (Hetherington et al., 2002) shows how these similarities and differences affect social work practice and the experience of families. In both Sweden and Germany, the child welfare systems put substantial resources into family support and value preventive work, but these two countries delivered services differently and had different expectations. In Sweden, the state is seen as representing the community of citizens and as the provider of social security (in the broadest sense). In Germany, it is expected that the delivery of service should be organized within local communities, although the state is responsible for ensuring that proper provision of child welfare services exists and that services are effective. The principle of subsidiarity, which is fundamental to German social structures, requires that all interventions take place at the least formal level that is feasible (Schäfer, 1995). In practical terms, these differences in culture mean that in Sweden there are very few nongovernmental organizations while in Germany there are many.

In Sweden, social workers participating in a comparative study (Hetherington et al., 2002) expected that families would accept state support. They thought that families expected the state to offer help and were likely to trust social workers. Mandatory reporting was seen as a means of ensuring that help was made available.

In Germany, social workers were very concerned about establishing trust with families because the voluntary engagement of families was considered pivotal. The German social workers thought that families had a right to receive help, but they knew that families also a had choice about the source of help because of the proliferation of different nongovernmental agencies. Families' trust had to be earned.

Social workers from both countries expressed a similar valuation of the importance of preventive and supportive work with families as an integral aspect of their child welfare systems. On the other hand, they had different political philosophies. As a result, in spite of similar values about preventive work, these child welfare systems were substantially shaped by different political philosophies, and the experience of families was different.

Child Welfare and Welfare Regimes

Esping-Andersen (1990) proposes a categorization of welfare regimes according to the socioeconomic philosophy underlying their health and welfare benefits systems. Countries where the state is heavily involved in the delivery of services are described as social-democratic. Countries that structure the delivery of services through other, non-governmental, means are considered conservative. In both of these groups, the philosophy requires that if citizens are sick or unemployed the state has a responsibility to see that they have access to help, whether assistance is provided by the state or by others. In the countries categorized as liberal, there are very low requirements for state responsibility and high expectations that individuals should make their own provisions for their health and social well-being.

If it is accepted that culture is the dominant force, this explains the convergence between Esping-Andersen's (1990) typology of welfare regimes and Gilbert's (1997) categorization of child welfare systems. All the countries that Gilbert describes as focusing on child protection are categorized by Esping-Andersen as having liberal welfare regimes. The countries that Gilbert describes as focusing on family services are categorized by Esping-Andersen as having social-democratic or conservative welfare orientations.

It is also the case that the countries with social-democratic welfare regimes have mandatory reporting of child abuse, while the conservative welfare regimes do not. For example, Sweden, which has a social-democratic welfare regime with a family support focused child welfare system, has mandatory reporting; Germany, which has a conservative welfare regime and a family support focused child welfare system, does not. The difference in political philosophy between Sweden and Germany identified by Esping-Andersen (1990) in relation to welfare regimes is reflected in the use or nonuse of mandatory reporting laws identified by Gilbert (1997).

Gilbert (1997) worked from formal descriptions of child welfare systems written by academics in each country. Working from intercountry comparisons based on qualitative data from social work practitioners, we identified the same divisions between types of child welfare systems. The English-speaking countries in our research (Hetherington et al., 2002) were England, Scotland, Northern Ireland, Ireland, and Australia (Victoria). All (except in some respects Scotland) have child

TABLE 2.1: Welfare Regimes and Child Welfare Systems

		Welfare regime		
Child welfare system		*'Social-democratic'*	*'Conservative'*	*'Liberal'*
Holistic system: 'Family service' orientation	*state service delivery*	Nordic countries[1]		
	subsidiarity		Continental European countries[2]	
Dualistic system: 'Child protection' orientation				English-speaking countries[3]

All the countries listed below were covered by Gilbert (1997) and/or Hetherington et al. (1997; 2002).
[1]Norway, Sweden, Denmark, and Finland.
[2]Belgium, France, Germany, Greece, Italy, Luxembourg, and the Netherlands.
[3]The UK, Ireland, California, Canada, and Australia (Victoria).

welfare systems characterized by a focus on child protection, distrust of state intervention, and a legalistic approach. These systems are crisis oriented, with an emphasis on rights and individual responsibility. Their systems treat family support and child protection as discrete processes.

The Nordic countries, with social-democratic welfare regimes, and the other European countries with conservative welfare regimes, have 'family service'–oriented child welfare systems. The differences between the two groups in relation to child welfare is reflected in the role of the state in delivering services. In spite of differences stemming from a very different view of the relationship between the state and the individual, both the Nordic and the other European countries in our studies have holistic child welfare systems that treat prevention, support, and the protective responses to child abuse as parts of a whole. The dualistic child protection orientation, with a division between services for family support and for child protection, in our investigation appears to be a consequence of operating within a liberal welfare regime. Table 2.1 sets out the broad pattern of welfare regimes and child welfare services for the majority of countries in the European Union and some states in North America and Australia.[5]

Making Changes

Problems relating to the well-being of children take place within a complex and potentially conflicting web of interests among parents, children, the community, and the state. Parents are family members with responsibilities and duties towards their children, individual citizens with rights, and members of the community. Children are family members, but dependent on adult care, and they are also individuals and future citizens with restricted rights. We all have expectations of the role of the state in relation to the individual and family, the family in relation to the child, and the community in relation to children and families. These expectations find expression in the functioning of child welfare systems.

A study of the differences between child welfare systems can help us to develop new ideas about changes that we wish to see. It also makes us more aware of the challenges involved in making changes in child welfare systems. Comparisons with other countries show how decisions made about services for families reflect attitudes about family autonomy and state intervention that are part of the culture in which professionals, communities, families, and children live. It follows that if we are attempting to introduce changes into our child welfare systems, we must be very aware of the cultural context in which any changes will take effect. This is not to say that change cannot take place; it obviously does. But it is difficult to make intentional changes that achieve their objectives without unintended consequences. Changes need to address the expectations shared by workers, families, and policy developers about the relationship between the state and the individual, the responsibilities of the family and the community, and the needs of children. If the changes are not consonant with these expectations, they have much less chance of acceptance and success.

This may explain why in England the efforts of the Department of Health to shift the focus of the system from child protection to family support have had minimal success. England has a long-standing political philosophy, particularly emphasized since about 1980, that sets a high value on the freedom of the individual from state interference. This ethos of individual autonomy and state minimalism does not readily support changes that would increase the involvement of the state in the welfare of children. There is a contradiction between discouraging reliance on state support and encouraging more supportive interventions with families. In countries like England, initiatives to introduce a broader child welfare perspective and to encourage the development of preventive services need to make a strong case for such changes and use strategies that influence multiple levels of the community and the government system. More recently important changes to the English child welfare system attempt to integrate social services for children into local Children's Trusts. It remains to be seen if these structural changes will affect the culture of services. International comparisons reinforce our awareness of the complexity of attempting to change something as central to civil society as its child welfare system.

There is a specific problem in trying to develop a holistic, truly integrative child welfare system in the context of a liberal welfare regime with an emphasis on individual responsibility. Front-line service workers can do a certain amount, perhaps more than they realize, by making use of existing structures. But there are limits to what they can do. In order to legitimize the changes that would need to be made, the challenge to existing expectations and assumptions needs to come from high levels of influence and power. Moving from child protection to child welfare entails a shift of resources and attention from protection to prevention. This raises anxieties that abused children will not be protected and that children will die. Making changes will entail taking risks, and risks that involve children are sensitive politically. Policy makers and politicians who want to change the system will have to rethink structures, reallocate resources, and be prepared for criticism that children's lives are being put at risk. It may help them to know that in other countries, strategies that seem so dangerous to us are seen as the safest and the most truly protective.

NOTES

1 The Centre for Comparative Social Work Studies was set up in 1991 by Professor John Pitts. It is part of the Department of Social Work at Brunel University in London and works in cooperation with practitioners and researchers in social work agencies and universities across Europe.
2 See, for example, Jones (1985), Esping-Andersen (1990; 1999), Øyen (1990), Hantrais and Mangen (1996), and Clasen (1999).
3 The specialist journals, the *European Journal of Social Work*, and *Social Work in Europe* are good sources, but there are increasing numbers of papers in mainstream child welfare journals. There is also a small body of literature on the use of comparative studies in social work research and education,

e.g., Soydan and Stål (1994), Hetherington (1996; 1998), Soydan (1996), Mabbett and Bolderson (1999), and Baistow (2000).

4 The author and colleagues have adopted the use of 'administrative' from the French, to fill the gap, and use it to describe the 'voluntary' or 'non-statutory' parts of the child protection system.

5 All the European countries studied by Gilbert (1997) and Hetherington et al. (1997; 2002) are members of the European Union, except Norway, which conforms to the same pattern as the other Nordic countries. Neither Gilbert nor Hetherington et al. includes Austria, Portugal, or Spain.

PART TWO

Child Protection Systems

The state is a regulator of social and moral arrangements, with an emphasis on individual rights and responsibilities. There is a clear division between private and public domains that protects the privacy of the family. Intrusion into families by child protection authorities is permitted only when parents violate minimum standards for the care of children. The primary focus of child protection is to protect children from harm in their own homes. Child protection service providers increasingly rely on adversarial judicial systems to confer authority on their work (Freymond, 2003). Reliance on state care of children has increased in recent years in many jurisdictions, and providing support for parent-child relationships is a secondary consideration. The child protection mandate is conferred to a stand-alone authority with minimal formal involvement by other service sectors or the broader community. The child protection chapters in this volume focus on England, Canada, and the United States.

3 Promoting Change from 'Child Protection' to 'Child and Family Welfare': The Problems of the English System

RACHAEL HETHERINGTON and TRACEY NURSE

Introduction: The Development of the System

Child welfare systems are fundamentally shaped by earlier aspects of a country's welfare systems and have a long and complex history. Parallel developments taking place in other aspects of welfare and in the support of people who are poor, disabled, and unemployed also affect them. Understanding the way the child welfare system functions now entails some consideration of how it used to function, and why changes have been made. After a brief historical introduction, this chapter will describe the framework of the present system formed by the Children Act of 1989 and the guidelines published by the Department of Health. This will be followed by an analysis of the problems of the system and a description of one project that is trying to bring about changes. In conclusion, we will look at the current dilemmas and opportunities facing English policy makers.

We will begin our history at the point when the British welfare state was set up in the late 1940s and 1950s, after the Second World War. In the United Kingdom, the civil experience of the war had important repercussions on child welfare policy in several respects. In particular, the evacuation of children from the major cities to the country brought to everyone's attention the fact that many children were living in poverty, were malnourished, and were lacking in many fundamental necessities for healthy physical and emotional development. The problems of children who were separated from their families were observed and recorded. The intervention of the state during the war had become commonplace, and relatively acceptable, and the well-being of the child had become a valid concern. This development in public awareness was reflected in the research of John Bowlby, whose influential work on the origins of depression followed from the work done at the Anna Freud clinic during and after the war (Bowlby, 1969).

The social welfare services for children set up after the war were administered and largely financed by Local Authorities (elected local government). The services developed in part as a response to the report of an inquiry in 1947 into the death of a child, Dennis O'Neil, who had been fostered. This set the pattern for a very characteristic aspect of the English child welfare system; changes have often been prompted by reaction to the reports of inquiries into child deaths or other child welfare scandals. However, for some years following these developments, the structures of the system were quite stable. The changes were mainly within the culture, ideology, and theoretical perspectives of the social work professions. New services were developed and the 1960s and early 1970s saw an increase in attention to community social work, the development of family work, and the introduction of systemic family therapy. These developments were in tension with an increase, both on the left and the right, in concerns about individual rights. During the late 1970s and early 1980s enormous social and political changes took place. The intervention of the state was actively discouraged and individual responsibility was promoted. Specialization was introduced, with an emphasis on the social worker as provider of services.[1]

At the same time as these changes in the wider national political philosophy were taking place, there were events within the child welfare field that had major repercussions. In the 1980s, there were several child death inquiries, the most important being those into the death of Jasmine Beckford in 1984 (London Borough of Brent, 1985) and Kimberley Carlile in 1986 (London Borough of Greenwich, 1987). Social workers were blamed for failing to pay enough attention to the children and being too ready to accept the protestations of the parents.

A review of the legislation relating to the welfare of children and young people was undertaken and looked likely to support a 'child rescue' agenda. However, in 1987 this was overtaken by events in the northern English town of Cleveland. It became known that large numbers of children were being taken into care on the basis of allegations by paediatricians that they were being sexually abused. This was very actively covered by the press, and became a major scandal. It was clear that the police and the social services were at odds, and that there were deep divisions in the medical profession over the actions and views of the paediatricians. There was an inquiry into what had happened (Secretary of State for Social Services, 1988) which emphasized the failure of the system to listen to the child, but also emphasized the rights of parents and the need for social workers to work in partnership with parents.

All these inquiry reports affected the outcome of the review of child welfare law. The Children Act of 1989 reflects the tension between giving priority to the welfare of the child and respecting the rights of parents. The changes in the law made by the Children Act of 1989 were accompanied by cultural changes. Parton, Thorpe, and Wattam (1997) point out:

> Increasingly our energies have been focused on refining and modifying the systems and procedures themselves. We have been concerned not so much with trying to do something about *child abuse* but *doing something about child protection.* (p. 18, original italics)

The Role of the Law and the Children Act of 1989

For about thirty years, the functioning of the child welfare system had been dominated by the thinking of welfare professionals using a welfare discourse and a medical model. King and Piper, writing in 1990, described how the language and the way of thinking about child welfare had shifted from a welfare discourse to a legal discourse. Thus the forces driving subsequent developments used the language of rights, looked for proof and evidence, and sought to name a responsible – or guilty – person.

The Children Act of 1989 consolidated previous legislation and developed a new court structure. It united in one Act the legislation relating to child protection, the support of families in difficulties, and decisions about the care of children whose parents were divorced or separated, but it did not include adoption law. It confirmed the separation between child welfare and juvenile justice. It also confirmed the social services department of the Local Authority as the responsible agency for child protection. Many aspects of the old legislation reappeared in the new Act, sometimes, as with the role of Guardian ad Litem (see below) with an expanded role. However, there were some important new developments. Some of these changes were intended to safeguard the rights of parents, particularly with regard to children in Local Authority care. Parents whose children were in care on a voluntary agreement, without a court order, were now able to take their children out of care without giving notice. If parents did not maintain contact with their children, the Local Authority could no longer assume the parental rights on children in voluntary care, as had previously been the case. Parents now continued to have some parental responsibility for their children when they were on an order and in Local Authority care. However, the most important change was encapsulated in the statement at the beginning of the act that the interests of the child were paramount.[2]

Children 'At Risk'

The Children Act 1989 is a law that *enables* the Local Authority to provide supportive services for children 'in need' and *requires* the Local Authorities to provide services for the protection of children 'at risk' of 'significant harm.' Part III of the Act covers the services for children 'in need.'

> It shall be the general duty of every Local Authority ... a) to safeguard and promote the welfare of children within their area who are in need: and b) so far as is consistent with that duty to promote the upbringing of such children by their families, by providing a range and level of services appropriate to those children's needs. (Children Act, 1989, s. 17)

The definition of 'in need' includes children with a disability. Under part III of the Act, the Local Authority has a specific duty to provide accommodation for children who would otherwise be homeless, and must also provide accommodation on a voluntary basis for children assessed as being 'in need.' Young people aged sixteen to eighteen can request accommodation without the agreement of their parents. The duties of the Local Authority to assist young people leaving care at eighteen until they are twenty-one have recently been extended (Children [Leaving Care] Act, 2000). The Act gives power to the Secretary of State to make detailed regulations for a case review system for children looked after by the Local Authority (s. 26), pointing the way towards an increase of central guidance on the conduct of cases.

Children 'In Danger'

Part IV of the Act sets out the grounds on which a court order can be made and describes the orders. The grounds are as follows:

The child concerned is suffering or is likely to suffer, significant harm; and b) that the harm, or likelihood of harm, is attributable to – (i) the care given to the child ... not being what it would be reasonable to expect a parent to give him; or (ii) the child's being beyond parental control. (Children Act, 1989, s. 31[2])

The orders that can be made are a care order or a supervision order. A care order commits the child to the care of the Local Authority. It gives the Local Authority parental authority over the child, and control (subject to challenge in the courts) over the amount of contact between parent and child. A supervision order gives the supervisor (a designated Local Authority or a probation officer) the duty to advise, assist, and befriend the child, and to take the necessary steps to do so. An application for a supervision order has to meet the same conditions as for a care order.

In a situation where there may be immediate danger, the Local Authority or the police can apply for an emergency protection order which lasts for seven days. Alternatively, the Local Authority can apply for a child assessment order. This order (which is not much used) requires parents to bring the child for assessment to a specified person or agency at a specified date. The order lasts for seven days from the specified date.

Leaving Local Authority Care

A care order is not time limited (beyond the age of eighteen), but after six months, anyone with parental authority, the child, or the Local Authority can apply for the order to be discharged. A child on a care order should have reasonable contact with parents and family and this can be specified in detail when the order is made. If parents want more contact than the Local Authority allows them, they can request a court order to regulate this. The child or the Local Authority can ask the court to forbid contact. However, in spite of the protection offered by the courts, the great fear of all parents who deal with the child protection system is that their child will be taken into care, and they will lose contact, and that this will be made permanent through adoption. If the child is not able to safely return to her parents, and looks likely to remain in Local Authority care until the age of eighteen, adoption is considered by the social services as a possible option. The use of adoption for children in state care is actively encouraged, particularly, but not only, for younger children. Adoption law is being reviewed, but at present a child can be freed for adoption at a point when there are as yet no named or identified adoptive parents available. The child then remains in the care of the Local Authority until such time as suitable adoptive parents are found. It is possible for the court to make an order for a child to be adopted or freed for adoption against the wishes of the parents.

The Philosophy of the Children Act

The philosophy of the Children Act of 1989 is strongly child centred. As well as setting out the primacy of the child's welfare in the first section of the first part of the Act, the next section goes on to state the circumstances to which the court shall have regard:

> (a) the ascertainable wishes and feelings of the child concerned (considered in the light of his age and understanding); (b) his physical, emotional and educational needs; (c) the likely effect on him of any change in his circumstances; (d) his age, background and any characteristics of his which the court considers relevant; (e) any harm which he has suffered or is at risk of suffering; (f) how capable each of his parents ... is of meeting his needs; (g) the range of powers available to the court. (Children Act, 1989, s. 1[3])

Any report to the court, whether in care proceedings or in relation to the responsibility of parents after divorce or separation has to take these circumstances into account.

In this way, the legislation reflects the concerns that were voiced after the inquiries into child deaths referred to above. These inquiries (and others) made a point of the lack of attention paid by social workers and other professionals to the experiences, to the feelings, and to the wishes of the child, and to the lack of awareness of the child's physical state and emotional well-being. Another way in which the legislation attempted to look after the child's welfare was through the consolidation and extension of a service which had originally been put in place in the Child Care Act of 1980. This was the Guardian (originally Guardian ad Litem) Service. The Guardian is an independent social worker, appointed by the court to represent to the court the wishes and interests of the child and to give the court an independent opinion on the child's best interests.

The Effect on Practice

Although only a very small minority of cases that cross the threshold of the social services ever come to court,[3] the law relating to child protection has a powerful defining effect on all the work of children and families services. Proceedings for the removal of children from their parents' care are initiated by an application to the court made by the Local Authority. The social services department also has a duty to make enquiries, if they have 'reasonable cause to suspect that a child ... in their area is suffering or likely to suffer significant harm' (Children Act, 1989, s. 47). The social services department of the Local Authority is thus central to the system of child protection.[4] They have to investigate allegations of harm and they decide whether to make the application to court for an order. All other services have to refer to them. The social workers are identified in the minds of the public as people who take children away from their parents – or who fail to take children away when they should.

The effect of the law on social work practice is compounded by the nature of proceedings in the English courts. The English Family Proceedings Court is formal, adversarial, and evidence-based. Although the Children Act of 1989 mitigated these aspects of procedure to some extent, the adversarial approach and the need for evidence still play a very large part. All parties usually are legally represented; the child and her parents have separate (free) legal representation and it is possible for grandparents, another parent, or other relatives to seek leave of the court to be represented. The Local Authority too has its lawyers. The combination of the need to investigate all allegations of suspected harm, the need to provide evidence of harm, and the adversarial nature of the proceedings influences the social workers' approach to their work. Their initial contact with a family, even sometimes if the parents themselves have asked for help, takes place in the context of their knowledge that, if the child turns out to be 'in danger,' as social workers, they will be expected to provide evidence in court against the parent.

The fact that this chapter has started by outlining the legal situation reflects the importance of the law in determining English child welfare practice. However, there are other important influences on the functioning of the system; first, the central control of the Department of Health and, second, the level and the focusing of the resources that are made available.

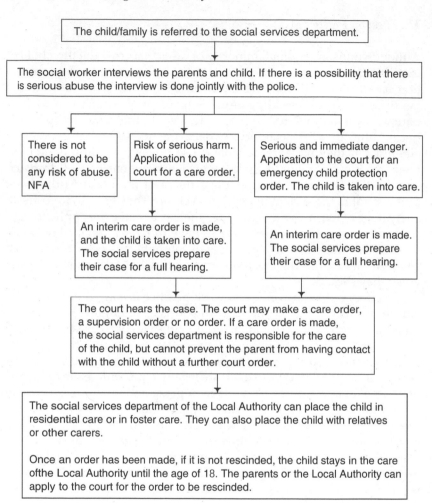

Figure 3.1: The Legal System of Child Protection.

Central Control, Local Control, and the Administrative System

Although the level of central control of the child protection system has grown steadily, it increased markedly from the time that the Children Act was passed. If the years leading up to 1989 were marked by the shift from a welfare to a legal discourse, the shift after 1989 from a legal to a managerial discourse was equally profound. The language of debate moved on from evidence and proof to accountability and transparency. Team leaders became team managers and clients became users.

The managerial approach permeated all levels of the system and each Local Authority has its guidelines and handbooks of procedure. But although the social work service for child protection is the responsibility of the Local Authority, it is heavily regulated by guidelines published by the Department of Health (DoH). The DoH aims to promote cooperation between different services and agencies and consistency between the responses of different Local Authorities. The level of regulation has grown steadily over the last twenty years. The most important of the guidelines are outlined below. The guidelines and other DoH publications provide the structure for the formal child protection procedures that precede and accompany the legal system for child protection.

'Working Together to Safeguard Children' (Department of Health, 1999)

This document outlines the most important of the DoH strategies for ensuring inter-agency cooperation. The first version of this document was published in 1976 and it has been developed and updated at interval – the latest version came out in 1999, with a significant change in name from *Working Together to Protect Children* to *Working Together to Safeguard Children* (DoH, 1999). Its main principle is that safeguarding children should be considered in the broader context of meeting the children's needs and offering the family support, and that services should be provided to strengthen parenting capacity. It dictates that each area should set up an Area Child Protection Committee (ACPC), with members from social services, the police, education, and health services.

The ACPCs have a number of tasks, which they delegate to different services. They are responsible for the establishment of the Child Protection Register (CPR), which holds the names of children in the area deemed to be 'at risk.' They are responsible for the management of Child Protection Conferences (CPCs) and for the provision of interdisciplinary training. The CPC makes the decision whether a child's name should be placed, or remain, on the CPR. The guidelines define child abuse in four categories: physical abuse, emotional abuse, sexual abuse, and neglect.

If a child is assessed as being 'at risk' or 'in danger' of abuse in any of these categories, the social services department must call an Initial Child Protection Conference (ICPC). A member of the social services department usually chairs the ICPC. All those concerned with the child should be invited, so the meeting can be quite large and could include, if relevant, the health visitor, teachers, nursery school employees, a school nurse, the general practitioner, a paediatrician, residential child care staff, or a foster carer. The Local Authority social worker will always be present and, if necessary, the police. The Local Authority solicitor may be present in an advisory capacity, and the guardian (if one has been appointed) as an observer. The parents are normally invited, although they may be asked to leave for some part of the meeting. Teenagers are sometimes invited, younger children very rarely. The purpose of the conference is to decide whether the child's name should be put on the CPR, and if so, to decide on a protection plan for the child's safety. The conference does not decide whether an application will be made for a court order; that is the responsibility of the Local Authority, (although the ICPC chair may recommend this). Following the ICPC, a core-group meeting (which includes the parents) has to be held within ten days. After the initial child protection conference, there are regular follow-up conferences until it is considered safe to remove the child's name from the register.

In complex and risky situations, it is sometimes necessary, before calling an ICPC, to discuss joint action with other agencies. In this situation, a Strategy Meeting is held between those agencies most directly involved, which will usually involve the police as well as the social services. At this meeting, plans will be made for taking any necessary emergency action, holding a child protection conference and/or initiating further inquiries.

The Guidelines to the Children Act 1989, Introduction and vols 1–10
(*Department of Health 1991–2*)

A series of guidelines to the Act were published by the Department of Health giving more detailed instructions on the implementation of the Act. They cover, among other things, court orders, residential child care, foster care, and the work of the Guardian Ad Litem. An introduction to the Act (Department of Health, 1989) sets out a principle which is of great importance for the everyday practice of the social worker, that the social services should work 'in partnership' with parents. This requirement to work in partnership is not stated in the Act, but the guidelines have a quasi-legal importance for social workers; they are expected to follow them unless they can produce a *very good reason* not to do so. So the social workers' duty to work in partnership with parents is second only to the duty to make the child their prime concern. These potentially conflicting priorities reflect the responses to, on the one hand, the inquiries into child deaths of the 1980s (London Borough of Brent, 1985; London Borough of Greenwich, 1987) and, on the other, the Cleveland inquiry of 1988 (Secretary of State for Social Services, 1988).

'Protecting Children: Messages from Research' (Department of Health 1995)

After the Children Act of 1989 (implemented in November 1991) had been in operation for four years, the Department of Health published a summary of research projects, usually referred to by the abbreviated title *Messages from Research*. The research projects provided evidence that the child protection system was drawing in many children who were found not to need protection. The summary of the conclusions drawn from the research gave two messages that were of particular importance to the Department of Health: first, the importance of the context of abuse; second, that too many cases were initiated as child protection and then, when the children were found not to be at risk, no services were offered. There was a call for professionals

> to work alongside families rather than disempower them, to raise their self-esteem rather than reproach families, to promote family relationships where children have their needs met, rather than leave untreated families with unsatisfactory parenting style. (Department of Health, 1995, p. 55)

One study (Gibbons, Conroy, & Bell, 1995) found that rates of registration between Local Authorities with similar demographic and socio-economic profiles varied widely and that only one in seven children whose situation was investigated were placed on the register. Farmer and Owen (1995) found that parents experienced the child protection procedures and the conference as intimidating and that even those mothers who had themselves asked for help, rather than being referred

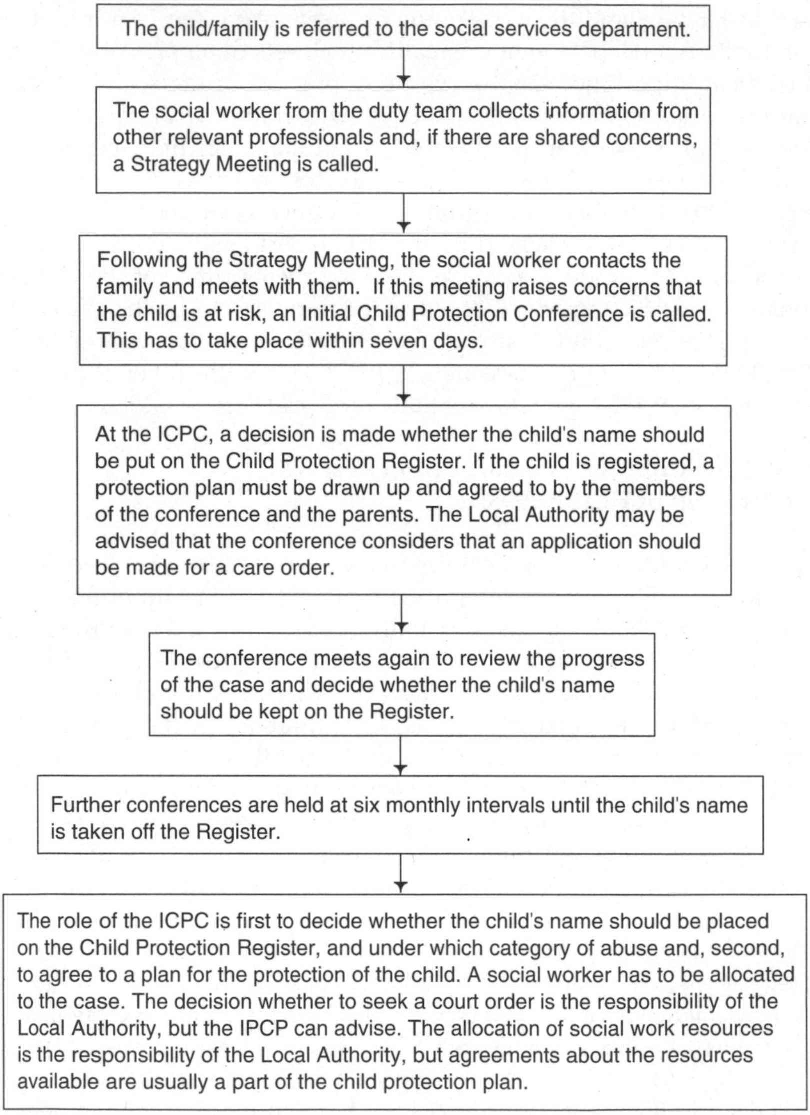

The child/family is referred to the social services department.

The social worker from the duty team collects information from other relevant professionals and, if there are shared concerns, a Strategy Meeting is called.

Following the Strategy Meeting, the social worker contacts the family and meets with them. If this meeting raises concerns that the child is at risk, an Initial Child Protection Conference is called. This has to take place within seven days.

At the ICPC, a decision is made whether the child's name should be put on the Child Protection Register. If the child is registered, a protection plan must be drawn up and agreed to by the members of the conference and the parents. The Local Authority may be advised that the conference considers that an application should be made for a care order.

The conference meets again to review the progress of the case and decide whether the child's name should be kept on the Register.

Further conferences are held at six monthly intervals until the child's name is taken off the Register.

The role of the ICPC is first to decide whether the child's name should be placed on the Child Protection Register, and under which category of abuse and, second, to agree to a plan for the protection of the child. A social worker has to be allocated to the case. The decision whether to seek a court order is the responsibility of the Local Authority, but the IPCP can advise. The allocation of social work resources is the responsibility of the Local Authority, but agreements about the resources available are usually a part of the child protection plan.

Figure 3.2: The Pre-Legal System of Child Protection.

by others, felt blamed and let down by the system. After the conference [ICPC], 70% of the parents were unhappy about their experience. More encouragingly, a study of parental participation (Thoburn, Lewis, & Shemmings, 1995) found that, in most cases, it was possible to achieve a significant degree of partnership with parents, even where there was disagreement. Whether or not parents agreed with the professionals, they valued workers who showed warmth and listened to what the parents had to say.

'The Framework for the Assessment of Children in Need and Their Families' (Department of Health, 2001)

The most recent guidelines reflect the impact of *Messages from Research* and demonstrate a shift in official thinking from concerns about failures to protect children to concerns about the failure of the system to make family support available where there were problems but not (or not yet) abuse. The *Framework for Assessment* (as it is usually called) sets out a structure for assessing children who may be defined as being 'in need' under s. 17 of the Children Act of 1989. The theoretical basis for the framework is holistic and ecological. There is an emphasis on the importance of taking account of the child's surroundings, her cultural context, her family and wider family, and the child's life experience as a whole. As a textbook, it gives a clear, well-researched and well-organized account of the process of a thorough assessment of a child's developmental state, the family strengths, and any needs for social support or specialist intervention. However, it is more than a textbook. It is accompanied by procedural requirements defining the time within which the assessment should be made and forms on which the assessment should be recorded. The time schedules depend on the complexity of the assessment required. An initial assessment should be completed within seven working days and a core (more detailed) assessment should be completed within thirty-five working days. The form to be completed for the core assessment of a child of three or four years is very detailed, being thirty-two pages long.

Resources

The Supporting Structures of Universal Services

The resources available for child welfare and child protection are part of a wider resource base for all families. The most important aspects of this are health services, education services, and family income support benefits.

HEALTH SERVICES

The National Health Service is a universal health service free at point of use. Hospital services, child and adolescent mental health services, and some community services are provided by independent trusts. Changes currently taking place aim to shift power from the hospitals to the primary care sector (general practitioner [GP], community nurses, and other community based resources). Each person is on the list of a GP and it is the norm for family members to have the same GP. Community paediatric health services provide a mother and baby health service. All children under five are 'on the books' of a health visitor (community paediatric nurse) and there is a school medical service. The health visitors have an important role in child welfare services. Although they focus mainly on infants and the early years routine health checks and immunizations, they also give advice on child rearing, and they are often the first people to know that families are in difficulty. Because they are a universal service, they are generally seen as a more acceptable and less stigmatizing source of help than Social Services. As well as being a major source of referrals, health visitors have a role in monitoring parents where there are child protection issues and are usually involved in child protection plans where there are children under five. Like all the other health services, they are underresourced and understaffed.

EDUCATION AND PRESCHOOL CARE

Compulsory school is from five to fifteen. Increasingly there are nursery school places available for children of four, and nursery school provision is being extended to three-year-olds. Some Local Authority Social Services Departments run nurseries which take children referred by the social services for welfare reasons, and which are open during school holidays and for longer than school hours. There are also many private nurseries and nursery schools, serving mainly families where both parents are in paid employment. There is a shortage of provision for preschool care for single parents or one-income families. There is also a shortage of afterschool centres. The Youth Service, which runs clubs for young people, is part of the education sector. Its services have been much reduced in the last ten years and there are far fewer youth clubs than there used to be. In many areas, leisure facilities for young people are very poor. Schools are supposed to have a designated teacher who acts as a source of information and consultation for the staff on child protection issues and handles liaison with social services in cases of possible abuse.

WELFARE BENEFITS

There is an extremely complex system of benefits for parents with children. It remains one of the least generous in Europe (Lobmeyer & Wilkinson, 2000), although child benefit levels have improved recently and there are some tax reduction supports for working parents on low incomes. There is an effort to help mothers to return to work and some benefits are focused on enabling this (e.g., financial support for child care). There have been recent government initiatives to increase support for families in socially marginalized areas.

Services for the Support of Families in Difficulties

Local Authority Social Services Departments provide some family support, delivered by their social workers and by 'family workers,' who usually lack formal qualifications. Most family support services are now provided by nongovernmental organizations (NGOs). They are usually charitable organizations employing qualified staff. There are also services provided by commercial or private for-profit agencies (mainly residential care services). The NGOs include residential care, family placement (fostering) agencies, family centres of various kinds, drop-in centres, case work and counselling services, and advice agencies. The NGOs are funded partly by the money that they raise as charities, and by charging the Local Authority for their services, and/or increasingly by direct government grants. The Local Authorities used to provide most of these services themselves, but since the early 1980s they have been expected to contract them out to NGOs.

Sources of Funding

The main source of funding for Child and Family Services is through the Local Authority, either from the revenue of local taxation or through support from central government. There is considerable debate over the realities of the levels of funding available. Practitioners feel that resources are continually diminishing; politicians (both local and central) say that there is more money in the system than there used to be. What is quite clear is that there are fewer social workers and there currently are many unfilled social work posts, particularly in Local Authority Children and Families Teams in the inner cities.[5] At the same time, the workloads steadily increase. There has been some transferring of resources. For example, residential care services have been reduced and there has been an expansion of foster care, which is a cheaper option. The legal system absorbs substantial resources, both indirectly and directly through the costs of social workers attending court and writing reports for the court, as well as through the work of the Guardian, and the legal departments. The child protection conference system also requires a great deal of time for meetings and report writing. Money is not usually available for preventive work, although there may be services that can be used *after* a crisis. A social worker's time is *always* in limited supply.

Resource Problems

The Children Act of 1989 was put into operation in 1991 in a wider socioeconomic context of increasing resource constraints on all aspects of Local Authority spending. This prevented the hoped-for developments in services for children in need. Restricted resources had to be reserved for meeting the Local Authorities' statutory duties in relation to child protection. There was also a drive by central government to develop a more hands-off approach by local government, so that Local Authorities were told to contract out services. In child-welfare, this encouraged the development of independent agencies in residential child care, fostering, the provision of aftercare for young adults leaving state care, family services, and family support.

The new diversity had advantages, but was affected by the focusing of services on child protection, so that agencies which had previously provided broader family support services were now only funded to provide child protection services. For example, a family centre run by a well-established family welfare charity previously offered residential services for the whole family and was originally intended to provide a program of assessment and treatment for dysfunctional families. Families were expected to stay for three to six months (sometimes more). The Local Authorities using the centre ceased providing funding for families attending the centre, except for the purpose of an assessment of their parenting for the court. For this assessment, families were expected to stay for six to eight weeks.

There are two central resource problems. First, the resources available to Local Authorities have diminished and, second, what is left has been focused on mandated child protection concerns. The Audit Commission (1994) pointed out that the lack of preventive work with families led to more being spent on child protection and state care, which was not cost effective. There is an effort to create a better balance between child protection and family support, but this has proved difficult. The *Framework for Assessment*, published six years later, is a continual effort to foster an improved balance. A recent Children Act Report revealed that the Social Services Inspectorate found the following:

> The general picture was one of scarcity, and thresholds for services were high. Other agencies continued to report that identifying child protection concerns was the key to unlocking service. (Department of Health, 2001, p. 49)

Recent Changes in Patterns of Resourcing

Recently, there have been central government initiatives to promote the development of local services and support social inclusion. The Sure Start program is a system of grants for local initiatives for services for children under four and their families. This was created in 1998 and the services and supports that it finances are just beginning to become available. In 2000, the Children's Fund, a similar program of support for services for older children (roughly five- to thirteen-year-olds) was announced. Connections is another initiative aimed at providing support for thirteen- to nineteen-year-old children (twenty-one if they have a disability). These developments have the effect of shifting more of the control of resources from local to central government. New money is going to initiatives shared between local communities and central government (the Sure Start model), rather than to restore the diminished services of Local Authorities.

How the System Works in Practice

Up to this point, we have looked at the system in terms of legislature mandates and service delivery structures. But a description of the legal frameworks and structures does not give a picture of the system in action. What does it all look like from the point of view of parents who, whether they like it or not, are involved with the system? What is their journey through the system? The following case is based on a parent's account.[6] All names have been changed and identifying details altered. The events in this story took place in the mid-1990s, before the *Framework for Assessment* was published, and illustrates the problems that the *Framework* seeks to address.

Elizabeth's story unfolds over several years, and started when she was herself in care as an adolescent. She had a social worker then, and again later, when she was in a mother-and-baby unit, but she moved to another borough, and for two years she was out of contact with social workers. Her health visitor introduced her to a support group in a family centre run by parents. She went to social services because she was hitting her eldest daughter, who was three years old. The children were put on the Child Protection Register and she was allocated a social worker. Nursery school places were arranged for the children. Then the children were taken off the Register after about six months, and the social worker stopped offering her appointments. Things went downhill again and, in December, Elizabeth asked her social worker whether she could go to the residential family centre. She was put on the waiting list – and waited. She commented, 'I can't see the sense in someone asking for it and then having to wait till something drastic happens for them actually to do something.' The children were put back on the Register. Elizabeth knew that being on the Register was the best way of getting help. 'I just went along with whatever they said, because they know best ... That's the only way to get the help that I'm getting now – to let them be on the Register.'

However, she found the conference (ICPC) frightening. 'It was like I wasn't there, as if they were talking about someone else.' She felt that the family centre worker was there 'to give evidence' and, although she was told that the conference would only consider matters of fact, not hearsay, she felt that this was not the case. She felt that she was being judged. Elizabeth had mixed views about her experience. She had got on quite well with her most recent social worker. She was able to go and tell her when depression was coming on so that 'it's like I've warned her.' But she could have done with being given help before the children were registered. 'They [the social workers] have to see that there is a major problem first.'

Elizabeth's experience demonstrates the problems caused by lack of resources and by the redirection of resources. She risked losing support if her children's names were taken off the Register. When she waited for a place at the residential family centre, she experienced the effects of the switch in resources from family support to child protection. She wanted help, and used it thoughtfully to prevent problems, warning her social worker when things were going badly. She could see how destructive it was to have to wait while things got worse before being able to get help; as doubtless could her social worker. She found the process of the Child Protection Conference (ICPC) intimidating. It was frightening because it could lead to her children being taken away. But she knew she needed help, so she had to go along with the system. Elizabeth's views echo the findings of *Messages from Research*. Although she was able to build a good enough relationship with her social worker (although she continued to trust her social worker less than she trusted the support group at the family centre), she found the system alienating.

Elizabeth's story does not illustrate all aspects of the process. Figure 3.3 summarizes the pathways that a referral can take, depending on the assessment of risk and need. The exact arrangements vary from one Local Authority to another and the description given below sets out the procedures of one borough.

All *new referrals* are processed by the centralized duty team, which covers the whole authority (in this case a large borough). A decision has to be taken whether or not further action is required. Action could be limited to referral to another agency, but might be for an initial assessment (under the *Framework for Assessment*) or for a child protection investigation (under s. 47 of the Children Act 1989).

If an *initial assessment* is undertaken, it might still be decided that no further action is needed, or that the case should be referred to another agency. However, it might be considered necessary to carry out a more detailed, 'core assessment' (see *Framework for Assessment*). During the core assessment, it may be necessary to consider a specialist assessment, for example, an assessment by a clinical psychologist. This should be carried out within thirty-five days and the family should be offered supportive services while this is going on. Following the initial assessment or during the core assessment, if it were thought that the child was at risk of significant harm, a child protection investigation (s. 47) would be carried out.

Following the *core assessment*, there might be a further, multiagency core assessment alongside the provision of services. A Child in Need Plan would be developed which would be reviewed every six months. If the core assessment had identified that the child was at risk of significant harm, there would be a child protection investigation.

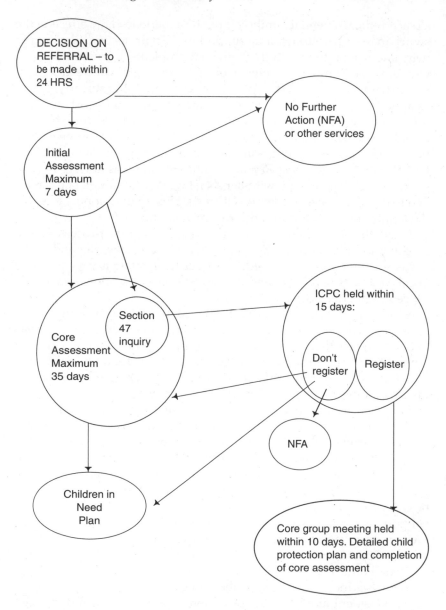

Figure 3.3. Using the *Framework for Assessment*: A journey through the child protection system.

Problems with the System

It is proving difficult to make the changes necessary to respond to the criticisms levied in *Messages from Research*. Practitioners did not disagree with the aims of working to empower parents and to improve unsatisfactory and harmful family relationships, but these are not easy goals to achieve. It was possible to make cosmetic changes to such things as numbers of children registered, but working successfully with families in difficulty and parents under stress required time and other resources that were no more available at the end of the 1990s than at the beginning. It also required social workers and their managers to shift their focus from child protection without providing them with much reassurance that, if things went wrong, they would themselves be protected from public and media vilification.

The English system is difficult for both social workers and families. It is felt by practitioners to be inflexible and bureaucratic (Hetherington, Cooper, Smith, & Wilford, 1997; Parton, Thorpe, & Wattam, 1997). There are many forms to fill in, deadlines to be met, and guidelines to be absorbed and followed. The social workers are very aware of the problems for parents and children that the system creates. A social worker participating in the Nottingham Project (see below) said:

> The child protection register itself is highly stigmatising and works against the concept of consent and undermines people ... Going to an initial child protection conference must have a massive impact on families. The process is almost like a judicial process, where at the end of the meeting we decide whether they are guilty or not of the abuse. (personal communication)

Social workers feel that they do not have the resources to respond to more emergencies and that this prevents them from supporting families. Yet they are being told that they should work with families and this is what they would like to do.

Parents find the processes of child protection intimidating, both the Child Protection Conference and the courts (Baistow & Hetherington, 1998; Thoburn, Lewis, & Shemmings, 1995). They are very aware that to get resources you have to present yourself as failing and that this is risky, as well as undermining to their self-esteem. They do not feel supported by the system when they are in difficulty, but feel blamed for failing to 'manage.' Asking for help is a last resort.

Responding to Current Problems with the System

In spite of the intensive efforts of the Department of Health [DoH] in issuing guidelines and providing summaries of research, training material, and a wide range of supporting information, there is a great deal of dissatisfaction with the system. Rebalancing family support and child protection is difficult. Research with social workers in Children and Families Teams undertaken in 1999 showed that children in need would get an assessment, but probably very little else unless they were assessed as being at risk (Hetherington, Baistow, Katz, Mesie, & Trowell, 2002). Major problems with limited resources, particularly professional time, continue. On a more positive note, a recent project in Nottingham demonstrates that, with supportive management and a motivated work force, it may be possible to make important advances without any major structural change.

The Nottingham Project

The Nottingham Project is a cooperative venture between Nottingham City Council Social Services Department and Children Across Europe, a network of European researchers working on international comparisons. One of the aims of Children Across Europe is to promote the development of good practice through the study of alternative approaches. Nottingham was selected to pilot some innovations since it has a high volume of child protection activity, with a high number of children on the Child Protection Register and high numbers involved in care proceedings.

A project manager was employed to develop and implement a twelve-month action plan.[7] A focus group is being used to gather the views of workers from different agencies about to child protection practice. The focus group will also look at various European models and, using case studies, consider the development of different approaches.

The Issues Identified

At the beginning of the Project, an analysis was made of statistical information. One important finding (reflecting the findings of *Messages from Research*) was the inequity between the numbers of children going to the ICPC and the numbers actually registered – the average over a nine-month period (April 2000 to December 2000) for children registered was 61%. This meant that 39% of children presented to Conference were not subject to registration and therefore did not require a child protection plan. Many families experience these meetings as stressful and feel their parenting is judged as being inadequate, so there is good reason to look for alternatives to such families being presented to Conference. The following figures regarding child protection activity in the month of June 2000 supported the need for further scrutiny of practice, decision making, and risk management:

- 32% of all enquiries led to a child protection investigation (Children Act, 1989, s. 47)
- 46% of child protection investigations resulted in an Initial Child Protection Conference (ICPC).
- 54% of children who were the focus of an ICPC were registered.

At the same time as the Nottingham Project was developing, the local implementation of the *Framework for Assessment* was taking place. The project needed to take account of the current climate in which social workers and other professionals work, and the historical influences that have shaped the way they work with children and families. As already described, social work in the United Kingdom has become proceduralized and bureaucratic. Ensuring that children's needs are met can be secondary to the actual process of investigation. Social workers have to face contradictory messages in working with children and families and in assessing and managing risk.

In order for change to occur, practitioners need to feel safe and supported. They need to know that there will be shared responsibility and accountability for decision making. The Project sought to introduce ways of working with families which would ensure that child protection processes are not invoked unless necessary and which would ensure that workers feel safe to practice in this new way.

The Themes

The Project drew on comparative research that looked at the child protection systems of some other European countries.[8] Key themes of subsidiarity, negotiation, and reflective practice emerged from the comparison of different systems (Hetherington, Cooper, Smith, & Wilford, 1997).

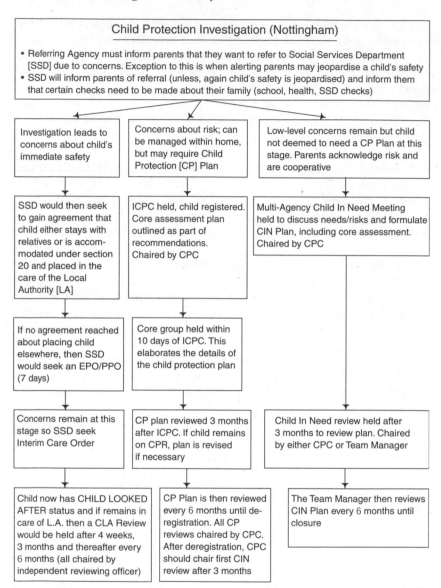

Figure 3.4: Flow Chart of a Child Protection Investigation.

SUBSIDIARITY

The political philosophy of subsidiarity promotes the use of the lowest level of intervention consonant with the effective resolution of the problem. The first resource should be the family, then the local community, then the region, and then the national state. What can be done by a nongovernmental organization should be. Schäfer (1995) describes subsidiarity as an ambiguous concept open to widely varied interpretation:

> The liberal, anti-collective and anti-state aspect of the principle of subsidiarity demands abstinence and non-interference by the state ... On the other hand [the principle] allows neither the state nor any other 'large community' to escape from its duties ... The larger community must support the smaller ones in their activities. (p. 53)

In relation to child welfare, subsidiarity leads to an emphasis on the importance of working at the most local and least formal level that is effective:

> This means that whatever smaller and more localised institutions or groups can do on their own must not be removed by a higher level of competence or by power of the state. Responsibility and decision making should rest with the people most involved. (Hetherington et al., 1997, p. 83)

NEGOTIATION

The resolution of disputes through negotiation is commonplace in some contexts, but requires a formal space where discussion and argument can take place before the law is involved. When the law could and might be invoked, there is an impetus to reach agreement or the partial resolution of a conflict and this can be used to support a negotiated rather than an imposed solution. Conflicts over the protection of children and the rights of parents are conflicts between the state and the parent. In many countries, there is some provision for reaching a negotiated solution to child protection disputes between parents and social workers. The location of this provision within the system varies, but a space is created for negotiation between the parents and the social workers under the auspices of another person or group. There is a link to the principle of subsidiarity in the assumption that, in most situations, a resolution should be found at the voluntary level and that negotiation should be tried before compulsion is used.

REFLECTIVE PRACTICE

The professional authority and confidence of the social work profession depends on a readiness to use their relevant knowledge base in conjunction with a critical awareness of the impact of subjective experience on practice. The development of reflective practice requires the input and support of a supervisor or team who will enable the worker to reflect on the process of her work and explore alternatives. The support of a team can help the social worker to locate her own responses to a family's situation in the wider context of the expectations of the community. Without a well-founded professional confidence, social workers neither could nor should abandon the safety of following rules and guidelines.

The project manager focused on developing strategies that would incorporate the main principles from these themes. The Project aims to create structures that flow from the application of general principles to particular situations, rather than seeking to correspond primarily to managerial and administrative expectations.

The Strategies

Subsidiarity

In order to translate this principle into local practice, the Project is developing strategies promoting the use of nonstatutory approaches. One of these is to ensure that consultation structures are put in place before Child Protection Conferences [ICPC] are needed. This will help to avoid the introduction of a higher level of power than is necessary. It also will filter out families where risk is manageable by means of a 'child in need' plan, negating the need to have a Child Protection Conference (or register the child) by promoting voluntary agreements between the Social Services Department, children, and families.

The Structure of the Child in Need (CIN) Meeting

The new procedures will state that consultation should take place with a Child Protection Coordinator (CPC) before a decision is made to proceed to hold an Initial Child Protection Conference (ICPC). This will serve to share responsibility and accountability between the social worker, her team manager, and the CPC. In addition, it will allow an opportunity for the social worker and her manager to reflect on their decision making and explore other options, prior to holding an ICPC. Holding a multidisciplinary CIN meeting would be one option.

New developments have to respond to the likely anxieties of the social workers. Workers will feel anxious about cancelling an ICPC, so the official status of the CIN meeting needs to be raised. It has therefore been recommended that an independent worker should chair this meeting. The impartiality and independence of the chair potentially will give preventive/family support work the same status and authority as child protection work, where there is an independent chair.[9]

In December 2000, there were approximately 415 children on Nottingham City's Child Protection Register. In December 2001, there were 307 children on the Register. The work of this project has contributed to this 26% reduction.

Negotiation

Negotiation and mediation are key issues in seeking to find solutions/ agreements to keep processes at the lowest level possible. Systems need to be in place to act as a buffer to more intrusive legal intervention into family life. A negotiation meeting will be introduced to operationalize these goals. This will be led by two workers acting as 'mediators,' from agencies other than the Social Services Department. A Family Mediation Service has agreed to second a worker to this project one half day a week. This worker is skilled and experienced in mediation, but also has significant child protection knowledge; the second worker is a manager from a local Sure Start program. This worker also has both family support and child protection experience.

The Structure of the Negotiation Meeting

Use of the meeting will be open to families, social workers, and other professionals. Families will be able to request a negotiation meeting if they feel that they are experiencing problems with their social worker. Social workers who feel they were not making any progress in their work with a family will also be able to request a meeting. Workers from social services and other agencies will be able to request a meeting if, for example, they feel that the family of a child on the Child Protection Register is not being cooperative, or where plans are seen as not working and concerns remain.

The aim of the negotiation meeting will be to hear the views of the main parties involved and to attempt to broker an agreement to avoid the use of the child protection system. The two mediators will first meet with the family in order to ascertain how they view the situation and why things have become 'stuck.' They will also seek to find out how the family members feel communication could be improved and how they might be helped to work together with the Social Services Department to try to avoid more intrusive intervention into their family life. The mediators then will speak to the social worker and her team manager to identify any perceived barriers to working effectively with the family. Following this, the negotiation meeting will be set up and both parties will attend. The mediators will try to reach a voluntary agreement between the parties. This is the only role of the mediator, who will not seek to make an assessment of concerns but will try to clarify with all parties what improvements are needed and what the Social Services Department might do if the situation fails to improve and concerns remain about a child's welfare.

Currently, many of these cases go to court in the absence of any other options. The court process is difficult for parents, expensive for the state, and time consuming for everyone. Although negotiation will not be successful in all cases, and decisions to invoke care proceedings will be appropriate in certain cases, the use of negotiated solutions has the potential to prevent unnecessary stress and to save money.

This is a new way of working and information sheets have been circulated to all team managers requesting them to discuss the proposals with staff; a leaflet will be available for parents inviting them to take part in the Project. At the time of writing, the Department is undergoing a major restructuring program and as a result the introduction of the negotiation meeting is being delayed.

Reflective Practice

Social workers and their managers often are responsible for working with families seen as presenting high risk and complex challenges. They carry multiple, often contrasting responsibilities, providing both assistance and policing. Ideally, these complexities require discussion and reflection involving many different perspectives. With current pressures on social workers and their supervisors, time for this type of discussion and reflection usually is lacking in supervision. Furthermore, organizational cultures are bureaucratic and proceduralized. As a consequence, space for workers' use of professional judgment is limited and they struggle to act with confidence and authority.

The Project is setting up a Consultation Forum which will provide staff with the opportunity to refer cases to a multiagency group for discussion. The hope is this support will permit social workers to engage with families with more confidence and authority. The Forum will use reflection and discussion to develop individual workers' professional skills and enhance their confidence. The cases that will be bought to the Forum will be considered high risk and complicated, where the team manager and the social worker may feel unsure about how to proceed.

The Structure of the Consultation Forum

The Forum will have a core membership (which will include a Social Services Department manager). Since the Forum will accept responsibility for the advice and guidance that it gives, this core membership will give the meeting Departmental authority allowing workers to feel protected. The Forum will have access to a pool of multiagency personnel, whom they can invite to the meeting depending on the issues involved. Having access to such broad consultation will provide social workers with opportunities to develop a wider understanding of issues and options for helping. Having action plans underpinned by a Departmental strategy for working with a particular family will increase their professional confidence and authority.

As with all such ventures, the development of the Project is affected by events in the broader system. The reorganization of local government structures and the introduction of new public initiatives to combat social exclusion are two recent developments that have impinged on the Project and may have unforeseen implications.

The Future of the Child Welfare System

The kinds of change being promoted by the Nottingham Project are not dependent on specific service delivery structures. They are an application of particular principles to processes which are already in place, an attempt to modify and/or support what already exists.[10] The principles that currently guide the functioning of child welfare in England are managerial principles of accountability, transparency, and service delivery controls within a hierarchical framework. Applying these managerial principles gives the system some benefits. For example, there are formal structures for cooperation between agencies. The publications of the Department of Health disseminate new research and provide the basis for a common approach and cooperation between services and professions. The system is formally transparent and families know what is happening to them.

But managerialism leads to increased rigidity, paperwork, stricter time scales, and an emphasis on the use of approved procedures. Managerial principles do not foster trust in the professionalism of individual workers, either by service users, other professionals, or service managers. The current emphasis may hinder the negotiation of ways forward that are, in reality, the best of several imperfect options. Improving family support, the current goal of the system, is not likely to be compatible with existing managerial methods. Families have complex and untidy needs, which change unpredictably or may fail to change, and require long-term assistance. Successful preventive work is hard to measure, and stasis may not be failure; it may be the best possible outcome. Trust takes time to build but without trust between families and professionals as well as between different professionals, communication with children and partnerships with parents lacks substance and reliability. More effective intervention requires trust, the ability to negotiate disagreements, and the authority to take action.

The development of the English system demonstrates how changes in the underlying discourse have shaped the way in which the work is carried out. It is not possible or desirable to go backwards, and a return to the welfare discourse of earlier years is not the solution. The issue now is how to develop a new discourse that incorporates attention to rights and to the accountability of the legal and managerial discourses, while responding to the human complexity of family life and to children's needs. There is an opportunity to dismantle the parallel tracks of child protection and family support and to realign the system on the unifying concept of children's welfare. Changes in formal structures might support such a change, but will not of themselves bring it about. We need to change how we think about child welfare.

[Addendum (November 2005)] Major changes are taking place moving toward integrating all health, education, and welfare services for children in local Children's Trusts. Child welfare responsibility has moved to the Department for Education and Skills and a Children's Ombudsman has been set up. Child protection social workers are being amalgamated into multi-disciplinary teams located in primary schools. Area Child Protection Committees are being reorganized into Safeguarding Boards and will no longer have to maintain a Child Protection Register. The impacts of these changes on English child welfare are unknown.

NOTES

1 See Parton, Thorpe, and Wattam (1997) *Child Protection: Risk and the Moral Order*, chapter 2.
2 For a full account of the developments leading to the passing of the Children Act 1989, and a discussion of the changes made, see Parton (1991).
3 In 1999/2000 there were 6,298 care orders (SSI 2001).
4 There are specialist teams within the social services department, the Children and Families teams, which undertake work with children in need, children at risk, and children in need of protection.
5 In 1999 there were between 20% and 40% unfilled social work posts in London boroughs (SSI report 2001).
6 This story was told to us by one of the participants in a research project comparing parents' experience of the child welfare system in England and France (Baistow & Hetherington, 1999).
7 The project is organized by a part-time project manager funded initially for one year by the National Society for the Prevention of Cruelty to Children (NSPCC). The project has the support of the British Association for the Study and Prevention of Child Abuse and Neglect (BAPSCAN). The impetus for the project came from comparative research carried out by researchers at the Centre for Comparative Social Work Studies (Brunel University), the Tavistock Institute, and the Practice Development Unit of the NSPCC.
8 The countries were Belgium (Flemish-speaking and French-speaking communities), France, Germany, Italy, Netherlands, Scotland, and England.
9 Currently the team manager chairs CIN reviews unless it is a borderline case in terms of risk, in which case the chair will be a child protection coordinator.
10 See Cooper, Hetherington, and Katz (2003) where the outcome of the Nottingham pilot project is discussed. Its success is attributed, in part, to the dual emphases on cultural change and structural change as part of the same process, an implementation process that was not rushed, and that allowed leadership and endorsement of new ideas to come from all system levels. Outcomes suggest that this Project aptly illustrates the possibilities for changes at the local level.

4 Forming and Sustaining Partnerships in Child and Family Welfare: The American Experience

PATRICIA SCHENE

In the current child welfare environment in the United States, one of the more positive developments is the formation of partnerships at the community level to share the responsibility for child protection beyond the formal public child welfare agencies (U.S. Advisory Board on Child Abuse and Neglect, 1993). This development is closely aligned with a strengths-based approach to vulnerable families as well as a willingness to serve more children and families reported for child abuse and neglect in a less adversarial manner (Farrow & Executive Session, 1997). The convergence of these developments is changing the face of child welfare in many communities in the United States. Of course, policy in this area is ultimately the responsibility of states, counties, and local governments and therefore changes more slowly and less evenly than if it were centralized. Nonetheless, the concept of building partnerships for child protection is *one* of the major current positive forces operating in the country.

Building community partnerships for protecting children arises from the recognition that it takes a community to protect children from abuse and neglect. The formal child protection agency cannot do this work alone (Waldfogel, 1998). The development of partnerships at the neighbourhood and community level is fundamentally directed towards involving more of the important formal and nonformal resources in every community in the work of protecting children.

There is a growing recognition that communities need to have reliable services and supports to prevent child maltreatment, to share in the intervention when maltreatment does occur, and to provide sustainable ways to connect children and families to supports after cases are closed to formal services.

The Development of the Response to Child Maltreatment

The response to child abuse and neglect in the United States has always depended on some level of partnership between the official child protection agency and the community. Statutory responsibilities to report child abuse connected reporters to the agency. Law enforcement personnel have long been involved in those cases where the abuse or neglect reaches the level of criminal conduct. Courts have always had a major role to play in determining whether the harm the child experienced or could experience warranted removal from the home and placement in some form of out-of-home care. Child protection agencies have had purchase-of-service contracts or memoranda of understanding with private and public agencies to provide some of the specialized services needed by abused and neglected children and their families.

The current focus on partnerships in child protection, however, goes well beyond what has been established in the past in terms of the participants and the roles played by the partnership. Community partnerships for child protection encompasses a more comprehensive form of involvement to prevent, respond to, and ameliorate the conditions that contribute to child abuse and neglect. Moreover, the concept of partnerships also includes, in some communities, actually sharing responsibilities for decision making on open cases. Partnerships also are expanding to include people in the community who do not have a formal role to play as part of an existing human service agency.

To understand the reasons communities are moving in this direction, it is necessary to briefly address the development of public involvement in the abuse and neglect of children, the processes underway fostering partnerships, and the emerging pattern of shared responsibility for protecting children.

Background/History of Public Involvement in Child Maltreatment

The protection of children is a value shared by all cultures and communities around the globe. Although the role of parents varies across cultures, it is always important and usually the primary source of protection, but the community also has a stake in the well-being of its children. In the United States, independence, privacy, and parental rights are highly valued. The legal system supports the right of families to rear their children according to their own values and requires evidence of danger of harm before the state may intrude on the sanctity of the home to protect children (Schene, 1998).

The pattern of intervention in child abuse and neglect throughout much of the nineteenth century was largely focused on the poor, and oriented towards the 'rescue' of children perceived to be neglected or abused. Much of the early work in child protection was provided through private agencies financed by both public and charitable dollars. The forerunners of the child protective service agencies of today were private associations known as 'anti-cruelty societies' formed in many eastern and some mid-western cities in the late nineteenth and early twentieth centuries. These agencies (more than three hundred by the early 1900s) were supported by both public and private funds and investigated reports of child abuse and neglect, filed complaints against the perpetrators in court, and aided the courts in their prosecution (Antler & Antler, 1979; Costin, 1985).

By the mid-twentieth century, the issue of child protection was transformed in the eyes of professionals from one of law enforcement to one of rehabilitation through social services. Efforts to protect children gradually became part of the growing array of human services provided by governmental agencies. By the 1940s, functions once performed by the private societies were taken over by a variety of public and voluntary organizations such as juvenile courts, juvenile protective associations, family welfare societies, and some newly formed governmental bodies (Costin, 1985).

The federal government became more consistently involved with the passage of the Social Security Act of 1935, establishing not only Aid to Dependent Children, but also Title IVB – Child Welfare Services. Limited federal funding encouraged states to develop preventive and protective services for vulnerable children. In practice, however, states used these funds mainly to pay for foster care, not to provide supportive services to families whose children remained at home. This remains the main way federal funds are utilized today.

In the 1960s, medical professionals focused public attention on evidence that many physical injuries to children were apparently inflicted by parents or caregivers. X-rays and other documentation of these injuries brought widespread coverage to what was named the 'battered child syndrome.' Child abuse became an issue of national importance and the role played by government agencies in identifying and responding to the problem expanded significantly.

In 1974, federal legislation – The Child Abuse Prevention and Treatment Act (CAPTA) – encouraged states to pass laws requiring professionals and others to identify children who needed protection, and to support public social services to investigate these reports and keep track of substantiated cases. Buoyed by growing public awareness of child maltreatment, this federal leadership helped to establish a nationwide system of child protection, including state statutes that mandate the reporting of physical abuse, neglect, sexual abuse, and exploitation. Child Protective Services (CPS) agencies were to investigate reports, and central registries of perpetrators and victims were established in all states.

The formal system through which we respond to child abuse and neglect is now largely a governmental one. The private child advocacy organizations and private child welfare agencies who led initial actions on behalf of vulnerable children made important contributions, but they only reached a small portion of the children experiencing abuse and neglect. Reporting laws greatly expanded the number of children identified, and governmental programs were established in every state to respond. These laws were passed out of a widespread and growing concern that many children were being abused and neglected by their parents and caretakers. There was a strong sense that society needed to protect children whose parents were unwilling or unable to provide that protection.

Primary responsibility is currently vested in public Child Protective Services agencies that receive, investigate, and respond to reports of child abuse and neglect from professionals, family members, and the general public. CPS is usually linked to child welfare departments with broader responsibilities, including foster care and adoption. CPS functions are funded through state or local authorities and are governed by state statutes, which are often shaped by federal legislation and funding. At the local level, the work of CPS is done in close coordination with the courts, law enforcement agencies, and local social service providers.

The construction of the response to child maltreatment has been based on several core assumptions. One of these assumptions is that parents would resist intervention and offers of help for their families. It is also presumed that legal authority to intervene in family life could only exist if reports were carefully investigated and clearly substantiated. Finally, child protective services have normally been considered a nonvoluntary service provided with the support of the courts. Many of these assumptions have been challenged as we have moved forward to build partnerships with families and communities to address child abuse and neglect and serve more families voluntarily.

Why Partnerships?

There is a growing recognition that communities need to have reliable services and supports to prevent child maltreatment, to share in the intervention when it does occur, and to provide sustainable ways to connect children and families to supports after cases are closed to formal services (Farrow & Executive Session, 1997). Although the work of the formal child protection agency (CPS) will always be central, there is a strong sense that many cases reported to CPS might be better served by a different system of supports and services. Moreover, of the cases that belong with CPS, many require resources that go beyond what can be offered by one agency. A coordinated approach using a variety of supports and services is needed by most families served by CPS.

Coordinating resources and developing needed services are key roles for community partnerships. It is also clear that many vulnerable children and families are not being reached by any agency. A key part of the community partnership agenda is to reach out to such families, building visible and accessible ways to connect families to support. Making it easier to both offer and receive help has been a shared goal of partnerships.

Processes Underway Fostering Partnerships

The development of support for partnerships arose out of a broader child welfare reform agenda that has been taking form for more than a decade. Every state in the union has made some significant changes in its response to child abuse and neglect. The agenda for reform, although generated from different groups and different immediate pressures, is largely consistent. There has been wide agreement that we needed to address concerns in a number of key areas.

Federal legislation has played a key role over the past decade. There is widespread recognition and understanding of the limitations of the existing system of reporting and response. There is also a growing sense of community concern about vulnerable children and a clearer willingness to play a greater role in their protection. Models of community partnerships now exist and provide models for other communities. There is an increased focus on outcomes and accountability that many recognize cannot be achieved unless a variety of services and supports form partnerships to achieve these outcomes.

FEDERAL LEGISLATION

The Family Preservation and Support Initiative (Public Law (PL) 103-66), passed in 1993, was the catalyst for communities to come together to identify what resources they had and what they needed in the way of services for family support and family preservation. The state plans emerging from this process became the foundation for using federal funds. It is assumed that partnerships between public and private nonprofit agencies are the mechanisms through which services are delivered, both to support families to prevent initial or further child maltreatment and to preserve families undergoing crises that could lead to the placement of their children in foster care. Funding to support these services was a new entitlement and this funding has increased since 1993 (Family Preservation and Family Support Initiative, Public Law 103-66, 1993, amended 1997).

Federal policies in recent years focused on the three major outcomes of intervention in child welfare – child safety, permanency, and well being. Statutory language and policy clarifies the requirement that state plans have to be based on community input about the best ways to achieve these outcomes. The Adoption and Safe Families Act (PL 105-89), passed in 1997, focused on promoting safe and stable families by moving children in foster care more rapidly into permanent homes and encouraging adoptions. Reasonable efforts still had to be made to rehabilitate the family to enable reunification when children were removed from their homes, but permanency for children had to occur within a shorter time period – usually within twelve months of placement in out-of-home care. One effect of the legislation has been to increase efforts to bring community resources together early in the process to help multiproblem families with children in placement in order to meet the time frames for permanency planning.

Limitations of Existing System of Reporting and Response

One area which has received much attention is the need for earlier intervention with troubled families. It has become clear that we cannot wait for a report of child maltreatment to offer help, nor can we screen out so many cases without offering assistance. Reporting skyrocketed after reporting systems were implemented in all states in the 1960s, with maltreatment reports increasing more than 300% from the early 1970s to the early 1990s. Reporting is not currently increasing at the same rate, but has levelled off in recent years. Still, more than 2.9 million children were reported in 1999, representing an enormous burden on the resources of CPS agencies to respond adequately when someone in the community suspects child maltreatment. Almost 40% of the reports were screened out without an investigation; of those investigated, only about 30% were judged to be substantiated. Of the 461,000 children in substantiated reports, only 55.8% received services after the investigation; an additional 217,000 children on reports that were not substantiated also received some services (United States Department of Health and Human Services, 2001).

The volume of reporting, the volume of abused and neglected children who do not come to the attention of CPS, and the limitations on the resources of CPS agencies to provide sufficient and effective services has led many to look for alternative ways to respond. Added to these factors is the fact that many families who come to the attention of CPS cannot or do not have access to the variety of social supports and services that could enhance their parenting and stabilize their families. Moreover, many families reported to CPS would be willing to utilize such supports and services without the coercive, nonvoluntary intervention associated with being identified as abusing or neglecting their children. Undergirding these considerations was the long-standing value that protecting children and strengthening families is the responsibility of the whole community, not just the CPS agency and the courts.

The cumulative impact of these limitations and the reexamination of some of the underlying assumptions of our system of reporting and response has led to a greater openness to reaching out beyond CPS to the wider community to form partnerships for the protection of children.

Community Concern and Willingness to Play a Greater Role

The pressure to engage families more effectively to enhance their commitment to positive changes has also played a major role in the reform of the American CPS. Moreover, there are many people and groups in many lower-income communities who have become increasingly concerned about the welfare of their children. They have seen many parents caught up in the problems of substance abuse, domestic violence, and the demands associated with getting and keeping a job. Housing is often precarious and childcare unaffordable, leading many parents to

accept less than safe options for their children. Violence in neighbourhoods and the presence of gangs exacerbate the underlying concerns
about children (Center for the Study of Social Policy, 1997).

Faith groups, schools, civic organizations, and neighbourhood associations have found many ways to contribute to the care and protection
of children. However, there is a strong sense that these efforts are not
well coordinated and normally are totally separate from the efforts of
public child welfare agencies. Moreover, vulnerable families need longer-
term supports for their parenting responsibilities than would be reasonable to expect from a CPS agency or other formal resource. It is recognized
that coordination of a comprehensive and integrated system of resources is needed to protect children and strengthen families. Furthermore, it is acknowledged that these resources must be able to respond
flexibly to the variety of cases that come to CPS. Children benefit
enormously from the active involvement of caring adults in their lives
and many concerned people recognize that building those partnerships
can produce better outcomes for the children and their families.

Some communities are trying to build on the concerns and commitments of individuals and groups to form more coordinated partnerships for protecting children. These communities' experiences speak to
the willingness of many to become involved, extend existing efforts,
and work with others to protect children. This willingness stems from a
belief that these efforts can be sustained and effective only if the major
forces in the community are making decisions together.

Focus on Outcomes and Accountability

Public policy in recent years has focused increasingly on outcomes. This
can be seen in almost any area of public policy and has particular
relevance for child protection. All agencies receiving any public funds
must demonstrate the effectiveness of their efforts. Moreover, the clear
direction is to define effectiveness with the same outcomes; increased
attention on child safety, the need for permanence, and the well-being
of children also have motivated CPS agencies to rethink some of the
traditional ways in which they work with families. Children who die or
are profoundly harmed by abuse and neglect land on the front pages of
many newspapers. News about abuse within foster care, concerns about
the health and conditions of many children in poverty, the disaffection
of many inner-city youths, and other issues have contributed to a readiness to examine what we are achieving from our efforts and interven-

tions. Thus it has been quite useful not only to focus accountability on outcomes, but to have a shared sense of what those outcomes should be.

It is clear that no one agency working alone can achieve the desired set of outcomes for children. The recognition of the relevance of these outcomes has led many organizations, public and private, to come up with similar or common assessment tools, to generate shared methodologies for measurement, and to be more open to forming the necessary partnerships for their achievement.

There are a variety of overt and subtle forces impacting the willingness to pursue partnerships for protecting children. Federal legislation, the limitations of the existing system of reports and response, community concern and willingness to play a greater role, and a generally increased orientation towards accountability to broad community outcomes, rather than agency-specific accountability for processes, are all illustrative of the forces that promote partnership development.

Who Are the Partners?

It is important to understand that partnerships grow and develop, adding new people and agencies over time. There is no set number or type of partner that must be represented before it could be known as a partnership. The idea is to expand responsibility for and participation in the mission of protecting children. Therefore, there will always be a growing list of actual partners, as well as another list of potential partners.

An important distinction is often made between formal partners and nonformal partners. Formal partners are those whose professional responsibilities or direct involvement in cases give them a defined and even expected role to play. Nonformal partners are those who represent natural settings or service agencies very relevant to the lives of children and families, but with no defined role with child protection cases. Perceptions can vary about where any particular agency falls depending on the degree of integration of the community's protective service system.

Appendix A provides a partial list of formal and nonformal partners who may be involved in the protection and well-being of children. This list is neither definitive nor comprehensive. It is illustrative of the types of organizations that could be part of any community's partnership for child protection. Moreover, even among the most clearly formal partners, roles usually have the potential to expand and, more important, their participation could include varying degrees of coordination as well as varying degrees of commitment to building the partnership. It is also clear that many of the less formal partners are not necessarily directly involved in the protection of children as their main focus and would have to be recruited into the work of the partnership.

LEVELS OF INTEGRATION

Community partnerships for protecting children can take different forms in different communities. One of the distinguishing characteristics of any partnership is the level of integration – in other words, what types of activities reflect 'partnership' decisions or actions, as opposed to the decisions or actions of individual agencies. Table 4.1 demonstrates the range of integration levels possible in partnerships and provides examples from communities which have embraced the various levels of integration in their partnership efforts.

Integration in these partnerships can range from lesser involvements, in which information is exchanged and appropriate resources are planned, to deep integration in which all partners in the community are equally accountable for the outcomes for children and families. At lower levels of integration, agencies may work together to help the families in the community connect to existing resources and to integrate advocacy efforts for acquiring more resources for vulnerable children and families. Another level of integration also may involve shared planning for meeting existing needs in order to assure the most efficient use of available services and supports and to avoid redundancy.

A higher level of integration could involve efforts to understand the services offered by other partners. This education process may involve cross-training or job-sharing. It might also involve a lead agency, probably CPS, hosting regular meetings of all actual or potential partners to convey information about identifying and serving abused and neglected children, for example, or to showcase the services of one of the partner agencies. At this level of integration, the agencies also could focus on the volunteer opportunities in the community that staff from any of the partner agencies could participate in and, possibly, receive some compensatory time from their agencies for volunteering.

Partnerships also can work to generate a common intake form across agencies, enabling families who need the services of multiple agencies to complete the intake process only once. Additional integration can occur when agencies share decision making on cases through family team meetings. This process could also lead to higher levels of inte-

Table 4.1: Levels of Integration

Level of Integration	Ways of Working Together	Examples from Partnership Communities
Coordinating to help families connect to existing resources	Working together to provide outreach to families in the community, recruiting neighbours and concerned citizens to contribute their time to support families, and to make it easier for people to both offer help and request help in order to keep children safe.	Cedar Rapids developed 'block links' people who are fundamentally volunteers who initiate contact with their neighbours in about a 2–5 block area. They offer information about the available resources and services related to children and families and encourage residents to participate in community meetings and celebrations. They are connected to each other, receive some training, and a staff person works closely with them. Communities often choose to establish family friendly hubs where a variety of formal and nonformal services and resources are co-located or accessed. Schools, family resource centres, churches, community centres, etc. are chosen as hub locations.
Joint planning for existing needs to avoid redundancy	'Resource mapping' to identify and organize the existing sources of formal and nonformal supports and services. It may also involve some of the initial members of the partnership recruiting others or tapping into the natural systems of support and connection within the community.	Michigan and Washington have formal ways that the state government funds and works with coalitions of community agencies. The expectation is that in order to receive state funding, these coalitions will jointly plan to meet existing needs without redundancy, ensure families are connected to resources, and share in the tracking of common outcomes. The Clark Foundation demonstration sites in St Louis, Louisville, Jacksonville, and Cedar Rapids have all engaged in a partnership process to map existing resources and communicate that information to all members of the partnership. When partnerships form governance bodies, the work of identifying existing resources and needs often leads to joint planning around how to build what is needed or expand what is available.

Table 4.1 (continued)

Level of Integration	Ways of Working Together	Examples from Partnership Communities
Understanding partners' ways of working	This could take the form of cross-training, or even shadowing staff of other agencies. It could also involve co-locating various agencies and using the opportunities of proximity to foster partnerships.	In Jacksonville, staffs from the local domestic violence shelter and the child welfare agency shadowed each other – meaning they went out together on the cases served by either agency. This led to strengthened relationships as well as an increased understanding of the parameters of policy and practice as well as opportunities for working together at key points in case decision making. The public child welfare agency in St Louis has hosted periodic meetings where all community agencies are invited to attend. These meetings provide information about the work of the partnership and they help the community as a whole to understand the variety of resources available. Questions are responded to about policies, procedures, and criteria for decision making. New partners are often recruited through these meetings. Moreover, more of the community gains an understanding of how the agencies operate.
Developing common intake forms	Families who need multiple services only ave to complete one form that satisfies hall the initial informational needs of all the agencies. This could lead to the partnership supporting a 'no wrong door' policy, whereby any needed service could be accessed for a family through any of the partner agencies.	St Louis has worked on identifying a set of information they all commonly need and developed shared forms to collect that information, no matter what agency first sees the family. This not only saves the family from completing redundant forms, it also sets the stage for each agency seeing itself as part of a network.

Table 4.1 (*concluded*)

Level of Integration	Ways of Working Together	Examples from Partnership Communities
Sharing decision making on cases	Involved agencies, as well as family members and informal supports, come together at a *family team meeting* at key points in the case to identify the priorities to be worked on, the changes needed to protect the child, the services and supports to be offered to the family to make the needed changes, and the outcomes anticipated by the family.	All formal and nonformal resources working with a family as well as people the parents themselves see as their supports meet together at a family team meeting at the outset of case planning and intervention. This is not done for all cases, but communities choose the type of case most likely to benefit from this way of work. Commonly, families with multiple prior reports or particularly complex situations would be selected. In addition to formal meetings, some communities who have service resources co-located in the community have multiple opportunities for less formal case consultation and shared decision making.
Sharing accountability	Shared accountability for a set of outcomes for families served by the partnership. The case would belong to the partnership, not to only one agency. The commitment would be to work together to achieve those outcomes and engage in any necessary course corrections or changes in supports and services that would be essential for their achievement.	The self-evaluation processes undertaken in a number of communities depend on shared commitment to a set of criteria to measure progress and outcomes. The governing body of the partnership reviews data collected by all members and there is the opportunity for course corrections if needed. The community collaboratives funded by the state in Michigan and Washington are examples of multiple agencies having a stake in achieving common outcomes related to child safety, permanency, school achievement, etc.

grated case management and service coordination across the partnership on the cases that are appropriate for such involvement.

Possibly the highest level of integration would involve shared accountability for a set of outcomes for families served by the partnership. Even though one agency might take the lead at any one time, all partners would have an equal responsibility for the outcomes.

THE CONTINUUM OF INVOLVEMENT

It is clear from the above discussion of roles and activities that community partnership involvement does not necessarily begin with an official report of child abuse or neglect or end when CPS closes the case. The continuum of involvement covers the entire gamut of primary prevention and early intervention, investigation and service provision after a report has been received, and the provision of care when formal agency involvement is no longer needed. Figure 4.1 describes a continuum of interventions and supports for community partnerships. It is also clear that this continuum of involvement can only be effectively brought to fruition when community partnerships include an adequate range of formal and nonformal resources committed to the protection of children and to the strengthening of families.

Communities with Partnerships

In the United States, building partnerships has usually begun with leaders in the community willing to explore new ways to support vulnerable children and their families, combined with the visionary leadership and sometimes the resources of private foundations. As the concept of partnerships has become more widely disseminated, many communities are moving in this direction without any formal foundation sponsorship. Two community partnerships are described below, as illustrations of what is being attempted in many American communities.

Jacksonville, Florida

This Community Partnership focuses on five public housing developments near one of the full-service high schools in the city. The five communities have fewer than 1,000 households, all living at or near the poverty level. The Partnership's mission is to make children safer by strengthening the community. Relationships have been built among local service providers, between caseworkers and family members, and

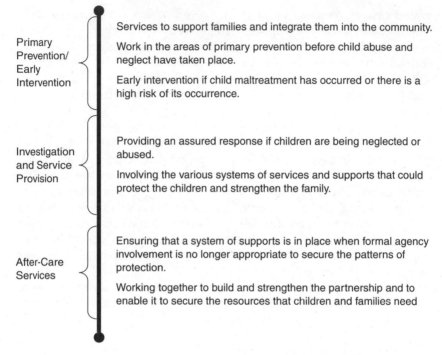

Figure 4.1: Continuum of Interventions and Supports for Community
Partnerships.

among individuals who live in these public-housing communities to
support each other and protect the children (White, n.d.).

Most of the women and children in the housing developments attend
church regularly and thus are connected to larger social institutions.
As the public child welfare agency began focusing more on the
neighbourhoods, administrators, supervisors, and caseworkers became
knowledgeable about the formal and informal leadership in the communities and have worked together to connect families with needed
services and supports both within and outside the community.

Other social service resources, such as Project Reach, a comprehensive counselling and referral centre, are housed in the same full-service
school and has staff representing six different agencies to help guide
families and children directly to the help they might need. They are
connected to domestic abuse counselling, drug treatment services,
tutoring, youth programs, and prenatal care resources. The Neigh-

borhood Network includes dozens of service agencies, governmental offices, grassroots associations, churches, and civic groups, such as the Urban League and the Boy Scouts, who attend meetings and play a role in the Partnership (White, n.d.).

The core of the Partnership, however, is the residents of the five housing developments. Placing great emphasis on identifying indigenous leadership, reaching out broadly to all the residents and the surrounding neighbourhoods, and organizing neighbourhood celebrations have all contributed to a strong sense of how to both ask for help and offer help.

A small circle of residents make up the Governance Committee, the Partnership's board of directors. Most live or work in the housing developments; the others come from nonprofit organizations and government agencies. The Governance Committee has five subcommittees co-chaired by a community resident and an agency official. These include Community, Family Awareness, Domestic Violence, Neighborhood Network, and Self-Evaluation. There is also the Integrated Service Team, a subcommittee of professionals who discuss specific cases to coordinate interventions and decisions, but keep information confidential.

Some of the key ingredients for change have been the sustained commitment and follow-through of those closest to the Partnership, the continued development of grass-roots support, the strengthening of the fabric of relationships across public and private, formal and nonformal resources, and the respect with which everyone is treated. It takes talent and commitment from the leaders to mobilize residents and to build the Partnership, continually recognizing that everyone has strengths and assets to contribute to the community.

St Louis, Missouri

The St Louis Neighborhood Network operates mainly in two zip codes in an area characterized by high rates of child abuse and neglect reporting, poverty, and transience. Neighbourhood hubs, based at community schools, a church, and a neighbourhood organization, serve as centres for the coming together of child welfare staff, social service agencies, teachers, clergy, family support workers, and parents from the communities.

An important context for the Partnership in St Louis is that the city was one of the original pilot sites for the state initiative to create two tracks for responses to reports of child maltreatment – an assessment track as well as an investigation track. The same set of zip codes were also the focus of Caring Communities – a statewide program to improve outcomes for children through greater emphasis on coordination among educational, health, economic development, and social services agencies. All of these forces shared some common goals related to building the community's capacity to protect children, providing families with supports accessible in their neighbourhoods, and preventing initial or continuing patterns of child abuse and neglect (Schene, 2000).

The St Louis Division of Family Services (DFS), part of the state child welfare system, has been a leader in the Partnership and has made many changes in its own policies and practices to foster community partnerships. It has stationed its staff in the neighbourhood hubs, appointed specialists in chronic neglect who work in partnership with neighbourhood family support workers, and developed specialized services for drug-exposed infants and their families. It also routinely shares case decision making with other formal and nonformal resources involved with the same families and serves as partners with schools and others to help respond to vulnerable children and families, before there is a need for an official report of child maltreatment. For example, DFS and the schools work together on cases of educational neglect or truancy; without filing a formal report, DFS staff work with the school social worker to help get kids to school regularly (Schene, 2000).

The Sigel Community Education Center – a community school – provided space and utilities for Partnership agencies at the Center, in addition to developing a 'welcoming center' for parents in the neighbourhood. An entire DFS child protection unit – a supervisor and several caseworkers – continues to be based at Sigel School. In the process of assessing reports, the staff often connect families to community supports and services. Most of the reports are closed at intake, but the intake period can extend as long as from 90 to 120 days allowing many stabilizing services to be put into place, removing the need to open about 20% of cases to ongoing services (Schene, 2000).

Particular tools and processes have been developed to support the Partnership, including common assessment forms, which are shared across agencies; community support agreements, where nonformal resources voluntarily commit to work with the family and provide oversight around child safety; and the use of family team meetings early in the case planning process by DFS and partner agencies. These meetings are also attended by all those considered significant to supporting the family in their process of change.

Facilitating Partnerships

There are a number of ways the development and operation of partnerships has been facilitated. These include making statutory changes, generating mechanisms of governance for the partnerships, and changing some policies and practices of child protective services to incorporate partnerships.

Statutory Changes

The major statutory change that has facilitated partnerships has been in the direction of differential response – or the formal distinction among reports/cases of child abuse and neglect in responding to some family situations through more voluntary participation in services, as opposed to handling all reports through investigations followed by involuntary involvement in child protective services. Called 'differential response,' 'dual track,' 'multiple track,' or 'alternative response,' this approach recognizes the variation in the nature of reports. Without expanding the existing state definitions of abuse or neglect, the use of differential response allows agencies to provide services to some cases without a formal determination of abuse or neglect. These families often are rapidly connected with a variety of community services that could stabilize the family and help to protect the children (Schene, 2001).

Working with the broader human service system at the community level is critical for differential response to work well. Partnerships are facilitated due to the need to collaborate and coordinate services and supports. Agencies outside of child welfare take on new responsibilities with the families referred for services. There are more opportunities and expectations for working in partnership to assess the safety of the children, for the progress of parents, and for making decisions about ongoing involvement (Schene, 2001).

Another form of statutory change used by some states involves state funding of community partnerships or alternative response systems that work with CPS to serve those families meeting the state criteria for abuse or neglect, but constituting low to moderate risk of subsequent harm. Examples of such approaches are seen in the states of Washington and Michigan.

In 1997, Washington state both required and funded the alternative response system to serve low- to moderate-risk cases through public health agencies and community support services. Three models of partnership were identified; each received funding, managed cases, and referred families to community services and provided services directly. All cases were reported initially to CPS and met the basic criteria of abuse and neglect. Although these lower-risk cases are not opened to CPS, the public agency can remain involved to monitor, help with services, and respond when needed. Before 1997, Washington had referred the lower-risk cases to communities, but did not provide any funding for services. Research at that time indicated that many of the families did not receive needed assistance (English, Wingard, Marshall, Orme, & Orme, n.d.).

In 1999, the state of Michigan implemented a five-category disposition system for child abuse and neglect cases, ranging from court involvement to voluntary community services. In two of the categories where community services are needed or recommended, there is evidence of abuse/neglect and CPS must assist the family in receiving community-based services on a voluntary basis. Michigan set up Multi-Purpose Collaborative Bodies (MPCBs) to facilitate system reform. These bodies include a wide variety of service providers and community members. The state funded those MPCBs that involved a broad spectrum of community stakeholders and developed a community plan to qualify for the funds. At-risk families in unsubstantiated or low-risk cases referred by CPS are given priority for their services (Michigan Family Independence Agency, 2001).

In both Washington and Michigan, the local partnerships collect evaluative data on state-determined outcomes related to re-referral to CPS and other indicators, or child and family well-being. Continued funding is tied to outcome achievement.

Lessons Learned in Building Partnerships

The development of community partnerships for protecting children is not a completely new approach, but what is relatively new is the explicitness of this strategy. Accompanying this more deliberate approach is a level of conceptualization, proactive design, planning, and continuing tracking of progress which allows us to perceive those factors that seem to facilitate partnership development.

There also is a heightened sense of the importance of identifying the salient facilitating factors in order to disseminate partnerships across many communities. This more analytical process has been reinforced by the fact that sponsoring organizations – foundations, state child welfare systems, national associations, for example – are working in multiple communities at the same time. The communities themselves are very aware that they are being looked upon as 'leaders' or 'pilot projects' in new approaches to the protection of children and the strengthening of families and communities. All of these conditions allow us to identify some of the lessons being learned in developing community partnerships.

Centrality of Leadership of Public Child Protective Services Agencies

Partnership development can be driven by a variety of organizations and led by any one of the partners. However, it has become clear that, when the focus of the community partnership is the protection of children, the leadership group has to include the public child welfare agency. If not as the original catalyst, certainly early in the developmental process, the child protection services system has to be more than just a participant. It has to be fully committed to the partnership in order to make the necessary changes in its policies, practices, and ways of working that enable partnerships to be successful.

CPS need to be in the forefront of bringing partners into the process of protecting children and strengthening families. It is essential that the purposes of partnerships are well understood and articulated by CPS in order to communicate effectively with the larger community. It is especially important that the community does not see partnerships as a way of 'unloading' CPS responsibilities, but rather as a way of working together to keep more of the community's children safe. CPS also plays a facilitating role by initially inviting others to discuss what is meant by partnerships for child protection and how they can work together. Other agencies within the partnership also can take significant steps to facilitate partnership development; when the community as a whole supports the work of CPS and is supported by CPS, it adds greatly to the strength of partnerships. For example, in St Louis, the director of the public child welfare agency became the chairperson of the community partnership when there were some concerns about continued commitment of some of the partners. This stabilized partnership development for an important period of time. In Jacksonville, when the public agency decided to have staff assigned to one of the community full-service schools, others also chose to place their staff in the same location.

Table 4.2: Summary of Lessons Learned in Building Partnerships

Issue	Lessons Learned
Centrality of the leadership of CPS agencies	• The leadership group must include the public agency • The purposes of the partnerships must be well understood and articulated to the community • The community must not see the partnership as a way of unloading CPS responsibilities • CPS agencies play a vital role in bringing together various partners and resources
Locating services together in the neighbourhood	• Co-location: – is more convenient for families – facilitates information sharing – assists in coordinated interventions across agencies – allows workers to get to know the community they work in – normalizes the use of services – places a strong focus on prevention and early intervention – must be accessible and neutral
Formalizing new agency agreements and ways of working together	• Agencies should provide opportunities for cross-training/job shadowing • Integrated service teams can provide more effective services to multi-problem families • Family team meetings can be an effective means of securing commitments from family members and community resources • CPS agencies should host open meetings to actively involve the community • Partnerships should develop a means of coordination, such as memoranda of understanding or contracts with other agencies
Developing tools for partnerships	• Useful tools for partnerships include: – common assessment forms – community-wide documentation of formal and nonformal resources – community support agreements – methods for maintaining confidentiality – means of providing flexible funding
Community outreach	• Encourage existing neighbourhood leaders to serve as block links to help families find the services they need • Find neighbourhood helpers who provide assistance such as childcare, transportation, meals, etc. • Encourage staff to volunteer time and/or receive compensatory time • Support ways to bring the community closer through celebrations
Development of governance	• Governing groups should include representation from formal agencies, nonformal resources, and community members • The governing bodies must track and evaluate progress • Outcomes/indicators should be shared with the community

Table 4.2 (*concluded*)

Issue	Lessons Learned
Evaluation	• Tracking progress against outcomes necessitates joint planning about collection of data and report production • Self-evaluation can be vital for identifying areas for improvement within the partnership
Involvement of nonformal resources	• Generate significant and specific roles for nonformal partners • Include nonformal supports at key points in the decision-making process • Respect and acknowledge the role nonformal supports have within the partnership • Understand the varying levels of, and motivations for, participation

Locating Services Together in the Neighbourhood

The co-location of services in particular neighbourhood settings such as schools or community centres has facilitated the development of partnerships. Agencies, such as CPS, domestic violence specialists, housing agencies, family counselling, job training, high school equivalency degree programs, being located together are not only much more convenient for families, but facilitate information sharing and coordination of interventions across agencies. Maybe even more important, they allow relationships to build among professionals and allow workers to get to know the community they work within and its resources.

The co-location of needed resources in a neutral setting, such as a school or family resource centre, has the effect of normalizing the use of services. Neighbourhood settings also help ease access to services as well. Under community partnerships, there is normally a strong focus on prevention and early intervention, as well as on more coordinated interventions. To enhance prevention and early intervention, it is essential to have an accessible, neutral setting where parents can gather in order to provide information about relevant community resources and build the type of trusting relationships that enable families to ask for help. The co-location of resources in a neighbourhood hub contributes in many ways to strengthening families and protecting children.

Formalizing New Agency Sgreements and Ways of Working Together

Successful partnerships are characterized by agencies that are flexible enough to incorporate significant changes into their conventional practices to support the coordination of interventions with families. These changes include opportunities for employees to cross-train and/or job shadow, the establishment of integrated service teams, the use of family team meetings, and other nontraditional organizational agreements and responses.

Cross-training occurs when staff from several agencies are trained together either in new practices or in becoming familiarized with each other's clients, methods of case acceptance, case planning, decision criteria, objectives of intervention, service content and delivery, and case closure processes.

Job shadowing allows for an expansion of cross-training when front-line staff from one agency join with a staff member from another to actually go through their working day. In the process, they not only gain an understanding of how the agency works with their clients and the needs of the families, but also have the opportunity to develop relationships across agencies that foster partnerships.

Integrated service teams provide a mechanism for shared decision making in cases where families face issues that cross agency lines. Often multiproblem families are receiving services from more than one agency without the agencies coordinating interventions. By working together in a team, assessment information is shared (with the permission of the family) and decisions related to planning, intervention, case closure, and after-care supports are made collectively. An illustrative example from Louisville, Kentucky, is the Comprehensive Services Team, which represents the variety of agencies involved in the case to plan together on how to coordinate their interventions and track overall progress against shared goals.

Family team meetings have been incorporated in many partnership sites. This involves a range of public and private agencies in the partnership agreeing to hold joint family team meetings with family members, extended support systems, and others of the family's choosing. These meetings provide an opportunity to discuss the positive and negative factors impacting the patterns of parenting and to develop a plan of intervention based on the priorities of the family, the safety needs of the children, and the willingness of available services and resources to commit to supporting necessary changes. These family team meetings are called by any member of the partnership and attended by all relevant partner agencies.

Nontraditional organizational agreements and responses are often needed to develop successful community partnerships. Hosting open meetings often is an effective means to help community members to understand each other's resources and to discover ways to access services, and to understand the greatest priorities or needs in the community. It is also important to develop means of coordination among the various resources available. These links can be accomplished through memoranda of understanding with other public agencies or contracts for purchased services from private agencies. However, it is also beneficial to allow some cases to be served on a voluntary basis primarily by community resources within the parameters of maintaining child safety.

Developing Tools for Partnerships

Communities have found it important to create specific mechanisms and concrete agreements to make partnerships operational. These have included common assessment forms, community-wide documentation of formal and nonformal resources, community support agreements, methods for maintaining confidentiality, and ways to provide flexible funding.

Common assessment forms can be used by all members of the partnership to collect standard information about those being served and to avoid multiple assessment processes. Beyond initial assessment, many sites have developed comprehensive assessment forms and processes that explore and document a broad spectrum of family strengths and needs to put together a case plan that often involves more than one agency or resource.

Community-wide documentation of formal and nonformal resources is often necessary to ensure that families can utilize all available resources to support parenting responsibilities. These efforts go beyond an information and referral resource. The process has normally required hours of volunteer time interviewing residents about what they might need or could offer to support other families. Among formal resources, the documentation process has agencies describing their services in ways that foster their utilization; in some cases, this documentation process has led to commitments to programs that have emerged only through the partnerships. For example, Cedar Rapids families experiencing both domestic violence and child protection concerns have access to a specialized network of services for children who witness violence. In St Louis, a partnership developed between a hospital, CPS, and a church-based team of volunteers to intervene with specialized supports to mothers of drug-affected newborns to keep the infants safe with the parents (Schene, 2000).

Nonformal resources often examine ways in which they can offer specific volunteer opportunities or programs of support. Churches, for example, have organized themselves in certain communities to offer parenting classes, childcare, one-on-one mentoring, Bible study programs, and other supports to families in the community. In Jacksonville, the residents of the public housing communities, all of whom are low-income, largely single-parent families, have joined support groups and volunteered their time to mentor other mothers, provide child care, and even have children stay in their homes when necessary.

Community support agreements are written agreements between a parent, the CPS, and a community support resource that specifies the mutual expectations. Often these agreements are concluded after initial CPS involvement with a family, when there is no immediate prospect of removing the child from the home, but where there are ongoing safety concerns. CPS agrees to close the case, but be available if needed; the parents agree to certain actions that will enhance the safety of the children; the resource person, often a close friend or relative of the parents, a minister, a school counsellor, or even a neighbour, agrees to pay special attention to the well-being of the children and to support the family in particular ways.

Methods to ensure confidentiality of information are needed for formal and nonformal resources to work together and share information about families. Families often are receptive to this and willing to sign release forms when that information shared is seen as helpful to them. The partnerships need to assure the proper safeguards are in place and all involved must receive some confidentiality training. Parents often are asked to give permission to share information across the partnership, rather than simply releasing it to one agency. This can happen only when the trust in the partnership is developed sufficiently.

Ways to provide flexible funding need to be developed to enable families to address their specific needs. Agencies have removed many categorical barriers to the use of funds in order to bring some flexible resources to the partnership. Partnerships often develop a shared pool of flexible funds that any of them can use to help a family in an emergency, such as potential evictions or utility cut-offs.

Community Outreach

Active outreach to the residents of communities is a vital part of partnerships' success. All of the partnerships are engaged in efforts to strengthen families to prevent child abuse and to intervene early to change patterns of parenting that threaten child safety and well-being. Prevention and early intervention requires reaching out to families before there is a substantiated case of child maltreatment. Outreach has taken various forms in different communities. Some sites have looked to existing leaders in the neighbourhood to serve as block links to help families find the services they need. There are also neighbourhood helpers who provide some direct assistance to families around child care, transportation, or meals. These individuals receive a very modest stipend for committing ten to fifteen hours a month. For example, Cedar Rapids, Iowa, has block links, people who volunteer to contact all those in their immediate area to help acquaint them with the community's resources and to encourage them to participate in general community events.

The process of identifying neighbourhood assets and recruiting volunteers within the neighbourhood has been used in many communities. This process also has served as an outreach mechanism as well as a way of educating the community about the partnerships. Agencies can also reach out by encouraging staff to volunteer their time, and/or giving them compensatory time for working with others in the partnership. Likewise, being available for consultation with partnership members about the need for reporting an incident of suspected maltreatment or exploring other ways to maintain safety is also beneficial to partnerships. Supporting ways to bring the community closer through celebrations and other efforts have been fundamental in increasing the sense of connectedness and support.

Development of Governance for the Partnerships

It seems essential for the viability of the partnerships to have a formal structure responsible for overseeing participation, decision making, needs assessment, resource development, and ongoing problem resolution. There is normally a governing group for the partnerships with participation from the formal agencies, other groups, and concerned residents of the communities. The governance mechanisms have taken different forms depending on mandates and funding arrangements. Tracking and evaluating progress and outcomes is another responsibility of partnerships and their governing bodies. Sharing information about outcomes for children and families, as well as other indicators of child and family well-being, with the community has played a key role in the success of these partnerships.

The Multi-Purpose Collaborative Bodies (MPCBs) established in communities across Michigan have somewhat different responsibilities. These governance institutions are designated by the state to receive and distribute funding to the variety of community agencies involved in the partnership. To qualify for funds, the MPCBs have to develop a community plan, get commitments to the plan from stakeholders, and define in the plan how they plan to serve the families referred by CPS. They also are responsible for collecting quarterly evaluation data from all components of the partnerships (Michigan Family Independence Agency, 2001).

The state of Washington has taken a similar approach, allowing community-based organizations to receive state funds to serve the lower risk cases. These organizations must bring together a set of relevant services and monitor some key outcomes to receive the funds.

Evaluation

Many of the partnerships are committed to monitoring and measuring their collective achievements against a set of specified criteria related to child safety, child and family well-being, service utilization, and community participation. Positive impacts on these outcomes cannot be achieved by any one agency acting on its own. Moreover, tracking progress against outcomes requires some joint planning around the data to be collected and the reports to be completed. The utilization of self-evaluation procedures for each partnership in the four cities supported by the Edna McConnell Clark Foundation has been a vital part of identifying needed course corrections. Each partnership has developed its own plan for self-evaluation; data is collected and regularly reviewed by the governance groups. In addition, the Foundation has contracted with Chapin Hall at the University of Chicago to undertake both evaluations of implementation and a formal outcome evaluation.

Involvement of Nonformal Resources

Of all the characteristics of community partnerships, the one that attracts the most interest is the way communities are involving a variety of informal resources in the work of strengthening families and protecting children. As mentioned earlier, informal partners cover a broad spectrum of individuals and organizations. The common denominator is that they have no formal or statutory role in interventions in child protection beyond the obligation to report maltreatment. Given this lack of formal regulation, it is important to generate significant and specific roles for nonformal partners. Including nonformal supports for families at important points to help guide decision making and provide ongoing supports to the families is essential for the partnerships to be successful.

In addition to specifying roles for nonformal partners, respecting their role and acknowledging them as significant members of family team meetings or on the governance committees of the partnerships must be emphasized. General efforts to educate the community about the shared responsibility for keeping children safe often can be the context for the involvement of nonformal partners. However, it is vital to understand the varying levels and types of participation as well as the different motivations for becoming involved.

Many nonformal supporters are interested in helping with specific cases because they know the children and families. Others are willing to provide help to, for example, a group of mothers who may need mentoring or a group of young people who are involved in a sports or recreation program. Energy and resources must continually be expended to nurture the involvement of nonformal partners; their participation is voluntary and sustaining their important contributions is an ongoing responsibility of the partnerships.

This discussion of the lessons being learned in developing and sustaining community partnerships for child protection clearly underscores not only the complexity of the process but also the variability across communities and the need for flexibility in constructing and sustaining partnerships. In addition to these lessons, there are more specific principles that have guided the work of building successful partnerships. These principles include keeping the safety of children as the paramount concern for the partnership, focusing on specific communities or neighbourhoods, including all people in the neighbourhood, offering a full continuum of services, and ensuring respectful approaches to dealing with families (see Appendix B for a detailed list of guiding principles for building partnerships). As communities continue to move forward with their partnership efforts, it will be essential to keep these lessons and guiding principles in mind as partners face both the challenges and the opportunities that such initiatives can provide.

Challenges and Opportunities

Challenges

WORKING WITH FORMAL PARTNERSHIP RESOURCES

Working as part of a community partnership is clearly quite different from working within the parameters of any one organization. In partnership, any one participant has responsibilities for joint decisions and shared interventions as well as within his/her own agency. Every organization has its own set of policies, practices, and way of relating to families. These are not always the same as the decisions and interventions of the partnership. Not only do front-line staff and supervisors have to accommodate to this reality, administrators have to understand how to hold staff accountable in the context of the partnership. Moreover, issues of accommodation have to be identified and sometimes brought to the attention of the governing body of the partnership in order to be addressed effectively. Table 4.3 lists some of the common challenges encountered by agencies when working in partnerships.

WORKING WITH NONFORMAL COMMUNITY RESOURCES

These differences in ways of working are magnified when contracting how the formal systems of intervention work with nonformal or voluntary ways of helping. As mentioned, some of these informal resources include organizations such as schools, churches, and recreation centres, who do not share a formal or statutory role in intervention in family problems, but share an interest in the safety and well-being of children and the strengthening of families. Other parts of the nonformal system include extended family members, relatives, and neighbours who are generally not part of any service organization, but also share a concern for children and families.

THE AVAILABILITY OF NEEDED RESOURCES AND
FAMILY ACCESS TO RESOURCES

Availability and access to resources is also a challenge that many partnerships face. Partnerships generally encompass work with children and families that fall within categories of prevention and early intervention as well as shared intervention on open CPS cases. Resources for prevention and early intervention usually are harder to obtain because there is no statutory obligation for the public child welfare agency to intervene until there is a report of child abuse or neglect. This presents

Table 4.3: Overview of Challenges in Developing Partnerships

Partnership Issues	Specific Challenges
Involvement of formal partnership resources	• Differing approaches and forms used for assessment • Different criteria for agency involvement and time periods for keeping cases open • Differing policies related to confidentiality of information – especially relevant when domestic violence resources partner with child protective services and/or family preservation resources • Differing modes of meeting with and relating to families – especially relevant in terms of how much has to be accomplished within the family home and expectations related to office visits as well as the voluntary nature of client participation • Practice differences related to the relative balance in focus on family strengths vs. the identification of dysfunction • Differing approaches to case planning, types of interventions, tracking of progress, and case closure
Involvement of nonformal partnership resources	• Need to recruit such resources • Lack of predictability of their involvement • Need to define roles together to ensure meaningful as well as appropriate involvement • Careful and different approach needed to sharing confidential information on cases • No clear place of work for consistent contact, sharing of information about the partnership or about specific meetings on cases • Lack of agency guidelines on the incorporation of the views and involvement of nonformal resources • Need to develop different patterns of accountability for nonformal resources in carrying out their roles and commitments • Nurturing sustained involvement of voluntary resources • Identification of patterns of communication and coordination and assignment of responsibilities for those patterns
Staff training	• Knowing where the major faith communities are and how they serve their congregations • Understanding the services schools provide including any specific programs for families to help their children succeed academically, GED or literacy services for adults • Knowing the range and locations of services related to physical and mental health, counselling, domestic violence, substance abuse evaluation and treatment, income support programs, housing services, welfare to work programs, special services for new parents, child care resources, etc.

Table 4.3 (*concluded*)

Partnership Issues	Specific Challenges
	• Familiarity with the recreational, after-school programs, family resource centres, parenting classes, Parents Anonymous groups, Boys and Girls Clubs, YMCAs etc. • In specific neighbourhoods there are often natural leaders – people whom residents turn to for advice or assistance; staff helping families can sometimes utilize such leaders, but need to be trained in ways to approach them.

obvious problems in finding families, but even after identifying families in need of intervention and prevention services, the partnerships are hard-pressed to secure funding. Agencies that provide what is needed may have funding criteria that limit access to these services. Some partnerships have assigned staff specifically to the task of identifying and developing needed resources. This is a continuing challenge.

PROMOTING THE PARTNERSHIP TO THE WHOLE COMMUNITY
A related challenge is that of promoting the partnership to the community. Partnerships rest on the premise that the protection of children is in the interest of the whole community. Furthermore, partnerships promote increased help-seeking and help-providing propensities in neighbourhoods and communities. There has also been a commitment in some community partnership settings to building greater community awareness through 'celebrations' or the solicitation of 'great ideas' that might receive funding. All of these types of efforts contribute to promoting the partnership to the whole community. Yet is it difficult to reach everyone in the community and to translate awareness of the partnership into some form of participation. This challenge might be addressed over time with the continued presence of the partnership and the continued invitation to become involved. This, of course, depends on the value members of the community place on the partnership.

GOVERNANCE
Governance offers a distinct challenge to community partnerships. There are no existing governance institutions at the neighbourhood or community level in most of the United States. City and county governments cover too large an area and do not address some of the governance

functions relevant to partnerships. There is a need for governing bodies not only to organize and coordinate the work of the partnerships, but also to reflect authoritative community decisions on the identification of needs and the allocation of resources. Since other entities such as governments, the United Way, and foundations currently make resource allocation decisions, one function of partnership governance is to influence those decisions. They sometimes have been able to ensure that funds flowing into neighbourhoods and communities enhance partnerships and address needs identified by the partnership. Moreover, in every community, residents need services that do not or cannot be reproduced in every neighborhood – such as a residential drug treatment facility. A function of partnership governance is to understand and attempt to increase the access to such needed resources. The internal functioning of the partnership, the access of residents to outside resources, and the articulation of governing and allocation processes are part of the responsibilities of partnership governance.

Training

Not only do front-line staff and supervisors need to be trained within their own agencies to undertake their responsibilities, they need to understand how other agencies operate and they need to be trained on coordinated intervention policies and practices. Partnerships depend on a high level of staff specialization by neighbourhood or community. To be effective, staff need to understand the broader context of resources and needs within the community and how residents use and access services and supports. The nonformal system of resources also needs to be understood by staff. Training also is necessary in helping staff make decisions in cooperation with extended family members or other supports, as well as with other agencies serving the same families.

Resource development. There is also a need for training staff in resource development. Most communities have more needs than existing resources can address. As needs are identified by the community partnership, some identified staff need to be assigned to work on resource development.

Sustaining partnerships is a continuing challenge. Often begun by a core group of committed individuals, partnerships have to become institutionalized as the normal way of working. This is necessary for the development of partnerships and for their survival. New generations of partners have to be committed to this concept and see its value.

Opportunities

There are many opportunities in building community partnerships for protecting children and supporting families. These opportunities manifest themselves in relations with individual families as well as in how agencies and communities function. In terms of individual cases, the response to vulnerable children and their families normally will be perceived as less adversarial, more sensitive to the needs of particular families, more comprehensive, and more likely to involve a range of supports when partnerships are in place. The reasons go beyond the presence of partnership resources to the philosophical foundation of partnerships. Community partnerships are normally motivated by a family-strengths perspective, based on the assumption that most parents want to do a good job, but may lack the resources, knowledge, supports, or stability to parent well.

In partnerships, the assessment process is normally more comprehensive and yields more substantive information about the priorities of the family as well as the network of support the family might naturally draw upon. Bringing those nonformal supports into intervention planning can greatly increase parental motivation to change as well as provide help in the change process. The assessment and case planning process in community partnerships can lead to a shared commitment to objectives by parents, their supporters, and formal as well as nonformal agencies providing services.

When a case is closed in a more traditional child protection agency, there is usually little likelihood of having aftercare services in place. With the involvement of nonformal supports in partnerships, CPS case closing is not the end of supportive involvements with the family.

Opportunities are also presented by community partnerships beyond work with individual families. Generally, the total resources available to serve vulnerable children and their families increase. There is a larger constituency for the protection of children when communities come together. There is a greater chance that there will be a continuity of care system developed through partnerships.

Conclusion

Forming and sustaining partnerships in communities to better protect children from abuse and neglect, and to improve support to vulnerable families is one of the most positive developments emerging in the

United States in recent years. Few families at risk of child abuse and neglect have only one challenge in their lives. Partnerships provide the opportunity for more holistic responses to the daily living realities and periodic crises families experience. As more resources are coordinated, a synergy can develop for continued expansion in the ways communities support parents and protect children.

The United States has concentrated the responsibilities for the protection of children in public child welfare agencies with the support of law enforcement and the courts. Moving from that mode of operation to one of community partnerships is not accomplished quickly or easily. The motivations for moving in that direction are growing, and early successes in building community partnerships help in the dissemination of this more inclusive way of working.

5 Problems and Potential of Canadian Child Welfare

KAREN SWIFT and MARILYN CALLAHAN

Canadian child welfare has hit troubled times. The system has been widely and publicly criticized. Its processes have become highly litigious and, in many communities, rigidly managed. For many front-line workers, time spent on paperwork outstrips, by far, time spent working directly with families and children. Perhaps as a result, recruitment and retention of staff have become critical problems across the country. At the same time, caseload numbers are climbing steeply, while more and more children are being brought into already burdened alternate care arrangements. When things go wrong, individual parents and workers are blamed, while systemic problems are patched up or glossed over.

That child welfare should be so troubled is not surprising. It is a residual or last-resort service in an increasingly mean-spirited social and economic context. The last decade has seen a substantial retrenchment of the Canadian social safety net, once a source of much national pride. Health care, education, and virtually all social services have seen drastic budget cuts in the last few years. Our politicians justify these changes through claims of otherwise insurmountable deficits and loss of competitive edge in the new global markets. Of course, the major victims of this reorganization of wealth and distribution of resources are the poorest and most vulnerable of families, the same families most likely to become involved with mandated child welfare services.

The Partnerships for Children and Families Project asks participants to reexamine our current child welfare paradigms. Given the problems facing the mandated system, and the stressful social and economic conditions in which this system must operate, this is a timely invitation. We take the opportunity in this chapter to explore past, present, and potential Canadian child welfare services and directions. The first part describes some historical roots of the Canadian child welfare system and current trends across the country and concludes with a brief critique of the present situation. Part II explores some contemporary initiatives to address the problems with the present system. In part III, we examine the contributions of these initiatives to a new paradigm and the organizing that will be required to make significant change.

Part I. History, Structure, and Current Trends

In Canada, responsibility for health, education, and welfare is provincial rather than federal. Since ten provinces and three territories have legal jurisdiction over child welfare, we cannot describe child welfare in Canada as a single, unified system. Nevertheless, some common traditions and understandings across the country provide the basis for describing Canadian child welfare.

The origins of child welfare in Canada have been described as a gradually evolving response to social and economic conditions of the nineteenth century (Harris & Melichercik, 1986). The two traditions shaping Canadian child welfare, according to these authors, were the long-held traditions of viewing children as the property of their parents and the more recent British doctrine of *parens patriae*, or the state as parent of the nation. This is the doctrine allowing intervention into the private family for the protection of children.

The first Canadian child welfare organization was established in Toronto in 1891, followed closely in 1893 by the country's first legislation, Ontario's Act for the Prevention of Cruelty to and Better Protection of Children. Most other Canadian provinces soon followed suit, developing similar legislation. In Quebec, child protection was carried out under the auspices of the Catholic Church; legislation generally following the principles of other provinces was not passed until 1977. Newfoundland, which did not become a province until 1949, also has a long tradition of religious influence over child protection matters. The recently proclaimed Territory of Nunavut, formed in 1997, is in the process of developing its child welfare system. Jurisdictions developing protection legislation later in the twentieth century have tended to pattern provisions on the principles already established by other provinces, while retaining some specific forms and concepts reflecting their history. Consequently, child protection legislation across the country, while not identical, follows similar principles and often uses the same or similar language and concepts. Generally speaking, child welfare services are residual, or 'last chance' services, and are highly regulated. Most provincial legislation originally focused on child neglect, while allowing cruelty to children a less prominent place. Ozment (1983) argues that harsh parents were viewed as less blameworthy than lax or indulgent parents. Discipline, however harsh, seemed to demonstrate attention and concern for the child, while ignoring children signified a lack of affection and concern. This focus on neglect also likely derived from urban conditions of the late nineteenth century, a time of obvious homelessness for many abandoned children. Early advocates, many of whom were members of the growing middle class, were concerned not only for the safety and futures of these 'street urchins,' but also for their own children's safety and for the security of their accumulating property (Swift, 1995b). This dual concern was succinctly captured in the motto of the first Children's Aid Society in Toronto: 'It is wiser and less expensive to save children than to punish criminals' (Kelso papers, 1890s, cited by Chen, 2001, p. xiv). This vision remains embedded in Canadian child protection law and policy today.

For the first half of the twentieth century, few changes were made in the original provincial laws. Archival documents show that the everyday responsibilities for protecting children were carried out mainly by women, some trained as social workers, some not. These women responded to complaints about the behaviours of reportedly irresponsible parents (often mothers) and unruly children, wrote copious case notes on what they observed, and intervened sometimes quite actively in the lives of families brought to their attention (Chen, 2001; Swift, 1995b). Gradually, these workers became more professional as social sciences developed and as social work created schools and training programs (Swift, 1995c). Historical records suggest, however, a strong leaning towards British moral traditions of individual responsibility, the nuclear family, and at least the appearance of 'proper' morality as central to the style and direction of much child welfare work during this period (Swift, 1995b).

In mid-century, a series of changes to child welfare legislation and focus occurred. Attention to the best interests of the child as the proper first principle of child protection decisions was among the first of these changes. In Canada, as elsewhere, Kempe's 'discovery' of the battered child led to changes in legislation, the most notable of which was the addition of mandatory reporting requirements in the child welfare legislation of most jurisdictions. Another significant event in Canada was the release of the Badgley Report (1984) reporting that one in two

Canadian females and one in three males have experienced unwanted sexual acts, and that four in five of these acts occurred in childhood. The report also stated that most of the perpetrators were known to the child and, in fact, often were family members. Prior to the Badgley Report, according to Wells (1990), sexual abuse was not viewed as either a widespread or serious problem. By the mid 1980s, however, sexual abuse rose to the forefront of attention in child protection. Law reform followed, in the form of Federal Bill C-15 (1988), which amended sexual assault provisions of the Criminal Code of Canada and also changed the Canada Evidence Act in order to facilitate the pressing of charges and giving of evidence by children. Some sixteen specific sexual offences were added to the Criminal Code, ranging from unwanted touching to assault with a weapon. This legislation does not remove responsibility from child protection authorities to investigate and intervene in sexual abuse cases, but it does ensure that police will be involved in both the investigation and criminal charging of offenders.

Changes to other related legislation have also affected the way child protection laws and mandates work. The introduction of the Canadian Charter of Rights in 1982 has not yet influenced child welfare significantly (Vogl & Bala, 2001), but may have long-term implications for practice if successful Charter challenges related to security of the person and to apprehension of children without court authorization are mounted. The 1984 federal Young Offenders Act relieved child welfare authorities of direct responsibility for youth convicted of breaking the law, resulting in a substantial change in focus for some jurisdictions. Among other effects of these changes are increased attention to legal issues in child welfare and intensified relationships among child protection workers and both police and the court system.

Through the 1980s, changes in ideas about child protection relating to the notions of risk and harm as criteria for involvement by authorities developed, tending mainly in the direction of raising the threshold of state involvement in the family. The idea of least intrusive action, always a thread in Canadian child protection practice, was encoded in protection legislation, imposing a requirement for child welfare intervention to be at the least intrusive level consonant with protecting children from harm.

During the second half of the twentieth century, the language and racial composition of the country also began to change. Through the 1960s, immigrants to Canada were primarily white Europeans, especially from Britain. A 1967 federal policy change, based on characteristics of individual immigrants, resulted in a significant shift in source countries. Immigrants from dozens of countries in Asia, Africa, South America, and the Caribbean now arrive in Canada and settle primarily in Ontario, Quebec, and British Columbia. In the major reception centres – Toronto, Montreal, and Vancouver – many different languages are spoken, and people of colour make up a large proportion of the population. This demographic change has required the development of new and different social services and has taxed the traditional child welfare service delivery model, as various groups express concern about overrepresentation of their children in care and inappropriate services provided (Hutchinson et al., 1992).

The Organization of Child Welfare

The institutional arrangements through which child welfare is administered in various jurisdictions reflect the complexity of Canadian society. Different organizational arrangements across the country relate to religion, language, history, and geography. The original structure of child welfare in Ontario has been retained. Following from the first Children's Aid Society in Toronto, fifty-four different Societies have evolved, serving different geographic and religious populations. These are quasi-governmental organizations, with individual boards of directors guiding their functions, but deriving all of their legal mandates and funds from various levels of government. In Ontario, two separate societies serve Catholic and other religious groups. Quebec has separate organizations for serving French-speaking and English-speaking populations. The overall organization of child protection in Quebec was overhauled in 1993, with the creation of Child and Youth Protection Centres (CYPCs) as agencies mandated to carry out legislated protection activities. The separation of mandated protection from local social service centres (Centre local des Services Communitaires – CLSCs) has created a potential for prevention work, as CLSCs are expected to work with local communities to provide a range of services for families at risk (Davies, Fox, Krane, & Schragge, 2002). In a number of other jurisdictions, the organizational structures of child welfare have developed as provincial departments, while Nova Scotia offers a mix of public and private services.

The most recent structural developments relate to Canada's First Nations. Although child protection is a provincial matter in Canada, status (legally registered) Indians come under federal jurisdiction. Until the 1960s, little child protection activity occurred on reserves, where status Indians were likely to reside, because the federal government generally resisted providing services that were under provincial jurisdiction, while the provinces resisted providing services that officially fell under federal jurisdiction. In addition, many Aboriginal children whose families lived on reserves were required to attend residential schools off reserve for most of the year, reducing the number of children likely to be in need of protection. Beginning in the 1960s, and coinciding roughly with the phasing out of required residential schooling, provinces began to extend child protection services to reserves. Within a short time, Native children became overrepresented in the in-care population. This history became widely known when two studies were published in the early 1980s (Hepworth, 1980; Johnston, 1983). Further research into the issue made clear that Aboriginal children were taken into state care far more frequently than other children, moved to foster care more often, and returned to their own parents much less often than Canadian children generally (Rosenbluth, 1995).

Beginning in the 1980s, some provinces began to create tripartite arrangements for the delivery of child welfare services to families on reserves. These agreements allowed bands of First Nations peoples, or groups of bands, to deliver services on reserves, with various combinations of provincial and federal funding and mandated through the relevant provincial legislation. By 1997–8, according to the Department of Indian and Native Affairs (DIAND), First Nations Child and Family Service agencies were delivering services to 70% of on-reserve children. The Department predicted an increase to 91% by 2002. This is an extremely important development, especially given the history of child welfare and Aboriginal people. The agreements now in place mark a new, if still limited, kind of partnership between child welfare authorities and First Nations peoples. The limitation is that protection services remain subject to provincial legislation, and are restricted in their possibilities of defining and delivering services consonant with Aboriginal history and cultures.

FUNDING ISSUES

Although child welfare is a provincial responsibility, programs, clientele, and levels of service are affected by federal funding arrangements that support health and welfare programs. Between 1966 and 1996, funding for services to children, including child welfare, was shared between the federal and provincial governments under the Canada Assistance Plan (CAP). These arrangements called for the federal government to provide 50% of the costs of provincially administered services to children and 100% of the costs of Aboriginal child services. Along with other cost-cutting measures taken in the 1990s, the Canada Health and Social Transfer (CHST) replaced the CAP. In the new plan, federal funding arrangements were changed from cost sharing to a lump sum contribution, based on a per-person calculation. Generally, federal funding of all health and welfare services decreased by as much as 40% with the introduction of CHST in the mid-1990s (Durst, 1999). The new funding arrangement also eliminated the principle embedded in CAP that the federal government had an obligation to ensure national standards of service to protect the interests of the poorest Canadians. This change in funding arrangements has affected child welfare services directly, especially since no special funding has been provided federally specifically for child welfare under CHST. In addition, reduced social assistance, health, and education funding has adversely affected families involved with the child welfare system, who tend to be among the poorest Canadians. With a federal surplus accumulating by 1998, and child poverty rates rising, the federal government attempted various policy measures designed to alleviate poverty levels of some of the poorest families. These efforts eventually produced the National Child Benefit, a supplement for working families, based on net income level. However, as critics have noted, the plan creates a two-tier system of the poor; in most provinces the employed poor benefit at least minimally while the unemployed poor do not (Durst, 1999; Swift & Birmingham, 2000).

In order to contain costs, and perhaps for other reasons as well, some provinces have changed their methods of funding child welfare services over the past few years. Ontario, for instance, has developed a funding formula that, while not formally tied to the standard risk assessment instrument, is frequently evaluated against it. A case rating low in risk is unlikely to qualify for funding. Obviously, less serious cases, that might be amenable to preventive measures, are less often opened since the organization must carry the costs of doing preventive work.

Another trend in child welfare funding is workload measurement, an often complex method of identifying core tasks of child protection work, assigning benchmark times for carrying out these tasks and developing funding formulas in relation to these data (Ontario Association of Children's Aid Societies, 2001). At least eight of the thirteen jurisdictions are developing or have already developed workload measures intended to guide funding levels. The northern and less populated provinces and territories demonstrate less interest in this form of management.

CHILD DEATH REVIEWS

A recent development has been the role of high profile media reports of deaths of children known to child protection authorities. Such reviews have taken place in a number of provinces in the past few years, and have led to or influenced policy shifts in those provinces (Swift, 2001). The first of these was the Gove Enquiry in British Columbia (1995) into the death of Matthew Vaudreuil, an in-depth investigation leading to major changes in legislation and service delivery in the province. In Ontario, a series of reviews was instrumental in producing changes in legislation and producing pressure for better funding for the child welfare system. In New Brunswick, three death reviews in the late 1990s produced a number of recommendations involving changes in legislation and service delivery. In general, reviews attempt to locate problems with individual worker activity and in organizational systems. General directions of recommendations have been to lower the legal threshold of risk required to intervene to protect a child and also to expand definitions of abuse and neglect in order to ensure cases are identified. Taken together, these changes are sometimes referred to as a child-centred approach. Because enquiries focus on mistakes by individual workers and systems, other recommended directions include the development of training programs for child welfare workers and installation of computer-based information systems. In addition, some jurisdictions have toughened up mandatory reporting clauses in legislation and have introduced risk assessment instruments for use by front-line protection workers. Some of these trends are discussed in following sections.

CHANGES TO LEGISLATION

Recently, legislation in a number of provinces has broadened and clarified criteria for determining that a child is in need of protection. Ontario, for instance, has added the phrase 'pattern of neglect' to its definitions of children in need of protection. Several provinces (British Columbia, Saskatchewan, Alberta) have expanded definitions of need for protection to include children engaged in prostitution. In Alberta, which claimed to be the first to add this issue to its legislation, children thought to be engaging in prostitution can be confined to a safe house for up to seventy-two hours. British Columbia can issue a restraining order, while in Saskatchewan, those who put a child at risk can be prohibited from contact with the child. Several provinces have also included domestic violence in their descriptions of conditions indicating that a child is needing protection. These additions to legislation undoubtedly increase the potential populations likely to come in contact with child welfare services.

The trend towards lowering the threshold for determining need for protection is another policy shift likely to increase the client population. In the 1980s, a heated debate in Ontario concluded with the decision to place the level of risk to a child at the *substantial* level to justify protection intervention. Ontario has now reversed its contested decision, replacing the requirement of *substantial risk* to *risk* of harm as the threshold for intervention. Also changing are policies allowing forceful intervention. British Columbia and Alberta have expanded powers to intervene if abuse is suspected. British Columbia allows power to arrest and to enter dwellings to *facilitate investigation* and, in Alberta, force can be used to enter premises to investigate. These directions stand in some contradiction to the Canadian Charter of Rights protections, but appear to have public support at present.

Since the 1960s, mandatory reporting of suspected child abuse or neglect has been increasingly focused upon in legislation as a mechanism for protecting children from harm. At present, most jurisdictions have mandatory reporting in their legislation. Most acts specify that anyone with concern for a child's safety should report, and many focus on professionals as having a special responsibility to make reports. In the past, legal counsel have generally been exempt from reporting, but some jurisdictions now include them specifically as nonexempt. Failure to report, and making malicious reports, are punishable in various jurisdictions by fines or short-term imprisonment.

Following the introduction of mandatory reporting clauses, introduced in most provinces and territories during the 1970s, the recorded incidence of both abuse and neglect dramatically increased. For instance, in Quebec, the number of reports increased 100% between 1982 and 1989. For protection staff, this increase involved 11,000 additional reports to investigate during this period (Swift, 1997).

There is a general belief that numbers of reports of abuse and neglect and investigations into these allegations continue to climb dramatically across the country. Data from the Federal/Provincial Working Group Report (2001) show that this assumption should be treated with caution. In fact, patterns and volume of both reports and investigations for the larger provinces vary greatly from smaller jurisdictions. For instance, during the month of March 1997, British Columbia authorities received 2502 protection reports. In that same month, the Northwest Territories authorities handled twenty-four such reports. For March 1999, numbers of reports grew by 19% to 3094 in British Columbia, while the NWT report number grew 33% to thirty-six. Both experienced a healthy increase in percentage terms, but the impacts are obviously greatly different.

Another kind of comparison can be shown between Newfoundland/ Labrador and Ontario, although the dates are not quite comparable. From 31 March 1997 to 1999, Newfoundland's number of protection investigations actually decreased by twenty-four cases to 2900. In Ontario, the number of investigations increased by some 3,270 cases to 66,759 between 1996 and 1998. These data remind us that trends are not homogeneous across Canada. Based on the limited data available, it would seem that the larger, more populous provinces indeed are experiencing steep increases in the investigation function of child protection, and that workload increases are heavily weighted to the front end of the system. Perhaps we should be looking to the smaller provinces, less burdened by huge numbers of cases, to design and try innovations at the service and partnership levels of child welfare.

INVESTIGATIONS

Formal risk assessment has become a staple of child protection in English-speaking countries over the past decade and some jurisdictions in Canada have recently followed suit. Both British Columbia and Ontario have adopted complex risk assessment instruments, which are required for use by intake workers attempting to make determinations of risk of harm to children. Other jurisdictions, for instance Saskatchewan, have introduced simpler measures, designed as guides for workers conducting investigations of protection concerns. Nova Scotia, New Brunswick, and Manitoba all have safety and risk assessment instruments. This approach is controversial for a number of reasons, including insufficient testing for validity, uneven implementation, and the wasting of scarce resources on unsubstantiated cases (Colclough, Parton, & Anslow, 1999).

Recently, the first national study of the investigation and substantiation of child abuse and neglect has been published (Trocmé et al., 2001). The data for this study were collected from child welfare workers across the country about reports and investigations of maltreatment in which they were involved. A sample of 7,672 investigations was used to derive estimates of annual incidence and some characteristics of cases of abuse and neglect, using 1998 as the base year. Findings of the study estimate an incidence rate of 21.52 investigations per 1,000 children in Canada for that year. Maltreatment was officially substantiated by investigating authorities in 45% of investigations. The rate of unsubstantiated cases, 55%, is similar to estimates in the United States in recent studies (United States Department of Health and Human Services, 1999).

The Canadian study confirms some beliefs about the protection system and contradicts others. The study does document a long-suspected truth about child welfare: neglect is the most frequently investigated form of maltreatment at 40% of total investigations. In 13% of investigations, physical harm to a child was documented and only 5% of investigations led to court applications. These data may contradict an image of child protective services as regularly rescuing children from physical harm, and also correct a misperception of most investigations leading to court proceedings for families. However, a common perception that single parents may be more vulnerable to investigation received some validation. Investigations by household type show that 46% of investigations involved children in single-parent households, the great majority of these female headed. Another perception, namely, that many children's living situations change as a result of investigations, received some confirmation. According to Trocmé and his colleagues' (2001) report, '12% of investigated children experienced a change in their living arrangements on completion of the initial investigation' (p. 58). Unfortunately, although the study examined income source, no data were collected about income levels of families investigated. Source data show just over a third of investigated families relied on social assistance (36%). Because of extremely low rates of social assistance in Canada, it is confirmed that at least this population of child welfare clients lives well below the poverty line. A higher figure, 39%, of families investigated report that they derive income from full-time employment. Since many are female lone parents, however, it is a reasonable assumption that many of these families also live at or below the poverty

Table 5.1: In-care Population in Selected* Jurisdictions, 31 March 1997 to
31 March 2001, and Per Cent Change

Jurisdiction	31/3/1997	31/3/2001	% Change
Alberta	5,543	7,948	43.4
British Columbia	8,232	9,956	20.9
Manitoba	5,203	5,440	4.6
Nova Scotia	1,767	2,019	14.3
Ontario	11,260	15,792	40.2

Source: Federal/Provincial-Provincial Working Group, 2001; Provincial annual
reports.
*Jurisdictions shown are those for which relevant data were available.

line. Canadian studies show that families headed by lone female parents fare badly in income level, even when working full time (Swift &
Birmingham, 2000).

CHILDREN IN CARE

The turn of the century has seen a dramatic increase in the in-care
population. In all jurisdictions, this population increased in the late
1990s, and in three of the larger and more wealthy provinces, Alberta,
British Columbia, and Ontario, the increases are dramatic. Some plausible explanations for an increased care population relate to trends cited
earlier, including policy shifts towards lowering criteria for protection
involvement, increased focus on mandatory reporting and investigation, the introduction of risk assessment instruments, and changes in
funding criteria in some jurisdictions that formally or informally link
provincial funding to involvement with higher risk and in-care cases.
Reports of children in care show that the trends of the 1990s (Swift,
1997) towards older age children in care continued to the end of the
decade. Jurisdictions have legislated varying ages as the cutoff for
identifying a *child in need of protection*, ranging from sixteen to nineteen,
making comparisons difficult. Nevertheless, as Table 5.2 shows, older
age children account for at least half of the children in care in a number
of jurisdictions.

Given the high proportion of adolescents in care, it would be interesting to examine the care biographies of these children. Many likely have
entered care at earlier ages and become 'stuck' in the system in adolescence. Another explanation for these figures is that many older children

Table 5.2: Proportion of Total Care Population Represented
in Children 12 and Older in Selected Jurisdictions

Province	Proportion (%)
Alberta	48.9
British Columbia	56
Nova Scotia	48.9
New Brunswick	62.1
Yukon	48.3

Source: Federal/Provincial Working Group, 2001. Those
selected (a) displayed figures for children in care, and (b)
categorized ages as 12 or older. These criteria allow for
some comparability, although it should be noted that they
do not necessarily have the same definition of age for a
child in need of protection, and also they have varying
policies concerning keeping children in care after that age.

are being brought into care. In relation to placement types and planning
for future alternate care needs, more examination of age figures across
the country should be done.

Western provinces, which have experienced the most severe criticism
over the last three decades concerning their treatment of Aboriginal
children and families, regularly include information in their annual
reports about Aboriginal children in care. Alberta, for instance, provides separate statistics for children of Aboriginal status, and further
breaks down the Aboriginal category to several different groups and
legal statuses. This information shows that very high percentages of
children found to be in need of protection are Aboriginal. In British
Columbia, 30% of children in care on 31 March 1999 were Aboriginal; Saskatchewan's Annual Report acknowledges that the majority of
children in care are Aboriginal. In that province, a comprehensive program approach to protection is being developed, one which includes
several specific plans to create partnerships with Aboriginal organizations in order to serve these children in appropriate settings and with
services that address cultural issues. Recent figures from Manitoba
(31 March 2002) show that over 80% of children in care are Aboriginal. These figures demonstrate that issues of overrepresentation of
Aboriginal children in the care system identified twenty years ago
remain to be adequately addressed.

All jurisdictions collect information on types of placements occupied
by children in care. Because the definitions and categorization of types

vary considerably, comparisons across the country are not valid. However, figures from 1999 in the Federal-Provincial Report (Federal/Provincial Working Group on Child and Family Services, 2001) do suggest that foster care remains the most common type of care, at around 50% of placements in several jurisdictions (e.g., Alberta, New Brunswick, Nova Scotia, Prince Edward Island), and in some cases much higher (e.g., Manitoba, Newfoundland, Northwest Territories, Saskatchewan). According to this report, care in group facilities and in specialized or treatment homes, where specifically shown, remains much less frequently used. This is much the same picture as reported in a previous survey (Swift, 1997). Many jurisdictions do not count care by kin separately, so accurate comment about trends in this form of care, strongly advocated in the United States and in some Canadian jurisdictions, cannot be made. It does seem, from limited available data, that foster homes are in short supply in many jurisdictions. Ontario, for instance, shows an in-care population in 2001 at 15,792, but only 6,707 approved foster homes.

Part I Summary and Conclusions

Canadian child welfare has changed over a century and a half, but its British and middle class roots remain strong. Individual responsibility, care by nuclear family, and moral as well as behavioural standards of care enforced by the state remain hallmarks of the system. At the same time, social, economic, and technical changes render the system inappropriate in a number of ways. Increased non-British, non-European immigration, changed relations with Aboriginal groups, and reduced standards and support by the welfare state of the country's poorest people are some of the changes that have not been adequately addressed. These changes have been accompanied by increasingly sophisticated technology for tracking and surveillance of problem populations and for containing costs; all have produced a pressing need to question and challenge a number of traditional assumptions and methods of child welfare practice.

The child welfare system has embedded in it a number of contradictions that remain powerful and often problematic. It rests on tensions between helping and punishing parents and between its focus on parents and on children. These tensions lead to constantly changing thresholds of intervention, guided at least as much by ideological and political interests as by any evidence of what works.

From the outset, the populations coming in contact with child welfare services have been poor mothers, and this remains true today. With new technology and increasingly rigid management and tracking systems, these women are under unprecedented scrutiny and control. The same management systems also track the efforts of front-line workers and managers, who also are predominantly women. The intense focus on reporting and investigation, and the high costs of such efforts, mean a substantially reduced focus on providing service and support. The result, in a harsh social and economic context, is highly punitive for many mothers and their children.

The combination of increasing numbers of reports, investigations, and placements of children for protection reasons across the country, along with problematic and insufficient alternate care arrangements, is causing alarm among all key constituencies in the system. In addition, widespread negative media coverage of the child protection system and the very substantial increase in some jurisdictions in paperwork, forms, and accountability procedures (Swift, 2001) contribute to worker recruitment and retention becoming the most worrisome problem in Canadian child protection at present. Even the usual critics of social workers and the protection system publicly identify worker retention and insufficient resources as blameworthy in contemporary child death reports (Malorek, 2000). Some social workers have expressed their concerns in the form of protests and strikes against the high level of paperwork involved in child protection, and the concomitant low levels of time for face-to-face work with clients and the lack of resources available to help children and families.

Not every jurisdiction or agency reflects these problems in the same way. Quebec's efforts to develop community services and the plethora of different arrangements with Aboriginal communities provide evidence of different possibilities. Smaller jurisdictions appear to display more flexibility in service delivery than larger ones.

PART II. Learning from Innovations in Child Welfare in Canada

The intent of this section of the chapter is to identify some innovations in child welfare in Canada and determine how they inform the development of a positive vision of child welfare.[1] We selected innovations based on publications and conferences in recent years that highlight new developments. These initiatives are featured prominently in current thinking about child welfare, although some may be only brief projects or recently implemented ideas. Further, we tried to feature projects and ideas that reflect the regional, cultural, and jurisdictional differences in our country and those that span the broad spectrum of child welfare: broad policy and preventive measures, investigations, out-of-home care, and research and education. None of these ideas are without drawbacks and we will suggest some of these. Given space restrictions of this book and the size and diversity of our country, many important and creative efforts will go unmentioned.

Broad Policy Initiatives: Increasing Income and Other Supports to Address Family Poverty [2]

Some will argue that focusing upon poverty and material resources in child welfare is a waste of time and energy and that such solutions require large-scale reform, beyond the capacity of child welfare organizations. While we agree that it is difficult, we believe that a positive vision of child welfare must include action to alleviate poverty. As noted in the first part of this chapter, most of the families and children involved in child welfare do not have the luxury of ignoring poverty, but must live it on a daily basis and are further alienated from child welfare services that do not address these fundamental realities (Prilleltensky, Nelson, & Peirson, 1999). As a nation, we have the capacity to ameliorate poverty; we have tackled it for the elderly with some notable success. Certainly, other countries with similar histories and challenges as our own have made more progress than we have in this area (Battle & Mendelson, 2001). While this section highlights federal initiatives regarding child poverty, it is important to remember that First Nations people have proposals for tackling poverty for their nations, mainly land claim settlements, that go beyond this particular discussion but which address poverty through economic and social development, a more holistic and potentially more beneficial approach.

One of the most significant issues on the family policy agenda in the 1990s in Canada was child poverty, provoked in part by a unanimous resolution in the House of Commons in 1989 seeking to eliminate child poverty in Canada by the year 2000. Campaign 2000, a coalition of more than eighty-five local, provincial, and national organizations, has demonstrated that little, if any, progress has been made on this issue in subsequent years. While poverty rates have gone down slightly over the past few years, the depth of poverty, the gap between the poverty line and the actual resources of families, has remained almost steady (Campaign 2000, 2001).

The Child Tax Benefit (CTB) and the National Child Benefit Supplement (NCBS), introduced by the federal government in 1998 to address child poverty have been widely criticized. Most provinces have chosen to deduct the NCBS from welfare payments with the result that families on income assistance have received little if any increase in benefits to date (Swift & Birmingham, 2000). Benefits are thus tied to source of income rather than to amount. Abrupt cut-off lines make irrational divisions between families with almost the same incomes. The program is not universal, it is insufficiently funded, and, finally, it results in little if any relief from poverty (Durst, 1999; McKeen, 2001).

However, we include it in this discussion because of its potential. It is administered federally through the income tax system, is less stigmatizing than current welfare programs, is paid to the main caregiver, usually the mother, and has the potential to provide relief from the assortment of provincial and federal programs for families. Federal funding has increased from 6.2 billion to 8 billion (2001 constant dollars) from 1998 to 2001. To achieve its potential in reducing poverty, benefits must not be deducted from those receiving income assistance. It must also provide sufficient levels of income. Freiler, Stairs, Kitchen, and Cerny (2001) propose a universal child tax credit for all and an income tested child allowance for families earning less than $40,000 to provide a base amount of $4000 per child per year with indexing, a sum supported by Campaign 2000 and the Caledon Institute (Battle, 2001; Battle & Mendelson, 2001). Such aims could be accomplished by revising the present program. The other contribution of the Child Tax Benefit and National Benefit Supplement is unexpected. It has produced a much more knowledgeable, committed, and connected policy community with practical proposals for tackling poverty and some growing consensus about what would work.

Preventive Work: Building Community

Probably one of the most well-known and least implemented innovation in child welfare is working in a community to foster healthy environments for children and families. Those favouring a community approach to child welfare challenge the definition of child abuse and neglect as individual problems amenable to clinical solutions (Dominelli,

1999; Wharf, 2002). These authors argue that, although child welfare has always emphasized working with individuals, mandatory reporting and risk assessment has reified this focus. As an alternative, they propose community solutions to the challenges facing families involved with child welfare agencies. Wharf (2002) suggests three overlapping strategies that exist in Canada: community social work, community organizing, and community control.

The first of these, community social work (Adams & Nelson, 1995; Smale, 1995), includes the practice of locating child protection workers in community facilities where they work in a more open, collaborative fashion with community members and professionals from other organizations. Presumably, this is the least difficult strategy to implement in the current system. For instance, in Huron and Renfrew counties in Ontario, some child protection workers are situated in the local schools. In Victoria, British Columbia, child welfare staff work out of neighbourhood houses in local communities. The Children's Aid Society of Toronto (CAST) has developed joint protocols with Toronto Family Resource Programs that provide clear guidelines for staff in family resource programs, enabling them to consult with CAST staff before or instead of making a report (MacAuley, 2002).

There are many positive outcomes of these efforts that are well documented. The child who comes to school hungry may not result in a 'complaint' to child protection, but rather the involvement of neighbourhood house staff who know the mother and her difficulties. Community locations provide less threatening settings than child welfare offices. They can also improve assessment of concerns about children within the context of family, school and community realities and encourage the development of resources in the community, so that children who require alternative care remain within their neighbourhoods and have smooth transitions between care and home (MacAuley, 2002; Wharf, 2002).

There are challenges to collaborative work. Staff in Family Resource Programs report feeling intimidated by the power of child welfare workers, overlooked as partners in the reporting process and sometimes coerced into taking inappropriate referrals (MacAuley, 2002). This latter point is particularly compelling when family resource programs are to be funded primarily through contracts with the child welfare organization. Child welfare workers under pressure may look to staff in their contracted family resource programs to offer the services that they cannot, even if these services do not fit with the philosophy and mandate of the family resource program. Moreover, as managing risk becomes paramount within child welfare, family resource programs fear that their funding may be reduced if they do not appear to be dealing with high-risk families. They may have to describe their participants in terms that emphasize the negative aspects of their functioning rather than strengths, a demand that stands in opposition to their central philosophy.

Wharf's second approach to community work, community organizing, seeks to change oppressive conditions in neighbourhoods and build community capacity to care for residents. The Children's Aid Society of Toronto has taken long-standing leadership in this regard, assigning specific staff to promote and develop local resources, coordinating social planning efforts, and taking actions to promote progressive policies (Lee & Richards, 2002). Their achievements are many and parallel those reported by other community workers (Ife, 1998). Perhaps most important are the opportunities for previously alienated citizens to become participating members of community organizations. Developing useful community resources for families, building connections among organizations, creating positive identities for disparate communities, including the confidence to tackle sometimes overwhelming problems, and learning the skills to face new ones are clear outcomes. Fuchs (1995) has documented how these and other efforts of inner city organizing in Winnipeg resulted in fewer removals of children from families and more likelihood that those removed could remain within the community.

Community control involves transferring authority for child welfare to community systems. First Nations people have pioneered this approach to child welfare, in spite of difficulties in mounting effective responses in communities devastated by poverty and cultural annihilation (Brown, Haddock, & Kovach, 2002).

Altogether, community work makes the case for improving individual and family circumstances by developing community capacity to respond to its residents. Although the outcomes are consistent across these efforts, financial and organizational support for community work in child welfare remains marginal. Our vision for child welfare would underscore the central place of community building.

Collaborative Investigations: Protecting Children by Responding to the Circumstances of Their Parents

The long-standing contradiction in child welfare practice and policy, to exert authority while offering help, confronts child welfare workers on a daily basis. Community workers and child protection practitioners have developed significant approaches to engage parents in relationships, founded on the belief that 'mother the mother and you mother the child.'

Family resource programs encompass a wide range of services promoting 'social support, co-operation, collective responsibility (civic mindedness) and citizenship through a mix of education, information activities, material support and other resources to family members and groups of families' (Kyle & Kellerman, 1998, p. 55). These programs place emphasis upon voluntary services that build on the strengths and needs of family members and encourage collective action. Located in every province and territory, and funded by a range of federal programs (Community Action Program for Children, Canada Prenatal Nutrition Program) as well as provincial, Aboriginal, municipal, and nongovernment funding sources, they constitute a valuable resource for many Canadian families. Their usefulness in confronting daunting issues, such as the use of substances during pregnancy and violence against women, is encouraging (Rutman, Callanhan, Lundquist, Jackson, & Field, 1999). Another strength of these services is the thousands of hours of volunteer labour that they generate, often provided by those with few resources (Reitsma Street & Neysmith, 2000). Family resource programs are a major asset for child welfare in Canada.

While evaluations of the effectiveness of these diverse research programs are fraught with all the difficulties of assessing prevention programs, some encouraging evaluation studies have been done, demonstrating the positive contributions of these mutual aid, informal helping, and prevention program approaches on several levels, including decreasing the need for protective intervention and reducing the removal of children from their families (Cameron, 1995; Fuchs, 1995).

Child protection workers within statutory services also have a lengthy, if largely unknown, history of protecting children by supporting parents. Their innovations take place quietly, often behind the closed doors of homes and offices. One study of best practices in the British Columbia child protection services focused upon the definitions and outcomes of best practice provided by parents, child protection workers, their supervisors, and community agency staff (Callahan, Field, Hubberstey, & Wharf, 1998). Remarkable consistency emerged in each group's responses, even though participants experienced child welfare practice from very different vantage points. Best practice is a complex process whereby parents and workers move to the same side, setting aside their differences, jointly planning for the care of children and developing necessary and appropriate resources so that plans can be realized.

While there are obstacles to achieving best practice, workers and parents using this approach reported their immense satisfaction with their work together and positive outcomes for children, even though some children were removed from parental care. These findings were reaffirmed by another study in the United Kingdom (Farmer & Owen, 1995) in which researchers identified families who had a successful outcome with child protection services. Success was identified as children being protected from harm, children's welfare being enhanced, and parents' needs being met. In those cases where all three outcomes were positive (23% of the cases), the researchers concluded that 'the alliance between the social worker and the parents, which occurred when the parents' needs were recognized and at least partially met, was an important factor in securing the protection of the child' (p. 294).

What these studies and others demonstrate is that it is possible to protect children through the development of collaborative rather than combative relationships with parents and family members, and through relationships that acknowledge that parents' own well-being as individuals is directly linked to their parenting capacities. While these truths seem obvious, child welfare policies and practices rarely reflect them.

Reforming Court Process: Group Conferencing

Child welfare work is often dominated by formal legal processes that can be daunting, even to experienced social workers and lawyers. One approach to making these processes less formidable and more useful is illustrated by family group conferences. These conferences, introduced in New Zealand in 1989, have their roots in Aboriginal understandings of justice that concentrate upon restoring harmony between offenders and their communities through a problem-solving process, generally implemented in circles including offenders, victims, and community members (Barsky, 1999; Hudson, Morris, Maxwell, & Galaway, 1996). The theory of reintegrative shaming explains the power of the process whereby the offender experiences the disapproval of victims and the community, seeks genuine forgiveness, and then works with community members to plan reparations and a return to the community.

In Canada, family group conferences in child protection have taken hold here and there,[3] but the outcomes have been most thoroughly examined in Newfoundland and Labrador (Pennell & Burford, 1996). Three distinct cultural and geographical communities participated in the Family Group Decision-Making Project, a demonstration project designed to implement and evaluate family group conferencing for children and families where abuse had been confirmed through child welfare investigations. In their analysis of twenty family group conferences, Pennell and Burford make some interesting observations. Family group conferences unfold in similar ways, but have the potential to respect cultural and community differences, including differences among an Inuit community in Labrador, a rural community with French, English, and Mi'kmaw residents, and an urban community in St Johns. Family members' interpretations of the causes of difficulties overlapped somewhat with those of professionals (single mothers neglecting their children, fathers abusing women and children, children being out of control), but family members emphasized day-to-day struggles with poverty and deprivation. For instance, one family in Labrador noted that neglect was a certainty without wood for the fire.

Although families' reactions to their common experiences of shame differed among communities and cultures and between genders, researchers report that this collective feeling of shame helped families move to struggling for solutions. These solutions for the most part require ongoing involvement and support from child welfare services, a finding supported by other studies, but change significantly the role of child welfare workers. The sheer exhilaration of families, many of whom were considered multi-problem through multi-generations, creating their own solutions and being heard is perhaps the most important outcome.

Provincial court judges in British Columbia have introduced another approach to conferencing, one that substitutes for a family court hearing in cases of child protection (Metzger, 1997). Under the authority of the British Columbia Act, 1996, all child welfare apprehensions that are not settled by consent are subject to a mandatory case conference chaired by a provincial court judge. Attendance for parents, their lawyers, and social workers is required. If not successfully mediated, the judge can refer the case for a formal trial. Since the inception of this requirement, two-thirds of the cases that would normally be heard at trial have been successfully dealt with at the case conference level.

Although these and other studies indicate the success of finding consensual processes to replace adversarial ones, many issues are still unresolved, including the potential for cultural tokenism, the assurance that less powerful members of families are not subsequently punished, and that governments do not renege on the resources required to carry out conferences and implement plans. However, there are several nuggets contained within these approaches. They show potential in addressing the alienation of parents resulting from traditional investigative and court processes. They also can reformulate definitions of problems and solutions in ways understood by families and children themselves, rather than solely based on the views of professionals, and can identify alternative ways of working in non Anglo-Canadian traditions.

Improving Life in Care: Monitoring Child Well-Being

Many more children are entering the care system in Canada and a long-standing problem is the quality of the care offered by government. The Looking After Children program (LAC), introduced in the United Kingdom in 1991 and implemented in fifteen countries, attempts to address the issue of children 'lost in care.' It identifies seven dimensions of development: health, education, identity, family and social relationships, social presentation, emotional and behavioural development, and self care skills. Social workers, caregivers and others are trained in the implementation of the guidelines, called Assessment and Action Records (AAR), to help them monitor progress of children over time in each of these developmental areas.

LAC found fertile roots in Canada in the 1990s when various scandals and concerns about accountability were featured regularly in the media and when many, including foster parents and youth in care, continued to express long-standing concerns about the quality of government care. In 1997, three pilot projects were launched (in the Maritimes, Quebec and British Columbia) resulting in modifications of LAC to better suit Canadian realities, leading to additional funding from the federal government to support implementation in all participating provinces and territories,[4] and further development of models for diverse communities, including First Nations.

There are some crucial elements of the Looking After Children initiative that have the potential to contribute to positive child welfare systems. Most importantly, LAC shifts attention to the day-to-day caregiving of foster and group home parents and to the realities of children in care. Moreover, LAC can promote broader cooperation, as it is not fraught with the ideological and professional divisions that torment other child welfare processes. The initiative emphasizes consistency in record keeping for children to provide continuity and a basis for assessing how well children are managing individually. As well, information can be aggregated at provincial, national, and international levels. This steady, comprehensive, and comparative data can influence policy to improve conditions for children in care. For instance, a study using LAC data documents the major educational needs of children in care (Kufeldt, Simard, & Vachon, 2000). Finally, from the outset, the LAC involved a wide range of constituencies in child welfare, including those most likely to advocate for and implement findings: youth in care, foster parents, and social workers, as well as members of interprovincial networks, federal and provincial governments, Children's Aid Societies and other child welfare organizations, and university researchers.

Expanding Choices for Out-of-Home Placements

While recent developments in child welfare have resulted in more out-of-home placements for children and youth, child welfare has been slow to recognize the potential of variations to traditional permanent placements in a nuclear family. The introduction of open adoption policies, permitting parents, usually mothers, to choose adopting parents for their children and to have some kind of continuing contact with their children and the adoptive families, is one response to this need. The Adoption Council of Canada supports open adoptions and recently consulted with provinces on this issue, using the British Columbia statute as a model (British Columbia Adoption Act, 1996, s. 59). In British Columbia, openness can vary from sharing letters or pictures through a third party, to birth parents having personal contact with the adoptive family throughout the child's life, or adoptive parents entering into agreements with other important people in their child's life, such as foster parents, grandparents, or Aboriginal community members. As a result, adopted children may de facto have two sets of parents, larger extended families, and continuing community affiliations. Mothers who have resisted adoption in the past, because it permanently separated them from their children, may now be amenable to this option if they can continue to have a place in the lives of their children.

The British Columbia Adoption Act also recognizes the possibilities of customary adoption for First Nations communities, whereby the court can recognize adoptions carried out under the custom of an Aboriginal community or band as having the same status as adoptions carried out under the Act. Customary adoption recognizes the traditional approach of some First Nations who place children with families within their communities when parents are unable to offer care.

Over the past fifteen to twenty years, a growing volume of social science research has addressed questions about children being raised by gay men and lesbians. Studies have failed to find significant differences between parenting abilities of heterosexual and homosexual families or significant mental health differences between children raised by lesbian and gay parents and those raised by heterosexual parents (Arnup, 1995; Laird, 1993). A national study, *Adoption in Canada* (Daly & Sobol, 1993), which prompted national debate on the topic concluded:

> Policies and attitudes with respect to home study criteria and selection guidelines are strongly focused on marital status and stability as the pivotal criteria. This focus no longer corresponds with increasing diversification of family forms. There is no evidence to demonstrate that the best interests of the child are better served in any particular family constellation. Thus, the increasing acceptance of various family constellations should be reflected in the selection criteria. Among other things, this will require a change in policy and legislation that allows for the adoption of children by single and unmarried couples, regardless of their sexual orientation ... (p. 103)

Since that time, some changes have occurred making it easier for gay and lesbian individuals to adopt the children of their partners. While child welfare laws make no mention of same sex couples, each provincial statute (with the exception of Manitoba's) allows for single adults to adopt children. Select provinces allow for two adults, married or not, to adopt, paving the way for same sex couples to adopt children outside their own families. For instance, in British Columbia 'two *adults* jointly may apply to the court to adopt a child' (British Columbia Adoption Act, 1996, section 29[1]). In Quebec, 'any *person* of full age may, alone or jointly with another person, adopt a child' (Quebec Civil Code, SQ 1991, c. 64, article 546, as amended by SQ 1995, c. 33, ss. 30–2, article 549). These initiatives stimulate a rethinking of the concept of family emphasizing instead the importance of supportive relationships to nurturing children.

Improving Advocacy: Listening to Different Voices

One of the developments occurring over the last decade is the development of local, provincial, and national advocacy groups designed to give voice to those who are the children, parents, and workers in child welfare.[5] While there are many such groups, we feature in our discussion, the National Youth-in-Care Network [NYICN]. This organization began with the organizing efforts of Kathleen Kudfeldt, who coordinated a conference for youth-in-care entitled 'Who Cares' in 1979. This conference, and other developments during the International Year of the Child in 1985 (Strega, 2000), prompted the formation of a nonprofit organization run by youth aged fourteen to twenty-four who are or have been in care in Canada. The organization aims 'to facilitate an empowering, constructive dialogue between young people in care and adult service providers in which youth are taken seriously and treated with respect, dignity, and sensitivity' (National Youth-in-Care Network, 1998, p. 2). It emphasizes mutual support, giving voice to issues as youth experience them, research, public education, and lobbying for change.

The accomplishments of this group are remarkable. In 2001, their public education efforts alone included over fifty presentations and consultations. Representatives gave press conferences on Parliament Hill, addressing issues related to section 43 of the Criminal Code as well as family violence and education. Also, documentaries on the organization aired on CBC TV's The National, CBC Radio, and CPAC. Members undertake their own research and lobby other research organizations to focus on youth issues. Along with other priorities, they have identified the lack of policy supporting youth leaving care, including those youth who are also mothers (Martin & Palmer, 1997). Most provinces provide little if any sustained services and youth are expected to make their own way at age eighteen or thereabouts.[6] It seems obvious that the opinions of those who receive child welfare services should be central in policy and practice development, but the venues for hearing their voices are few and far between. It is essential that such advocacy groups speak out and that they have access to those in child welfare who can make changes.

Building Capacity in Research and Education

Until recently, most child welfare research has taken place within provincial jurisdictions,[7] and this creates difficulties in making comparisons across jurisdictions. Recent developments are making national research more possible. The Federal/Provincial/Territorial Working Group on Child and Family Services Information produces intermittent bulletins (www.hrdc-drhc.gc.ca) on child welfare developments within each province and territory, and occasional statistical reports on child welfare that, while not providing comparative data, can at least present some overall picture of trends. Funding for five Centres of Excellence for Children's Well-Being, part of the federal government' s National Children's Agenda (agreed to by the Federal/Provincial/Territorial Council on Social Policy Renewal in 1997) has provided support for a number of research ventures. One of these is a long overdue national study detailing the incidence of child abuse and neglect in Canada (Trocmé et al., 2001), a snapshot that can provide some base line data for future comparisons. These centres also have the potential to develop national networks of researchers and enter into partnerships with advocacy and professional organizations.

An overlooked feature of research in child welfare is that the research agendas have been largely controlled by academics, senior policy makers, and those in research institutes and rarely shaped by the families and workers within the system. As a result, we know a lot about particular subjects and very little about others. The development of advocacy groups, their presence at conferences, and their insistence that research address their concerns are very positive developments. Not only do these advocacy groups suggest areas for research, but they also promote research methods that incorporate their understandings of the system and involve them from the outset in the research process.

Finally, although schools of social work are pressed to prepare more workers for immediate practice in child welfare, particularly frontline child protection, and to teach competencies developed by child welfare organizations, new partnerships that have the potential to respect the roles of the employer and the academy in preparing practitioners are emerging. The development of child welfare specializations within three schools of social work in British Columbia, which feature antioppressive knowledge and skills for work in communities and with Aboriginal peoples, as well as with general child welfare populations, is an example of partnerships that may support retention of workers and improved practices (Armitage, Callahan, & Lewis, 2001).

Part III. Towards Reform in Child Welfare

We have identified several characteristics of many of these child welfare innovations that contribute to new conceptions of child welfare.

Collaborative Decision Making

Most initiatives are based upon a fundamental belief that decisions affecting the lives of children and families are best made in an open fashion with the important parties involved and within the context of relevant values and realities. This approach challenges traditional perceptions of professional expertise and confidentiality.

Attention to Diversity

These initiatives emphasize the importance of context in individual decision making and call into question the application of universal standards of child well-being, measured by yardsticks developed from scientific and professional standards. This presents a fundamental challenge to Eurocentric thinking about children and families that is usually ignored.

Strength-Based

Implicit throughout these innovations is the belief that most situations, however challenging, contain positive elements that can be enhanced. The movement away from documenting shortcomings of parents to open discussions of strengths and development of practical child safety plans is decidedly different from what occurs at present in most jurisdictions.

Balance

At present, the child welfare system seems out of balance. The majority of funds are provided by provincial governments to investigate complaints of child neglect and abuse; in many cases, however, nothing further happens for children or their families and they are often undermined in the process. Little money remains to fund innovations like these highlighted in part II, yet their potential to change the need for and the process of investigations is clear.

Child and Family Focused

Much of our activity in child welfare at present is shaped by organizational requirements, funding formulas, and workload management. Social workers are increasingly charged with administrative tasks. Yet all of these innovations have as their focus the well-being of children and families and attention to their definitions of issues.

Building Relationships

These initiatives demonstrate the need for positive relationships between child welfare workers and those they serve.

Partnerships for Reform

Can these innovations lead us to a new paradigm for child welfare? We conclude that these ideas are necessary, but not sufficient, building blocks of a reformed system. In spite of these initiatives, many of which demonstrate courage and creative thinking, child welfare remains isolated from the forces that might shape positive reforms. Thus, we conclude with a discussion of the nature of the types of partnerships necessary for real reform.

First, this notion of partnerships involves a rethinking about the definition and nature of work. Those traditionally seen as clients and lay people are in fact undertaking a large part of the work involved in child welfare. The idea of their role as receiving help rather than as working, usually without remuneration, requires change. Current funding formulas do not recognize the labour involved in developing and maintaining real working partnerships.

Second, although these initiatives have much in common, they appear as somewhat isolated endeavours. For real change to occur, child welfare has to become active in social reform, and to do this strong connections have to be forged. Our key partners in this endeavour, at the ground level, should be social movements advocating for reform: women's groups, anti-poverty organizations, Aboriginal governments, and groups concerned with resource issues such as housing, employment, and the environment. Child welfare can provide direct evidence of the impacts of current policies on the most vulnerable Canadians, while these advocacy groups can help us work toward a vision for change.

Finally, child welfare should develop partnerships at national and international levels. At present, child welfare agencies are constrained by provincial mandates and have few opportunities to develop national perspectives and to create partnerships on overarching issues such as poverty and child care. On the broader stage, local child welfare organizations should form partnerships with child welfare efforts in other countries. If we remain in isolated constituencies, we diminish our resources and our power.

NOTES

1 Conference organizers provided writers with some criteria of a positive vision. These criteria included (a) providing assistance in ways that are welcomed by the parents and children involved; (b) using helping strategies which take advantage of up-to-date knowledge of programming for disadvantaged and distressed families; (c) focusing on holistic concepts of well-being for children, parents, families, and communities; (d) placing a priority on keeping children safe from harm; and ensuring that service providers in the system feel their work is meaningful and worthwhile.
2 The term 'child poverty' in current parlance and government initiatives is misleading and ignores the connection between children and their families.
3 British Columbia is the only jurisdiction to include family group conferences in child welfare legislation.
4 In February 2002, all provinces and territories had named a LAC coordinator and all with the exception of Manitoba, Saskatchewan, and Nunavut were at some stage of implementation. See http://www.lacproject.org/pubs/Canadian_LAC-Eng.pdf for a complete review.
5 A few key groups include Caring for First Nation Children Society (www.fernweb.com/cfncs); Child Welfare League of Canada (www.cwlc.ca); FRP Canada (www.frp.ca); Parents Anonymous (www/parentsanonymous .org); Canadian Foster Parent; Caledon Institute (www.caledoninst.org); and Campaign 2000 (www.campaign2000.ca).
6 Post majority legislation and services are poorly conceived in Canada. A few provinces have taken some action. For instance, the province of Saskatchewan has included specific sections in its child welfare legislation permitting the director to continue services beyond majority for youth between eighteen and twenty-one who are continuing education and need support to do so or who have particular mental and physical impairments requiring special attention (s. 56.1).
7 Exceptions include the National Council of Welfare, the Laidlaw Foundation, Status of Women Canada, and occasional national publications by individual authors.

PART THREE

Family Service Systems

The state supports child and family welfare systems that reflect communal ideals about children, family, and community. Principles of social solidarity and, in some settings, of subsidarity (local responsibility) are emphasized. Fostering the proper care of children is seen as a shared responsibility. Providing support for parent-child relationships and the care of children are primary focuses. Demonstrating risks of harming children is not a necessary precursor for families or children to receive assistance. Some child and family welfare services are not separate from services to the general population. Legal systems are inquisitorial, and mediating dialogues with specialized judges and mandated officials are common in many settings. Ideally, there is an emphasis on reaching consensual agreements with families. The chapters in this section examine family service orientations in France, the Netherlands, and Sweden.

6 The Plight of Paternalism in French Child Welfare and Protective Policies and Practices

ALAIN GREVOT

Evolution of the French Child Welfare and Protective System between the Seventeenth Century and 2002

1638–1945: The Prehistoric Years[1]

In 1638, the first Charity Organization for Lost Children was founded by Saint Vincent de Paul in Paris, followed more than a century later by the Lost Children's Hospital in 1761. Until the revolution of 1789, charity action focused on the consequences of poverty, and mostly on abandoned children. The well-known tower system was the only official form of state intervention (the tower was a state-sanctioned building where mothers could leave their children in a small enclosed room where they were cared for by nurses; confidentiality was preserved).

The French revolution introduced a completely new concept: the primacy of paternal power. Paternal power was the father's legal right, based on the Roman civil code, to limitless power over his children. For revolutionary legal experts, the aim was less to develop a child protection strategy than to break up the family model of the aristocracy, a symbol of despotism. Nevertheless, this reform defined a key paradigm still at work in 2002: the child as supported by the state, not simply because of the child's susceptibility, but because of a sentiment that the child is also a future citizen of the state.

In 1810, the first penalty for serious abuse of a child emerged in the Napoleonic criminal code, despite the fact that the Napoleonic civil code (1807) had restored the central power of the father in the French family. In 1814, the state began to play a (limited) role in the supervision of children living in foster care. In 1832, the first mention of sexual abuse appeared in the criminal code with the indecent behaviour offence.

By the end of the nineteenth century, children had assumed some legal rights, with laws on children at work and compulsory schooling – one of the most symbolic of the First Republic's policies. In 1889, a new breach in paternal power appeared with civil code provisions that left a father open to the possibility of forfeiting his parental rights. In 1892, the very first law on child abuse and neglect was formed and, at the same time in Paris, Dr Tardieu published his forensic study on child physical abuse syndrome.

The beginning of the twentieth century saw the formation of several key initiatives in legislation for the protection of children. The first child welfare administration (Service d'aide à l'enfance) was established in 1904, as the responsibilities of church and state were officially separated. In 1912, the position of Children's Judge – a professional and specialized judge in charge of juvenile delinquency cases – was created. The judge worked with a probation service, employing the ancestors of *Éducateurs spécialisés* (child social workers) – one of the two main corps of social workers, the other one being *Assistantes sociales* (generic social workers), modelled after the role of social nurses. With the 1933 law on neglected and abandoned children, the first stage in constructing the French system was complete.

The Welfare Years and the Birth of the Existing French System

As in many western European countries, the role of the state greatly expanded in 1945, leading to the creation of a welfare state, which provided social insurance and family allowances. The 1946 French Constitution declared France to be an indivisible, secular, democratic, and social republic.

One of the first legislative decisions of the 1945 national union government was a pivotal law about juvenile delinquency. Firmly centred on the priority of *educative* (education and treatment) answers to juvenile delinquency (until age twenty-one), this law established the Children's Judges as the moral authority of the child welfare system, far ahead of the social services, then still in their infancy. Since the public child welfare social services focused primarily on abandoned children, for nearly fifteen years it was common for 'pioneer judges' to use flexible interpretations of the law to allow social workers to deal with a much broader range of troubled children. This group of very committed Children's Judges pushed hard for the development of local non-profit organizations to help children and families in trouble; very often the Judges were personally involved in the creation of these Associations for the Protection of Childhood and Adolescence (Association de sauvegarde de l'enfance et de l'adolescence).

In 1958, Charles de Gaulle returned to power, and with him a large group of influential Social Democrat or Christian Democrat civil servants. In the wake of a new constitution (the Fifth Republic), they developed a wide range of public policies, more attuned to social development through the role of state and public services, with the goal of creating a stronger French economy.

It was a time of rapid urbanization, immigration, and growth. In the first months of this new political and economic era, social work emerged as an integral part of national development. The contemporary child and family welfare and protection system is rooted in the spirit of the Fifth Republic, with a symbolic alliance between the state and the family for the up-bringing and education of children – child being understood both as a member of a family and a citizen-to-be.

In 1958, the Children's Judges obtained what they had been lobbying for since 1945: a new law regarding children in danger. The law concerning *Assistance éducative* became the foundation of judicial protection. As a result, Children's Judges were responsible for responding to instances of juvenile delinquency and for more general cases of children in trouble. Because of this shift in responsibility, Children's Judges found themselves as often involved with parents as their children. The law on *Assistance éducative* made Children's Judges the secular arm of the state with a responsibility to support parents in their role. Children's Judges had the power to limit parental rights, but not to suppress them or to definitively separate children from parents. Since the core concern of the law was the existence of danger for the child, it left the gates open for two actions: the first, a rather informal and open dialogue between the judge, the parents, and the children; and the second, implementation, by a new kind of social and educative service (called AEMO: Action éducative en milieu ouvert), of judicial orders offering help and counselling to the family, with the stipulation that judges be able to monitor the development of the child's living conditions with parents and relatives.

The next step occurred a year later, in 1959, with the publication of the Act regarding administrative protection – the precursor to the modern French child protection system. The code included a duty for social services, at that time administered by the state, to develop a large repertoire of social work strategies to bring help, support, and counselling to families facing social difficulties likely to endanger their well-being. These forms of intervention included voluntary or negotiated care for children. For judicial protection, the key concept was 'danger,' while for the administrative field it was 'risk of danger.' No one was able to provide a precise definition of danger, but work went along on this basis for nearly thirty years. The structure of the system designed in 1958–9 can be represented under two separate levels, each divided into two fields completely funded by the state.

The first level covered proactive global social action, aimed at leading the way for the health and social development of the country (primary prevention), and the administrative protection of children, based on voluntary or negotiated interventions (secondary prevention). This level was under the responsibility of the state's National Health and Social Affairs administration (DASS), with a national management and ninety-nine local administrations (DDASS) – one for each *département*, an administrative and geographical jurisdiction created by the French revolution. Each local DDASS had three departments: (1) the Social Services Department; (2) the Mother and Infant Health Protection Department (PMI); and (3) the Child Welfare Department (Aide social à l'enfance), responsible for administrative protection. Each DDASS was organized in a local health and social team, called Circonscription d'action sanitaires et socials, serving an average of 25,000 inhabitants. These local teams were composed of members of each of the three DDASS departments: a group of general social workers (*Assistante sociale de secteur*), one for every 5,000 inhabitants, along with nurses, midwives, paediatricians, home aid workers, family economy social workers, child social workers (*Éducateurs spécialisés*), and one psychologist. The Mother and Infant Health Protection Department (PMI) worked closely with the École maternelle – a free public preschool for three- to six-year-old children that is available everywhere in France – and developed mobile health centres in rural areas. The Aide social à l'enfance (ASE) departments of DDASS worked not only with their own teams, based in the local units, but also with the network of children's homes and foster care services from the nonprofit sector. The French nonprofit sector was formed in the postwar period as the state developed its social policies using its own public services and nonprofit organizations (by means of agreements generating financial and technical control over the nonprofit organizations).

The second level of the 1958–9 system included the judicial protection field, led by the Children's Judges and their close partners, the large social and educative service of the Action éducative en milieu ouvert (AEMO). These officials implemented supervision and educative orders for children living with their parents or relatives. Care orders were implemented by the local DDASS–Aide sociale à l'enfance departments with their own children's home (emergency units) or foster care services and the network of children's homes and foster care services from the nonprofit sector.

Between 1975 and 1979, the national social affairs policy focused on a concept of global social action, and on the strong link between global social policies and prevention and protection social policies. A 1979 report from the Social Affairs Inspectorate (Bianco & Lamy, 1980) promoted a preventive and global approach to difficulties. Its guiding principles were widely implemented. The DDASS local units encouraged collaboration among all their members, and the 1975–85 period was characterized by the substantial development of the human and technical resources of both public and nonprofit sector services. The impact of this policy between 1973 and 1983 can be assessed by the decrease in the number of children in the care of the child protection system on a judicially enforced or voluntary basis. The number of these children fell from 235,000 in 1973 to 140,000 in 1983 – 50% of whom were under state care on a voluntary or negotiated basis (http://www.sante.gouv.fr/drees). It was the peak of the welfare-oriented period in France.

Soon after came a period during which the state ordered its administrations and nonprofit partners to place priority on the economic and social development of France, and in particular to focus on populations not conforming to those expectations. Major changes in France were placing pressure on the generous and rather paternalistic family and children welfare system. The impact of a 1974 economic crisis (e.g., runaway unemployment), increasing awareness of a large multiethnic (mostly North African) adolescent population in urban areas, the impact of the evolution of women's rights (equal parental rights between father and mother, 1971; contraception, 1971; legalization of abortion, 1975), and the transformation of the traditional family model all contributed to strain on the welfare system. The nonprofit organization ATD–Fourth World (ATD: Help for All in Distress), a voluntary organization working with poor families, focused at that time on promoting a minimum income allowance (created in 1988). Their militant criticism of social work, especially child protection strategies, gave both service providers and politicians a poorer public image.

Two Sources of Change: The Sudden Awareness of Intrafamily Maltreatment and the Decentralization of Child Protection Responsibilities

In addition to the pressures noted above, the destabilization between 1983 and 1989 of the child welfare and protection system came from two other sources: the decentralization of child protection from the state level to the local level, and the newly introduced concepts of physical and sexual abuse.

The 1981 socialist government decentralized many state powers to local authorities. This was a significant change in a country that had had a deeply rooted culture of centralized powers. The state put social work and child welfare and protection responsibilities in the hands of *Conseils généraux* – a level of local authorities all but unknown to the majority of French people and whose role had been for two centuries a very minor one. The government intended to bring decision making in social affairs closer to the people directly affected by the decisions, and also wanted to harmonize the French system with those in other European countries. One factor that severely inhibited progress was that the state had lost control over child protection expenses (+10% per year) at a time of economic crisis (1974–84). Furthermore, no national data recorded which children were being named 'at risk' or 'in danger,' why they were so named, and for what purposes.

All the DDASS administration personnel (social services, PMI, and Aide sociale à l'enfance) were transferred from state control to *Conseils généraux*, but a substantial number of technical decision makers from DDASS chose to stay with the state rather than go to the local authority. This created a serious loss for the child protection system, because very often the new technical decision makers were unskilled in social work and child protection.

More generally, the decision to decentralize child protection responsibility was made in spite of the reservations and criticisms levelled by social workers. For most academics and social work practitioners, the intrusion in the private family sphere was legitimated by the original Republic's alliance between the state and the family. They viewed the move of the main responsibility for child protection from the state level to the weakest level of the French democracy (*Conseils généraux*) as a poor one. As a result, mandates from the justice system suddenly became, for a majority of child protection practitioners, the only source of credible involvement in cases dealing with children in serious trouble. This change would have important consequences five years later when an increased awareness of the issue of child maltreatment further destabilized the system.

At the Montréal International Society for the Prevention of Child Abuse and Neglect Conference, a small group of paediatricians and Ministry of Social Affairs civil servants – all founding members of the French Association for the Information and Research on Child Abuse (AFIREM) – came in contact with, and reacted positively to, North American ideas about child abuse and neglect. They were especially impressed by initiatives from Québec. In France, they lobbied for action by the government, and the Ministry of Social Affairs launched its very first campaigns against the physical (1985) and sexual (1987) abuse of children.

These two campaigns, based on television and newspaper advertisements, had a strong impact. The messages were reinforced by new nonprofit organizations created by survivors of abuse and by media stars. These new groups developed aggressive strategies towards the official child protection system and effectively exposed the general public to the dark side of family life. Everywhere in the French-speaking world (especially in countries in the Caribbean and Indian Ocean), children and adults began to talk about serious abuse of children and social work practitioners changed their perspectives on these issues. On 10 July 1989, the Prevention of Abuse of Children legislation was enacted. The Act gave local authorities the duty to set up a permanent plan of action to collect information about abused children and to investigate all suspected cases in cooperation with the justice sector. Compulsory reporting of abuse was required for everyone involved in the primary and secondary prevention service sectors. At the same time, the education system became involved in this national fight against child abuse. After years of silence and secrecy (that often served to protect abusive teachers), a very clear order was given to all teachers and school staff: refer all forms of suspected abuse to the judicial prosecutor.

The new law also required that local authorities train all service providers in the subject of maltreatment, and collect data about the incidence and prevalence of abuse. To share in this mission, the local authorities set up jointly with the Ministries of Social Affairs and Justice a national registry of children in danger (ODAS). Having found that it was nearly impossible to collaborate without a common language, ODAS (http://www.odas.net) made it a priority to develop a comprehensive glossary, since words such as danger, referral, and maltreatment had no agreed-on common meaning within the field.

Under the basic ODAS definitions, *maltreated or abused children* are children who are victims of physical violence, mental cruelty, sexual abuse, or neglect producing grave consequences for their physical and emotional development. *Children at risk* are children who are subject to living conditions that can put in danger their health, safety, morality, education, or upbringing, but who are not otherwise maltreated. *Children in danger* encompass the whole of the two preceding categories.

These definitions were used for the annual data collection that began in 1994. For the first time, an overview of who entered the French child protection system was anticipated. However, these new definitions brought some confusion with them. The 1958–9 system was based on the idea that children at risk of danger were under the charge of administrative protection and children in danger were under the charge of the judicial system. In 1991–2, as the use of the *ODAS* glossary spread across all child protection services, nearly all children at risk of danger became labelled in danger, as a result of the change in definitions. Some Children's Judges were critical of this change, but the social pressure for a quick and effective answer to child abuse negated any voice of opposition.

The July 1989 Act had a deep impact not only on the new local authority social services but also on service providers working with children perceived to be in trouble. The ensuing ten-year period was a time of more emphasis on child protection than child and family welfare.

The Recognition of the Reality of Abuse and Neglect and the Power of the Public Response

The 1994–7 period saw a dramatic increase in reported maltreatment cases (especially sexual abuse, which moved from 5,500 recorded cases in 1995 to 6,800 in 1997), though in the following years the numbers stabilized for this sort of case (Table 6.1 shows the number of children referred to Aide sociale à l'enfance [ASE] between 1994 and 2000).

The emphasis on more protective approaches had some positive effects: the French community was made to face the reality of the dark side of family life and, as a result, was forced to make significant

Table 6.1: Children Referred to Aide sociale à l'enfance between 1994 and 2000

	1994	1995	1996	1997	1998	1999	2000
Maltreated Children	17,000	20,000	21,000	21,000	19,000	18,500	18,300
Children at risk	41,000	45,000	53,000	61,000	64,000	65,000	65,500
Total	58,000	65,000	74,000	82,000	83,000	83,500	83,800

alterations to institutional life (in schools, children's homes, etc.). In the report to parliament published in September 2000 (GIPEM, 2000), the Ministers of Social Affairs and Justice gave evidence describing cases being served of child physical, emotional, and sexual abuse. In 1996, police forces followed social services in setting up annual data collection procedures for these cases. The results showed that child sexual abuse investigations and prosecutions were growing – from 14,211 in 1997 to 16,434 in 1998. Criminal Justice recorded a similar trend – 575 sexual crimes (rapes by parents/adults with responsibility for the child) in 1994, 715 in 1997, and 602 in 2000; 2,579 sexual assaults on minors were reported in 1994, 4,233 in 1997, and 4,666 in 2000.

The severity of sentencing increased dramatically during the first five years of the 1990s. An incest case (with rape) is now sentenced to five to twenty years of imprisonment. In 1997, the government supported a national campaign on child abuse and neglect. On 7 July 1998, a new Act concerning perpetrators and victims of sexual abuse dramatically improved the support offered to child victims of sexual abuse in criminal proceedings. Instructional video recordings, the development of the child advocate (*Administrateur ad hoc*), therapeutic support, and other services were offered to victims of abuse. In 1999, the Ministry of Social Affairs published a guidance report on the prevention and treatment of institutional violence. During the same period, sentences against teachers and sports trainers, as well as judges, priests, and bishops, made national news headlines.

Between 1997 and 2000, the annual national conference on child abuse and neglect addressed, in succession, the issues of physical abuse, emotional abuse, sexual abuse, and the benefits and costs of long-term care for maltreated children. In 1998, 272,050 children and adolescents (less than 0.2% out of 15 million people aged under 19) were the subject of some form of child protection interventions (see Table 6.2).

Table 6.2: Child Protection Interventions in 1998

Actions	Number
Home aid	25,000 families
Financial aid	450,000 families
Family supervision orders (Action Educative en Milieu Ouvert)	128,850 children
Administrative Care based on negotiated basis, implemented by local authorities	• Foster care: 62,000 • Residential care: 41,000 • Other forms of care: 12,500
Judicial care orders implemented by local authorities	84,500 children
Judicial care orders implemented by family or other individuals	27,700 children

The Destabilization of Child Protection System: Red Lights on the Dashboard

Despite support from substantial investment in a program of continuous training, the rapid implementation of compulsory child abuse referrals to the Local Authorities' social and health workers who were in charge of most preventive actions had negative effects on these personnel. They lost confidence in their ability and in their right to work with families in trouble if they feared for the safety of the children, or had any doubt about the parents' capacity to face and solve their children's problems. The result was a growth in referrals to the justice system (see Table 6.3). Also of significance is the change in the ratio of children who were put in care based on judicial orders: 1 out of 2 in 1980, 3 out of 4 in 1998.

Due to the increase in referrals, the 352 Children's Judges had to respond at any point in time to 145,000 cases of children deemed to be in danger. The increase meant an average of 440 files for the judges' civil activity – at a time when a dramatic growth of juvenile delinquency was already exposing them to greater public pressure.

A study published in January 2001 (Deschamps, 2001) provides some telling statistics:

• 100% of parents or children had no access to their files prior to the hearings
• 98% of reports sent by fax or given by social workers on the day of the hearings were used for the proceedings

Table 6.3: Children Newly Referred to Aide sociale à l'enfance (ASE) and the Ratio of Cases Passed on to the Justice System

	1994	1995	1996	1997	1998	1999	2000
Referrals to Justice by Aide sociale à l'enfance	31,000	36,000	42,000	49,500	49,000	47,500	47,500
Cases treated by local authorities (Aide sociale à l'enfance)	27,000	29,000	32,000	32,500	34,000	36,000	36,300
Total of new children in danger cases	58,000	65,000	74,000	82,000	83,000	83,500	83,800
Proportion of total new children in danger cases referred to the justice system	53%	55%	57%	60%	59%	57%	57%

- in 87% of hearings, social workers and family members were heard at the same time during the hearing
- in 61% of hearings, Children's Judges gave full information about the file's content (referral report, investigation report, review report)
- the average time for serious case hearings was 41 minutes
- only 5.2% of Children's Judges' orders were subject to appeal.

Most of the investigative services (Action éducative en milieu ouvert) had a long list of cases waiting many months to be served. For example, the workforce of the JCLT investigative service increased three times between 1998 and 2002, but many cases, equal to one third of its operating capacity, were still waiting to be served in January 2002 (Deschamps, 2001).

Strengths and Weaknesses of the System in 2001: The Challenge of Preserving the Positive Nature of the System

As mentioned above, the French child protection system involved roughly 300,000 children and adolescents in 1998. This section will look first at some financial ambiguities of the current system. Then we will examine why and how the system has been placed under scrutiny in recent years. Finally, we will present a thematic summary of the results of five official studies of the French child protection system published between 1999 and 2001.

More Money, Fewer Children, but What about Prevention Interventions?

As the Social Affairs Inspectorate concluded, some elements of the French child protection system are very hard to define (Naves & Cathala, 2000). A striking example is the system's financial ambiguity. The overall French social protection expenses were, in 1999, 389 billion Euros. Local Authorities' social service expenses (which cover the elderly, people with disabilities, and children and families – some 830,000 people in all) were 12 billion Euros. Child welfare and protection's part of the social service expenses were 4.6 billion Euros, and the Family Allowances System's special social action funds were 2.3 billion Euros (global Family Allowances expenses are 38 billion Euros).

There are two main fiscal consequences of the decentralization of child protection from the state to local authorities: (1) more money spent on fewer children; and (2) more money spent on placement, and less on other forms of intervention. Child protection expenses grew by 85% through the 1984–99 period as the number of children involved in child protection interventions fell from 333,000 to 269,000. Care cost an average of 120 Euros per day in residential care and 80 Euros in foster care. Child care (placement) costs consumed 75% of the budget, as the balance of expenditure patterns shifted towards placement and away from prevention and treatment interventions. Interventions by Action éducative en milieu ouvert, the largest unit working with children in danger and their families, saw social workers with caseloads of fifteen to twenty-five families at a time, even if their teams included psychologists and psychiatrists. State expenses for Juvenile Justice (courts and investigative services) are unknown, as are health expenses related to child protection.

A Child Protection System under Scrutiny: Why and How?

By the end of the twentieth century, three new elements affected the balance between welfare and protection, and disturbed the relations between families and child protection professionals. One came from the users of these services, another from the jurisprudence of the European Human Rights Court, and a third from the evolution of professionals' awareness about the importance of evaluating service and management practices.

The nonprofit organization ATD–Fourth World – the voluntary organization working with poor families that lobbied the 1988 socialist government to provide a minimal income allowance – strengthened its links and influences with the Minister of Social Affairs directly and through the media. ATD–Fourth World called for an enquiry on the impact that poverty and precarious living conditions had on childcare decisions during child protection interventions. The Minister of Social Affairs and the Minister of Justice, two major members of the socialist government, asked the Inspectorates of Social Affairs and Justice to investigate how voluntary and judicial care orders in the child protection field were decided. The investigation included interviews with professionals, parents, children, decision makers in Aide sociale à l'enfance administration, and Children's Judges, and also analyses of referral contents and judicial files. The Naves-Cathala report was published in mid-2000 and was actively reported by the media which, for the first time in France, began to make bitter critiques of service providers. In the wake of the report, the Minister of Family and Children set up a commission of service providers, decision makers, and academics to consider the evolution of relations between parents and professionals. Their final report (Roméo, 2001) was widely commented on by the media and officially presented by the Minister at the Etats généraux de la protection de l'enfance in November 2001 (*Etats généraux* is a very symbolic phrase in French as it was the name of the first revolutionary national assembly in 1789).

The feeling that the French *Assistance éducative* judicial proceeding was somehow too specific and constrained had grown within the corporate body of judges, and especially among Children's Judges. The principal concerns were the lack of direct access by families to the judicial files and the place and role of barristers. To keep the humanist spirit of the 1958 founders safe, and to prevent criticism from the European Human Rights Court, it was considered important to review the proceedings. The *Garde des sceaux* (Minister of Justice) asked a group of judges and practitioners to recommend changes. The methodology included a questionnaire that was sent to every Children's Judge in France.

At the same time, the ODAS national observatory of children in danger published a pilot study on the ways that children and parents move through the child protection system. For five years, the work of

ODAS had influenced the evolution of Aide sociale à l'enfance professional culture. The pilot study, based on the work of small groups of
Aide sociale à l'enfance officers, helped to increase the awareness of
French decision makers about the importance of observation and evaluation. The influence of JCLT's European comparative studies was extremely significant at this level as well (Grevot, 2001). ODAS's work
impelled the politically powerful Local Authorities Assembly to produce a study of the functioning of the child protection system in sixteen
Local Authorities (DPJJ/ADF, 2001) jointly with the Ministry of Justice.
In addition, the first annual report of the newly named Child Ombudsman was published in 2000. A large part of the report focused on child
protection interventions.

Thematic Summary of Five Official Reports (Children and Families)

First and foremost, the five reports share an assessment that contemporary family models are widely diverse, complex, and fragile. The
reports also conclude that users of protection services are calling professionals to account for their methods. They agree that professional
workforces demonstrate questionable ways of thinking about two main
service user groups.

FAMILIES LIVING IN SENSITIVE URBAN AREAS
MAKE UP THE FIRST GROUP
France faces a considerable crisis in its inclusion model, which had
worked quite well for the last two centuries with immigrants arriving
from all over Europe or from Christian cultures overseas. Members of
the large North-African population that had immigrated to France in
the 1960s and the West-African population that is part of the current
flow of immigration, are the major victims of recent economic and
social changes. The French republican model is based on individual
inclusiveness, with new arrivals progressively internalizing French values and social models, even if they maintain links to their original
cultures. For many years, immigrant North-African families had a difficult decision to make in determining whether they would remain in
France or return to Algeria, Morocco, or Tunisia. Children born during
the 1970s and 1980s were guided by ambivalent parents, who were
facing both a breakdown of cultural perspectives and economic uncer-
tainty as industrial changes made them susceptible to unemployment.

During the 1980s, the role of fathers and women's status became the subjects of ideological disputes between French social workers and North-African families. Things became more complex as the classic North-African family model faded and both social work and juvenile justice failed to develop an appropriate understanding of the new French North-African family ways of living. If many young people from North-African communities became involved in community-based activities (sports, culture, day care), a very limited number continued in the education system to become qualified social workers. Neither was there significant representation of people from minority cultures and races among French political and administrative staff. Day by day, the weight of negative representations grew between immigrant families, families with limited resources, and social workers. As a result, more families avoided contact with public social services.

National social programs were designed to reduce the social costs connected with urban social housing areas built in the 1970s. These housing areas were seen as having very negative effects on child development, especially in educational attainment. Residents were deeply stigmatized. A social and cultural divide had developed, concealed by the public image of France reflected, for example, in the multiethnic 1998 world championship soccer team. These issues continue to be underestimated in local and national political discourse, because they challenge the inclusive image of our nation.

ADOLESCENTS MAKE UP THE SECOND GROUP
The Child Ombudsman's Annual Report (2001) stated that in 2000–1, our country saw adolescents as a major threat. The trend started during the 1980s with the dramatic increase in aggressive behaviour of young male groups in sensitive urban areas. As schools increasingly revealed, violence at school was becoming commonplace, due to the impact of government child abuse policies. Daily media coverage of serious incidents (barbarous murders, group rape, assaults of young people by peers, etc.) involving adolescents from all social classes and cultures found audiences across the political spectrum. Public perceptions put enormous pressure on child welfare and on other social workers and therapists, including Children's Judges. Some of the official reports described serious panic among professionals at the time of the 2001 investigations.

The third major agreement about families is that economic and social precariousness increase the pressure on parenting skills and family education responsibilities. The reports also point out that child protection professionals focused on intrafamily relationships more than on contextual parameters like daily living conditions.

Professional Practices

The five official reports agree that it is a matter of urgency to bridge the gap between the worlds of service users and service professionals. The preferred method to reduce resistance is to link supports for the parental role with child protection interventions. The reports promote the concept of coeducation and mutual good treatment (*bientraitance*) between service users and professionals, even if these practices may generate a profound upheaval in professional practice and the nature of qualifications of social work teams. Recommendations include the development of methods to assess family resources and strengths, moving beyond the exclusive focus on family weaknesses and poor functioning to include the nature of the wider family and social environments.

For the first time in France, official documents recommended that a limit be placed on the involvement of the Children's Judges in child protection work. The ideas in these reports about the child protection system focus on agreements, contracts, and partnerships among service users and social workers. They provide an alternative to the monopoly of the concept of 'beneficiary,' where users call for service and the concerned administration decides whether or not to offer the service in ways defined only by itself. The studies conducted by the JCLT Research Department show that French professional practices involve negotiation less often than do those of other continental European child protection systems, in Belgium or Germany, for example (Grevot, 2001).

Nearly all of the reports identify a need for more formal and informal support for front-line service providers. Most generic social workers, such as *Assistante sociale de secteur*, or community-based health professionals, such as PMI nurses and paediatricians, are facing paradoxical expectations, since the introduction of compulsory abuse reporting in 1989 merged with their professional welfare orientation. Facing more complex and fragile family cases, service providers in local authorities are seen generally as receiving poor support from their management. The reports' main recommendation is for much clearer reference to social work principles and procedures, specifically in child welfare and child protection work, after more than forty years of legal emphasis.

Institutional Missions

The 2002 French child protection system was the result of many legal texts accumulated from 1958 to 2000; areas of serious confusion among the texts have been identified by these official reports. The most serious confusion arises in the numerous overlapping areas in the Children's Judges' (Justice) and Local Authorities' (administrative) legal responsibilities. Belgium and Germany faced the same problem before 1990–1, but defined a more distinct role for these two sectors. By means of a new law, priority has been given to voluntary child welfare work by official social services, with the justice system playing a subsidiary role.

However, in France, efforts to clarify jurisdictions proceeded by noncompulsory local negotiations. It proved nearly impossible in 2001–2 to introduce explicit and binding changes in the structure of the system as each party to the negotiations was reluctant to interfere with the jurisdictions of other parties.

Nevertheless, local authorities, social services, and Children's Judges continue to try to improve the clarity of the system for its users. This objective is supported by the January 2002 Social Work Act, legislation that requires all public and nonprofit welfare and protection institutions to prepare documents describing their internal rules and procedures, develop service plans for individuals, collect and take into account service users' points of view, and offer service users access to their files.

The 2002 Social Work Act also introduced a new concept for French service providers: the duty of all institutions to design self-assessment methods for their performance and to call for external evaluation every five years. A National Council of Evaluation has been created including administrators, academics, service providers, and service user groups. The Council's mandate is to approve assessment methods and personnel, and to promote good service practices.

Legal Aspects

Though the new laws were intended to enhance the rights of service users in 2001–2, it was not the first attempt to realize this ambition. The 1984 law on the relations between Local Authorities' child protection social services and their users was, like many other official rules, not implemented correctly by staff and social workers. So the government intends to begin anew official inspections by the General Inspectorate of Social Affairs, a state department.

For the first time in France, in the spring of 2002, national television channels and newspapers castigated child protection professionals for the way they treated families and children in child protection proceedings and interventions. To this author, it was a media storm resembling those in England, where this kind of event has occurred regularly for many years. Even if the attack was based sometimes on stereotypical cases, it resulted in pressure on professionals and helped those working to change their way of thinking about service users. For example, the Deschamps report (2001), based on an analysis of child protection judicial proceedings, gave birth in March 2002 to a new act giving parents and children direct access to their judicial files in Children's Judges' courts.

Conclusion

The Plight of Paternalism and the New Balance between Welfare and Protection

The first years of the twenty-first century could be an important benchmark for the French child welfare system. Initially designed during the 1950s as a welfare-oriented system at a time of rapid economic development and population growth, the French system takes as its model the spirit of a republican state-citizen relationship, which was characterized for many centuries by the responsibility of the state to define and safeguard the common interest. The state appointed a large network of professionals throughout the whole French territory, established important strategic links between all resources, like the École maternelle and PMI department, and exhibited a preoccupation with coherence and consistency. The Children's Judges were the key actors in this system, mixing a paternalistic role with an active promotion of parental responsibilities.

The difficult confrontation with the extent of serious abuse and neglect cases, beginning in the late 1980s, opened the way for the influence of criminal proceedings on child protection work and, during the 1990s, very much reduced opportunity for dialogue and negotiation among service professionals and users. But it also revealed that French practices were in many ways highly discretionary and confusing. In the context of the social evolution of French society (family models, multicultural communities) and with the impact of more liberal economic and social policies, counterinfluences came to light especially through legal proceedings and in the media. The entire system (service providers, policy makers, judges) began to question its practices and values.

The content of many different official documents (national surveys, inspection reports, and laws) published between 2000 and 2002 demonstrated that the system is changing. These texts demand more transparency in interventions and decision making, call for a new balance of powers between service users and professionals, and support assessment of family potential and of the quality and impact of possible interventions.

At the core of these changes is a modification in the relationship between professionals and service users through coeducation, a French Republican version of Anglo-Saxon enabling and empowering. The new priority for social workers and all professionals in child welfare is to be clear about what they propose to do to be closer to families' daily realities, and to help families to discover and to use their own resources to reduce the dangers for their children as far as possible.

The first decade of the twenty-first century will see the retirement of nearly 60% of the child welfare and protection workforce. Young professionals are entering the system at a pivotal moment. In the French context of social and moral crisis, they begin their work with multiproblem families with clearer institutional references and much more awareness of issues like emotional, physical, or sexual abuse than their older colleagues had at the same stage of their own careers. Though some criticisms of the new procedures are surfacing, the public message sent to professionals still focuses more on the need to help families in trouble than to blame them. There is general consensus about the legitimacy of coeducation (between service clientele and service providers) and a shared state-parent responsibility for child rearing.

Coeducation could be at the heart of a new direction for the French system. Many professionals are deeply committed to it. However, the inertia created by a strong paternalistic culture and poor methodological preparation may curb its evolution. The short-term development of the French democracy will weigh heavily on the child protection system, as no social work practices can be too far from the nation's core values. Is it possible to promote negotiation, balance of powers, and open-mindedness in a country lost in fear of change, responsibility, and openness to other cultures? The next years will provide the answer. French child welfare and protection practitioners have a role to play in that evolution, as they build on legislation that supports clearer values and more open ways of working.

NOTE

1 See the Glossary for terms in use in the French child welfare system. For a timeline of the evolution of the French child protection system, see Appendix C.

7 Child and Family Welfare in Sweden

GUNVOR ANDERSSON

Introductory Facts about Sweden

Sweden is a relatively large country in northern Europe, with a population of not quite nine million inhabitants. The king, who is head of state, does not have political power. There is a parliamentary form of government, and the dominant political ideology is social democratic. Sweden is a member of the European Union, though not a member of the European Monetary Union, and there are intense discussions among individuals and political parties for and against membership in the EMU.

Reports on conditions for children in Sweden typically describe a high standard of living compared to many other countries, and suggest that most children in the country are physically and psychologically well. Nevertheless, the same reports often note that many children have difficulties and suffer from adult maltreatment or neglect, and that too many young people use alcohol and drugs and commit crimes. Refugee children are said to need more help, especially those coming to Sweden without their parents.

The Children's Ombudsman, established in 1993, is a national authority mandated to represent the interests of children, to collect information about their needs, and to safeguard their perspectives in legislation and regulations. The value base for this work is the UN Convention on the Rights of the Child (1990). The term 'child' refers to people from birth to eighteen years of age, as stipulated in the Convention and, since 2002, in Swedish law. Each year the Children's Ombudsman delivers a report to the government on the welfare of children in Sweden and points out the constitutional changes necessary to realize the intent of the Convention. The Children's Ombudsman has also published a statistical report based on children (but not on households or families as is the case in many other national reports).

According to the Ombudsman's report *Up to 18: Facts about Children and Young People* (BO, 2001), the Swedish parents' allowance provides 80% of salary and is paid over a twelve-month period, but the recipient (usually the mother) must allow the other parent (usually the father) to stay at home with the child for at least one of these months. An additional three months of parental leave has a lower rate of compensation. Most children from fifteen months to six years are entitled to a place at a day-care centre (preferred by most parents) or at a registered child-minding home. Municipalities have an obligation to provide children a place in day care, if that is the parents' choice. From the age of six or seven most children go to schools administered by the local government. A small proportion of children attend private schools. Eighty-three per cent of mothers (with children living at home) are employed in the workforce, but half of them work part-time. Ninety-three per cent of fathers have full-time work (in 1999). Seventy per cent of children live in a detached or semidetached house and 30% in an apartment. Twenty-six per cent of all children (under eighteen) have divorced or separated parents, most of them living with their single mother (18%). Four per cent live with their mother and a stepfather and 3% with their single father.

In the three big cities, Stockholm, Gothenburg, and Malmoe, it is more common than in other areas to have a foreign background. In these metropolitan areas, 43% of all children under eighteen are either born in a foreign country or have one or two parents from a foreign country. Nationwide, this proportion is 24%. The most represented foreign countries are, in rank order, Finland, Yugoslavia, Iraq, Turkey, Iran, Norway, Bosnia-Herzegovina, Poland, Denmark, and Chile. I mention this to show that Sweden, though once rather homogeneous, has become a multicultural country where many different languages are represented. Many are followers of Islam. In social work caseloads, children and families with foreign origins are overrepresented, not least in the city of Malmoe and the district of Rosengaard, as will be shown below.

An official commission was recently struck to consider whether a Swedish welfare model still exists. One of the commission's first reports, *Welfare at a Crossroad: The Development during the 1990s* (SOU 2000:3), suggests that there has not been a crucial shift in the model for welfare services, although there have been some problematic changes. There were marked governmental cutbacks during most of the 1990s as state finances were undermined by a rapid decline in labour supply and a high rate of unemployment and, at the same time, an influx of refugees. The cutbacks led to a decline in service standards and in staff resources for day care, education, and publicly funded leisure time activities for children. The report shows, for example, that the mean number of children per adult in preschool (including day-care centres) in 1990 was 4.4, but in 1998 it was 5.6. There were 9.1 teachers per 100 children in schools in 1991, but only 7.5 teachers per 100 children in 1998. There are signs of increasing disparities between the well-being of the majority of children and the well-being of children in poorer environments.

Compared to some other welfare states, political power in Sweden is rather decentralized, with considerable authority given to the municipalities. During the 1990s, decentralization became widespread, from the state and county level to 289 municipalities or even smaller districts. The responsibility for health and social services, day care and education, and for children with learning difficulties and psychiatric problems was transferred to the municipal level. Consequently, there are local differences in the organization and delivery of welfare services. The report *Welfare at a Crossroad: The Development during the 1990s* (SOU 2000:3) notes that children of single mothers, immigrants, and refugees have lower material standards and more health problems, and that there are signs of increasing class gaps in Sweden. But the report also suggests that there is a lack of knowledge about children's living conditions, especially from the child's perspective.

Child and Family Welfare – An Overview

The terminology of child welfare has, in some countries, clear associations with child protection. The term child and family welfare[1] is appropriate for Swedish conditions, because there is no dividing line between family support and child protection. Family support can protect children from neglect or abuse when they are living at home, but is also important when children are placed outside the home, to prepare for their return home, or to ensure that parents maintain contact with their children in foster and residential care (Andersson, 1992). In his comparative study, the American researcher Gilbert (1997) points out that Swedish child welfare has a family service orientation rather than a child protection orientation, although reporting of child abuse is mandatory.

What follows is an overview of the Swedish child and family welfare system, including the legal framework, services and interventions available, and two examples of support services for dependent children (0–18) and their families. Contact persons/families, a statutory support service, is described, as is child and family welfare in the district of Rosengaard, in the city of Malmoe. As social services in Sweden are decentralized, generalizations about organization or support programs are difficult to make. Rosengaard is one of ten relatively autonomous districts in Malmoe, and will serve as an illustration of the local organization of social welfare. The chapter concludes with reflections on child and family welfare and issues currently under debate in Sweden.

Approaches to child welfare vary among countries. As the American researcher Furstenberg (1997) writes, the differences may relate to the balance between family and state in the responsibility for children. The privatized ideal of family-state relations in the United States, which maximizes the authority of parents, stands in contrast to the collaborative model present to varying degrees in most European nations and most fully developed in Sweden and Norway. Universal services such as day care and health care are seen as normal in the family – state relations in Sweden, and are not included in this paper's consideration of child and family welfare. Social services for vulnerable families and children in need, means-tested support services, and child protection interventions are, however, defined for our purposes as child and family welfare.

The Legal Framework

In Sweden there is no special Children's Act, because children are included in the 1980 Social Services Act (SoL).[2] This primary law is a goal-oriented enabling Act based on voluntary efforts, and stipulates general guidelines for municipalities concerning their social services obligations. According to section 12 in the Social Services Act, the social welfare committee in each of the 289 municipalities should endeavour to ensure that children and young people grow up in secure and beneficial conditions. The social welfare committee should be especially observant of children and young people who show signs of developing in an unfavourable direction and provide these children and young people with the protection and support they need in close cooperation with their families. The best interests of the child shall always be taken into consideration. The child's own opinion should be solicited as far as possible and allowance should be made for the child's wishes, consistent with his or her age and maturity.

According to section 71, it is the duty of authorities (and their employees) whose activities relate to children and young people, and of other authorities in health, medical care, and social services, to notify the social welfare committee immediately if, in the course of their activities, anything comes to their attention which may imply the need to intervene for the protection of a minor. The general public *should* report, but this is not formulated as a duty in the Act.

The social welfare committee shall, without delay, open an investigation of matters brought to its attention – by application or report – and determine whether the committee needs to intervene for the protection or support of children. An investigation or assessment should not be more extensive than is justified by the circumstances. The implementation of supportive measures, care, and treatment shall be documented.

The Social Services Act (SoL) is supplemented by the Care of Young Persons Act (LVU), which regulates the circumstances under which authorities may take children into compulsory care, if such an intervention is judged necessary and the parents (or young people over fifteen years of age) do not consent. A decision to take a child into care according to this Act is issued by the county administration court following an application by the municipal social welfare committee.

Family Maintenance or In-home Supportive Services

The Social Services Act contains guidelines for support for children and families, but the local authorities are free to plan various activities, programs, and projects. In most municipalities, there are programs to support vulnerable or insufficient parents in raising and caring for their children. There may be supportive groups for young parents or single mothers, or families may be seen on a regular basis by social workers or by family pedagogues working in the home. In most municipalities, there are group activities for children with parents who are abusing alcohol and drugs. Individual arrangements can be made in cooperation with the preschool or school and the child may be assigned a personal assistant, if he (or she) is disruptive to the group. There are programs for teenagers who need support (or activities) to refrain from using drugs or engaging in criminal activities. Child psychiatric treatment for the family or the individual child is always available. There are no reliable national statistics on supportive social services; if they are not statutory services, they vary among municipalities and parts of the country.

One statutory service called contact person/family is the most used statutory support service for children and families. During the year 2000, about 22,000 children and young people participated in the contact person/family service, which means 10 in 1,000 youths (Socialtjänst, 2001:8). Contact person/family is a flexible service for children and young people up to eighteen (or in some cases twenty). It is common for contact families to have children stay overnight regularly (e.g., every second or third weekend), and more common for contact persons to connect with older children or teenagers on a daily basis. Everyone has the right to ask for a contact person/family, but the local social welfare committee decides on the need for the service and appoints the contact family or person. It is also common for the social services to suggest the service following an assessment of the needs of the child and the family. The service will be discussed more fully below.

The contact person/family service introduced into social welfare legislation the possibility of children and families receiving social support from volunteers or laypersons. Child welfare in Sweden belongs to the public sector and there are no non-governmental or volunteer organizations serving as alternatives (Lundström & Wijkström, 1997). While contact persons/families do voluntary work, they must be officially approved, and are paid and supervised by public social services. As volunteers, they are ordinary people who have no special training, but do have the necessary time, a feeling of solidarity with people with social problems, and the ability to provide support to parents and children. According to the Children and Parents Code, the court can also appoint a contact person from social services. Such a decision might be made, for example, when divorcing parents are in conflict over access rights to the child, or when it is judged in the child's best interests that a contact person be present on visits with his or her (violent or drug abusing) father or mother. The service provided by the contact person/family is reviewed every six months, but it can continue for years.

Out-of-home Care

If out-of-home placement cannot be avoided, the consent of the parent(s) is recommended. About 75% of children in out-of-home care are placed with parental consent under the Social Services Act (SoL), and the remainder in accordance with the supplementary Care of Young Persons Act (LVU), which regulates placements under compulsion. During the year 2000, about 18,000 children (0–18/20), or 8 in 1,000, were in out-of-home placements (twenty-four-hour care) at some time during the year (Socialtjänst, 2001:8). Every six months, the social welfare board in the municipality or district is required to review all out-of-home placements. The law sets no time limits on care but it does not allow statutory permanency. For children under the age of twelve or thirteen, out-of-home placement is typically the result of parental neglect or abuse and not the behaviour of the child. Behavioural causes for placements do increase with the age of the child during the teenage years. On a particular day, 1 November 2000, around 75% of children in out-of-home care were in foster care and 25% were in residential care. Foster care is more common with younger children; residential care is more common for children in care by compulsion. There are different forms of both foster and residential care.

Foster Care

The ultimate aim in foster care is reunion of the child with his or her parents and there is no time limit on the rehabilitation of parents. As the U.S. researcher Barth (1992) writes: 'In Sweden, the underlying assumption of the law is that "every parent can be rehabilitated"' (p. 39). Nothing is said in law about how a case should be handled if reunion is not possible or is considered inappropriate. On the other hand, a placement with parental consent can be changed to a placement by compulsion, if assessment indicates that it is not in the child's best interests to return home. Although the Swedish system has no statutory permanency in foster care, there are children who cannot return home and who stay in long-term foster care (Andersson, 1999b; 1999c). According to a study of five cohorts of eighteen-year-olds (Vinnerljung, Langlet, Zaar, & Gunnarsson, 2000), 10% of those in foster care grew up in their foster home following placement at an early age.

The compulsory Care of Young Persons Act (LVU)[3] has been reviewed and a number of changes proposed (SOU, 2000:77). These include a recommendation that after three years, the social welfare committee should make a special assessment to ensure that children and young people, as much as possible, enjoy continuity in their relations and have a 'family for life.' If a child has lived in a foster home for three years or more, the social welfare committee should take more initiative to transfer custody to the child's foster parents. Currently, though there is a legal possibility of transferring custody to foster parents as guardians if the child has lost his or her parents or lost contact with them, this option is seldom used. In Sweden, it is not possible for children to be adopted without the consent of their parents, and since the 1970s, very few parents or single mothers have wanted their children to be adopted. Consequently, adoption is not used as an alternative for children in the child welfare system. If you want to adopt a child in Sweden, it has to be – with very few exceptions – an international adoption.

Legislation for foster care is rather strict in Sweden compared to other countries, as Hessle and Vinnerljung (1999) point out. Unregulated private foster care is illegal. Even a grandmother is required to notify the local authorities, agree to be investigated, and submit to semiannual inspections. In practice, we tend to talk about three types of foster homes: traditional, kinship, and emergency foster homes, though in national statistics, they belong to the same category. The child's continued contact with his or her natural family is considered to be important in all types of foster care. Over the last three decades, Swedish child welfare professionals have tended to be suspicious of kinship care (fostering by relatives). But since 1998, Swedish law has specified that primary consideration should be given to relatives or other close adults as substitute caretakers. Many local authorities use contracted foster homes for short-term or emergency placements. These families usually have a contract to care for a given number of children and are also paid for 'an empty bed.'

Residential Care

In Sweden, foster and residential care are not wholly separate entities, following a change in definition in the Social Services Act of 1980. The Act stated that if a foster home has four or more children, and if fostering is the main source of income for the parents, then the home is defined as a residential unit. The rationale behind this legal change was to bring professional care under stricter control; however, it also paved the way for an expansion of private care (Hessle & Vinnerljung, 1999). Some of these new private residential units would probably be defined as 'specialist foster care' in other contexts. Most of them admit teenagers, but they seem to have increased their 'market share' for younger children as well (Hessle & Vinnerljung, 1999).

In addition to these small, private institutions, there are also public institutions called homes for care and accommodation (HVB), where the staff is usually more educated than in private institutions. It is more common for younger children (twelve and under) than teenagers to be placed in these public institutions. It is also more common for these institutions to receive children for a short time, for a period of assessment, or during a transition stage between home and foster home. Of the homes for younger children, 90% admit children and parents together (Sallnäs, 2000). It is considered in the child's best interests not to be separated from his or her parent(s) when in residential care. These arrangements also facilitate the assessment of the family, and the family work required to prepare for the child's return home or for a move to a foster home. Most of these public institutions are small, and 73% are designed for nine children or less (Sallnäs, 2000).

In Sweden, the age of criminal responsibility is fifteen. Younger children caught by the police engaging in criminal activities, using drugs, or exhibiting other disturbing behaviours are the responsibility of social services. The social services have been criticized periodically for more talk than action. Sometimes these children are assigned a contact person, and sometimes they are sent to either a foster home or a home for care and accommodation (HVB) for a while. Youth between fifteen and eighteen can be involved in legal proceedings, but even if sentenced, they are usually referred to social services. Social services can, in turn, place the young person in a home for special supervision, where there are facilities to place violent youth in temporary solitary confinement. As of 2002, there were thirty homes for special supervision under the umbrella of a national government agency, which has the expressed aim to turn this form of care – traditionally punitive and confining – into evidence-based treatment (Hessle & Vinnerljung, 1999). In his study of a home for special supervision, Levin (1998) states, 'Beyond the rhetoric of punishment and treatment there is a praxis which is something quite different – neither treatment nor punishment' (p. 344). Levin notes that in the special supervision home he studied, only 20% of the boys and 50% of the girls managed well or reasonably well in life after leaving the home.

Only in exceptional circumstances would children under eighteen be sentenced to prison. In 1999 the system was reformed to permit young people aged fifteen to seventeen who have committed serious crimes to be sentenced instead to secure institutional treatment.[4] The reform was intended to prevent the harm that can result from a prison stay. The nature of the crime determines the length of sentence, and treatment is emphasized.

The same government agency is responsible for both special supervision and secure institutional treatment homes. Young people are sent to a home for special supervision according to provisions set out in the Care of Young Persons Act (LVU) while others are sent to the new secure institutional treatment facility under provisions set out in the Criminal Code. As young people are rarely sentenced to prison in Sweden, great demand for secure treatment facilities was not anticipated and the facilities were developed in connection with existing homes for special supervision. However, judges are more willing to sentence young people when there are such alternatives to prison. The number of secure facilities has increased from five to sixty in two years and there is demand for more.

Contact Person/Family as a Statutory Support

A colleague and I have recently reviewed the evidence about the contact person/family service (Andersson & Bangura Arvidsson, 2001). There is a conspicuous shortage of research on this support service. It appears to be an international phenomenon that preventive work and noninstitutionalized support services are less studied than foster care and residential care, for example. Our review was based on Swedish research reports and on papers written by students in their sixth or seventh semester of university social work studies. Contact persons/families is reported to be a positive service for all parties involved, including the client children and families. For contact persons/families, the satisfaction criterion is easier to apply. It is more difficult to find evidence for the curative effect of a normal everyday life in a contact family or with a contact person, or to determine the processes and potential benefits of identification with significant others, or the degree to which the service prevents future problems.

There are problems in the evaluation of contact person/family because it is used – and should be used – in a very flexible way and without unnecessary administrative constraints. Broadly speaking, there are two ways to use the service. The term 'contact family' is used for a family that is visited by a child in need one or two weekends per month and perhaps for a few days during summer vacations, or when there is a temporary need for accommodation because of problems at home. The contact family provides a support service by being a normal or ordinary family, prepared to include a child in need for a few days and nights at a time, but regularly and potentially for many years of childhood.

The term 'contact person' is used when a person, without involving his or her family, has contact with a child or young person on a daily basis. This is more common for older children and teenagers, who may need help with schoolwork, access to an adult outside the home with whom to discuss problems, company for constructive leisure time activities, or support in independent living. The contact person/family is expected to co-operate with the child's parents and provide support to the child's single mother (or father).

The Swedish contact family has some similarities to the British approach to respite care. According to the Children Act of 1989 in England and Wales (and later in Scotland and Ireland), children in need because of social problems as well as children with severe learning disabilities can get 'family-based respite services' (Aldgate, 1993; Aldgate & Bradley, 1999; Stalker, 1996). The British respite care or short-term accommodation is used much less than the Swedish contact family, perhaps because of the stigma associated with learning disabilities (Aldgate & Bradley, 1999). In Sweden, children with disabilities have their own supplementary legislation (Law on Support and Services for People with Disabilities, LSS), which gives them rights in addition to the rights in the Social Services Act. A support family providing respite care for children with learning disabilities is distinguished from a contact person/family according to the Social Services Act and is not included in the national statistics for contact person/family.

In Sweden, the contact family concept does not have a history of negative associations. The concept of contact person can, however, be associated historically with probation under the former Children's Act (Sweden had a Children's Act until 1980). To separate the association of control of teenagers and antisocial behaviour, the contact family/person concept was introduced in the Social Services Act of 1980 as a new and flexible voluntary support for families and children (up to eighteen). The Compulsory Care of Young Persons Act of 1985 introduced the possibility of appointing a contact person for fifteen-to-twenty-year-olds without their consent as a result of their behaviour, but this has been used rarely.

Because there is no obligation for contact persons/families to write reports, no obligation for the responsible social worker to supervise beyond joint meetings twice a year, and no pressure from the authorities to evaluate, there is no reliable assessment or descriptive information about the service. Here are some observations, however. Class differences between contact persons/families and user families are not obvious. Differences in family composition are far more obvious, as children with a contact person/family are, to a large extent, living in households with one adult, usually a single mother, while contact families usually include a mother and a father. While the mother typically initiates the move to become a contact family, especially for young children, there seem to be more men serving as contact persons, especially for teenage boys. It is common for contact families to live in a rural district and have a private house and pets, which can be important for the children. On the other hand, it is also common for contact persons to live in an urban environment, close to the child's home environment, in order to do things together outside the home.

On the whole, there are few reports about gender differences among younger children. For teenagers, there are differences in the contact persons' views about the needs of boys and girls and appropriate activities. Although there is an expressed intention to use services to support immigrant families in their integration into Swedish society, immigrant children seem to be underrepresented. On the other hand, immigrant children are overrepresented in out-of-home placements, especially in homes for special supervision.

Reports on user satisfaction suggest that most people are satisfied with their contact person/family. According to social workers, the contact person/family is the most frequently requested social service support. Contact persons/families are satisfied with their work, too, believing that it serves a useful purpose. There does not seem to be as much conflict between families and their contact persons/families as there is between families and foster families (Andersson, 1993; 1999a).

When young children are asked about the purpose of contact persons/families, many think they have a contact family because of their mother's need for relief (from the child) or her need to have some time for herself. The children comment positively on pets in the contact family, opportunities to play with the children in the contact family or other playmates, and access to sports and recreational activities. The negative issues they raise include homesickness and rules that differ from those at home. Some of our university students' papers suggest that social workers do not always inform young children about the reason for the service, or involve them in planning. Students who based their papers on client journals found that social workers do not describe children as individuals with specific needs and wishes until they are teenagers. There is a tendency for social workers not to see individual children until adolescence. More must be done here and elsewhere in social work to involve children and to understand their genuine experiences, and to ensure that services are supportive for the children as well as for the parent(s).[5]

Child and Family Welfare Work in the District of Rosengaard

As mentioned earlier, the organization of child and family welfare differs among municipalities and autonomous districts. The district of Rosengaard in Malmoe is one of many possible examples. Rosengaard reflects something of Sweden but, to a greater extent, it represents a suburban area in a Swedish city. In fact, Rosengaard (in translation: rose garden) is an area like a few other areas in the big cities, known for the poverty of the population and the extent of its social problems.

The city of Malmoe is the third biggest city in Sweden with a quarter of a million inhabitants. The city is divided into ten districts and in each district there is a social welfare board, a social welfare office, and an organization for child and family welfare. As the districts are relatively autonomous, each has organized its child and family welfare somewhat differently. Rosengaard, with 21,000 people, was built in the 1960s, when Sweden's goal was to build one million apartments to eliminate a housing shortage. The 'million program' was later criticized for its functional but not very attractive architectural style. Today a majority (84%) of the inhabitants in Rosengaard are immigrants or children of immigrants, and about fifty languages or language groups are represented. Social workers and other professionals in the district frequently need interpreters for their professional contacts. The proportion of children under eighteen in the population in the district is around 38% and unemployment is high, as is the dependence on social assistance (95% in some parts of the district).

In Rosengaard there is a social services office, which responds to different concerns and needs. In the office an administrative social worker responds if you wish to report suspected child abuse, apply for social assistance (supplementary benefits) or social support, or ask for help in handling your child's drug abuse problem or your husband's violence. The administrative social workers exercise public authority; that is, they assess needs, investigate home conditions, take grant applications for supportive services, and implement compulsory care orders, although the need for compulsory care is determined in the regional administrative court. If the administrative social worker handling your case finds that the most adequate help or support for the family or child is through contact with the child and family centre, this can be arranged readily because the two services belong to the same social services organization.

The child and family centre acts on the principle that the needs of families, children, and young people direct their work. No one should be turned away, but neither should anyone be forced to receive help from the centre. The centre's social workers co-operate with the administrative social workers at the social services office, but are not housed in the same building. They also cooperate with voluntary organizations in the district, such as immigrant and women's organizations. With their flexible approach to social work, they can act as an intermediary between the social services office and people in the district, although it is no longer possible to get help directly from the centre without a decision from an administrative social worker at the social service office.

The social workers at the child and family centre are divided into three working teams (see figure 7.1):

1 The working team for *community work* consists of five social workers who focus on general or commonplace social problems in the district. For example, they work at the four schools in the district and can mediate or intervene in conflicts between children or between children and adults. They deliver aggression replacement training (ART) in some classes where there are children with particular problems in handling aggression. The team also works closely with the district police and takes part in inquiries focused on children suspected of crimes or other offences. In connection with the inquiry, they visit the family and talk with the parents on at least one occasion.

2 The working team for *recruitment and support of caregivers* consists of four social workers. Their task is to identify foster caregivers and contact persons/families and assess their suitability. After these persons or families have been matched with a child, the social workers on the team are responsible for making up a contract, including payment, and for supporting the caregivers. Usually a contact person/family is recruited to provide preventive service, but they can also be appointed to provide follow-up support after the

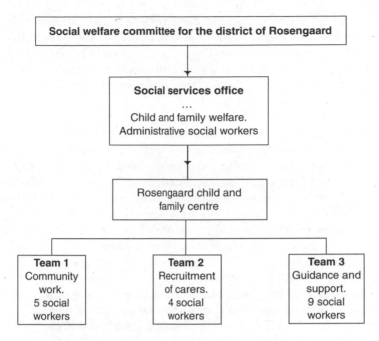

Figure 7.1: Rosengaard social services organization for child and family welfare

child has returned home from a foster home. A former foster family
may serve as a contact family to give the child continuing support.
In all cases there is an administrative social worker responsible for
the client family. However, the administrative social worker can –
and usually does – refer the continuous work with the natural
family and/or a particular child to the working team for guidance
and child and family support as described below.

3 The working team for *guidance and child and family support* consists of
   nine social workers. They provide guidance, support, and psychosocial treatment to families and/or individual children and young
   people up to the age of eighteen. Their objective may be to prevent
   out-of-home placements by supporting a family or a single mother
   in raising their children, especially during critical periods. They can
   do regular home visits and have a mandate to do whatever is supportive in the situation. They can support foster children, be helpful
   in conflicts between parents and foster parents, or prepare the
   natural family to take care of the child again after out-of-home

placement. They can support young people in independent living, for example, immigrant girls in severe family conflicts. In this child and family work, there is no fixed dividing line between support and protection, but if social workers discover a maltreated child, they must report the finding to the administrative social worker, putting the child's interests first.

In Rosengaard, as in many suburban areas in the Swedish cities, you cannot talk about social problems without noting immigration and its associated problems, including unemployment, language barriers, and other difficulties of integrating into Swedish society. Overcrowded apartments are a problem in some suburban areas because rental flats were not built for families with more children than are common in most contemporary Swedish families. In some places there is an educational gap between children with immigrant parents and children with Swedish parents. There are areas, like Rosengaard, where schools can be described as segregated, because few ethnic Swedes are living in the area. On the other hand, many immigrants want to live among relatives and friends and others who speak their language, or where there is a mosque for Muslims, for example. There is considerable changeover in the district as immigrants learn the language, get a job, and move away. Sweden has become a multicultural society. In the field of social work, an increased knowledge of international migration and ethnic relations is required.

Discussion

Does the official balance between parental rights and the rights of children have the same meaning in different countries? When comparing British and Nordic trends in child welfare, the Norwegian researcher Grinde (1996) comments that 'principles and methods may be easier to generalise than concrete results and experiences, which depend more on social factors, the legal framework, and national characteristics and attitudes' (p. 11).

When Parton (1997) writes about the great tension between family support and child protection policies and practices in Britain, the observations have no meaning in the Swedish system. In Sweden, the intention of family support is to protect the children in the family from maltreatment, neglect, or faring badly. If it is necessary to protect the children by using out-of-home placement, the family requires support to remain in contact with the child in care, to cooperate with foster parents or residential staff, and to be rehabilitated and prepared to take care of the child again. There is an element of protection in support and an element of support in protection. Walker (2002) writes that the renaissance of family support in Britain is seen as an alternative to child protection, rather than part of a connected network of resources to be used as different needs emerge. In Sweden, support and protection are seen as intertwined.

Still, in Sweden, the family services orientation has its critics, because it may reduce attention to the needs of individual children. During the last decade or so, it has been publicly noted that social workers spend more time talking to parents than to children and that the child's point of view is not always included in assessments and or in the decisions that affect them. From a gender perspective, the family orientation is, in fact, a mother orientation: in child and family welfare, single mothers (without job or education) are overrepresented and held responsible for the children's well-being to a much greater extent than fathers, as has been pointed out in the United Kingdom (Farmer & Owen, 1998).

There are problems in translating some concepts from Swedish to English. For example, in Sweden the broad concept 'fare badly' (the opposite of 'fare well'), includes abuse and neglect, but also more diffuse signs of problems at home. We have mandatory reporting of children who fare badly or are suspected of faring badly. When talking about voluntary services as opposed to compulsory care, it is more correct to talk about services with and without the consent of parents (or young people over fifteen). Partnership is stressed and may result in the parents' consent to out-of-home care for the children. Parents may realize that if they do not give their consent, the social worker (through the social welfare committee) can bring the case into the regional administrative court and the child can be taken into compulsory care. By consent, they can avoid compulsory care, even if the circumstances, maltreatment, or behaviour of the child is bad enough to warrant compulsory care.

Child and family social workers in Sweden have room for discretion. The relation between the client and the social worker is seen as important and flexible enough to accommodate different solutions to problems. Of course, discretion can make families vulnerable when they have poor relationships with their social worker. I am part of a network of social work researchers from eight different countries, which is investigating managerialism and discretion in child welfare. If Britain is on one end of the continuum (managerialism), Sweden is on the other end (discretion). As a (probable) consequence, while there has been ongoing work to improve documentation, Sweden has fewer requirements and has been criticized in this regard. At present, there is an experiment with British care and assessment models in seven Swedish municipalities (*Looking after Children* [Ward, 1995] and *Framework for the Assessment of Children in Need and Their Families* [Department of Health, 2000]). Numerous questionnaires need to be completed in a systematic way and at regular intervals in these approaches. There is as yet no evaluation of the applicability in the Swedish system of these models. There are some complaints from social workers that the writing takes too much time.

The degree of professional discretion, combined with the decentralized social services in Sweden, make it hard to generalize about the nature of child and family welfare in the country. While the law, intention, and ideology are the same, the resources, organization, experiences, and practices may vary. Social work has been a research subject in the university for only about two decades, and there is proportionately less research on child and family welfare than in other parts of the social services. There is much less research on support services for families and children living at home than on out-of-home care, and there is less research on younger children than on teenagers. When young people have problems – or cause problems in society – because of criminal activities and drugs, they become more visible in the media, in political discussions and in research.

Unfortunately, evidence gathered through research is seldom used as a guide to practice. It has recently been shown, for example, that the rate of breakdown in out-of-home placements is 30–7% for young people placed as thirteen-to-sixteen-year-olds (Vinnerljung, Sallnäs, & Westermark, 2001). A national sample of 776 adolescents was followed in local case files for up to five years from the original placement in 1991. First- and second-generation immigrant children were strongly overrepresented. The most common reasons for care were behavioural/antisocial problems and chronic adolescent/parent conflicts in the birth home. Sixty per cent were in foster care, 30% in private or public residential care (HVB), and 10% in (state) homes for special supervision. Seventy-five per cent of the placements were made with consent and 25% without consent. Forty-four per cent of all breakdowns were due to teenagers rejecting further placement and 36% were due to caregivers refusing to go on. 'In other words, it is a myth that teenage placement breakdowns are caused mainly by foster parents and residential staff throwing adolescents out of care' (Vinnerljung, Sallnäs, & Westermark, 2001, 246).

It is obvious that more research is needed, along with changed practice and more support services for teenagers – before, after, and instead of out-of-home care. Residential care for teenagers with criminal activities is very expensive, and it may be useless in the long run. Perhaps one of the most burning questions in Sweden today is how to support families in handling teenagers involved in criminal activities and drug abuse *and* how to find a rehabilitating place for them at school and in the labour market.

Swedish social workers in child and family welfare report that they are very concerned about the shortage of time for individual children and families. They complain about repeated reorganization of social services and the turnover of professionals. They are worried about reduced support to children in need at school and reduced preventive services for groups in risky situations or environments. In many municipalities, they are worried about high unemployment rates of immigrants, their problems with the Swedish language, and their lack of integration to broader society, which has a negative effect on their children's integration and well-being. There are forces outside social services that social workers cannot do much about, although they must respond to the consequences.

The schools of social work or departments of social work in Swedish universities offer a three-and-a-half-year generalist social work education after senior high school and not a specialist education (e.g., for child and family welfare workers). Some of these workers complain that they do not have enough education for the level of responsibility in their work and would like to have continuing training. However, training is up to the employer (or the municipality) and practices vary. There is still a gap between social work as a research subject at the university level and as social work practice at the municipality level, and there are ongoing discussions about how to improve social work education for professionals. There may be a gap between what works according to research and what politicians and the general public will welcome. Maybe it is as the British researchers Weightman and Weightman (1995) found in their comparison: 'Essentially, Swedish culture provides far higher levels of legitimation for state intervention than exist in England' (p. 79). However, that does not mean that the interventions are more successful, and lately there have been serious discussions, initiated by the National Board of Health and Welfare, that interventions should be based on knowledge of effects.

NOTES

1 This terminology was suggested by the organizers of the Positive Systems of Child and Family Welfare Conference held at Wilfrid Laurier University in Ontario, Canada, at which the print version of this paper was presented.
2 SoL ('voluntary' law), see *Social services act and care of young persons act.*
3 LVU ('compulsive' law), see *Social services act and care of young persons act.*
4 See *Secure institutional treatment for young offenders – instead of prison.*
5 For a review of research about contact persons/families in Sweden, see Anderson (2003) in Katz and Pinkerton, 291–308. These studies include the multiple perspectives of the contact families, the parents, the social workers, and the children. Andersson (2003) concludes: 'I have a positive perception of the system through the few studies presented in this chapter and have not found any evidence of damaging effects. The system has the potential to focus on children and their best interests, while still including the whole family and contributing to an extended network for vulnerable children and families' (pp. 304–5).

8 When One Door Shuts, Another Opens: Turning Disadvantages into Opportunities in Child and Family Welfare in the Netherlands

A.W.M. VELDKAMP

Introduction

The child and family welfare and child protection systems in the Netherlands have been under heavy criticism for many years. Numerous experts in these fields have advocated more co-operation and greater coherence between the systems (Bisschops, 1998; Doek, 1991; Van der Linden, 1992; Van Nijnatten & Van Montfoort, 1992; Veldkamp, 1997b). The connection between the two fields seems to be a never-ending issue for political and public discussion, one that has filled many bookshelves in recent decades (Doek, 1991). In spite of this, the relationship has not fundamentally changed until now.

In the first part of this chapter, the characteristics of the child and family welfare and child protection systems in the Netherlands will be described and compared. Subsequently, these characteristics will be explained in light of the historical argument on which the dichotomy in the welfare and protection systems is based. Attention will be paid to the harmful effects of the existing structure, in particular for multiproblem families, which make it clear that changes are necessary. Finally, ideas for changes to the child and family welfare and child protection systems will be discussed.

Description and Comparison of the Child and Family Welfare and Child Protection Systems

The Child and Family Welfare System

Child and family welfare is founded on the fairly recent Youth Services Act. Child and family welfare services consist mainly of private institutions that, although funded by the government, can act with a certain degree of autonomy. Administrative responsibility for the (private sector) youth services rests with the Minister of Health, Welfare, and Sport, and provincial and municipal executives of the four largest urban regions, Amsterdam, Rotterdam, The Hague, and Utrecht.

In the Act, child and family welfare is described as 'the activities aimed at preventing, reducing or solving problems or disorders of young persons of a physical, social or pedagogic nature that could have an adverse effect on their development towards maturity' (Youth Services Act, s. 1). This is a very broad definition that, in principle, encompasses all conceivable preventive and curative activities connected to favourable development from childhood to adulthood. By definition, child and family welfare is geared to the individual child and his or her personal context and circumstances, and proceeds from an attitude of assistance. In other words, assistance is not imposed, but provided at the request of the young person and/or his or her parents. Participation is voluntary, and the person requesting assistance must be motivated to accept it. The person's description of the complaint or problem should be the starting point for treatment. In this way, the right of self-determination is acknowledged and respected; in principle, the client is held responsible for his or her own situation and determines if and when he or she has had enough assistance. The client is considered to have some (potential) problem-solving ability and to be capable of making choices. Assistance focuses on enhancing the development and self-sufficiency of the clients and on improving the quality of their life. In the Netherlands, parents and children do not have any legal right to assistance, and therefore the child and family welfare services have no obligation to provide it (Veldkamp, 2001).

If we look at the resources used in child and family welfare, we find a range of non-residential and semiresidential facilities, often with a multidisciplinary staff of behavioural experts. These facilities, instead of being oriented towards the demands of children and families, are predominantly focused on the services they supply and do not appear to be well coordinated or cohesive. The sector has advanced diagnostics and diverse treatment methods at its disposal and utilizes the results of behavioural research to refine both.

The Child Protection System

Child protection originated in and was legitimized by the now rather ancient Children Acts of 1901, which were not enacted until 1905. The sector falls under the administrative and political responsibility of the Minister of Justice, and is a mixture of government and private initiatives. A government organization, the Child Care and Protection Board, is authorized to investigate the circumstances under which children are brought up, if the Board suspects that the circumstances could pose a threat to the child's development. If there is cause for intervention, the Board can enlist the services of the court. If the court finds that intervention is justified, intervention is delegated to a family supervision institution. Once again, this is a private institution.

The original objective of child protection was (and actually still is) to safeguard the moral development of children, when that development is at risk through the incorrect or improper exercise of parental authority. The assumption is that the cause of deviant behaviour and crime is poor upbringing, and that it can be blamed, more or less, on the upbringers.

Legal means – the so-called child protection measures – are provided in the Dutch Civil Code[1] (*Burgerlijk Wetboek*) that make it possible to breach parental authority. Initially, the law provided only for withdrawal and removal measures (Dutch Civil Code, Book I, ss. 266 and 269), which resulted in the complete withdrawal of parental custody. In 1922, the guardianship measure was added, which limited parental authority (Dutch Civil Code, Book I, s. 254). With the adoption and application of these measures, the legislator intended to kill two birds with one stone; the child could be saved from moral ruin 'by removing it from the pernicious influence of its degenerate parents,' and society would be protected against children who would otherwise come to no good (Van Montfoort, 1993; 1994).

To apply a child protection measure, it is necessary for the Child Care and Protection Board to make it plausible to the court that the relevant grounds laid down by law have been met. These grounds consist of rather abstract descriptions of characteristics and forms of parental (mis)behaviour that are not considered compatible with the proper exercise of parental authority: 'powerlessness,' 'unsuitability,' 'a history of bad conduct,' 'gross negligence of the obligation to provide care and upbringing,' and 'ignoring the instructions of a family supervisor to a serious degree.' It must be demonstrated that the parents have forsaken their parental authority or that they are exercising it incorrectly or improperly. In other words, the court must be convinced that the parents are demonstrably and thoroughly failing their children. The child protection service must therefore make statements about the failure or inadequacy of the parents. To protect children, the law compels the child protection service to disqualify the parents as upbringers. As a consequence, the initial focus in the child protection sector is more on the failure of the parents than on the needs of the children (Veldkamp, 1997b).

According to the government's official interpretation, and contrary to the assumption of many, child protection is not assistance (Van Montfoort & Van Nijnatten, 1991). Child protection consists of protecting the interests of children by taking responsibility through the exercise of legal authority (Van Nijnatten, 1995). It is the government's public responsibility to stand up for children whose development is seriously threatened by the faulty exercise of parental authority. Children only deserve protection when it has been established in court that they have been seriously harmed or have suffered through acts or omissions of their parents.

Parental authority is the main orientation point in child protection, on which virtually all activities are based. Problems with children and youth are attributed to the way in which parental authority functions. Social factors, such as social deprivation or poverty, are not considered. Expressed in simple terms, the historical argument is as follows.

The law confers parental authority on the parents, on the assumption that this will adequately safeguard the child's interests. Parental authority encompasses both the right and the obligation to care for and bring up children (Dutch Civil Code, Book I, s. 247). Originally, in the year 1900, the latter obligation meant primarily that parents had to teach their children socially accepted values, so that children could learn to behave themselves appropriately. Today, it includes enhancement of children's personal development and responsibility for their physical and mental welfare (Dutch Civil Code, Book I, s. 247). The legislator assumes that parental authority functions adequately if the parents properly fulfil their obligation to care for and bring up the child. If parents fulfil their obligation, which is expressed, for example, in how they and their children behave in society, there is no reason for the government or the child protection service to interfere in the family. If, however, the living and upbringing conditions of the child are seriously wanting, it is construed as failure by the parents to comply with the obligation imposed by law in a way that constitutes a direct threat to the moral development of the child and therefore an indirect threat to society. The government then has a legitimate reason to intervene. Parental authority can be withdrawn or curtailed and, after intervention by the court, partially or fully assumed and exercised by the child protection service. In theory, such intervention remedies the failure in the exercise of authority and adequately safeguards the interests of the child and society once again. During the term of the judicial measure, parents are given the opportunity to bring their behaviour in line with the expectations of society, and they may receive instructions in this regard. If the parents adjust their behaviour sufficiently, they can be considered worthy to exercise parental authority independently again and the judicial measure can be lifted. If not, the responsibility remains with the child protection service (Veldkamp, 1993).

In most cases, the child protection service is not called in by the parents or young person, but by others, including (youth) care workers, teachers, and doctors, or family members, neighbours, and family acquaintances. Although currently an initial attempt is made to obtain the cooperation of the parents and child, child protection measures can be imposed against their explicit wishes. Because of its far-reaching consequences, the use of force and coercion by the child protection service has provoked angry protests in the past (Van Montfoort & Van Nijnatten, 1991). On the one hand, these protests resulted in improved legal status for parents who have dealings with the child protection service, for example, the right to inspect reports and to complain about the actions of the child protection service. On the other hand, in some cases, the strengthened legal status of parents can make the protection of children considerably more difficult. The way in which the child protection service used power and coercion in the past has given it an unfavourable image, one that will be difficult to shake. Undoubtedly it has discouraged cooperation from the voluntary child and family welfare services, which tend to go to extremes to avoid the child protection service, and call on it only if attempts to assist are unsuccessful (Van Burik & De Savornin Lohman, 1994). As a result, children and their parents often remain in extremely difficult circumstances without help for long periods of time.

Resources available to the child protection service are limited, certainly in relation to the very complex problems confronting the sector (Doek, 1991). First, the service must work with a very outdated law, based on views about family, parenthood, and child-rearing problems from the beginning of the last century (Soetenhorst-de Savornin Lohman, 1998), as described above. Once the court has pronounced a child protection measure, concrete obligations of the child protection service with respect to the child and his or her family cannot be ascertained from the law (Doek, 1991; Veldkamp, 1997b, 1997c). Therefore, these legal instruments do not guarantee in any way that the circumstances of children will improve. Moreover, the child protection service is predominantly monodisciplinary. Although the number of behavioural experts has been increasing slowly for several years, social work is by far the most well-represented discipline in child protection service. There is a chronic lack of time and a serious shortage of options for placing children outside the home when their living circumstances make this necessary. There are as yet no unambiguous criteria for intervention (Scholte, 1997). The development of diagnostics and methodologies for the practice of child protection is still in its infancy (Doreleijers, 1995; Faas, 1991; Kalverboer, 1996; Mertens, 1996; Ten Berge, 1998). All in all, child protection is expected to tackle the most complex problems with entirely inadequate means (Doek, 1991) and does not succeed in doing so (Slot, Theunissen, Esmeijer, & Duivenvoorden, 2001).

Comparison of the Two Systems

Child and family welfare and child protection are two separate circuits, each with its own legitimacy, responsibilities, views and concepts, organizations, administrative relationships, and financing. Child and family welfare centres on the individual and his or her emergency situation. Assistance activities are developed only on request, are aimed at reducing or relieving the reported problem, and are based on the requester's own responsibility and ability to change. In child protection, the emphasis is not on providing assistance, but on applying the law. As described earlier, the interests of society receive as much consideration as those of the individual. In order to serve both interests simultaneously, legal means are used that may be applied under coercion and are linked with an encroachment on the parents' responsibility and autonomy in raising their children.

Assistance Versus Law: The Historical Basis of the Separation of Child and Family Welfare from Child Protection Systems

The separation of child and family welfare from child protection originated and still exists as a consequence of the central government's view, held and practised strictly since the beginning of the previous century, that assistance and law are separate powers (Committee on Child Protection Law, 1971). This view has been responsible for the failure of every attempt at the further integration of child and family welfare with child protection (Doek, 1991; Van Montfoort & Van Nijnatten, 1991). Throughout the 1990s, the strict separation of assistance and law dominated the relationship between child and family welfare and child protection, and has survived the various movements at the end of the century related to the upbringing and protection of children.

Soetenhorst-de Savornin Lohman (1993) distinguishes four fixed patterns in the relationship of assistance and law, which I will use here to clarify the differences created between child and family welfare and child protection. The first pattern relates to the difference between behavioural scientists and jurists in the approach to deviant behaviour, including problems in upbringing. This pattern concerns which strategy can be expected to produce most results in dealing with deviant behaviour: treatment and influencing the behaviour of the individual and family (assistance), or punishing the deviant behaviour and compelling the adjustment of behaviour through the use of legal means (law)? A balanced answer to this question has never been formulated, but simply circumvented by constructing a separation: behavioural scientists tackle deviant behaviour by providing assistance and jurists do this by applying the law; everyone for themselves, within his or her own framework, by their own means and using their own professional views and definition of the problem. A competence battle is avoided.

The second pattern consists of the varying political attention given to maladjusted young people, in this case for deviant behaviour and crime. As long as deviant behaviour and crime occur on a limited scale and do not constitute a great threat to society, there is not much government interest: the care of maladjusted young people can be left in good conscience to parents and welfare services, and the role of the state and the law can remain limited. However, where there is increased deviant behaviour and crime, political interest increases, the call for government measures becomes louder, and the role of the state and the meaning of the law suddenly become more important (Junger-Tas, 1997). After all, the interests of society are at stake, to which individual interests must give way if necessary and intervention in personal and family life must occur sooner and more frequently.

The third pattern is the interweaving of private enterprise and government. Welfare, the care for the person in need, has long been the domain of private institutions (assistance) in the Netherlands. In this area the government's task is to set out preconditions for private initiatives (law) and to supplement them, but the principal responsibility for the care of young people is borne primarily by private enterprise. The role and responsibility of the government and the law only come into play when assistance has failed, is inadequate (Doek, 1991), or when a higher interest is at stake, such as the safety of society or the protection of social morals (Van Montfoort, 1993; 1994).

The fourth pattern consists of the tension between the interests of adults and the interests of children: whether the interest of the child justifies a violation of the rights and freedoms of adults, in particular, the adults who have primary responsibility for the upbringing, the parents. This is a legal balancing of interests, which is the province of the courts. The weight attributed to those interests can vary, according to the views that prevail in a certain period, and are reflected in the law. The child's interest is not determined on the basis of the ideas of behavioural science, nor is it described in terms of assistance. The courts only use legal concepts and criteria, which must be derived from and tested against the law. Interests are expressed in law. The court must examine whether enough violence has been done to the child's right to care and upbringing to justify encroachment on the parent's right to bring up his or her child freely and according to his or her own views. In this balancing process, the court can assign an informative or advisory function to behavioural scientists to give more concrete substance to abstract legal terms, such as 'the interest of the child' or 'gross negligence.' However, this is done only with a view to substantiating the court's decision. Taking the decision remains the responsibility of the court, so that the court ultimately has the last word.

The Harmful Effects of the Separation of the Systems

In the relation between child and family welfare and child protection, the patterns discussed above can be clearly recognized in the distinction between assistance and law. The government does not interfere in the decisions of adults to have children or in the consequences that this decision can have. Problems in upbringing are seen primarily as a private matter and not a matter for government intervention. People are deemed to be responsible for the solution of their own personal problems, including problems in raising their children. There is almost full consensus on these issues in the Netherlands. Parents have a large measure of freedom to bring up their children according to their own views. That in itself is a good starting point. As long as things go well, there is no need for the law or child protection, and both remain in the background. The government's role is limited initially to creating and maintaining private facilities for child and family welfare, which people can rely on if they are unable to solve their own problems. Voluntary assistance by behavioural science disciplines is preferable to use of the coercive legal measures at the disposal of the child protection service. These only come into play if parents use their freedom to the detriment of the child, assistance fails, and harm may be or has already been done to the child and society.

The distinction between assistance and law has had a definite effect on the relation between child and family welfare and child protection in practice. We see that both sectors address similar problems (Deboutte, 1989; Doek, 1991; Soetenhorst-de Savornin Lohman, 1993) and, amazingly enough, it is more or less a matter of chance whether a client ends up at child and family welfare or child protection with his or her problems (Van der Linden & Hendrickx, 1991). Both sectors operate in the same territory, but each does so in its own way, seeking solutions that usually do not extend further than the limits of its own frame of reference.

Though pursuing the same purpose, the best interest of the child, child and family welfare and child protection operate from a different viewpoint and attitude and use different means of intervention. Over the course of time, the separate sectors have developed in quite different ways. Generally speaking, child and family welfare keeps reasonable pace with social changes, and attempts to anticipate new problems and find contemporary solutions for traditional problems. In contrast, from its inception, child protection has remained virtually unchanged and still uses the same instruments (and their underlying ideas) with which it was equipped almost a century ago (Soetenhorst-de Savornin Lohman, 1998; Veldkamp, 1993, 1997a). This has only widened the differences, and child and family welfare and child protection have grown further apart with time (Doek, 1991); it really makes a difference for the child and family in crisis whether they have to deal with assistance or law.

The Multiproblem Family

The dogmatic and organizational separation of child and family welfare and child protection leads to considerable problems in practice and to a dichotomy in the care of young people. Those seeking and in need of help – parents and children in the middle of a serious crisis – are the main victims of this division. These problems are felt most strongly where assistance and law should come together, for example, in cases of violence, abuse, and neglect.

Such situations usually involve long-term, multiple problems, where the possibilities for the clients to change are limited, as are the possibilities for the child and family welfare service to make changes (Ghesquière, 1993). In these situations, the clients are not usually able to meet the treatment conditions of voluntary assistance and motivation set by the child and family welfare service. Multiproblem families are steeped in misery and are often in a state of social incapacitation. They have little confidence in society and social workers and are therefore barely motivated to seek help. Often parents have had a troubled upbringing themselves and, through lack of alternatives, perpetuate the problem in the lives of their children. In these situations, the starting points used by child and family welfare, based on the client's freedom, aim too high. The client does not really have any freedom; freedom presumes a choice. The clients do not choose their miserable circumstances, but lack the knowledge, insight, and skills to get out of them on their own or to express a request for help. If child and family welfare nevertheless continues to require that the client request help and be motivated to accept it, the families who need help the most are precisely the ones to be deprived of it, and their hopeless situation could, if it were possible, become more hopeless.

The risks to the health and development of the child, and the educational incapacity of the parents that gives rise to these risks, can make it necessary for child protection to intervene. It is necessary for someone outside the family to call the attention of the child protection service to the multiproblem family, and this is anything but a matter of course in the Netherlands, where there is no obligation to report a suspicion of child abuse, sexual abuse, or serious neglect of children. Reporting to the child protection service is the responsibility of the individual social worker, and there is not much willingness to report. In the present system, if a report is made, interference with the family must be justified on the basis of the seriousness of the threat to the child. If this threat is not yet serious enough, or if the parents show a minimal willingness to cooperate (meaning that the legal grounds for protective measures are not met), the child protection service will refrain from further action, refer the matter, or wait until things gets worse and intervention is possible. In these situations, the parents and child are deprived of help. If the child protection service does take protective measures, help for the child and family is not guaranteed. A child protection measure is only a legal framework to impose help on the family; it is *not* assistance. In other words, the institution charged with implementing the child protection measure must rely on child and family welfare facilities to organize assistance. However, the child and family welfare service tends to view the child protection service not as an applicant for assistance or a promoter of the interests of the child and family, but as a judicial organization with which it would rather not deal. To be eligible at all for assistance, the clients for whom assistance is requested must be motivated, and things come full circle. In the worst case, the child and family are left to pick up the pieces.

The Need and Suggestions for Change

Making a theoretical distinction between assistance and law is not wrong in itself. Nor is it wrong to translate that distinction into a child and family welfare system, provided the system continues to fulfil its purpose, fits in with the character of the modern age, and answers a need felt by society. It is wrong only if the elements of assistance and law are not connected in a balanced manner within the system, if the distinction is maintained solely for its own sake, or if it determines the organization and design of child and family welfare. Then we deceive ourselves into thinking that assistance and law, or child and family welfare and child protection, are exclusive of each other, while in reality they cannot do without each other. The distinction leads to great confusion and ever more bureaucracy, while those who are dependent on child and family welfare do not benefit from it in any way (Veldkamp, 1995b). It is much more important to try to increase the accessibility, range, and effectiveness of youth services by discouraging compartmentalization and facilitating connection, so that children and families with problems will not be shifted around fruitlessly or fall between two stools.

Formally, the distinction between assistance and law still determines the relation between child and family welfare and child protection. Nevertheless, new ideas in both sectors are shaking the foundations of the traditional relationship. The main sources of the rapprochement between child and family welfare and child protection are the changing status of the child and altered ideas on important aspects of upbringing. For example, there is more restraint in issuing care orders for children, partly as a result of diminished confidence in the effects of residential care. At the same time, child and youth psychology and education are paying more attention to the importance of the bond between parent and child and to the significance of mutual loyalty in that relationship. More emphasis is being placed on the relational aspect of upbringing, on the value for children of a good relationship with their parents. These shifts in value and attitude require an approach in which assistance to the child involves an investment in maintaining and improving the relationship with his or her parents and preventing a separation of child and parents. The approach also requires a common vision from the child and family welfare service and the child protection service concerning families with serious problems.

An important reference in such a vision is the (International) Convention on the Rights of the Child (CRC). The Convention came into effect in the Netherlands in 1995 and should be regarded as providing adults (parents, other adults, *and* government) with nonvoluntary guidelines to promote the health and development of the child and protect him or her against any form of violence, abuse, and neglect. It centres on the child and his or her right to safety, upbringing, and development.

In the Convention, the child is seen as an independent bearer of rights, and not as the property or extension of his or her parents. The starting point is that 'the child, for the full and harmonious development of his or her personality, should grow up in a family environment, in an atmosphere of happiness, love and understanding' (preamble to the CRC). For that reason alone, according to the Convention, 'the family should be afforded the necessary protection and assistance so that it can fully assume its responsibilities within the community' (preamble to the CRC).

The granting of rights to the child creates obligations for adults, without whom the child would not evolve. Parents are deemed to have primary responsibility for compliance. In the event that the parents do not succeed in their child-rearing responsibilities, social facilities, such as child and family welfare and child protection, are partly responsible for implementing the rights of the child. In this connection, the Convention refers to an obligation to 'render appropriate assistance to parents ... in the performance of their child-rearing responsibilities' (CRC, Art. 18).

For the child and family welfare service, the introduction of the Convention means that the child must be seen as the primary client and requester of help, not the parents. This means, for example, that the child should not have to depend solely on the cooperation or motivation of his or her parents to receive help. Volunteer engagement can still apply as the starting point for treatment; however, the responsibility of the child and family welfare service does not end if the child is obviously in need of help, but the parents are not willing or able to express the need. Limits to the parents' freedom in raising their child arise when the child is denied necessary help, and the parents' right to bring up their child at their discretion conflicts with the rights of the child to healthy development. The child's right to safety, upbringing, and development requires that steps be taken to enable that child to be helped, if necessary by disregarding certain rights of the parents. With that goal in mind, one of the responsibilities of the child and family welfare service can be to call in the child protection service.

The letter and spirit of the Convention also have consequences for the child protection service. As early as 1991, the Child Care and Protection Board formulated a contemporary vision of child protection based on the Convention, which emphasises the connection between child and family welfare and child protection in the event of problems in upbringing (Beaufort-Caspers & Veldkamp, 1991; Koens, 1992). The vision has been followed through in guidelines for the Board's actions in the event of serious problems (Veldkamp, 1995a). Both express the idea that directed assistance to the child and his or her family is the primary purpose of the child protection service. In this context, protection should not be viewed as putting up a screen between parents and child, which would only further weaken the already weak functioning of the family (Colapinto, 1995). Protection primarily means strengthening the functioning of the family and/or the functioning of the child, for the purpose of solving the problems or making them bearable. Out of recognition that they have primary responsibility for rearing their child, initial attempts should be made to motivate the parents to accept help on a voluntary basis. The court will only be enlisted when it is evident that a conflict of interest exists between parent and child: help is necessary for the child, but the attitude or incapacity of the parents makes it unattainable. The assistance of the law is then required because the child will suffer harm if he or she is deprived of help. From this point of view, the child protection measure is only the key to unlock the door to child and family welfare (Van der Linden, 1992).

This vision of child protection argues for tailor-made child protection measures to enable specific assistance to the child and family when parents do not succeed in providing adequately for the developmental needs of the child. I am an advocate of the replacement of the present measures for withdrawing and curtailing parental authority with a varied system of legal provisions that must bring specific forms of assistance within the reach of the child and family. The provisions set out duties and create obligations to the child. After intervention by the courts, other adults, either with or in addition to the parents, must fulfil such obligations. These provisions should be geared to the individual situation of the child in question and his or her parents, and aimed at compensating the deficiency in meeting the child's developmental needs. To determine the nature and extent of that deficiency, a thorough diagnosis and assessment are required of the child's development, the entire family circumstances, and the capacity of the parents to bring up the child. In addition, a thorough forecast needs to be made to create realistic, feasible prospects for the child. The diagnosis, assessment, and forecast should be based on insights from education, developmental psychology, psychopathology, family pathology, and so forth. To the extent possible in the current state of the art, it should also be determined which resources, persons, disciplines, and services can help to remedy the educational deficiencies the child encounters in his or her present upbringing circumstances and how long this might take.

Because imposed assistance is always coupled with an encroachment on people's rights and freedoms, this assistance should be tailor-made in such a way that the encroachment is kept to a minimum. Legal provisions could include protection of the child when his or her physical or psychological integrity is in danger; care, upbringing, and location of the child; treatment and support of the child and/or his or her parents; and, with prevention in mind, education, training, or coaching of the parents (Baartman, 1997). According to the circumstances, one or another provision or a combination could be used.

To impose one or more forms of assistance, the court must be asked to render a decision. A request for this purpose must be based on reports in which the assessment, diagnosis, and forecast are described, along with a plan of action. The plan of action should preferably and as far as possible be drawn up in consultation with the parents and the children. The plan should state the relief requested to remedy the deficiency in the child's needs. The court should review whether the right of the child to safety, upbringing, and development requires the relief and also whether the circumstances justify an encroachment on the rights and freedoms of the parents for the purpose of enforcing the rights of the child.

If the court decides to allow the requested relief, the parents will have to tolerate the required encroachment on their rights and freedoms. The decision, which should outline the implementation of the plan of action in the most concrete terms possible, would create the power and obligation of the child protection service to involve certain child and family welfare facilities in solving problems, and the obligation of the child and family welfare service to provide the assistance (Veldkamp, 1997b). With such a varied system of powers, assistance and law could complement each other well, the interest of the child could be served in the best way possible, and parental responsibility could remain intact as far as possible. This is a combination of assistance and law that is completely in keeping with the definition of child and family welfare; at the same time the need for an administrative and organizational separation of assistance and law would cease to exist.

Summary

The separation of assistance and law has led to a division in youth services, which creates disadvantages especially for children and parents who are suffering from serious upbringing problems. Under the influence of changed views on the parent-child relationship, the status of the child, the role of parents, and the approach to serious upbringing problems, it is becoming clear that assistance and law can help each other. Both assistance and law are gradually taking on a different meaning, through which they may develop into allies. I hope that the children and parents who need both protection and assistance will be able to reap the benefits of these developments in progress.

An Update on Recent Changes in The Netherlands System of Child and Family Welfare
MIA LAMERS[2]

The dichotomy between assistance and law, as described in the preceding chapter, has led to sharp distinctions between welfare and protection approaches to child and family welfare in the Netherlands. Numerous political debates have culminated in initiatives designed to overhaul the existing system. Currently, the child and family welfare system in the Netherlands is undergoing a major transition, and substantial changes in service delivery processes are under way. A new Youth Services Act is expected to become law in 2005. Establishing one portal for child welfare services that encompasses welfare and protection approaches has been a priority to address concerns about the separation of service delivery systems.

The Bureau Jeugdzorg has been formed to establish a more integrated and efficient system of service delivery. This organization has a broad mandate to provide assistance to families where there are problems in the social and/or psychological functioning of young people or if there are issues related to upbringing, including child abuse. The Bureau has four departments. The first is the voluntary department of the Bureau Jeugdzorg (formerly called Youth and Family Welfare), which assesses the type of assistance required by the family. The voluntary department does not provide ongoing treatment; workers have a maximum of five contacts with the client. During the assessment phase, appropriate ongoing treatment services for the family are determined and referrals are made. Youth Mental Health, which functions separately from the Bureau Jeugdzorg, is one organization that provides ongoing treatment services to families. Workers from Youth Mental Health and Bureau Jeugdzorg may collaborate during the assessment phase.

If there is a question of child abuse or neglect, the family may be referred to the Advice and Reporting Centre for Child Abuse and Neglect (ARCAN), the second of the four departments of Bureau Jeugdzorg. Every province and metropolitan centre has an ARCAN where families can go to receive advice or to report child abuse or neglect. In total, the Netherlands has fourteen ARCANs. When a community member approaches ARCAN for advice or consultation, support is provided but no investigative action is undertaken unless the person making the report can do little to remedy the situation. Cases are most likely to be transferred to ARCAN when the family does not cooperate with the voluntary department of the Bureau Jeugdzorg or Youth Mental Health or when suspicions of abuse or neglect require further substantiation. ARCAN has the resources to facilitate investigations. If a community member generates the referral and the family is prepared to receive assistance, the case may be handed over to the voluntary department of the Bureau Jeugdzorg. Depending on the nature of the problem, ARCAN may also refer the case to the medical sector (i.e., Youth Mental Health).

If ARCAN is not successful in supporting the family adequately with voluntary assistance, or in situations where the abuse is severe, the family is referred to the Council for Child Protection. The Council is part of the Ministry of Justice and separate from the Bureau Jeugdzorg. It attends to matters of child abuse, custody, and access rights following divorce, and criminal proceedings against minors. When compulsory assistance is necessary, the Council for Child Protection will provide investigative services and may recommend a child protection measure. The range of measures include a family supervision order where a family guardian will be assigned to give advice to parents, relieving the parents of parental authority (while they remain involved with the child as much as possible), or dismissing the parents from their parental authority. If a judge grants a protection order, the family is referred to the third department of the Bureau Jeugdzorg (formerly called Youth Protection). This department coordinates compulsory assistance for the family. The fourth department of the Bureau Jeugdzorg works with youth who have a criminal order.

Under this new structure, the expectation is that intake functions will be centralized and service delivery to families will be streamlined. The reorganization aims to decrease the dichotomy between welfare approaches, where confidentiality is emphasized, and protection approaches where the public reporting of suspected child abuse is more likely. Under the proposed legislation, local authorities will receive a single budget to finance the services provided by Bureau Jeugdzorg.

Under the old system, Youth Mental Health organizations frequently exercised the prerogative to refuse cooperation with organizations involved in compulsory assistance to families. Many practitioners are opposed to using coercion with families, believing that forcing a family to receive services is counterproductive and unjust. Under the new law, when Bureau Jeugdzorg specifies a treatment for a family, practitioners will be obliged to provide services and to share their diagnostic knowledge with other organizations. This is a highly contentious issue in the Netherlands. Currently, there are discussions about potential consequences for an institution that is not able, or not willing, to provide the treatment specified by Bureau Jeugdzorg. One of the fears is that families will sue the organization or the government if they are unable to get the specified treatment. Debates surrounding this issue are delaying passage of the new Act.

NOTES

1 For an English translation of the Dutch Civil Code, see Haanappel, Mackaay, Warendorf, & Thomas (2002).
2 Mia Lamers is a registered child psychologist. From 1992 to 2001,

Ms Lamers worked with the Council for Child Protection coaching social workers as well as developing interventions and policy. Since 2002, she has worked in a similar capacity at the Bureau Jeugdzorg in Rotterdam. Ms Lamers also has a strong interest in cross-national research and in 2000 spent six months studying the child protection system in England.

PART FOUR

Community Caring Systems

Community care models are unfolding in many Aboriginal communities in various parts of the world. Ties to extended family, community, place, history and spirit are considered integral to healthy individual identities. Ideally, community caring relies on consultations with parents, extended family and the local community about the protection and care of children. Because of the devastating effects on Aboriginal populations of colonialism, residential care, and child protection systems, a strong connection is made between caring for children and fostering a healing process for whole communities. A strong value is given to keeping children within their families and communities. Respect for traditional Aboriginal values and procedures is integral to community care processes. Two papers in this volume assess First Nation community caring orientations in Canada, and another focuses on the Maori experience in Aotearoa/New Zealand.

9 From Child Welfare to Child, Family, and Community Welfare: The Agenda of Canada's Aboriginal Peoples

DEENA MANDELL, CINDY BLACKSTOCK,
JOYCE CLOUSTON CARLSON, and MARSHALL FINE[1]

Child welfare is an issue of critical importance in the evolving relationship between Canada and its Aboriginal peoples.[2] The education and care of Aboriginal children embody much of the painful history between First Nations and the Canadian government. Elsewhere, we have considered the major historical and contemporary issues in Canadian Aboriginal child welfare in a review and synthesis of current theory and research (see Mandell, Clouston Carlson, Fine, & Blackstock, 2003). In this chapter, we focus primarily on the current context, recognizing that some familiarity with the historical and cultural background is a sine qua non for understanding the relevant issues.

Colonization had a devastating and lasting impact on Aboriginal societies, traditions, and values, effects that are manifest in the history of child welfare (see Bennett & Blackstock, 2002, for a bibliographic guide). Mainstream child welfare services, among them the residential school system introduced in the 1870s, have been an instrument of disintegration of Aboriginal communities in Canada. The First Nations are engaged in a struggle to gain control of child welfare in their own communities, and this issue has a significant place in the First Nations movement towards self-determination.

Implications of Overrepresentation in the Child Welfare System

The widespread separation of successive generations of children from their families and communities has produced social, cultural, and economic disruption. The effects are traced in the Royal Commission on Aboriginal Peoples (RCAP, 1995; 1996a; 1996b; 1996c), and in Armitage (1993), and Johnston (1983).

Aboriginal children remain significantly overrepresented in the child welfare system. Timpson (1995) cites federal data showing that in 1991 the number of Native children taken into care was ten times that of non-Native children. Data from Indian and Northern Affairs Canada (INAC) show an increase of 71.5% in the number of children in care (defined as status Indian children resident on reserve) between 1995 and 2001 (McKenzie & Morrissette, 2002). British Columbia reports that Aboriginal children currently compose 43.8% of the province's children in care; Saskatchewan reports Aboriginal child-in-care populations exceeding 70%; and, in Manitoba, where Aboriginal children constitute about 21% of the population under the age of fifteen, they account for 78% of children in care in the child and family services system (Aboriginal Justice Inquiry Child Welfare Initiative [AJI-CWI], 2001). A submission to the Ontario government by that province's Association of Native Child and Family Services Agencies (2001) indicates that in some northern Ontario Aboriginal communities up to 10% of the children are in care. As in the past, many children are placed in non-Aboriginal foster homes and residential facilities (McKenzie & Morrissette, 2002).

In Aboriginal cultures, child welfare is inseparable from family and community welfare, and, as a consequence, mainstream child welfare services are often at odds with the needs and wishes of Aboriginal peoples. Cross-cultural insensitivity and racism are present to some degree in the relationships between the child welfare system and all nondominant groups (see, for example, Korbin, 1994; Owen & Farmer, 1996; see also Courtney, Barth, Duerr-Berrick, Brooks, Needell & Park, 1996). But the issues associated with colonization and assimilation are unique to Canada's Aboriginal peoples, and for this reason, a multicultural analysis is inadequate to describe their experience (Bennett & Blackstock, 2002).

Much has been written about Aboriginal beliefs and values concerning children, family, and community (see, for example, Connors & Maidman, 2001; McKenzie, Seidl, & Bone, 1995; RCAP, 1996a). While there are significant differences among Aboriginal communities in the expression of these value systems, common elements include a holistic world view and belief in interdependence. Broadly speaking, traditional Aboriginal cultures regard children as gifts from the spirit world, part of the web that connects all life forms, the environment, and the world from which they come. As they mature, they bring to their communities, the gifts of '[renewing] the strength of the family, clan and village ...' (RCAP, 1996c, p. 23). Elders and members of the extended kin network have a responsibility to nurture and guide children according to the traditional teachings, anchoring the child's identity and helping him or her make sense of the world (Blackstock, 2001).

A child removed to residential school, foster care, or adoption outside the community is placed in what Johnston (1983) describes as 'triple jeopardy' (1983, p. 59): separation from parents, and simultaneous loss of the kinship network and cultural context, typically including the child's birth language and connection with the land. In essence, the child loses ways of relating to and understanding the world. Because the socialization process involves complex communication of values and expectations, the displaced child may not understand the expectations in the new environment, or know how to relate to people or to the new community. He or she may be confused about the place of Indigenous knowledge and language (McKay & Clouston Carlson, 2003; RCAP, 1996c).

Identity in community is a core value in Aboriginal traditions. The nature and extent of relationships with the people and world around them have a far greater place in developing and sustaining personal identity in Aboriginal than in non-Aboriginal children (Chandler, 2002). It follows that the forced removal of children to residential schools or child welfare settings produced devastating effects in Aboriginal communities (see Carlson, 1995; MacDonald, 2002; McKay & Clouston Carlson, 2003; RCAP, 1996c). All children raised in institutional settings, for example, grew to adulthood without parenting models, whether or not they were subject to more profound abuse and neglect.[3] The disruption of parent-child relationships was passed to succeeding generations (Hodgson, 2002).

It is important to note that this is a generalization – despite their circumstances some Aboriginal children in the residential schools were able to maintain relationships with family or to benefit from other role models (Canadian Broadcasting Corporation, 2000; Cook & Carlson 1997)[4] and succeeded in developing independent judgment skills and the capacity for emotional attachment.

Child Welfare in Aboriginal Communities

While the painful story of the residential school system and its devastating effects has been well documented (See AJI, 1991; AJI-CWI, 2001; RCAP, 1996a), Armitage (1993) argues that in some ways the child welfare system may have been more damaging than the residential school system. Children in care were cut off from their families and their peers as well.

A brief history is in order. In the early 1950s, it was recognized that services to Aboriginal communities in health, welfare, and education were inferior to those in the rest of Canada, and these provincial services were extended to reserves (Johnston, 1983). Little attention was paid to the question of compatibility between provincial services and the needs of Indian communities (Johnston, 1983), or to the problems inherent in transferring services developed in an urban context to remote rural communities (Armitage, 1993). Historical, social, cultural, and economic contexts were ignored, and the extent of social breakdown and economic disadvantage in Native communities went largely unacknowledged. Social agencies were set up to deal with individual problems in individual families (Timpson, 1993). Child welfare services were often initiated by non-Native authorities, and children were frequently removed to non-Native foster homes. During adoption proceedings, the requirement for voluntary consent through the courts was often waived (Armitage, 1993).

Inadequate funding arrangements amplified the problem (Johnston, 1983). In provinces providing only federally funded child-in-care services, provincial social workers were called 'only when conditions had deteriorated to the point that no alternative to apprehension was possible' (Awasis Agency, 1997; Timpson, 1993, p. 39). There was no incentive for provinces to develop preventive services or avoid apprehensions (Timpson, 1993). At both levels of government, willingness to pay child-in-care costs, combined with reluctance to fund preventive services, family counselling, or rehabilitation, made permanent removal the preferred solution in problem situations (Timpson, 1993). By the 1980s, the national ratio of Native to non-Native children removed from their families was 5 to 1, although at the time First Nations and Métis constituted only about 6% of Canada's population (Awasis Agency, 1997).

Prior to the introduction of the federal funding formula in 1991, funding of First Nations Child and Family Services agencies was 'inconsistent and often inequitable' (McDonald & Ladd, 2000, p. 9). Even the federal formula has been deemed inadequate by the Joint National Policy Review (McDonald & Ladd, 2000). As a result of jurisdictional wrangling between federal and provincial governments, and disparity across provincial jurisdictions, many reserves continue to receive funding inferior to other Canadian communities.

Towards Self-Determination

Although active protest by First Nation communities against removal of their children occurred throughout the period of colonization, First Nation child welfare agencies first appeared in the mid-1970s, reflecting a growing desire for self-determination (Johnston, 1983; Koster, Morrissette, & Roulette, 2000; McKenzie, Seidl, & Bone, 1995). Increasing recognition of the over-representation of Native children in the child welfare system, and the United States's Indian Child Welfare Act of 1978, contributed to the rising demand for change in the early to mid-1980s (McKenzie, 1989). Jurisdictional issues between federal and provincial authorities continue to be dealt with differently across the country, as Aboriginal peoples press for more authority in child welfare.

Ontario's first joint initiative between a First Nation and the local Children's Aid Society occurred in 1979, with provincial funding. The initiative was intended to promote care within the community and reduce the need for children to come into the care of the Children's Aid Society. It led to the appointment of the first Native child welfare prevention workers in two northwestern Ontario Aboriginal communities. Soon after, the program was expanded to all First Nation communities in the province.

In 1981, also in Ontario, a Band Chiefs resolution forbade Ontario and Manitoba to remove Native children from reserves and demanded the return of children previously removed. The Chiefs also declared their intention to create their own child welfare laws and services.

In 1984, the Child and Family Services Act gave official recognition to the rights of Aboriginal people, including the right to develop child protection agencies. Under the Act, a band or Native community may designate a particular body as a Native child and family service authority, and the Ministry is obliged to negotiate the provision of services with this authorized group on request. Resulting agreements may allow the Aboriginal authority to provide services, and the authority may be designated a Children's Aid Society under the Act. Currently, there are five Aboriginal agencies so designated in Ontario, serving 55 of Ontario's 136 First Nations (Association of Native Child and Family Services Agencies of Ontario [ANCFSAO], 2001; Koster, Morrissette, & Roulette, 2000). This number is low compared to other parts of Canada; British Columbia, for example, currently has nineteen First Nation Child and Family Service Agencies, and five of these are delegated agencies with full child protection authority.

By the 1980s, Canadian child welfare experts publicly acknowledged that the system did not operate in the best interests of Aboriginal children or families (Johnston, 1983). Protests in Manitoba by Aboriginal people against international adoption placements resulted in a public enquiry early in the decade. The report by Family Court Judge Kimelman (1985) was strongly critical of the child welfare system, concluding that the Aboriginal community was justified in its claim that the child welfare system was practising 'cultural genocide.' The report blamed the cultural biases and inadequate training of social workers, but ignored the context of overwhelming social, cultural, and economic disruption, systemic biases, and structural inequities (Carlson, 1994; McKay & Clouston Carlson, 2003; Timpson, 1993). Nor were the profound differences in values in child care, family life, and community addressed (Timpson, 1993).

Since the early 1980s (and in a few cases, the late 1970s), while child welfare legislation has remained under the control of the provinces, Aboriginal communities have developed initiatives and negotiated or implemented programs designed to fit their needs (Armitage, 1993; McKenzie & Morrissette, 2002). There is considerable variation among these initiatives and in the role that First Nations now play in child welfare, due in part to differences among First Nation communities themselves, to the history between First Nations and local governments, and to differences in provincial policies (Armitage, 1993).[5] Armitage compares, for example, the relatively comprehensive approach in Manitoba and the ad hoc approach of British Columbia. But, despite the differences, a gradual shift in awareness has led to less aggressive intervention by social workers than had been true in the 1960s and 1970s, and to an increasingly respectful and collaborative way of working with Aboriginal communities (Armitage, 1993). Many Aboriginal communities, however, aspire to a very different kind of arrangement.

The effects of the justice system on Canada's Aboriginal peoples appear in patterns strikingly similar to those produced by the child welfare system. By the early 1990s, two-thirds of the men and 90% of the women in Manitoba jails were Aboriginal. Incarceration rates for youth aged fifteen to nineteen are nine times higher among First Nations people than among non-First Nations, and seven times higher for those aged twenty to twenty-four (McDonald & Ladd, 2000). In addition, there is a recursive interaction between the effects of the child welfare and justice systems. Research by the Manitoba Métis Federation in 1989 determined that 'the single most determinant factor of

Métis people becoming offenders was their experience in the Child and Family Services system' (as cited in Awasis Agency, 1997, pp. 1–2). In Ontario, 40% of the offenders in the Aboriginal justice program in Toronto in the late 1990s were found to have been adopted or to have spent their adolescence in foster care (Koster et al., 2000). The Aboriginal Justice Inquiry (AJI, 1991) identified other contributors, namely changes in the province's liquor laws, new policing agreements that stationed Royal Canadian Mounted Police (RCMP) closer to Native communities, and the demoralization of Native World War II veterans. Many Aboriginal people who appeared before the AJI argued that the removal of children, and the resulting disruption of communities and value systems, ultimately led to the breakdown of traditional social behaviour patterns (AJI, 1991). And, in turn, these behaviours put children at risk. McKenzie and Morrissette (2002), for example, connect the widespread violence against Aboriginal women – a justice matter – with the prevalence of family breakdown and child care problems – a child welfare issue.

The justice literature identifies parallels between the justice and child welfare systems including their assimilationist histories, institutionalized racism, and disregard for cultural differences, and the economic and cultural disruption for which they are responsible. The demands for recognition of Aboriginal law and for control over child welfare have been closely linked for several decades (Zlotkin, 1994).

Jurisdictional Models for Delivering Child Welfare Service in Aboriginal Communities

Child welfare services have entered Aboriginal communities at different rates, with many inconsistencies and with varying degrees of acceptance by First Nation communities across Canada. It is difficult to develop a comprehensive view in light of jurisdictional and legislative differences, and variations among Aboriginal communities themselves, including relative acculturation or traditional identification; rural, remote, or urban location; proximity to services, among others. These issues complicate the development and delivery of child welfare services that would be in the best interest of all Aboriginal peoples.

Zlotkin (1994) classifies Canadian legal models for First Nation child welfare systems in two broad categories: tripartite agreements and the statutory model. Tripartite agreements are those between a First Nation government or tribal council, the federal government, and a provincial government. They enable First Nation child welfare agencies to administer provincial, but not First Nation, law in matters of child welfare. Federal funding is guaranteed during the term of an agreement. The model Zlotkin refers to as 'statutory' is used in Ontario, and was introduced with provincial child welfare legislation in 1985. This model is discussed under the heading 'Premandated model.'

The range of jurisdictional models is expanding as increasing numbers of Aboriginal communities and First Nations operate child and family service agencies. We have identified five models currently in operation or in development across the country. Each model has important implications for funding regimes, and references to various funding methods are included in the discussion.

Currently, the Department of Indian and Northern Affairs Canada (INAC) accepts financial responsibility only for funding First Nation child and family service agencies providing services to eligible children resident on reserve. The funding is provided pursuant to a national funding formula known as Program Directive 20-1 (Chapter Five), 1989 (amended 1995), commonly termed INAC Policy Directive 20-1.[6] In Ontario, First Nation child and family service agencies are exempt from Directive 20-1, as they are funded by the Province of Ontario in accordance with the Memorandum of Agreement Respecting Welfare programs for Indians between Canada and Ontario, known as the 1965 Indian Welfare Agreement. Off-reserve service delivery is typically funded by the provinces and territories.

The Delegated Model

This is the most common jurisdictional model, in part because the INAC funding formula, Directive 20-1, requires that First Nation child and family service agencies operate according to its conditions to receive funding for child welfare service delivery on reserve. In this model, the provincial or territorial child welfare authority designates Aboriginal agencies to provide services to Aboriginal peoples either on or off reserve, according to their provincial or territorial child welfare statute(s). The mechanism for delegation varies from province to province, but in all cases delegation is formalized either through an agreement or by an Order in Council. Delegation can include full authority (operating with full child protection and prevention authority) or partial authority (providing support and prevention services to families, while the provincial authority provides child protection services).

While the delegated model provides an opportunity for Aboriginal peoples to care for their children and families, it has notable weaknesses. For example, the provincial/territorial child welfare statutes are founded on the individual rights philosophy of British common law. This philosophy is often in conflict with the interdependent, communal, and holistic basis for Aboriginal concepts of justice, and the traditional means of caring for children, youth, and families. Managing the disparity between traditional values and beliefs and the legislation is a significant challenge for most Aboriginal agencies.

In addition, this national funding formula does not adjust for differences in provincial/territorial legislation, which can result in gaps between what a First Nation child and family service is delegated to do and the funding available to support its efforts (McDonald & Ladd, 2000). Under this formula, little emphasis is placed on funding for community development and the preventive services required to support First Nation families in caring for their children at home.

In June 2000, the Assembly of First Nations and INAC published a report reviewing Directive 20-1 and providing seventeen recommendations for improvements to the current policy (McDonald & Ladd, 2000). The recommendations included the need for mechanisms to coordinate provincial jurisdictions with federal funding, an increase in funding for 'least disruptive measures' programs, and recognition of First Nation jurisdictional models. The recommendations have not yet been implemented.

Off-reserve Aboriginal child and family service delivery is funded by provincial/territorial agreements. The nature and extent of these agreements vary from province to province. The Aboriginal Justice Inquiry-Child Welfare Initiative (AJI-CWI) in Manitoba provides a promising model for funding off-reserve service delivery that recognizes both the right of Aboriginal peoples to care for their children and the diversity that exists within the Aboriginal population. The model provides for the formation of four child welfare authorities, two of which are First Nations, one is a Métis authority, and one is for non-Aboriginal clients. Aboriginal peoples are included in drafting child welfare legislation, standards, and funding mechanisms (AJI-CWI, 2001).

Many Aboriginal organizations, particularly those working with communities involved in active self-government processes, regard the delegated model as an interim approach to governance, pending recognition of Aboriginal laws. Delegation is seen as a capacity-building measure as exploration continues for more meaningful, culturally appropriate, and community-based paradigms. Brown, Haddock, & Kovach (2002) conclude that the best thing about the delegated model – which they characterize as neocolonial – may be the resistance it generates in First Nation communities, as they do the work of empowering themselves to sustain their traditions and values.

Premandated Child and Family Services

Aboriginal and First Nation child and family service agencies operating under the premandated model provide prevention and family support services pursuant to agreements, including licensing agreements, with the provincial/territorial government. These agencies, principally located in Ontario, are incorporated as nonprofit transfer payment agencies with their own boards of directors (Koster et al., 2000). Their goal is to ensure that families have access to culturally appropriate preventive and foster care resources. The 1984 Child and Family Services Act, which provides the legal basis for the establishment of child welfare agencies by First Nation governments and organizations in Ontario, also permits exemption of a First Nation child and family service authority, band, or Native community from any provision of the Act or its regulations. These exemptions are the mechanism for allowing the delivery of culturally appropriate services that might not meet certain requirements of the original legislation (Koster et al, 2000). Six Nations of the Grand River in southern Ontario, for example, recently reached an agreement under the Child and Family Services Act that allows children placed in customary care[7] not to be considered in the care of the province, yet Six Nations still receives funding to support the customary care arrangement (Six Nations of the Grand River, 2002). The First Nation agencies of Ontario have called for clearly defined guidelines for achieving full mandated status (ANCFSAO, 2001). As mandated agencies, they would offer the 'full range of child protection services' to Native children (ANCFSAO, 2001, p. 73).

The Self-Government Model

This model recognizes the jurisdictional authority of Aboriginal peoples in the area of child and family services. The authority often is based on treaties, such as the Nisga'a Treaty, which includes provisions for the development of Nisga'a laws governing child and family services as long as those laws meet provincial standards. Although the Nisga'a are currently operating a delegated child and family service agency as a capacity-building measure, plans are under way to draft and implement tribal laws. The model of self-government has the benefit of being based on the world view, cultures, and histories of Aboriginal peoples, and affirms rather than competes with traditional child and family caring processes.[8]

There are many First Nation and Aboriginal groups in Canada that have expressed interest in establishing self-government models of child welfare, and this is likely to be a growing area of development in the coming years. The drive for self-determination in issues of child welfare is clearly bound up with broader issues of empowerment in First Nation communities, at least in part because self-determination is seen as crucial to socioeconomic development.[9]

The Band By-law Model

The Indian Act allows for Indian Band Chiefs and Councils to pass band by-laws that apply on reserve. As described above, the Spallumcheen First Nation of British Columbia passed a by-law establishing sole jurisdiction for themselves over child and family services on reserve. The Minister of Indian and Native Affairs Canada at the time resisted signing the by-law, but did so after much advocacy by the Spallumcheen. With additional advocacy, funding and provincial support eventually followed. The Minister has since refused to recognize any further by-laws associated with child welfare, and the Spallumcheen First Nation is currently the only agency operating under this model (Union of British Columbia Indian Chiefs, 2002).

The Tripartite Model

Under this model of governance, the provincial and federal governments delegate their law-making authority to a First Nation, usually with the requirement that provincial standards of child welfare be followed. The name refers to the three parties involved. While this model offers more recognition of tribal authority than the delegated model, it is, like that model, administered under delegated authority from the province/territory and federal governments, and gives First Nation child welfare agencies the mandate to administer provincial, but not First Nation, law (Zlotkin, 1994). Accordingly, some First Nation and Aboriginal groups prefer to pursue models that recognize in full their jurisdictional authority to care for children, youth, and families. A case in point is the Sechelt First Nation in British Columbia, which has adopted the tripartite model. By the terms of the agreement, the provincial government delegates its law-making function to the Sechelt First Nation; within certain limits, Sechelt has the authority to develop and implement tribal authority for child and family services. Consultations have begun with community Elders, leaders, and members to design the child and family services model. Adoption of the new jurisdictional model is anticipated within the next couple of years (N. Simon, personal communication, December, 2002). As this model relies on delegation of law-making authority from provincial and federal governments, it is seen as a step towards self-government, though not full recognition of Sechelt law-making authority.

Issues in the Development of Culturally Appropriate Practices

Child welfare services to Aboriginal people that are designed, administered, and delivered by mainstream agencies under laws that are not Aboriginal can at best aim to be 'culturally sensitive.' As Rooney and Bibus (1996, p. 64) argue, 'While cultural sensitivity is useful with recent immigrants who have not had extended contact with the dominant culture, work with historically oppressed minorities requires a perspective which recognizes the power differences between representatives of the dominant culture's agencies and members of oppressed groups.' Understanding the historical relations between groups can help child welfare practitioners 'to look beyond their own backgrounds or training in cultural sensitivity to recognize that they represent a powerful, potentially hostile threat to families' (p. 64). Morrissette, McKenzie, and Morrissette (1993) distinguish between 'culturally sensitive' and 'culturally appropriate' practice and emphasize their preference for the latter. 'While culturally sensitive service advances awareness of issues in the Aboriginal community in the context of involvement with an ethnic minority, culturally appropriate service integrates core Aboriginal values, beliefs and healing practices in program delivery' (p. 101). Even when First Nation agencies have authority to deliver and administer some services, limits to their mandate and role places constraints on the cultural appropriateness of those services. Brown and colleagues' review of a British Columbia First Nations agency (2002) argues that full empowerment of First Nation communities is not possible in the context of power imbalances inherent in paradigms such as the delegated model.

The needs of First Nation communities are not comparable to those of non-Aboriginal communities. In some Aboriginal communities, unemployment, poverty, substance use, child abuse and neglect, violence against women, youth suicide, and communal disintegration are widespread (ANCFSAO, 2001; Koster et al., 2000). Poverty and marginalization increase stress on families and increase their participation in child welfare systems. Timpson (1995) finds this reality to be largely missing from the child welfare literature until quite recently, for what she deems to be political reasons. According to McDonald and Ladd (2000), 50% of First Nation children living on or off reserve live in poverty. In 2000, over 55% of First Nation children in Manitoba and approximately 35% of Métis children lived in poverty (Social Planning Council of Winnipeg, 2003). ANCFSAO (2001) claims that the application of Ontario's new risk assessment instrument to remote Northern Ontario communities would likely find most or all of the children to be at risk; yet the services to respond to these conditions are absent. The Tikanagan agency in Northern Ontario, for example, lists the following services missing in its catchment area: psychological assessment, residential treatment, intensive child and family intervention, day treatment programs, mobile crisis response programs, professional children's mental health counselling, early intervention and prevention, suicide prevention and response programs, programs for autism, attention deficit hyperactive disorder and fetal alcohol syndrome, sexual abuse treatment programs, residential services for children and youth with serious developmental challenges, special services at home, speech and language assessment and therapy, Healthy Babies, Healthy Children, Better Beginnings, Better Futures, and regular medical services (ANCFSAO, 2001).

The major issues at stake in the various delivery models for Aboriginal child welfare services are the right to self-determination and the suitability of services to meet the unique needs of Aboriginal communities in ways that further the aims of community healing, capacity building, and child well-being. Adaptations of social work education and practices to the needs of Aboriginal communities have been attempted, with mixed results (Castellano, Stalwick, & Wien, 1986; Morrissette et al., 1993). Because of the unique needs and conditions, the delivery of mainstream services is bound to be less cost-effective in First Nation communities, less culturally suitable, and more difficult with regard to meeting provincial and territorial standards or reconciling them in the cultural framework of community. If full consultation and collaboration are not in place, and if policy and requirements are not flexible, the result can be 'devastating' (ANCFSAO, 2001; MacDonald, 2002). No conventional model has yet been able to adequately address these needs (Morrissette et al., 1993). Organizational practices, accountability requirements, centralized control, political interference by band councils, practice modalities and methods, and staff development and training are especially problematic when services and the agencies which deliver them 'operate within legislative and policy frameworks created by the dominant society' (Morrissette et al., 1993, p. 103).

There has been a painful developmental process associated with the realization of these constraints, partly because the extension of child welfare services began in some communities before a full dialogue had taken place. The importation of existing mainstream models early in the development of an Aboriginal child welfare system meant that structures, policies, and practices designed for another culture were transposed uncritically (RCAP, 1996c).

The Awasis Agency (1997) draws on the work of Thomas (1994) and Shields (1995) in outlining mainstream approaches to social work that 'inhibit growth and development in children and families, particularly First Nation families' (p. 24). These limiting approaches include a focus on deficit reduction rather than promotion of capacities, and a reliance on a categorical approach to service delivery; they consider cases outside their larger context, failure to incorporate holistic healing, lack of power sharing in the system, family powerlessness combined with agency reluctance to share power, and the barriers created by language. Morrissette and his colleagues (1993) identify as problematic conventional approaches to direct practice, funding, and organizational structures that are incompatible with traditional ways of helping and healing. Even when new policies are family oriented and community based, prevailing practice continues to emphasize individualized understanding of causation and culturally inappropriate interventions, especially placement of children outside communities (Morrissette et al., 1993).

Structural issues. Jurisdictional issues are salient, insofar as they are linked to standards and requirements, funding, and the degree of autonomy First Nation agencies actually have over policy, programs, and practices. Without jurisdictional control, the development of culturally appropriate services is impeded (McKenzie & Morrissette, 2002). Despite some measure of control over policy development within a given agency, an ongoing tension exists with provincial child welfare laws and standards, and the accountability issues they raise (ANCFSAO, 2001; Koster et al., 2000; McKenzie et al., 1995). The fundamental struggle revolves around cultural differences conceptualizing child welfare and what its priorities will be. Since the 1999 Ontario Child Welfare Reforms, for example, practice, training, and funding give priority to child safety based on risk assessment and protection. The emphasis is on competency, goals, and 'business-plan objectives' (Koster, 2001, p. 3), rather than on the holistic values upon which practice in Ontario First Nations is based. This results in a poor fit between training, funding, and technology and the current capacities and resources of the First Nation communities involved (ANCFSAO, 2001). Official standards establish levels of child well-being and safety which the state can then legitimately enforce; child risk standards are the foundation criteria for intervention in families. In order for these criteria to be culturally appropriate, the standards must be culturally specific (McKenzie et al., 1995). Proper implementation of standards presumes, of course, that adequate resources will be provided.

In an attempt to identify such standards among First Nation communities, McKenzie and his colleagues (1995) conducted a series of focus groups with a broad range of representatives from eight communities. The topics addressed included the definition of a family, indicators of abuse and neglect, preferences regarding placement of children for alternate care, and how culture should shape provision of child and family services. After outlining the themes discussed in the focus groups, the authors conclude that the emergent principles reflect a 'holistic, family-and community-focused foundation for child welfare services' (p. 648). They note that many of the ideas expressed by the participants about what constitutes good child welfare practice also are consistent with mainstream standards. McDonald and Ladd (2000) indicate that only in British Columbia have First Nation standards been incorporated into provincial standards, although in several provinces, First Nations are at various stages of developing and implementing their own standards.

Funding is a particularly thorny problem (McKenzie, 1989). ANCFSAO (2001) identifies funding benchmarks and funding formulas related to programs – and to most aspects of organizational costs – as being inadequate or limiting at best, and at worst as being in conflict with the visions, law, and values held by the First Nation communities. Particularly problematic are funding formulas that are directed primarily at supporting children in care and do not allow the flexibility to provide the services deemed necessary by the communities themselves. In the context of an Aboriginal vision and cultural imperative to keep families together and children within their communities, the contradiction is obvious.

Block federal funding offers the significant advantage of affording First Nation agencies the flexibility to develop innovative programs and set their own administrative priorities (McDonald & Ladd, 2000); however, it is most suited to large agencies with established track records of operations (McKenzie & Flette, 2001). McKenzie and Flette's evaluation of one five-year block funding project at West Region Child and Family Services in the mid-1990s provides an example of how such funds have been used to develop accessible and culturally appropriate, community-based resources. The funding was used to develop alternative programming (e.g., a therapeutic foster home program for children with special needs), to add treatment support services to each local community team, and to coordinate and host other community services (such as family violence and day-care programs). New positions within the agency also were funded to develop new initiatives (e.g., a Community with Special Needs Coordinator developed a program for children and families struggling with fetal alcohol syndrome or its effects). Partnership with education authorities led to a program for youth who had dropped out of school, and another offering life skills, computer training, and support services for young parents with children in care or at risk of entering care. The goal of balancing protection with prevention led to the development of programs providing resources to families and children, such as groups for mothers to learn and receive support from Elders and other women. Decentralized management of such programs is emphasized and supported. Nevertheless, block funding has some disadvantages from the First Nation agencies' perspective, insofar as the agreements lack specific criteria for adjustment of funding and for establishing a starting budget base (McDonald & Ladd, 2000).

Other larger-system issues include agency development and the relations between Native and non-Native child welfare authorities, which are troubled by mistrust (ANCFSAO, 2001), differing research and evaluation methods (ANCFSAO, 2001; Koster et al., 2000; Morrissette et al., 1993), and power imbalances (ANCFSAO, 2001; Awasis, 1997). Recruiting, training, and retaining staff who can meet mainstream standards for social work education, English literacy, and technological competence under these conditions, coupled with negotiating the internal and external politics involved, pose enormous challenges (ANCFSAO, 2001; Castellano et al., 1986; McKenzie, 1989; McKenzie et al., 1995; Morrissette et al., 1993).

Finally, there are issues within First Nation communities themselves that contribute to the complexity of developing and delivering culturally appropriate services. Internal politics, divisions, and power struggles within communities have been mentioned above. In addition, communities are often quite small, and many or most of their members are related to each other. The social worker may be related to the families she or he serves (ANCFSAO, 2001). Where there is still a general lack of awareness about child abuse and sexual abuse (ANCFSAO, 2001), 'denial and minimizing' on the part of family and community members may compromise the principle of respecting parental rights by requiring intervention against their wishes (McKenzie et al., 1995).

There are inherent challenges in balancing individual and collective rights in a way that promotes child, family, and community well-being. On the one hand, the principle of restoring harmony to a family or community may lead to responses that ultimately fail to protect victims from abuse (La Rocque, 1997; Morrissette et al., 1993). On the other hand, there are significant potential benefits to the less formal and less structured ways of working in small, closely knit communities (Brown et al., 2002; MacDonald 2002). From a Canadian child protection perspective, it is difficult to fully comprehend how the inseparability of children's, parents', and communities' well-being, and the inevitable permeability of professional and community boundaries, can be addressed. This difficulty underscores the lack of cultural fit between mainstream child protection and the needs of Aboriginal communities.

Direct Practice Issues

Culturally sensitive practice essentially refers to the adaptations that mainstream services incorporate in dealing with cultural minority groups, Aboriginal and otherwise. It involves education of workers about values, customs, and practices that may differ from those of the dominant culture in order to establish cooperative relationships and avoid inappropriate judgments and interventions. It may involve specially designed programs, outreach, and hiring staff who are members of the cultural group being served. The main considerations in child welfare are profound differences in expectations and values that shape the ways that family is conceptualized and, hence, the ways that laws, policies, and practices are formulated.

Some fundamental principles taken for granted in mainstream Canadian social work are not appropriate to First Nations communities and traditional Aboriginal ways. The concept of child welfare as protection, for example, is in conflict with an Aboriginal paradigm of holism, community ties, and capacity building. A conflict of such substance points increasingly away from the idea of bridging cultures through cultural sensitivity training and practice models, and towards self-determined Aboriginal visions of caring for children, families, and communities (Mandell et al., 2003).

There are several models of practice in the academic literature, and some that can be inferred from the writing of First Nation agencies, that outline frameworks for culturally appropriate child welfare services. Castellano and her colleagues (1986) advocate the establishment of separate Aboriginal social services with small Native communities operating 'within a single budget.' They advocate a framework for distinctively Aboriginal practice that builds on the Aboriginal world view, which includes connectedness to creation, interdependence in community, responsibility of all 'for the benefit of the group,' and 'balance' in life. The other main building blocks identified are the cultivation of an understanding of colonialism, the lost possibility of 'a traditional self-sustaining economy,' and the 'creation of dependency.'

Morrissette and colleagues (1993) posit a framework for Aboriginal social work practice that combines principles grounded in an Aboriginal world view with developing consciousness about colonialism. In addition, they add the principles of 'cultural knowledge and traditions as an active component of retaining Aboriginal identity and collective consciousness, and empowerment as a method of practice' (p. 91), and an understanding of the range of cultural identifications among Aboriginal people. A continuum of cultural identification has been elaborated to aid in this understanding (McKenzie & Morrissette, 2002). The framework presumes the fundamental elements of a structural approach to social work: that is, the connection of individual experience to conditions of oppression. Also important is the strengths perspective that adds recognition of Aboriginal people's resilience and their capacity to recognize their problems.

Morrissette and colleagues (1993) argue that culturally appropriate practice goes beyond 'cultural sensitivity' to include using Elders and healers for traditional teaching and healing (e.g., the healing circle) and a community-based approach to the development and delivery of services. This would require flexibility in funding and in accountability regarding service requirements. To accommodate these goals, agency services would need to be restructured at the administrative and direct-service levels. Social work education would need to support these new approaches, and indeed to reevaluate and reshape current mainstream approaches. The intention of such a model apparently is not to create a parallel system, but to transform mainstream services.

McKenzie and colleagues (1995) endorse a framework for child welfare services in First Nations communities under legislation and standards that make the provider agencies responsible for prevention and family support services (as opposed to more narrowly defined child protection practices). A child's attachment to parents and caregivers, extended family, community, and culture all are seen as important, so that preferences for out-of-home care, when necessary, give priority to keeping the child within the community. In the study upon which this model is based, the authors found that the participating communities view a child-centred approach as necessary when a child otherwise might be subject to abuse, and recognize out-of-home placement as required at times. Access to trusted caregivers and counsellors may necessitate placement outside the community, and this too is acceptable when necessary.

The Awasis Agency of Northern Manitoba (1997) is an agency with 99% Aboriginal employees, whose explicit intention is a radical change in the way child welfare services and the appropriate training of Aboriginal social workers are conceptualized. Instead of emphasizing prevention of child abuse and neglect, the agency stresses 'well-being within families and communities' (p. 94). The developmental framework for practice integrates adult education and community development, emphasizing 'learning in the context of political involvement' (p. 92).

At the level of larger systems, First Nation and Aboriginal ways of knowing in child welfare need to be affirmed through legislation and resource allocations in order to augment the cultural fit and efficacy of child welfare services. At the organizational level, the necessary features include decentralized structure, recruitment and retention of a stable core of properly trained staff, funding benchmarks, and outcome measures that are suitable to the context, and participatory research to continue development of innovative, effective programs. In order to be consistent with holism, healing, and strengthening of families and communities, service delivery must be structured to include a culturally based system of care.

Although these systems necessarily vary in accordance with the traditions of various communities, the following are examples of dimensions of such a system: traditional healing, inclusion of Elders in supportive and preventive services, repatriation of children who have previously been removed, use of customary care or custom adoption whenever possible, cultivation of resources for foster care and adoption when needed, alternatives to an adversarial legal process between families and child welfare authorities, and a focus on the family as a unit as opposed to the child alone. Specific services at the community level may include community capacity building; community service teams; group programs and preventive/supportive service, such as recreational programs for youth and families; education about substantive and procedural issues regarding child abuse and neglect, sexual abuse, alcohol and substance use, suicide prevention, and so forth. At the level of families and individuals, services include family support services (e.g., in-home services, respite care) and individual and family counselling as needed. There also is a need for access to mental health and child development services within the community, or funding to gain access to them outside the community.

Brown and colleagues (2002) describe the experience of the Cowichan people's Lalum'utul'Smun'eem, a name for their child and family services agency that means 'Watching over, caring for our children, caring for our families and extended families' (p. 131). The story of this agency clearly conveys how political, structural, jurisdictional, funding, and practice issues are inseparably interwoven with one another and with principles of holism, reclaimed traditions, self-determination, empowerment, and community building. Because 'all children are the mandate' (p. 141) the agency interacts with the community through workshops, presentations at community events, contributions to the community newsletter, and participation in interagency projects. It maintains an open door to members of the community.

Four types of programs are involved in the aim of supporting the entire community and protecting all children: prevention, support, child safety services, and a community-based special care home for children in need of protection. Prevention includes a program for art therapy, one for grieving children, and one for children who witness violence, a women's group, and summer cultural camps. Support encompasses development of foster homes in the community for Cowichan children both on and off the reserve. The special care home utilizes a family-based model rather than a staff model. Prevention and support also include parenting programs, in-home support, respite care, and referrals to counselling. Reports on child safety are assessed and responded to by a Child Safety Team, which investigates situations where child safety is a concern. Children are placed in a safe environment if protection is deemed necessary. This team works closely with prevention and support services, with a view to avoiding apprehension if other services can strengthen the family while keeping the child safe.

Lalum'utul' Smun'eem is not yet fully autonomous due to jurisdictional and funding arrangements, this reflects 'an inherent contradiction between a community empowerment approach and a delegated model of child and family service practice' (Brown et al., 2002, pp. 139–40), a contradiction which the authors identify as the result of a neocolonial power imbalance. Professionalization remains another impediment to fulfilment of the agency's vision, since 'the concept of "professional" is still grounded in western educational and practice experience' (p. 140).

The changes to practice approaches such as those described above require changes to social work research, education, and training. Issues of who appropriately should do the work, recruitment and admissions, suitable curriculum design, program structure, and funding all need to be addressed in order to support the needed changes in policy, service design, and service delivery.

Summary and Conclusion

Aboriginal children are overrepresented in Canada's child welfare system, just as Aboriginal youth and adults are in the justice system. At the same time, child welfare services available to Aboriginal communities are often inferior and culturally inappropriate for their unique needs. Aboriginal peoples not only have distinct ways of knowing and being that are different from mainstream Canadian society, they are further distinguished from other cultural groups by a history of assimilation and colonization which has eroded their traditional cultures and imposed significant socioeconomic and political hardships. This history has established a relationship of marginalization that makes it extremely difficult for incremental changes from within the dominant child protection framework to be effective. Efforts at reform have stressed changing the Aboriginal peoples themselves, rather than mainstream institutions. Meanwhile, Aboriginal claims to the historical right of self-determination and self-government pose challenges to established institutions. Although the goal of Aboriginal-controlled child welfare services has been identified, and receives some support among First Nation people and governments, primary efforts to date have focused on adapting mainstream child protection services to provide culturally sensitive services, and on developing in piecemeal fashion alternative models for culturally appropriate services. There are no simple and obvious solutions, but solutions are clearly necessary and are being demanded by Aboriginal people.

The development of new models has had mixed success to date. Although the assumption of child welfare authority by Aboriginal peoples has increased the options for culturally based services, they are often predicated on Canadian child protection legislation. The result is lack of cultural fit for the child welfare ideology, law, and services delivered. In addition, Aboriginal agencies face even more acute socio-economic problems than mainstream agencies. These problems – along with experiences and assets – are now beginning to be addressed within Aboriginal communities, and in the mainstream child welfare system. Models of practice must arise out of the communities themselves, so that they can be congruent with the Aboriginal world view regarding community strengthening, traditional ways of healing, and addressing the effects of colonialism. Appropriate hiring practices, culturally appropriate social work educational programs, adequate and flexible funding, and administrative structuring are also crucial.

Relations based on marginalization, power imbalances, and racism will need to be transformed in order to make these elements possible. Given some fundamental common ground between the value base of Aboriginal people and the social work profession, it may be possible that with openness to critical reflection, and genuine respect for Aboriginal self-determination, the profession can contribute to the development of truly appropriate new systems of child welfare, not only for Aboriginal communities, but for the many communities that constitute Canadian society.

NOTES

1 All four authors have worked at one time or another in the field of child welfare in Canada and all of us have worked with Aboriginal families. Cindy Blackstock is Gitanmaax First Nation, Joyce Clouston Carlson is Métis, and the remaining two authors, Deena Mandell and Marshall Fine, are of European Jewish descent. Cindy continues to administer and develop programs in First Nations child welfare and has published in the field. Joyce is a social worker and doctoral candidate who has worked with Aboriginal leaders to assist in publication of several volumes of oral cul-

tural stories. Marshall and Deena are involved in various child welfare studies and teach about child welfare in multicultural contexts as part of their graduate courses on social work practice with families.

2 Terminology set out by the Royal Commission on Aboriginal Peoples (RCAP) (1996b) established 'Aboriginal peoples' as the term referring to political and cultural groups considered original in North America; this includes First Nation (replacing the term 'Indian'), Inuit (replacing Eskimo) and Métis peoples of Canada. First Nation people who lose their status when they leave the reserve are also included by the term Aboriginal. This terminology is not followed consistently in the literature. Different terms may be used in different parts of the country and by authors of varying backgrounds. It is a confusing issue, but we have chosen to err, when in doubt, on the side of inclusiveness. We have therefore tried to keep our use of the terms as close to the RCAP formulation as possible; but when referring to the literature, we stick to the author's own choice of term whenever appropriate. See also guidelines developed by the Department of Indian and Northern Affairs Canada (INAC) at www.ainc-inac.gc.ca/pr/pub/wf/index_e.html.

3 The death rate in residential schools in BC ranged from a low of 11% to a high of 40% at the Kuper Island residential school throughout its twenty-five years of operation. These staggering death rates were due, in large part, to the substandard care and housing provided to the children (Fournier and Crey, 1997).

4 These variable effects have not been well studied. One can speculate that they may be attributable to mediating influences such as positive relationships that may have been formed with teachers or schoolmates, or to families 'back home' whose own histories (communal and individual) enabled them to be more supportive of their children in the schools (S. McKay, personal communication, Sept. 2002). In general, however, the issue of what role the residential schools played in the lives of individuals, communities, and cultures is a highly complex one (see, for example, Canadian Broadcasting Corporation, 2000); the polarization around it does little to further our understanding of the complexities and variables involved. It is likely that some children's experience of the schools was neither entirely harmful nor entirely beneficial. Communities were likely differentially affected as well. It is also important to consider the effects of the schools in the broader context of the overall disruption of First Nations economy, social structure, customary practices, ways of living on the land, and so forth, rather than as an isolated variable.

5 The First Nations Child and Family Services' *Joint National Policy Review* (McDonald & Ladd, 2000) contains several tables comparing key aspects of provincial child and family services legislation, delegation of statutory child and family services, and provincial and First Nations service standards across Canada.
6 See www.tbs-sct.gc.ca/rma/account/sufa-ecus/fncfs-sef_e.pdf.
7 Customary care is the practice of placing Aboriginal children with relatives or members of their own band when it is necessary for the children to be removed from their parents' homes.
8 See the Nisga'a Lisims Government Website: www.nisgaalisims.ca.
9 Research on the question of why some First Nations communities in the United States and Canada prospered socioeconomically – while others continued to struggle – indicates that substantive community improvement in social and economic well-being is preceded, rather than followed, by First Nations self-determination and sovereignty (Cornell & Kalt, 2002).

10 Maori Perspectives on Collaboration and Colonization in Contemporary Aotearoa / New Zealand Child and Family Welfare Policies and Practices

CATHERINE LOVE

> Ko Taranaki toku maunga
> Ko Tokomaru toku waka
> Ko Te Atiawa toku iwi
> Ko Ngati Te Whiti toku hapu
> Ko Te Whiti O Rongomai raua ko Tohu Kakahi nga poropiti
> Ko Te Tatau O Te Po toku whare

Let me expand on the meanings beneath the lines of these statements for Maori.

'Ko Taranaki toku maunga: My mountain is Taranaki'
This indicates that I descend from the shared ancestors of Ranginui and Papatuanuku, the sky father and earth mother. You would know that I am a living face of the ancestors who lived and died around Mount Taranaki, and who are buried within the richly prized and fertile lands of Taranaki province.

'Ko Tokomaru toku waka: My canoe is Tokomaru'
These words tell you that my mettle is that of the people who traveled the Pacific Ocean in the canoe called Tokomaru, and whose crew populated a number of areas in the land of Aotearoa/NewZealand.

'Ko Te Atiawa toku iwi: My tribe is Te Atiawa'
These words speak of my mortal and immortal line of descent from Tamarau and Rongoueroa. They communicate that I am of the Northern Taranaki tribe, Te Atiawa, where the first shots in the wars between Taranaki Maori and the New Zealand Crown were fired.

'Ko Ngati Te Whiti toku hapu: My subtribe is Ngati Te Whiti'
My people are descendants of Te Whiti O Rongomai, whose ancestors lived in the area known as Nga Motu, and who kept the fires burning at Te Whanganui A Tara (Wellington Harbour).

'Ko Te Whiti O Rongomai raua ko Tohu Kakahi nga poropiti: Te Whiti O Rongomai and Tohu Kakahi are the prophets'
We are followers of Te Whiti O Rongomai and his uncle Tohu Kakahi, who led our people in active and peaceful resistance to European colonization 50 years before Mahatma Ghandi led his own people on a similar path. It was these ancestors who created the self-sufficient, prosperous and progressive village of Parihaka, known as the 'Village of Peace,' in the midst of war and devastation. Hence we are survivors of the so-called 'never-ending war' between Taranaki Maori and the Crown/New Zealand Government. This is a war that involved 40 years of armed conflict, a war that saw prolonged 'scorched earth' policies followed by concerted 'bush-scouring' by colonial troops, and payment provided for the heads of Taranaki Maori men, women, or children. You will know that I am involved in some way in a war in which 'the weapons have changed from the musket and taiaha, to pen and paper.'

This history provides a context that includes our history as some of many whose lands were confiscated, in their entirety, by the Government; whose villages, homes and cultivations were burnt; who were pushed off their lands in order to provide town and country sections and farms for eager settlers; whose surviving men were deported to the cold southern region of the country, many to be imprisoned indefinitely without trial, many to be used as slave labour to build the sea walls, roads and gardens desired by the European settlers; and whose women were systematically raped leaving many of us with the imprint of these events carried permanently in our genes.

'Ko Te Tatau O Te Po toku whare: Te Tatau O Te Po is my house'
The name of my ancestral house, Te Tatau O Te Po, signifies we are some of the many who were never able to return to our ancestral lands, and who settled in the region known as Te Upoko O Te Ika A Maui (the head of the fish of Maui), or Wellington, the capital city of Aotearoa/New Zealand. This is where the national Parliament was built on top of our own homes and cultivations. You will recognise that this Parliament sits directly atop the brains of Te Ika A Maui (the fish of Maui; the Maori name for the North

Island of Aotearoa/New Zealand); a graphic representation of the ambitions of successive governments to control the minds and movements of the people of this land. (Waitangi Tribunal, 1996)

The above words of introduction (*pepeha*) carry within them the stories of my history and identity, and that of my *whanau* (family), *hapu* (subtribe), and *iwi* (tribe). When shared with other Maori,[1] the effect of the *pepeha* or introduction is to supply a wealth of information about the speaker, and to make visible a network of relationships and intersecting histories that predate the existence and determine the relational positions of both speaker and listener. The relationships and histories carried within our *pepeha* provide a context which extends beyond the present situation, and often beyond the lives of both speaker and listener.

This chapter examines discourses around partnership, collaboration, and appropriation between colonized and colonizing peoples in Aotearoa/New Zealand, with particular reference to discourses around the child and family welfare, care, and protection arenas. Of primary concern are discourses around relationships between Indigenous Maori and statutory systems of child and family welfare and protection in our country. It is argued here that Aotearoa/New Zealand statutory welfare authorities and policy makers have engaged in lip-service to the notions of well-being and family focus, notions promoted and preferred by indigenous Maori communities, while in fact continuing to operate according to deeply embedded notions of risk identification and individualism. The two positions represent fundamentally different ways of viewing societies and the people within them. It is proposed here that the 'child protection' focus in Aotearoa/New Zealand is supported by entrenched colonial and racist mentalities which provide largely unexamined barriers to real movement towards meaningful ideological and systemic change. In order to subject these dual discourses to examination, the meaning systems and contexts that underpin the respective positions of colonized and colonizer must be made visible.

In Maori discourse, the process of examining context can be understood in terms of *whakapapa*. *Whakapapa* is often translated as genealogy; however, its meaning also extends to broader understandings. *Whakapapa* encompasses the layer upon layer that has been built upon to bring us to our present position. Tracking through the layers of Maori *whakapapa* will eventually connect us to our spiritual origins and to *Papatuanuku*.[2] In this context, however, it is the *whakapapa* of child and family welfare, care, and protection services in relation to the indigenous Maori of Aotearoa/New Zealand that will be traced.

Honouring *Whakapapa*; The Sacredness of our Stories

For Maori, meeting each other, coming together, and discussing issues, *whakapapa* is the first thing that is shared. *Whakapapa* provides the context through which connections are made and from which future relationships and directions develop. This is consistent with Maori beliefs that we understand by looking behind, beneath, and around the issue at hand, rather than directly at the current situation. We believe that in order to orient ourselves to our present and future, we need to firstly examine that which is 'behind.' Only then will we be able to see clearly where we presently stand and where our future directions may lie.

In discussing systems of child and family welfare, *whakapapa* and manifested meanings are clearly important. Welfare policies and practices develop within, and are reflective of historical, political, social, cultural, and economic contexts and relationships, which have evolved over time through the ongoing colonial enterprise. A key thesis of this chapter is that the layers of development of child welfare, care, and protection systems in Aotearoa/New Zealand correspond with the layers of colonialism on which the nation has been built. In Aotearoa/New Zealand, the contexts and relationships facing Maori include genocidal[3] and assimilationist strands, in which child welfare policies and practices have figured significantly.

A Historical Narrative

Early visitors to Aotearoa/New Zealand came, predominantly, from a Victorian English environment that featured a gender-based division of responsibilities for child care, and an emphasis upon private rather than public spheres influencing dress codes, asset ownership, and leadership roles. Alongside these was a particular perspective on the nature of childhood, including a common, and legislatively supported belief in the correctness of physical discipline for children, of the appropriate place of children in society,[4] and the correct way for children to behave.[5] From this perspective, early settlers to this country had some difficulty understanding and appreciating the communal living and working arrangements of Maori, the obvious affection with which children were regarded, the relatively relaxed mode of child rearing, the inclusion of children in all aspects of Maori life, the communal responsibility for child care, the comparative freedom (including sexual freedom) of Maori women, and the central involvement of men in caring for children.[6]

The first concerted wave of colonization was brought by missionaries who worked hard from the mid-nineteenth century particularly to save the souls of Maori, educate them, and turn them from their heathen ways. Missionary efforts, conducted with the noblest of intentions and certainly with the best interests of the people at heart, can be characterized as attempts to gain (appropriate), transform, and thus colonize the minds and spirits of Maori (Walker, 1987; Walker, 1996). Images of nineteenth-century Maori indicate that the missionaries were at least superficially successful in their endeavours. Maori children attended mission schools, and with their families donned the more decorous European clothing of the times, attended Christian services, and developed their literacy skills through regular reading of the Bible. However, while Maori had adopted a number of superficial aspects of British society, their fundamental social systems and structures remained largely intact. It may be argued that Maori appropriated some of what was offered, and added these to their preexisting values and beliefs.

As colonization gained momentum, imperatives to assert its systems, structures, and understandings became more pressing. Maori patterns of communal living, ownership, gender roles, and child-rearing practices, which clearly challenged and obstructed these imperatives, came to be viewed with open negativity.

The Treaty of Waitangi opened the floodgates for (primarily British) settlers. Over five hundred Maori *rangatira* (chiefs) signed the Treaty of Waitangi in 1840. At that time the Maori population was estimated to be around 100,000–200,000, with the non-Maori population estimated to be around 2,000 (Jackson, 1992). Maori systems and structures were dominant in Aotearoa/New Zealand at this stage. Maori were also economically and politically strong and well armed (Jackson, 1992).

In the decades following the signing of the Treaty of Waitangi, Maori vitality declined drastically. In a scenario familiar to many colonized peoples, Maori became subject to a combination of genocidal policies and practices by the colonial administration and settler population. Maori were alienated from their lands at an alarming rate through a combination of shady deals and 'sales,' official confiscations, and government policies designed to drive Maori from their land. The loss of land meant loss of *papakainga*[7] that provided the foundations for Maori *whanau*, *hapu*, and *iwi* cohesiveness, economic facility, and ultimately health and wholeness. Maori populations were decimated by diseases introduced by Europeans,[8] and in some areas 'scorched earth' policies and 'bush-scouring' were accompanied by payment for Maori heads and the large scale imprisonment without trial and deportation of Maori.[9]

By 1896, the Maori population had declined to an estimated 42,000, while Pakeha[10] numbers continued to grow (Pool, 1991). By the early 1900s, the impending extinction of Maori was officially acknowledged.[11] Contrary to popular expectations, however, Maori survived, making a remarkable recovery (Hirini, 1997).

Policies which included attempts to eradicate Maori language[12] and colonial strategies designed to keep Maori in the menial or servant class[13] continued to impact on Maori in the early decades of the twentieth century. In the post–Second World War era, Maori were encouraged and coerced to move from their largely rural settlements to the towns and cities, in order to provide a pool of unskilled and semiskilled labour for the growing urban industries. During the mid-1950s to the mid-1960s, Maori became very rapidly urbanized. Assimilationist policies coexisted with genocidal influences at this time. Maori housing was 'pepper-potted' amongst Pakeha suburbs, and statistical definitions of Maori were designed to ensure that, with intermarriage, Maori would become statistically insignificant, and be subsumed within the European ethnic category.[14] Prior to urbanization, Maori representation in negative social indices, such as prisons and psychiatric institutions, was negligible. Within the first generation of urbanization, however, the picture changed radically, with Maori beginning to feature at ever-increasing rates in negative statistics from the mid-1970s to the present day. It was at this time that the relationship between Maori and state welfare authorities began.

Maori ethnic group members now comprise over 15% of the population.[15] This proportion is growing, and the Maori are expected to make up 22% of the population within the next fifty years. Maori are also a young population, with 37% under the age of fifteen years.[16] However, Maori are grossly overrepresented in indicators of deprivation. Compared to non-Maori, Maori die earlier, are much more likely to be admitted to psychiatric hospitals, to be imprisoned, to die by suicide or accident, to be unemployed, to have children at a young age, to have large families, to live in overcrowded situations, and to live on low incomes.[17]

Colonial Responses to the Treaty of Waitangi: Collaboration or Appropriation?

The Treaty signed in 1840 has been consistently viewed by Maori as a sacred and seminal covenant.[18] Under the terms of the Treaty, Maori agreed to British settlement, and to the establishment by British Crown representatives of their own systems of governance over their own people.[19] British Crown representatives in turn affirmed and guaranteed *rangatira*[20] and *hapu* the continued exercise of *tino rangatiratanga* (absolute authority/chieftainship/sovereignty), and the undisturbed possession of all estates (lands, forests, fisheries), and other taonga (things treasured) including customs, beliefs, and values. However, for around a century, the Treaty of Waitangi was regarded by successive New Zealand governments as a 'nullity.'[21] The Treaty and provisions contained within it were invisible within mainstream colonial discourse, although they were consistently referred to in Maori narratives.

The Treaty of Waitangi is now acknowledged by the Crown and much of the population as the founding document of the New Zealand nation. However, this acknowledgment did not come easily. For some time in the mid-1970s, Aotearoa experienced civil unrest from Maori groups on a scale not seen since the land wars of the previous century. Maori demanded recognition of the Treaty of Waitangi and highlighted unresolved grievances through a variety of protest actions and occupations. To a non-Maori New Zealand population, who had oft proclaimed that the racial harmony in their nation constituted the best race relations in the world (Walker, 1996), the stridency of Maori voices proclaiming something very different came as a shock.

In the mid-1970s, the New Zealand government initiated Waitangi Day celebrations as a national holiday and day of celebration. The focus of the official celebrations was on the Treaty as the foundation of New Zealand nationhood, the coming together of two peoples as one and a source of legitimacy for the New Zealand government. These national celebrations have consistently provided an illustration of the dual discourses operating in relation to the Treaty and to the conflicting understandings of the relationships between Maori and non-Maori which were laid out in the Treaty. The celebrations have provided a forum for mainly Pakeha politicians to affirm the authority of the government of the day throughout the nation and to seek to move from a one people narrative theme to one emphasizing two peoples under one government. Simultaneously, Maori protests have focused on the failure of successive governments to acknowledge the Maori provisions of the Treaty and to implement these. The provision for *tino rangatiratanga* (absolute authority, chieftainship, sovereignty) of *hapu* and *iwi* is viewed as particularly pivotal.

From the perspective of Maori protestors, the national celebrations, while ostensibly honouring the Treaty of Waitangi, actually served to undermine the *hapu* and *iwi tino rangatiratanga* guaranteed in the Treaty of Waitangi. The emphasis on unity between peoples (races) within one nation meant that *hapu* and *iwi rangatiratanga* (tribal and subtribal authority) became invisible, while a focus on the Maori people/race/culture or *Maoritanga* was promoted. In Maori eyes this constitutes another act of cultural imperialism verging, once again, on being genocidal. In the words of John Rangihau, 'Maoritanga is a term coined by the Pakeha to bring the tribes together. Because if you cannot divide and rule, then for tribal people all you can do is unite them and rule. Because then they lose everything by losing their own tribal histories and traditions that give them their identity' (Rangihau, in King, 1992, pp. 189–90).

In recent years, the guarantees of *tino rangatiratanga* and the right to maintain our own values, beliefs, practices, and systems guaranteed in the provisions of the Treaty of Waitangi have been further redefined by government. The Treaty of Waitangi has been rewritten by the Crown as a series of 'Treaty principles.' Central among these are principles of:

• partnership: referring to a partnership between Maori and the Crown
• participation: referring to the right of Maori to participate in processes and structures affecting them
• protection: referring to the active protection of Maori values, culture, rights, and aspirations.

Many Maori consider the redefinition of the Treaty of Waitangi into a set of principles to be a mechanism designed to dilute the effect of the Treaty of Waitangi through the appropriation, assimilation, and transformation of Maori Treaty narratives into a Pakeha discursive framework. For instance, the partnership principle does not specify the nature of the partnership, allowing power imbalances to continue unfettered. The participation principle allows for Maori participation in systems and processes, but does not confer any decision-making power or authority.[22] The protection principle implies continued control by the dominant group, in the nature of a paternalistic Crown-driven power relationship.

The Waitangi Tribunal was formed at a time when the pressure of racial conflict, stemming from demands for the ratification of the Treaty of Waitangi, and demands for social justice for Maori, were reaching their twentieth-century peak.[23] The Tribunal provided an outlet for the heat generated by the race debate. In effect it was one of a number of vehicles designed to allow Maori to let off steam. While the Tribunal was sanctioned to hear Maori accounts, identify breaches relating to the principles of the Treaty of Waitangi, and make recommendations pertaining to these, unlike other judicial bodies, its powers stopped there. Tribunal recommendations were not binding; the government was under no obligation to take heed of recommendations and frequently did not do so.[24]

In the ongoing debates around the interpretation of the Treaty of Waitangi, three things are clear:

1 Maori see the guarantee of *tino rangatiratanga* as a key provision of the Treaty. This implies absolute sovereign authority and, in effect, the status of independent nation states for *hapu* and *iwi* groups. This is consistent with Maori custom and tradition. Within such traditions, *hapu* and *iwi* were responsible and accountable for their own members; they coexisted and worked alongside each other; and, one *iwi*, in the ordinary course of events, would not presume authority over another.

2 The Crown takes the view that the Treaty of Waitangi effected a ceding of sovereignty by Maori to the Crown. The Crown is particularly averse to acknowledging more than one source of sovereignty in the land. The principle of a single source of sovereignty, that being the sovereignty of the Crown, as represented by the New Zealand government, is fundamental to the ongoing colonial endeavour.

3 Maori and non-Maori often agree that the Treaty of Waitangi provides a framework for partnership between peoples. It is the nature of the partnership, and the implementation of it that is in dispute.

Current statutory interpretations of the Treaty inherently ignore Maori understandings of *rangatiratanga*. Maori expectations and aspirations from 1840 until the present have been that the rights guaranteed under the Treaty of Waitangi will be recognized and implemented. This includes the recognition of *hapu* and *iwi* as possessing sovereign authority over themselves and their *taonga* (treasures). Chief amongst the *taonga* that many Maori wish to reclaim is the capacity and autonomy to care for, educate, and protect our *tamariki*[25] and *whanau* (children and families).

Colonization in Social Welfare Discourses

Ethnic statistics relating to Maori children in state care and Maori families who have been subjected to interventions through welfare authorities have been poorly recorded in the past.[26] The result has been that researchers have faced obstacles to gaining a clear statistical picture of the extent and nature of interactions between Maori families and state welfare authorities. This, in turn, has operated first to prevent meaningful academic analysis and dialogue around the historical relationships and interactions between Maori and welfare authorities in Aotearoa/New Zealand and, second, to exclude the lived realities of Maori from official (statistical) discourse.

Anecdotal evidence indicates that large numbers of Maori children were removed from their families by well-meaning social workers, particularly in the post–Second World War era, when there was a massive migration of Maori from rural to urban areas. From the 1960s, through the 1970s, 1980s, and 1990s, many Maori *whanau* had been affected by the taking of children and this was reflected in a common injunction to Maori children to watch out lest the Welfare get you.[27] The removal of Maori children from their families, and the concomitant vilification of these families, was done, of course, 'in the best interests of the child.' It became something of a paternalistic fashion at this time also for middle-class Pakeha to foster or adopt Maori children, with a view to providing them with opportunities that their own *whanau* and communities were seen as unable to provide.

During the mid-1980s, in response to continuing demonstrations of Maori unrest, spaces (vents) were created in a variety of forums for Maori to give voice to their frustrations and their aspirations, and to provide new perspectives based on a Maori worldview. These spaces were created within the very systems identified by Maori as the prime instruments of colonial oppression. For many Maori leaders at the time, this represented an opportunity that was eagerly grasped. Some of our finest minds and senior leaders contributed to provide an extensive vision of social welfare, social policy, and justice systems that would work for and with, rather than against, Maori *whanau* and communities. The report of the Ministerial Advisory Committee on a Maori Perspective for the Department of Social Welfare, known as 'Puao-te-ata-tu' was released in 1986 (Ministerial Advisory Committee, 1986), followed by the report of the Royal Commission on Social Policy (1988), and the report on Maori and the Criminal Justice System (Jackson, 1988). These reports reflected the generous sharing by Maori of many facets of *Maoritanga*[28] and provided the government, officials, policy makers, and practitioners with a more extensive vision of Maori society, values, beliefs, and aspirations than most would have been privy to previously. Maori hopes during these processes were that the new openness to Maori aspirations and considerations signalled an unprecedented era of cooperation and collaboration between Maori and state agencies. Many Maori saw this as a chance to challenge, modify or recast the function of social welfare systems from being part of the appropriation, fragmentation, and colonization of Maori to ultimately providing possibilities for Maori cultural forms, systems, and institutions to coexist, on an equal footing, alongside Western cultural forms, systems, and institutions.[29] Alternatively and more optimistically, there was hope that a new social justice, an inclusive and family-focused Maori model of welfare, might be adopted for all.

In hindsight, the apparent new openness to Maori views signalled a discursive shift from a deficit model, which had positioned Maori and Maori perspectives as unworthy of serious consideration, to an additive discourse which provided for parts of Maori cultural narratives to be added to the existing philosophical framework. Maori people and Maori realities were added to the margins and were still defined as other measured against a centrally positioned Pakeha norm.

Conceptions of Self in Colonization Processes

The most fundamental Pakeha norm, one which underpinned the systems, structures, and understandings that the colonial administration sought to impose, was a particular, deeply rooted and largely unconscious understanding of what constituted a normal, healthy, and correct selfhood. Conceptions of self are culturally based and so pervasive within cultural systems, and ingrained within individual psyches, that they are usually invisible to those that subscribe to them. However, as Landrine (1992) has noted:

> What we assume a self is, by and large predicts our assumptions about how a self relates to others, takes control, develops, 'ought to' behave, think and feel, and 'goes wrong.' Thus culturally determined assumptions

about the self are beneath all Western cultural, clinical concepts and understandings of normalcy. (p. 402)

The conception of self underpinning ongoing colonial processes in Aotearoa/New Zealand has been described by Sampson (1993a) as self-contained individualism. It features these key tenets:

1 That the body is a container that houses the individual; thus the 'essence' of a person, the psychological qualities – will, motivation, emotion, and soul – are housed in the body
2 That all that is contained in the self is separate and distinct from that contained in other selves and other entities. Definitions of healthy selfhood, according to this conception of self, are those that have firm boundaries and function as self-contained units (Love, 2000, 22)

In discussing essentially the same individuocentric conception of self, Landrine (1992) considered that the self

can be described without reference to others ... It can be thought about, analyzed, and discussed in isolation ... Within this conception of self and other, self is seen as primary, with relationships being derivative (that is, the self is seen as pre-existing relationships) and relationships may be rejected if they do not meet the needs of self. (pp. 403–4)

Further, maintaining boundaries between that which is seen as intrinsic or self and that which is seen as extrinsic or other becomes vital to normal and healthy development. This supports assumptions of an internal locus of control and responsibility and hence of the individual accountability that underpins Westminster-style systems of justice, and British models of education as well as child care and protection.

I have identified elsewhere some implications of the self-contained model of self which impinge directly on Western welfare and justice systems. These are

that parents possess rights of ownership over their children; these ownership rights are limited by the authority of the state over its citizens; that the state is comprised of individual citizens who function as self-contained units of production; that responsibility and accountability are located within individuals; that culture (and I would add 'character') is a product of human learning and is contained within individual selves. (Love, 2000, pp. 22–3)

It is this conception of self, with a multitude of attendant implications, that underpins the laws, policies, practices, and institutions set in place by the colonial administration of Aotearoa/New Zealand. It is this conception of self which makes the notion of child protection as divorced from *whanau* (family) well-being seem rational; which can conceptualize a *separation* of the best interests of the child from those of family; which makes the removal of children from their family systems *appear* to provide them with opportunities for health and wholeness; and, which *makes sense* of the notions of ownership reflected in Aotearoa/New Zealand models of adoption and child and family legislation (Love, 2000). It is this individualistic ideology which

> makes the individual the basic unit of social analysis. It supports a politically conservative predisposition to bracket off questions about the structure of a society, about the distribution of wealth and power, for example, and to concentrate instead on questions about the behaviour of individuals within that (apparently fixed) social structure. (Tesh, 1988, p. 161)

This is the ideology which underpins historical and current child and family policy in Aotearoa/new Zealand.

In contrast to this self-contained individualism, Maori conceptions of self may be described as 'ensembled' (Sampson, 1988, 1993a, 1993b). Key features of ensembled conceptions of self include a fluid self-other boundary (maintaining distinctions between self and other is not vital to identity); an inclusive definition of self (the region defined as self may include a number of people, living and dead, and elements of the environment); and a field control orientation (power and control are located in a field of influences that may include but are not confined to self). Sampson (1988) described an ensembled self in the following way:

> Who I am is defined in and through my relations with others: I am completed through those relations and do not exist apart from them. In working for them I am working for myself. (p. 20)

This position accommodates perspectives based on notions of shared (group) responsibility and accountability, and the indivisibility of self from *whanau*, *hapu*, and *iwi* that characterizes Maori views, systems and processes.[30]

Te Wheke: A Model of Maori Well-Being

Pere (1988, 1991) has proposed a model of *whanau* health based on a Maori world view, which provides a useful illustration of an ensembled perspective of self. Her 'Te Wheke: te oranga o te whanau' model utilizes the octopus as a symbol of *whanau* health and well-being.[31] Within this model, the octopus symbolizes the *whanau* or extended family unit. Each tentacle of the octopus represents a dimension which requires sustenance if the *whanau* is to experience health and well-being. The many suckers on each tentacle represent the multitude of facets within each dimension. The tentacles of the octopus are intertwined, representing the interconnectedness of the dimensions. In common with people, the octopus has mechanisms which it can use to protect itself from external threats. If feeling threatened, the octopus may hide behind a black ink veil of its own making, and seek to avoid or flee from the threatening situation. Like people, the octopus is not totally benign and should be approached with care. If injudiciously handled, it can inflict a painful bite with the beak hidden on its underside.

The dimensions for the model proposed by Pere (1988, 1991) are as follows:

Wairua: the spiritual dimension which encompasses all aspects of life is carried with us through our *whakapapa* (genealogy) and is significant in all actions, processes, and destinations. Maori see this dimension as primary.

Mauri: the life force, essence, or ethos that binds together the *wairua* (spirit) and *tinana* (physical) and thus provides the conditions for life. All people and all elements of the natural world (for example, rocks, trees, rivers, birds, spiders) have their own unique *mauri*.

Whanaungatanga: 'family-ness,' *whanau*, *hapu*, and *iwi* relationships and social dynamics. This dimension incorporates notions of interdependence, complementarity of roles, *whanau*-based identities and group affiliation, commitment, and effort.

Tinana: the dimension of physical needs and that which provides sustenance and safety for the body.

Hinengaro: the dimension that encompasses the mind, cognitive processes, thoughts, and intuition. It alludes to the hidden female element and implies a need to respect the sacredness of our private thoughts.

Whatumanawa: the dimension that refers to the seat of deepest emotions and visions. Sustenance for this dimension requires conditions through which we fully experience and express our deepest emotions.[32]

Ha a koro ma a kui ma: *ha* is the breath. *Kui(a)* and *koro(ua)* are the senior elders and ancestors who have passed the breath of life to the generations following them. This dimension emphasizes the indivisibility of the generations and the unity of *whanau*, *hapu*, and *iwi* identity symbolized in the sharing of the ongoing breath of life. Knowledge of heritage and history, use of native language, songs, and traditions and *whakapapa* are important sources of sustenance for this dimension.

Mana ake: often translated as 'prestige, standing, authority,' this dimension refers to the standing of groups of *whanau*, *hapu*, and *iwi* within communities. *Mana* ultimately comes from the gods and is reflected in the spiritual power and protection accorded by them. It is recognized and affirmed by people and is maintained through contributions to the whole and through service and hospitality to others. The *mana* of *whanau*, *hapu*, and *iwi* is indivisible from the *mana* of individuals.

While described briefly here, it should be noted that each of these dimensions can take a lifetime to fully appreciate and develop. If Pere's 'Te Wheke' model is seen as an example of an ensembled conception of self (Sampson, 1988, 1993a, 1993b), it would imply that any actions or decisions relating to the well-being of Maori *whanau* should take into account and operate in ways consistent with the complex webs of meanings, relationships, and needs alluded to above.

Disparate conceptions of self and other underpin the competing realities and dual discourses that have characterized relationships between colonizer and colonized in the history of Aotearoa/New Zealand. While colonial authorities have possessed dominance in terms of power and access to resources for much of the relationship, Maori have maintained discourses of resistance over a number of forums. British colonizers brought with them ingrained cultural assumptions privileging self-contained individualism and they reconstructed systems and institutions based on this privilege throughout Aotearoa/New Zealand. Prior to colonization, Maori had long had their own systems and institutions based around ensembled individualism.[33] These systems and institutions still function in healthy Maori families and communities today.

Key principles of Maori child and family policy include the following: a view of children as products of significant *whakapapa* lines and hence as full spiritual beings with their own mana, shared (extended family and community) responsibility for the care of children,[34] the primacy of *tikanga* in all decisions about appropriate courses of action, and the significance of *utu* in all interactions. The latter two points perhaps require further elaboration.

Tikanga is based in the concept of *tika*, which may be translated as 'right, true, correct and just.' The concept of *tika*, and *tikanga* as the enactment of this is based in considerations of justice, according to that which is right, true, and correct. These considerations incorporate a variety of aspects including all those outlined by Pere (1988, 1991), with *wairua* being a vital core. *Utu* refers to the principle and processes of reciprocity. *Utu* provides a mechanism through which to practise and maintain *tikanga* or that which is *tika*. This principle demands that balance be kept in all relationships, and that respect and hospitality be reciprocated in order to maintain balance in relationships. *Utu* is also the foundation for Maori systems to ensure redress and rebalancing of relationships in cases of wrongdoing. Together these principles and processes provide mechanisms for the management of virtually all situations. Together, these principles and mechanisms account for the importance of justice to Maori people. Maori, even as children, tend to have a very strong sense of justice and injustice. Where there is perceived injustice or imbalance, significant efforts are made to secure justice and balance, utilizing notions and practices associated with *tikanga* and *utu*. This is the basis of traditional and contemporary systems of reconciliation and restorative justice as practised in Maori forums.[35]

Maori principles and practices, based on beliefs such as those outlined above, were marginalized and demonized in the past, and have been appropriated, redefined, and grafted on to individualistic and Eurocentric systems in the present. When considered in light of the totality of colonization experiences, it is not surprising that Maori, along with other colonized peoples, tend to come to any discussion of systems of child and family welfare with a keen awareness of these contexts and often with a profound distrust of such systems.

Ongoing Discourses of Colonization and Resistance

> New analyses and a new language mark, and mask, the 'something' that is no longer called imperialism. For indigenous peoples, one term that has signaled the striking shift in discourse is 'post-colonial.' Naming the world as 'post-colonial' is, from indigenous perspectives, to name colonialism as finished business. (Smith, 1999, p. 98)

The primary agenda of successive governments has been to maintain the sovereign control which is fundamental to ongoing colonization of indigenous peoples. When the hold of government on power and control over Maori was seen to be under serious challenge, Maori were encouraged to participate in governance systems to an extent. The limit of that extent has been to provide the dominant group with resources, including the cultural knowledge and language, which could be appropriated to further solidify the ongoing colonization of Maori. In relation to child and family welfare, care, and protection, there are several facets to this process.

First, Maori coopted to government agencies were required, in order to be intelligible to policy makers, to speak in 'a register' not their own (Sampson, 1993a).[36] Churchill highlighted the 'intellectual imperialism' which creates and maintains the 'compartmentalization' and 'departmentalization' of knowledge and 'the delineation of ... discrete organizational spheres' (1996, pp. 279–80), both processes that mitigate strongly against the possibility of contextual and holistic communications.[37]

Second, Waitere-Ang and Johnson (1999) have noted that

> inclusion and how we as Maori are identified as being included, continues to be a problematic process. Inclusion appears to be based primarily on rules that we have no control over and the result is actually one of exclusion ... the focus appears to be one of physically including us, yet remaining ideologically absent. (pp. 2–3)

In effect, invitations to Maori to participate in social policy discussions provided a forum for the expression of Maori frustrations and aspirations, and the opportunity to be heard at the level of policy within the institutions and systems that had enormous influence on the lives of Maori *whanau*, but simultaneously it presented the challenge of presenting Maori views in a way that was comprehensible and palatable to Pakeha policy makers. The opportunity came at a price. Aspects of Maori language and culture were pulled out of their holistic contexts and presented in a necessarily compartmentalized manner. Lankshear (1994) argued that 'the struggle for symbolic power through words, their meaning and ideological capture, often results in the loss of the conceptual validity of much that is embodied within language' (as cited in Waitere-Ang & Johnston, 1999, p. 10). Through separation from their *whakapapa* or contextual base, Maori language and culture become lifeless and empty. The result is a loss of *mauri* or life force and strength within the words and concepts.

A further layer within this process involves the claiming and appropriation of Maori resources, in the form of cultural knowledge and language, and the use of these to further assert control over the Indigenous population. This is, of course, a primary feature of ongoing colonial operations. In an analysis of intellectual and cultural property rights, Mead (1996) argued:

> Colonial powers are still in the infancy stages of looking back at the first wave of colonization and acknowledging that their violent acts of seizing foreign lands and territories in order to develop settlements and secure resources ... were calculated acts of genocide ... Some regard cultural and intellectual property rights as the second wave of colonization because the principles ... are seen as a continuation of the ideologies of foreign conquest and domination. (p. 23)

In utilizing Maori terms and appropriating Maori processes in child and family welfare and in care and protection legislation, policies, and procedures, state officials and workers assume, as previously noted, an authority to define, describe, and prescribe the nature and form of Maori terms and processes. Further, the information provided by Maori informants has been used to develop culturally sensitive strategies and programs which seek to be palatable to Maori, while maintaining the fundamentally oppressive premises and power dynamics intact. In relation to child and family welfare policies, this means that a veneer of extended family involvement, consensus decision making and collective, social justice has been added to a centralized, individualistic, authoritarian, and punitive frame.

During the time when Maori voices were not heard anywhere within the developing child and family welfare, care, and protection discourses, genocidal child and family social work was able to proceed, in the main, without challenge. As ventilation spaces were created for Maori to present their views and aspirations, others were provided with Maori narratives and presented with a variety of Maori language terms, concepts, and ideas. Dominant system representatives often appropriated the knowledge provided to them, presuming the right to reuse, redefine, and ultimately marginalize Maori narratives, as they were grafted onto Anglo-American systems.

This brings us back to a consideration of the nature of cultural narratives, and in particular, the issue of subtexts. For all of their fullness and clarity to Maori, the narratives presented in the various reports could only ever present a partial picture to those who operated outside of the discursive frameworks from within which the cultural narratives emanated. This is because, without the culturally constituted webs of meaning that are needed to generate whole (holistic) meanings in the spaces between the words, non-Maori could access only the overt narratives, and would normally never know the subtextual narratives on which the overt narratives were predicated. Hence, attempts to include Maori perspectives without a serious examination of existing subtextual dominant paradigms could not be truly successful.

Structural and Systemic Impediments to the Development of Positive Indigenous Systems

The Children, Young Persons and their Families Act (1989) was hailed by many as signalling a new direction in cooperation and collaboration between Maori and Crown (state) welfare and youth justice agencies. It drew on the reports mentioned above and sought to address some key issues that had been identified by Maori. These included an apparent recognition of the importance of *whanau, hapu,* and *iwi,* a reconstruction of the *whanau hui* process through the system of family group conferencing, the option to provide (cultural) lay advocates to represent Maori perspectives, and provisions for the development of Iwi Social Services[38] which would theoretically allow Maori the authority to provide care and protection for their own people.

Impediments to the realization of positive systems of child and family practice are both structural and systemic and relate, in part, to institutional and personal racism. In the years since the passing of the Act, Maori have been expressing concern at a number of aspects of the legislation and its implementation. In a review of a range of policies and Acts of Parliament relating to family law in Aotearoa/New Zealand, Durie-Hall and Metge (1992) concluded that the basic assumptions underpinning most family law and policy in Aotearoa/New Zealand were in conflict with Maori understandings and practices regarding family/*whanau*. The effect of these conflicting assumptions is that Maori social forms and practices have been largely ignored and, making no substantive accommodation for these forms and practices, can be seen as constituting an 'attack' (Metge & Durie-Hall, 1992, p. 50) on Maori beliefs, forms and practices regarding family/*whanau*.

While Metge and Durie-Hall (1992) would advocate for the accommodation of Maori perspectives within family related legislation, such accommodations do not address, and may well act to disguise the fundamental differences between Maori conceptions of self and the

Western conceptions of self that govern family law, child and family welfare policy, and psychological practices in Aotearoa/New Zealand. Accommodation as currently practised also fails to provide for the Treaty guarantee of *tino rangatiratanga*. In 1996, an authoritative voice on family law in Aotearoa/New Zealand noted:

> Article 2 of the Treaty guarantees tino rangatiratanga (autonomy) to Maori. This is not compatible with the statutory responsibility that is vested in the NZCYP Service by the CYP&F Act 1989. (Children, Young Persons and Their Families Service, 1993)

Love (2000) was also critical of the operation of the much heralded family group conferences on a number of grounds. These included the fact that a Maori process had been appropriated and transformed, thereby removing the very elements that were pivotal to its successful operation, including *whanau rangatiratanga*.[39] She also noted that there was no devolution of power and authority within the system, resulting in a situation where *whanau*, *hapu* and *iwi* were being asked to resolve problems within *whanau*, *hapu*, and *iwi*, but were not receiving the resources required to do so. Also, rather than moving towards the (Maori) goal of *tino rangatiratanga*, family group conferences could represent a further insidious encroachment into Maori *whanau* life and domains of authority. Jackson (1995) commented:

> Justice for Maori does not mean the grafting of Maori processes onto a system that retains the authority to determine the extent, applicability and validity of those processes. (p. 34)

A number of specific instances may be cited to illustrate the interplay of structural and systemic forces, based on colonialism and institutional and personal racism, which constitute the grafting process alluded to by Jackson (1995):

- 'Care and Protection Panels' include Maori community representation but decision-making authority rests with state-sponsored care and protection co-ordinators.
- There is provision for the use of lay advocates to represent child and family cultural perspectives within the Family Court system, but decisions about using lay advocates depends on the discretion of the

court. This is an example of an add-on approach which is dependent upon the goodwill of dominant system representatives.[40]

- A variety of culturally sensitized Anglo-American training and assessment instruments are used which feature decorative Maori border designs and footnotes.
- In relation to provisions for the establishment of Iwi Social Services, which many Maori saw as a potential pathway to the actualization of *tino rangatiratanga* aspirations, Bradley (1995a) noted:

By 1992 DSW was receiving considerable criticism from iwi for its lack of progress in determining standards for IA (Mason, 1992). Evidence mounted to show that Maori were gaining less information from businesses within DSW; that Maori organizations were monitored more harshly; that they were given fewer resources to cover a larger target group; and that they were discriminated against by care and protection co-ordinators who were failing to include or were actively excluding whanau members from Family Group Conferences. (pp. 30–1)[41]

- Although the Act apparently provided a legislative mandate and provided for resources to be allocated towards the establishment of Iwi Social Services, departmental staff prejudice and discrimination had not changed greatly from the previous decade (Bradley, 1994, 1995a, 1995b, 1995c; Rangihau, 1992).
- Structural impediments to the development of positive *iwi* systems are apparent when the notions of 'Iwi Authority/Iwi Social Services' contained in the legislation is examined. Under the terms of the Act, an 'Iwi Social Service' is a body approved by the Director-General in accordance with the terms of the Act. The *rangatiratanga* or authority of *iwi* is thus subsumed under the authority of the Director-General of Social Welfare, an arm of the state.
- Further, it is officials working within the Department of the Director-General of Social Welfare who determine the criteria that *iwi* groups must fulfil in order to be approved, and at what level. The regulations that officials have produced meant that Maori tribal entities must conform to a variety of processes, procedures, and regulations modelled on the very Pakeha institutions from which they are seeking to remove themselves. Some Maori authorities have declined to participate in this process as it is seen as in conflict with the *tino rangatiratanga* provisions of the Treaty of Waitangi. The

processes and structures required of tribal groups seeking to be recognized under the terms of the Act may be described as replacing white bureaucracies with brown bureaucracies (Walker, 1996).

• In the mid-1990s, CYPS (Children and Young Persons Service) initiated a public information campaign which targeted Maori radio and print media. The campaign depicted the service as having a family support orientation and encouraged families who were experiencing difficulties caring for their children to contact the service for help and support. When some Maori parents sought help, their contact with the service was recorded as an official 'notification.'[42] Some parents and children were subject to intrusive processes by social workers and children were sometimes forcibly removed as a result. By the turn of the century, the service had reverted to a 'dob in a neighbour' campaign, where communities were encouraged to protect children thought to be at risk by reporting suspicious families to the service.

In the conclusion of this section, I wish to discuss another aspect of the ongoing colonization of Aotearoa/New Zealand within the child and family welfare, care, and protection arena. This aspect concerns the cooption of Maori within the state welfare system. There are two avenues that have been tried in this respect. The first is the recruitment of more Maori into social work and social policy training programs, resulting in a larger pool of academically qualified Maori social workers. The second avenue involves the employment of *iwi* social workers (those who have worked voluntarily or under various schemes for their *iwi* or local communities in capacities outside of statutory systems). Both of these avenues have strengths and weaknesses. Positive outcomes include an increase in the number of Maori who know and understand how the system operates, an increase in the number of Maori who perhaps can work with whanau in culturally appropriate ways, and an increase in the number of Maori who are reaching senior positions and who may be able to effect positive changes within existing systems, structures, and processes.

The primary problem with this approach is that statutory systems, based on assumptions of self-contained individualism and with a strong punitive focus (the police and CYPFS[43] have a primary collegial relationship in child abuse reporting protocols),[44] are not designed to allow Maori (or other ensembled self) perspectives and ways of working to flourish.[45] As a result, Maori workers are employed for their Maori knowledge and standing, but pressured into conforming to institutional mores that are in conflict with *tikanga Maori*.[46] This is particularly problematic for workers who have come from *iwi* or Maori community practice, where the trust of their communities and their own standing among these people are pivotal to the success of their work. One of the side effects of the cooption of Maori into the current statutory regime has been that many of the social activists of the 1970s and 1980s have become the social service providers of the new millennium. Battling a system from within is a role that consumes enormous energy and can limit vision, particularly when competition for limited resources for Maori services is fierce. This position also leaves Maori workers exposed to being labelled by institutional representatives as incompetent or unprofessional, if we do not conform to institutional mores. On the other hand, Maori workers perceived as conforming to the norms within statutory welfare systems may be viewed by their *whanau, hapu, iwi,* and communities as brown faces doing the dirty work that was previously done by white social workers. It is an unenviable position.

The Children, Young Persons and their Families Act (1989) provided some potential for new and positive systems of child and family welfare and protection to develop in Aotearoa/New Zealand. However, meeting this potential is largely dependent on the understanding and goodwill of mainly non-Maori officials and practitioners. As I have argued elsewhere (Love, 2000), while

> the Aotearoa/New Zealand legislation ... features some elements of a complex system of Maori cultural values, beliefs and practices ... the danger ... is that the apparent state commitment to a culturally appropriate process is clearly limited. It may, in fact, serve only to provide a brown veneer for a white system that has historically contributed to state run programmes of cultural genocide and whanau dis-memberment. It may also serve to undermine Maori systems and institutions and to co-opt Maori people and cultural forms as agents in our own oppression. (p. 29)

Developing Conceptual Frameworks

In order to effectively recognize and analyse the processes discussed in this paper, it is helpful to have a conceptual framework. For understanding relationships between research and Maori, Waitere-Ang and Johnston (1999) identify 'four theoretically different ... frontiers that have impacted, and continue to impact on Maori' (p. 14). These four frontiers are as follows:

1 the unnamed frontier – characterized by a universalistic narrative and assumptions of objective truth based in dominant group realities and excluding indigenous voices
2 the colonial frontier – where culturally different 'others' may be 'physically present but [are] ideologically absent' (Waitere-Ang & Johnston, 1999, p. 4)
3 The indigenized frontier – characterized by an apparently 'Maori friendly' 'cultural additive' approach, within which 'ethnic additives become the adornment of unchanging structures and processes ... [and which erroneously assumes] that the inclusion of Maori equates to empowerment' (Waitere-Ang & Johnston, 1999, pp. 4–5, 10)
4 the Indigenous frontier – which provides a Maori-centred cultural, ideological, and structural framework, where the focus is on 'structures, decision-making and identifying how Maori are excluded ... a Maori centred/Kaupapa Maori approach places Maori at the centre' (Waitere-Ang & Johnston, 1999, p. 14).

Elements of all four frontiers exist in Aotearoa/New Zealand today. The colonial and Indigenized frontiers are dominant within statutory systems, while Maori are pushing to extend the fourth Indigenous frontier.

Whakapapa Moves On: Towards New Partnerships

I wish now to outline some of the positive initiatives that are happening in Aotearoa/New Zealand, and to identify key features of these. In my observation, these positive systems are pushing the 'Indigenous frontiers' (Waitere-Ang & Johnston, 1999). They are largely operating outside of the statutory systems of child and family welfare, care, and protection.

Maori social service providers working under the auspices of health, educational, church, and justice authorities frequently develop services that are consistent with Maori holistic philosophy. This means that, as well as attending to the immunization of babies, for instance, Maori health workers (often informally or from their positions of authority as members of the *whanau* or community) will advocate for the housing

needs of a teenage mother, facilitate her access to personal health services and benefit entitlements, provide personal counsel, link her with
extended *whanau* and community groups who can provide social contact and support, encourage her participation in cultural activities, and
teach her about the sacredness of her own *whakapapa* and that of
her child. Recalling the dimensions of Pere's 'Te Wheke' model (1988,
1991), these workers are effectively providing sustenance for *tinana*,
whanaungatanga, mana ake, mauri, wairuatanga, hinengaro, whatumanawa,
and *ha a kui ma a koro ma* (see pp. 248–9). This type of informal arrangement operates through the goodwill of workers, outside of official job
descriptions. Maori in mainstream organizations, who are working in
the connected, holistic, and strength-based ways consistent with *tikanga*
Maori, can run into conflict with management and colleagues as a
result. Love (1999) discussed how Maori workers operating holistically
within mainstream individualistic organizations are identified as unprofessional, incompetent, and as having boundary issues and anger
problems. However a number of Maori groups provide *kaupapa* Maori
services, with management who utilize existing funding categories cre-
atively to provide support for these ways of working.

Another site of the reclamation of *rangatiratanga* through use of *tikanga*
Maori processes are the initiatives taken within Maori *whanau*, communities, and *marae*,[47] which rarely come to public attention, but which
involve the utilization of Maori systems and processes to address issues
such as physical and sexual abuse within *whanau*. These processes often
involve the use of *whanau hui*, and practical utilization of traditional
concepts, such as those outlined in 'Te Wheke' (Pere, 1988). They are
typically initiated and led by *whanau* elders, often women, and they
operate outside of state regulated systems. These processes involve
whanau discussion and decision making and operate according to a
tikanga framework. Its principal aims are to uphold the *mana* of *whanau*
(which necessitates a focus on and building upon family strengths), and
to use shame based rather than guilt-based moderators of behaviour,[48]
which utilize powerful traditional processes based on *wairua* (spirit),
whakapapa (connections), and *utu* (reciprocity) to promote balance, reconciliation, and healing. Sometimes the consensus decision of the *whanau*
is to approach statutory authorities. However, this decision is an outcome of the *rangatiratanga* or authority of the *whanau* and represents a
mid-to-end-point rather than a beginning of the process. This model
provides for *whanau* to enter into engagement with statutory bodies
from a position derived from the authority of their own values, beliefs,

and decision-making processes and which ensures *whanau* and *hapu* support is provided throughout the process.

Te Wero is a new *kaupapa* Maori program targeting sex offenders in Maori communities. The program aims to work with *whanau* and communities in a pro-active manner, facilitating the institution of the above processes and providing access to appropriate therapeutic programs for abusers and those who have been abused. Te Wero is currently negotiating the terms of its relationship with its mainstream sponsor. One of the issues to be addressed is that the requirements of the primary funding body for community-based sex offender programs are seen to undermine the *rangatiratanga* principle and *whanau* empowerment philosophy of the *kaupapa* Maori program. As a result, alternative sources of funding are being sought.

On a more formal level, the Lower Hutt Family Centre has developed a structure that incorporates three autonomous sections: Maori, Pakeha, and Pacific Peoples. The centre provides a working model of partnership within which culturally appropriate models of family therapy have developed, and protocols put in place, to protect the rights of each section to have an authoritative voice in relation to its own peoples.[49] The Family Centre has developed a therapeutic model known as 'Just Therapy.' The model is based in *tikanga* (right, correct, appropriate, and just process) and uses the tenets of *whakapapa* (belonging), *wairua* (spirit), *mana* (sacredness), and *rangatiratanga* (liberation and authority).

The Lower Hutt Family Centre also has refused to be confined to the practice of family therapy. The Centre recognized that the process of family therapy, and the confidentiality that implied, kept stories of social disadvantage and oppression locked within four walls. Under traditional Anglo-American family therapy models, all the workers could do was to alleviate the symptoms as much as possible and then send families out to the same conditions as before. The Family Centre became involved in the active provision of community support, advocacy, and political activity in an effort to address the issues external to families, which were creating and maintaining their problems.

The Family Centre also recognized that community advocacy and political protest, while important, were not effectively getting the stories that families had to tell to the law and policy makers. The Centre created an independent social policy research unit, involving all three sections. The social policy research unit engages in social policy research designed to highlight the effects of political and economic policies on families, and to provide strong research-based arguments for social justice. Through the combined use of quantitative and qualitative research, the Centre has been instrumental in the introduction of a number of positive social policy changes.

Conclusion

Although there are some positive moves and individual success stories, the position of Maori as a group across a range of social indicators is uniformly negative. The place of Maori in negative social statistics is a direct result of the loss of resources wrought through colonization.[50]

Colonization, by definition, is an abusive process. It is a process designed to minimize the resources of the colonized group, stunting their ability to flourish, and to maximize the resources of the colonizing group. The preceding analysis of the *whakapapa* of statutory child and family services in Aotearoa/New Zealand tracked the colonization role of these services in the past and the present. However, statutory welfare services themselves exist within a wider colonial context which structures the power dynamics, ideologies, and perceptions permeating social services. In Aotearoa/New Zealand, this broader context is influenced through consistently negative media portrayals of Maori, many of which depict Maori as incorrigibly savage or incompetent. Such portrayals serve to reinforce racist stereotypes and undermine efforts by Maori to be seen as credible and capable thinkers, strategists, and providers of services for our own people. The tragedy of this situation is that as statutory agencies and individuals try increasingly hard to save us from ourselves, Maori distrust and (justifiable) perceptions of a punitive and controlling system grow. This, in turn, reinforces a bunker mentality that sees Maori *whanau* close ranks against the state welfare authorities. Consequently our people are seen as resistant to help and well-intentioned interventions. A second result is that we are increasingly identified as a problem group, and more resources are poured into helping to resolve 'our problems.' Inevitably, these resources are used to maintain the dominance of existing systems, processes, and the assumptions on which these are based, which is what Maori are actively resisting.

Two possible solutions are apparent at this time. The first involves a true devolution of power and resources to Maori. This is based on the premise that, if Maori had control over resources, systems, and structures, resistance would be less, outcomes would be improved, and the enormous social, emotional, and financial costs of propping up the existing system would be significantly reduced.

A second scenario would see a complete overhaul of existing child and family legislation, policies, and practices. This would be a major shift in attitudes and perceptions among the creators and appliers of these mechanisms. This would entail large shifts in conceptions of relationships between the state and families.

In order to move towards truly positive and liberating models of child and family welfare services for Maori and/or all citizens, we need to clearly identify the pitfalls that have plagued relationships thus far, as well as the gains that have been made. There are several points:

- The embedded assumptions of self-contained individualism that permeate our current legislation and policies need to be exposed and considered. We need to move from an exclusive focus on individuals, individual families, and pathologies to a focus on social conditions, social justice, and family and community strengths. Approaches based upon concepts of ensembled selves provide possibilities for new attitudes, practices, and processes.
- We need to explicitly acknowledge the ongoing impact of colonization, and the racism which supports it. Colonization and racism are often seen as historical issues. Yet they are very much alive in our country and elsewhere. In order to avoid collaborating in the modern forms of colonization and racism, we need to be able to recognize their evolving forms in contemporary contexts. We also need to work actively to remove the vestiges of colonial mentalities from our selves, our systems, and our structures.
- In narrative family therapy practice, we recognize the value of insider knowledge, and the fact that families are experts on themselves; they are the ones who best know their own problems and can best identify their own solutions. Movement in this direction has been apparent in our current welfare system. However, recognition of family and community expertise must be accompanied by community empowerment manifested in the generation and ownership of solutions. This involves a big step away from the other key tenet of colonialism, the investment in the power of a single sovereignty.
- The tendency has been for state employees to be defined as state servants, whose role is to fulfil the functions prescribed by the state. An alternative is to *really* view children, families, and communities as our customers. Maori currently represent a significant group of

unhappy customers. As dissatisfied customers, the choice not to use the service (voluntarily at least) is often the first choice. If the service were viewed as safe and supportive, rather than punitive and denigrating, the likelihood of Maori voluntarily accessing services at an early point would be significantly increased.

• A further issue is the need to understand the financial implications of continuing to operate welfare systems that consume large amounts of resources and frequently produce negative outcomes. The alternative of positive investment in communities may well be more cost-effective. Considering the relatively youthful Maori population, such investments are particularly important. Our nation cannot afford to continue to incarcerate and marginalize Maori at the present rate.

Poroporoaki – Final Word

Harakeke (the flax bush) is a key material in Maori society, providing the basis of much of our clothing, construction, artistic, and medicinal materials. The centre shoot of the *harakeke* represents the *mokopuna* (child), the next pair of leaves embracing either side of the centre shoot represents the parents, and the outer leaves represent the grandparents and previous generations, who are there to nurture and protect the younger generations. The centre shoot of the flax is the source of new growth and rejuvenation. It is the life source of the plant, which provides sustenance for the bell-bird that sings its song of welcome to each new day with joy and prosperity.

Hutia te rito o te harakeke	Pluck the centre of the flax
Kei hea ra te korimako e?	And where will the bell-bird be?
Ka ki mai koe	You ask me,
'He aha te mea nui o	'What is the most important thing,
te ao?'	in this world?'
Ka ki atu au	I reply
'He tangata, He tangata,	'It is people, it is life, it is
He tangata'	everything.'

NOTES

1 While I use the terms 'Maori' and 'Maoritanga' throughout this paper, I acknowledge and support perspectives which see the use of a homogeniz-

ing framework, while convenient at times, as contradictory to *iwi* (tribal) identities and *tino rangatiratanga* (authority).

2 *Papatuanuku (Papa)* refers to our Mother Earth

3 Genocide may be defined as 'the systematic attempt to destroy a race or people' and ethnocide may be defined as 'the systematic attempt to destroy completely the culture of a people' (Sluker, 1995). Both are characteristic of the cultural modification processes forced on tribal peoples by colonial governments around the world (Bodley, 1990). I have argued elsewhere that distinctions between genocide and ethnocide are moot, 'as the destruction of a culture and ethnic characteristics effectively equate to the destruction of a people' (Love, 1999).

4 Consideration of the appropriate place of children in society was also based, of course, on class considerations.

5 A common colloquialism still heard sometimes today is that 'children should be seen and not heard.'

6 See Mikaere (1999) for a discussion on the consequences of settlers from a highly gender-divided, patriarchal context interpreting and interacting with a nonpatriachal, communalistic Maori society.

7 *Papakainga* refers to home bases.

8 Several epidemics decimated Maori populations, with influenza and measles wreaking devastation.

9 The Waitangi Tribunal 'Taranaki Report' (1996) details these events in the province of Taranaki.

10 Pakeha refers to white-skinned New Zealanders.

11 The Superintendent of Wellington Province recorded that 'the Maoris are dying out and nothing can save them. Our plain duty as good, compassionate colonists is to smooth their pillow. Then history will have nothing to reproach us with' (Buller, 1884, p. 54, as cited in Pool, 1991, p. 28).

12 Maori were subject to compulsory state education, within which Maori language was often banned and many, many Maori were strapped or beaten for speaking their mother tongue.

13 Smith (1992, as cited in Waitere-Ang & Johnson, 1999) describes how 'native schools' prepared Maori men and women for menial and physical labour.

14 The definition of Maori as used in census and other official statistics was a person of half or more Maori blood. As Maori blood became diluted, they would theoretically cease to exist as Maori. This and other assimilationist strategies are fundamentally genocidal in nature.

15 Statistics in this section are drawn from the New Zealand Department of Statistics website: www.statistics.govt.nz as of June, 2002.

16 This compares to 22.8% of the total population.

17 For example, the fertility rate for Maori women at ages fifteen to nineteen is almost four times that of non-Maori and Maori women are almost twice as likely as non-Maori to have had five or more children. Fifty-three per cent of prison inmates were Maori in 2000, and Maori prison inmate numbers are forecast to grow to 59% by 2013. Although some of the low incomes received by Maori may relate to overrepresentation amongst welfare beneficiaries and in low-paid occupations, Maori receive lower median incomes than non-Maori in similar occupations, and also have lower median incomes than non-Maori with similar levels of education. (Statistics New Zealand, 2002)

18 There were in fact at least two versions of the Treaty of Waitangi, one of which is in the English language and carried different meanings to the Maori language version. I concentrate here on the Maori language version as this version was signed by over five hundred chiefs and is the version which should be recognized under the principle of contra preferentum.

19 This is consistent with Maori custom within which each *iwi* (tribe) has their own *rangatiratanga* (chieftainship, authority and responsibility) for their own people and resources. It was seen as proper that *te iwi Pakeha* (the white-skinned tribe), through their rangatira (or chief, in this case the queen of England) should have authority over and take responsibility for their own.

20 *Rangatira* here refers to chiefs.

21 This view of the Treaty of Waitangi emerged from an 1888 High Court decision by Prendergast, in which the Treaty was characterized as a simple nullity.

22 This principle can be interpreted in terms of participation through representation and consultation. This often means that a Maori person or perspective is included along with ten or more non-Maori in consultation processes, with little weight given to the Maori voice. The notion of inclusion (participation) without power is examined further at a later point.

23 The Waitangi Tribunal was established in 1975 and is composed of Maori and non-Maori members. It is charged with conducting hearings into, reporting on, and making recommendations in regard to alleged breaches of the principles of the Treaty of Waitangi. The Tribunal is empowered to accept claims made by any Maori person on an alleged Treaty breach either historical (from 1840) or contemporary.

24 In 1996, the Waitangi Tribunal issued the first report into events in Taranaki, those pertaining to my own history, as described above. The

Tribunal reviewed the events of 1840 to the present, including the scorched earth and bush scouring activites, destruction and burning of homes and villages, and human devastation. In its report, the Waitangi Tribunal described some of the actions taken by colonial forces and governments against Taranaki Maori as constituting 'a holocaust.' The use of this term created a furore amongst politicians, the media and a non-Maori public eager to deny that any such thing could have taken place. Numbers of non-Maori and the media expressed scorn for the notion that anything that could have happened to Maori in this country could possibly be seen to constitute a holocaust. Media reported that Maori members of parliament were banned from using the 'H' word, defenders of the use of the word in relation to Maori were vilified, and the use of the term was effectively excluded from public discourse. This despite the fact that the events referred to by the Tribunal undeniably met dictionary definitions of a holocaust.

25 *Tamariki* is a term for children

26 This may relate to the policies referred to previously, which were designed to render ethnicity invisible and replace it with a 'one people' philosophy, a philosophy related in turn to expectations that Maori were facing extinction and to mechanisms that were designed to eliminate Maori from statistical existence See Love (1999) for an elaboration on the transformation of expectations of extinction to mechanisms designed to statistically eliminate Maori presence.

27 The injunction to 'watch out' is used to remind us to listen, to behave well, and to be careful.

28 Maori culture, world view, way of being. However I refer to the previously cited comments of Rangihau (1992), and to note 1.

29 The extremely negative reaction of Pakeha politicians to Jackson's 1988 report, *Maori and the criminal justice system* (which openly proposed recognition and support for a separate Maori justice system) mitigated against this latter hope (see Love, 1999).

30 As a reminder; *whanau* refers to extended family; *hapu* to subtribal groups of extended families who share common genealogy; and *iwi* refers to tribes composed of *hapu* groups with an eponymous ancestor.

31 Literally translated as 'The octopus: The well-being of the family.'

32 The expression of emotion referred to here is not necessarily, or even primarily, verbal expression. Western practitioners often require people to 'describe' their emotions in words, or to 'talk about what they are feeling.' This can serve to negate the *whatumanawa* by reducing that which may be more profound than words can express to the level of cognitively mediated sentence structures.

33 I have discussed the nature of *tikanga* as a basis of Maori law and decision-making processes in more detail elsewhere (Love, 2000).

34 This includes shared responsibilities across genders and age groups. Older siblings participate in the care of younger children, and senior family members (rather than parents) had/have primary decision-making rights and responsibilities for younger *whanau* members.

35 It is important to distinguish between Maori forums, in which *tikanga, utu,* and related systems and meanings can have full expression, and those forums that are cloaked in aspects of Maori culture and form, but cannot be classified as *kaupapa* Maori, or Maori centred.

36 According to Sampson (1993a), in order to be heard, 'serviceable others ... must use the approved forms of the dominant groups ... merely having a voice is not sufficient if that voice must speak in a register that is alien to its own specificity, and in doing so loses its own desires and interest. While having a voice is preferable to being held silent, in so far as that voice is not reflecting one's own interests, desires and experiences, then one may speak, but only to further the dominant groups' agenda' (pp. 10–11).

37 Churchill (1996, p. 279) lists the domains of 'sociology, theology, psychology ... archaeology, geography, astronomy' and so on, as illustrating the compartmentalization of knowledge. I would add the departmentalization of social welfare, justice, education, and health as examples of the departmentalization of social systemic spheres. He lists the organizational spheres of 'church, state, business, education, art' as examples of these delineations (p. 280). He further proposes that 'the system of Euro-supremacist domination depends for its continued maintenance and expansion, even its survival, upon the reproduction of its own intellectual paradigm – its approved way of thinking, seeing, understanding, being – to the exclusion of all others' (p. 281).

38 Tribally based social services.

39 *Whanau rangatiratanga* here refers to the authority and decision-making powers of extended family groups.

40 Judges have had variable attitudes to the appointment of lay advocates on cultural grounds; some rarely if ever consider them to be necessary, some appoint lay advocates but may not give due weight to their submissions (possibly because of limited understandings of the cultural meanings that they provide). The fact that the appointment of such advocates is additional to the core process in Family Courts means that they represent an added extra cost, rather than an integral component.

41 DSW is the Department of Social Welfare, which has undergone several transformations and is now known as 'Child, Youth and Family' service

(CYFs). The service is still colloquially known as 'the Welfare' or 'DSW' in some Maori circles. IA refers here to Iwi Authorities. This article was written before amendments to the Act which resulted in a renaming and redefinition of Iwi Authority Social Services (IAs) to 'Iwi Social Services.'

42 That is, a notification of a risk or occurrence of abuse, neglect, or risk.

43 The statutory agency responsible for child care and protection in Aotearoa/ New Zealand has undergone several nominal changes, the most recent being a change in name from Children and Young Persons Service (CYPS) to Children, Young Persons and their Families Agency (CYPFA), and then Child, Youth and Family Service (CYFS).

44 For instance, the National protocol between the Ministry of Education, the New Zealand School Trustees Association, and the New Zealand Children and Young Persons Service (1996) requires school principals to ensure notification to NZCYPS or the police if abuse of a child or young person is disclosed or suspected.

45 By way of example, state social workers (including Maori) are required to have professional supervision. Maori workers may have cultural supervision in addition. Cultural supervision is viewed as an adjunct, an extra support for Maori workers, as opposed to a fully integrated alternative. The professional supervision remains central.

46 *Tikanga* Maori here refers to right, correct, appropriate, and just ways of acting as defined within a Maori cultural framework.

47 *Marae* are the bastions of *rangatiratanga*. They are usually comprised of land and a building or buildings and provide communal centres which operate in the main according to *tikanga* Maori.

48 There are no words in the Maori language that equate to the English language expressions 'sorry' or 'thank you.' Rather it is practical demonstrations of reciprocity, rebalancing, and processes of restoration across a number of dimensions that rule Maori processes.

49 In the case of culturally mixed families, negotiation takes place, but if the relationships are between Pakeha and Maori participants, Maori voices have authority in recognition of the principles of social justice and rangatiratanga.

50 The resources referred to here include physical, spiritual, emotional, and community or people resources as outlined, for example in the model, Te Wheke (Pere, 1988, 1991).

51 The arena that is currently exempt from these depictions is the sporting arena, where Maori are allowed to be heroes.

11 First Nations Child and Family Services and Indigenous Knowledge as a Framework for Research, Policy, and Practice[1]

MARLYN BENNETT and CINDY BLACKSTOCK

Introduction

Children of the First Nations were best cared for prior to colonization. True since the beginning, Indigenous knowledge informed the values, beliefs, and practices of caring for children, youth, and families. Although the specifics varied with the significant diversity of Aboriginal peoples in Canada,[2] care was generally provided according to a holistic world view in which children held a place as important and respected members of an interdependent community and ecosystem. The holistic world view is the antithesis of the individual rights basis on which Canadian child welfare legislation and practice are premised.

First Nations child and family service agencies face the difficult task of building on communal rights, interdependence, and knowledge, cultural strengths often diametrically opposed to legal requirements imposed by Euro-Western values, laws, regulations, and standards as embodied in the delegated model of service delivery (Taylor-Henley & Hudson, 1992). The requirement to use provincial legislation arises from section 88 of the Indian Act. Section 88 says that provincial laws of general application apply on Indian reserves whenever the Indian Act is silent on an issue, and such is the case in child welfare. For First Nations child and family service agencies to deliver services on reserve, they must received delegated authority from the provincial/territorial government according to the provincial/territorial child welfare statute and reach a complementary agreement with the federal government to fund such services. The complexities of delivering services under the delegated model are significant. It requires the ability to develop and deliver child welfare based on Indigenous ways of knowing and being, but within the ambit of Euro-Western child welfare legal structures that have largely failed to meet the needs of Aboriginal children (Aboriginal Justice Inquiry – Child Welfare Initiative, 2001). In addition, service inequities arise as First Nation child welfare agencies are funded by a national funding formula (known as Directive 20-1) that does not adjust for the differences in provincial/territorial child welfare legislation (Assembly of First Nations and Department of Indian Affairs and Northern Development, 2000).

The delegated model is an interim measure designed to meet the immediate and pressing needs of First Nations children and families while political leaders work to have Aboriginal laws recognized. Morse (1984) describes the limitations of programs predicated on Euro-Western values and beliefs, like the delegated child welfare model, as follows:

> The decision making power concerning critical issues affecting the colonized lies in the hands of the colonizers; the dominator gives little weight to the values, lifestyle and laws of the dominated; the colonialists interact with indigenous peoples in a manner that reflects the lower status and power of the latter; the colonizers import their standards, cultural values, laws and systems and impose them on the colonized so as to eliminate the latter's traditional structures. (p. 26)

Despite the significant challenges, there are many fine programs where First Nations have bridged this gap effectively, including the Yellowhead Tribal Services Custom Adoption Program (Alberta), the Caring for First Nations Children Society Aboriginal Social Worker Training Program (British Columbia), and the Aboriginal Justice Inquiry – Child Welfare Initiative (Manitoba). A fundamental key to success for all of these programs is that they are designed and delivered within Indigenous knowledge frameworks that reflect local cultures. Their successes inspire First Nations' efforts to affirm and promote Indigenous systems of knowledge, law, and practice that will result in ideologically cohesive systems of care.

This chapter focuses on the process of affirming Indigenous knowledge and research methods that support First Nations social work practice and ideologies. At the same time, we will identify the complementary and conflicting aspects of non-Aboriginal social work research and practice. To accomplish this, we provide a critical analysis of research as a tool for the legitimization of knowledge within a Euro-western framework and the implications for the colonization and marginalization of Aboriginal knowledge. We argue that academic research is itself inherently a colonizing process; before there can be meaningful progress in promoting and including Indigenous knowledge, the research process itself must be de-colonized. Finally, we advocate for greater means to connect research and policy processes with the realities of practising within an Aboriginal social work context.

This chapter also highlights the development of the First Nations Child and Family Caring Society of Canada (FNCFCS), a national organization that brings together Indigenous people, knowledge, and resources to validate traditional knowledge in the contemporary lives of First Nations children, families, and communities. The establishment of a First Nations research organization signals the development of a sustainable framework to support culturally appropriate systems of caring for First Nations children, youth, and families. Positive systems of child caring have endured as long as Aboriginal people have occupied North America.

A Contemporary View of Culturally Appropriate Social Work: Challenges and Opportunities

> Despite a United Nations' opinion that Canada is the best place in the world regarding quality of life measures, the reality of the Native child is bleak. A Native child is likely to be born poor and stay poor; she is, of all Canadians, most likely to die in infancy, to have fetal alcohol syndrome, to be sexually abused, to die in an accident, to drop out of school, and to commit suicide in adolescence. Almost every morbid statistic associated with the lack of child health and well being shows a gross and disproportionate representation of Native children ... Overall ... Native Canadian children can be ranked with children of the third world in both their quality of life and life chances. (Report on the Standing Committee on Health, as quoted in Awasis Agency of Northern Manitoba, 1997, p. 1)

For First Nations peoples, colonization is not just an artefact of the past. It is manifest every day as we live surrounded by Euro-Western legal, social, spiritual, and economic frameworks that continue to marginalize and encroach on First Nations peoples and Aboriginal knowledge and beliefs. In the child welfare context, in 2002, there were approximately 22,500 First Nations children in the care of Canadian child welfare authorities (Department of Indian Affairs and Northern Development, 2002). To put this figure in context, in 1940 there were approximately 8,000 First Nations children attending residential schools. There are more children in the care of the child welfare system today than were in state care at the time the residential schools were in full operation (Indian Residential School Survivors Society Newsletter, 2002). This is just one of the significant socioeconomic challenges facing First Nations children, families, and communities. Other challenges include issues such as poverty, youth suicide, accidental death, substance abuse, disproportionate incarceration rates, and low high-school graduation rates. Yet there continues to be a lack of awareness in Canadian society, and specifically in the profession of social work, of the cultures and histories of First Nations peoples and the effects of colonial policies such as residential school and the child welfare system on the well-being of First Nations children, youth, families, and communities. This ignorance, traceable to the inadequate telling of our history in Canadian schools and media, and the misinformation and misperceptions this generates, endures today as many Canadians believe that colonization and racism are issues of the past (Bennett, 2002). Vigilance is necessary to ensure that colonial thinking and actions do not continue to influence social work practice, policy, or research, or allow ill-advised social work practice to continue. Consider the following statement by a First Nations Child and Family Service Director in British Columbia:

> There needs to be political will on behalf of the province to truly evaluate their current practices within their commitment to stop colonial practices and ensure service availability to First Nations peoples. MCF [Ministry for Children and Families] in particular needs to critically analyze their own system and practice regarding First Nations peoples. Their current approach of demanding First Nations meet a myriad of standards for operations and practice whilst independent reviews consistently determine that MCF practice with Aboriginal children is extremely deficient is certainly open to skepticism and carves out a distressing reality for First Nations children and families. MCF must role model its voiced commitment to quality and culturally based service delivery. (Assembly of First Nations and Department of Indian Affairs and Northern Development, 2000, p. 67)

Correcting colonial practice takes more than good will and commitment. It takes ongoing, active critical analysis and engagement of the profession to ensure that research, policy, and practice work in partnership with Aboriginal peoples to affirm and promote their ways of caring for children, youth, and community. The significant socioeconomic challenges facing First Nations children and families can feel overwhelming, but must frame a call to action rather than numbing us into inaction. In effect

> [W]e must be careful of the dangers of academic detachment in reviewing the significant statistics demonstrating the crisis facing First Nations children, families and communities because numbers ... turn the brute facts into mathematical abstractions which camouflage feeling. (Snider, 1996, p. 38)

Detachment is too often reflected in academic research about First Nations peoples. If we succumb to detachment, we are robbed of the 'emotional leap into the reality of personal experiences which alone can penetrate specific dimensions of a human tragedy' (Snider, 1996, p. 38).

Active engagement and understanding require the development of an Indigenous research infrastructure to ensure that Aboriginal peoples are the beneficiaries, not simply the subjects of more research that portrays our realities as neutral abstractions. Emphasis must be placed on ensuring that Indigenous knowledge and practices are accepted as valid and respectfully included in our deliberations, dialogue, and practice as social workers. It is unfortunate that Indigenous knowledge continues in the main to be the purview of anthropology and not integrated into various academic and professional disciplines, including social work. Redhorse, Martinez, Day, Day, Pouport, and Scharnberg (2000) in their publication *Family Preservation: Concepts in American Indian Communities* described the practice implications arising from the marginalization of Indigenous child and family knowledge and practices:

> Tribal child welfare and family preservation service systems seek to develop models that integrate natural helping networks with mainstream practice, non-Indian county systems fail to recognize or keep pace with this development ... Most county service professionals continue to regard tribal programs as inferior or without merit and, in some cases, disregard cultural practice. Consequently there is a problem with planning and coordination of services. (p. 37)

The development of Aboriginal courses or programs within the social work discipline is an important beginning in establishing a respectful paradigm for working with Aboriginal peoples. Too often, however, Aboriginal social work is offered as a specialized and elective area of study rather than an integral part of social work education and practice alongside Euro-Western ideologies and theoretical frameworks. The development of Indigenous research capacity will inform social work, but it must be accompanied by significant and sustained efforts by social work professionals to value, understand, and include Indigenous knowledge and ways of caring for children, families, and communities in their education and practice.

Innovation Based on Indigenous Knowledge and Tradition

There are good examples of the respectful inclusion of Indigenous knowledge in social work. For example, significant modifications in the social work program at the University of Manitoba have been proposed, largely in response to anticipated restructuring of the child welfare system in the Province of Manitoba through the Aboriginal Justice Inquiry – Child Welfare Initiative (AJI-CWI). The AJI-CWI proposes substantial changes to the way in which child and family services will be delivered to the First Nations, Métis peoples, and the general public in Manitoba. The most profound changes to date are the increased participation by the Aboriginal peoples in the restructuring and decision-making process, and the willingness on the part of the Manitoba government to share some aspects of its child welfare jurisdiction with Aboriginal peoples in Manitoba in the following ways:

- recognizing a province-wide First Nations right and authority over the delivery of child welfare services by extending and expanding the off-reserve jurisdiction to provide child welfare services to First Nations citizens
- recognizing a province-wide Métis right and authority over the delivery of child welfare services to their constituents
- intending to restructure the existing child welfare system through legislative and other changes

The responsibility for management of services will be delegated to two First Nations (both on and off-reserve) child and family service authorities and one Métis child and family service authority. Responsibility for management of services to other children and families (non-Aboriginal) will be delegated to a General Child and Family Services

Authority. The new Authorities to be set out under this initiative are as follows:

- a First Nations of Northern Manitoba Child and Family Services Authority
- a First Nations of Southern Manitoba Child and Family Services Authority
- a Métis Child and Family Services Authority
- a General Child and Family Services Authority (for all other families)

Under these proposed changes, the province will continue to maintain ultimate responsibility for the safety and protection of children in Manitoba. It will establish laws, policies, and standards for the new system and will work with the four Authorities in providing services. The four Authorities will have new and expanded rights and responsibilities granted by the Minister to be recognized in new legislation. Each Authority will design and manage the delivery of child and family services throughout the province, assist in setting standards, and have the authority to select and provide funding to various agencies under its mandate that qualify to deliver services under the new system (AJI-CWI, 2001). Services delivered by the Aboriginal agencies will be culturally appropriate and based on an understanding of Aboriginal families and communities.

Under this system, the four Authorities (and their funded agencies) will work together to serve the needs of people across the province. All four Authorities (and the agencies operating through them) will have responsibility for services to the entire province at the same time, a structure referred to as concurrent jurisdiction. This marks a major change from the current system, in which only one child and family service agency has responsibility in any given geographical location in the province. The primary objective of the new system is to ensure that people receive services through the most culturally appropriate Authority. All families and children becoming involved with child and family for the first time will be guided through a streaming process to connect them with the appropriate Authority. The streaming process is based on the belief that families will want to receive services through the Authority with which they most closely identify (AJI-CWI, 2001).

Public feedback on the proposed child welfare system changes was solicited by the Aboriginal and provincial partners during a seven-week period that ended in September 2001. The objectives were to provide an opportunity to Manitoba citizens without formal representation on the AJI-CWI to comment on the proposed changes and to assist in identifying the strengths, limitations, and/or gaps. Public feedback reflected strong and widespread support for the overall vision for a restructured child and family services system as described in the *Promise of Hope: Commitment to Change* document (AJI-CWI, 2002). Support was indicated for the overall goals, the governance model, the use of a streaming methodology combined with choice in determining service jurisdiction, the service objectives proposed, the emphasis on the development of a culturally appropriate workforce, and proposed changes in how the system would be funded (AJI-CWI, 2002).

Because of the complexity and the ongoing nature of the AJI-CWI process, only some of the significant aspects of the proposed changes have been described. There is no doubt a great deal of work remains for those involved. Because of greater participation by Aboriginal people in the restructuring process, there will be increased demand for Aboriginal social workers familiar with an Aboriginal context. The University of Manitoba is developing a curriculum to address the need for an expanded Aboriginal labour force, educated in the Indigenous ways of helping in child welfare.

Yellowhead Tribal Services Agency in Edmonton, Alberta, has been widely recognized for its Custom Adoption Program, based on the culture of First Nations communities. The program is guided by a council of Elders and is responsive to Alberta's legal adoption requirements. It takes a holistic community approach to adoption, viewing the child as a member of a caring community and not the sole responsibility of one set of parents. It is an extension of the traditional practice of the community, assuming care for a child as a natural part of community life when a parent or extended family members are unable to do so. The program involves the community in supporting and affirming the important roles of biological and adoptive parents and extended families, eliminating much of the stigma and isolation resulting from mainstream adoption processes for First Nations.

The Caring for First Nations Children Society Aboriginal Social Worker Training Program provides comprehensive training for social workers employed by Aboriginal child and family service agencies. Development of the program followed an acknowledgment that mainstream social work education programs did not adequately prepare these professionals to work in an effective and respectful manner with Aboriginal children, families, and communities. A committee of First Nations child and family service agency staff, representatives from British Columbia's Ministry for Child and Family Development, and the Department of Indian and Northern Affairs Canada worked in partnership with the Caring for First Nations Children Society to develop this program.

The training is competency based and integrates three broad areas of understanding: (1) knowing about First Nations cultures and contexts; (2) developing best practices within a First Nations child and family service context; and (3), respecting the requirements of provincial legislation and practice standards. To enhance participant experience and appreciation of the diverse cultures of Aboriginal peoples in British Columbia, the training is provided, whenever possible, in Aboriginal communities and features a field training component which seeks to affirm and promote community-specific knowledge. The program also includes a graduation ceremony hosted by an Aboriginal community. The graduation programs affirm the important role the social workers will play in community life and underscore the shared commitment of social workers and the community in promoting the care of children and youth.

Since the program was introduced in 1999, more than 250 First Nation participants have completed one or more of the four modules of the training program (Caring for First Nations Children Society, 2002). Evaluation results show that participants strongly support this training approach. They find the training relevant and practical in their work with Aboriginal communities. The Caring for First Nations Children Society has recently expanded its range of training programs to include community workshops, supervisory training, and the development of training methods specific to Aboriginal child and family services.

These examples attest to exemplary results when programs and services are developed by Aboriginal peoples and informed by their traditions, knowledge, and cultures. They also indicate the need for enhanced infrastructures for Indigenous research, policy, and practice to support the development of culturally appropriate Aboriginal child welfare initiatives across the country and internationally.

The efforts of First Nations child and family service agencies in Canada to enhance Indigenous research and policy capacity culminated in a national meeting of First Nations child and family service providers at the Squamish Nation in 1998. From this meeting developed a new national Indigenous organization, the First Nations Child and Family Caring Society of Canada (the Caring Society). The primary objective of the Caring Society is to promote First Nations child and family services interests, knowledge, and best practices in First Nations systems of care. In partnership with the Centre of Excellence for Child Welfare, the Caring Society established a First Nations research site in Winnipeg, Manitoba, that will promote Indigenous knowledge, conduct research, and assist in building research capacity in First Nation agencies (First Nations Child and Family Caring Society, 2002). More important, the creation of this research site signals the establishment of research paradigms, as well as legal and policy frameworks that complement Aboriginal ways of caring for children.

The next two sections of this chapter discuss the pitfalls of traditional research approaches and the benefits of Indigenous knowledge as a research framework to guide the Caring Society in its study of First Nations child welfare agencies and the communities they serve.

Affirming and Promoting Indigenous Knowledge and Research

The primary purpose of the Caring Society's First Nations Research Site is to conduct research involving individuals working with First Nations child welfare agencies in order to enhance research capacities that are respectful of First Nations values and ways of caring for children. Research using traditional academic methodologies refined by mainstream learning institutions and presented as the primary means for the legitimization of knowledge is experienced by many Aboriginal Peoples as another layer of the colonizing process (Cajete, 2000; Smith, 1999).

Too often, a concept held as true for millennia by Indigenous peoples is accepted by non-Aboriginal social workers or scholars only if validated by established research evidence. This perspective highlights the conquest and control of nonwhite, non-European peoples and their ways of constructing knowledge. Yazzie (2000) notes that colonization is part of the theory of Social Darwinism:

> After Charles Darwin developed the theory of evolution, Herbert Spencer came up with the concept of 'survival of the fittest' ... He went on to argue that some people are 'fitter' and thus 'superior' to others ... The theory of Social Darwinism assumes that a certain group of people has the right to make decisions for others and to control the government and the economy ... Social Darwinism also assumes that there are 'inferior people,'

and history and contemporary practice show that they are women, non-Christian, and people of colour. In North America, that includes Indians and other Indigenous peoples. (p. 42)

To understand how research can be a colonizing process, one only has to look at the subtle ways in which First Nation students are indoctrinated by Canadian universities (Cajete, 2000; Hampton, 1995). Those of us of Aboriginal descent are not from homogeneous cultures and backgrounds, and yet in Western learning institutions we are expected to fit into 'one size fits all' institutions (Bailey, 2000). The unwritten rules of the dominant society require that we all speak English, write research papers and exams based on specific criteria outside of our Indigenous world views, and learn what others decide we need to know. Nor does what we learn in these institutions assist us in reaffirming and legitimizing our own ways of knowing and doing (Cajete, 2000; Colorado, 1992; Hampton, 1995; Martin, 2001). Furthermore, the language in which knowledge is imparted is not ours by birth.

Battiste and Youngblood Henderson (2000) note that these sorts of activities establish the dominant group's knowledge, experience, culture, and language as the universal norm. The educational experience of Aboriginal people exemplifies the continued colonization of Aboriginal peoples, where the colonizers (the dominant society in Canada) reinforce their culture by making the colonized (Aboriginal students) conform to their expectations (Battiste & Youngblood Henderson, 2000). Once we leave these institutions, we are expected to reflect what we have learned in everything that we do, even in our work with Aboriginal communities. But Western learning institutions and their research agendas do not mirror who we are as First Nations peoples. Structures, content, processes, and staff within these institutions are controlled primarily by members of the dominant society who, consciously or unconsciously, reinforce the marginalization of Indigenous knowledge systems (Bailey, 2000; Battiste & Youngblood Henderson, 2000; Kirby & McKenna, 1989).

The creation of knowledge is based on what Battiste and Youngblood Henderson (2000) call Eurocentricism. Eurocentricism supports the belief in the superiority of European peoples over non-European (Indigenous) peoples, with an inherent lack of recognition (or ignorance) of Indigenous knowledge systems and ways of knowing and doing. Discussing the Eurocentric need to define Indigenous knowledge, Battiste and Youngblood Henderson (2000) note in their treatise on *Protecting Indigenous Knowledge and Heritage*:

> Eurocentricism relies on arbitrary definitions that have no relationship with the life forces that Indigenous peoples use to understand life. Modern Eurocentric thinkers believe there are numberless ways in which they can classify ideas, objects, and events in ecology. The system of classification and the definitions used within it are based on the desires or purpose of those who created the system. The definitions are judged to be valid if they advance the desires or purposes of the people who fabricated them, allowing them to measure, predict, or control events. Since the validity of the system rests on its ability to contribute to particular ends, no basis exists for saying that one classification system portrays the 'real' world more accurately than another does. Given the principles of diffusionism and universality, however, Eurocentric thinkers automatically assume the superiority of their worldview and attempt to impose it on others, extending their definitions to encompass the whole world. Typically, this quest for universal definitions ignores the diversity of the people of the earth and their views of themselves. (pp. 36–7)

Aboriginal sources of knowledge and ways of knowing and doing are grounded in our languages, the land, animals, our Elders, and spiritual messengers (Auger, 1997). They are reflected in our own systems of child care. Each of these elements of knowledge is more complex when the plurality of Indigenous knowledge systems is considered (Cajete, 2000; O'Meara & West, 1996). While Indigenous knowledge is marginalized, there is no shortage of research on Aboriginal peoples being conducted by university researchers around the world. In fact, Aboriginal peoples globally feel that they are the most overresearched group in the world (Royal Commission on Aboriginal Peoples [RCAP], 1996d; Smith, 1999).

Research has long been the domain of the 'privileged.' Research about Indigenous peoples and their lands has been conducted by 'outsiders,' 'experts,' and 'authorities,' who too often have dissected, labelled, and dehumanized Indigenous peoples, acting as helpers in the colonial dispossession of Indigenous land and cultural heritage (Martin, 2001). Volumes of research have been generated on Aboriginal people in Canada, but relatively little research that Aboriginal peoples have been able to define for themselves (Gilchrist, 1997; RCAP, 1996d). This is beginning to change as more and more Aboriginal people attend university and begin to challenge the traditions of Western research methods and ethics.

Our purpose is not to question the legitimacy of the current institutions of higher learning, as this has been done many times by other Indigenous scholars in Canada and elsewhere (Battiste & Barman, 1995; Battiste & Youngblood Henderson, 2000; Cajete, 2000; Hampton, 1995; Martin, 2001; Smith, 1999). Rather, our intent is to highlight the significant limitations inherent in current concepts of learning and legitimate knowledge. There are many benefits that First Nations peoples have gained and will gain from formal education. We believe that academia will be enhanced by respecting and supporting Indigenous systems of knowledge.

The success of our own partnerships with the Universities of Toronto and Manitoba in setting up the First Nations Research Site attests to these specific institutions' willingness to explore reciprocity in knowledge development. However, to strengthen the capacity of Aboriginal people to conduct research in child welfare (and other fields), the Research Site faces the daunting challenge of decolonizing the research process to legitimize our own ways of generating Indigenous knowledge controlled, owned, and protected collectively by First Nations peoples.

We should not contribute further to the public silencing of Aboriginal voices (Kirby & McKenna, 1989). Instead, we recognize that we have an ethical responsibility to support initiatives that create opportunities for First Nations people to conduct research congruent with Indigenous values and priorities. Our research should be empowering, and lead to positive results for First Nations communities. Not only will the involvement of the community be instrumental in determining our research agenda and methodologies (Battiste & Youngblood Henderson, 2000), but community members must be given opportunities to benefit from training and employment opportunities that may be generated by conducting research. Local systems of knowledge must be respected too, as each system of knowledge is unique.

Snider (1996), quoting Wiesel, a writer and survivor of the Nazi concentration camps, remarks that 'knowledge burdens us with heightened responsibilities,' especially when it comes to the representation of 'truth' (p. 45). The First Nations Research Site will develop culturally appropriate ethical guidelines that support Indigenous values and ensure that the knowledge shared and gained is used to the legitimate advantage of communities. Issues such as the right to be included in relevant research and to be fully informed about the purpose, methods, and use of the research will be central in the development of these ethical guidelines (Gilchrist, 1997). By upholding these guidelines, we will affirm our Aboriginal philosophies and world views and, according to Fitznor (1998), move a step forward in decolonizing existing Western-centric research traditions by reaffirming culturally based ways of caring for children predicated on Aboriginal values.

The First Nations Research Site and the Partnership with the Centre of Excellence for Child Welfare

The First Nations Research Site is the product of a partnership between the First Nations Child and Family Society of Canada, the Centre of Excellence for Child Welfare (CECW), and the University of Manitoba. The Site resulted from discussions between the board members of the First Nations Child and Family Society and management of the CECW. The dean of the Faculty of Social Work, on behalf of the University of Manitoba, agreed to house the First Nations Research Site and provide administrative and resource support within the Faculty of Social Work. The First Nations Research Site is one of four research sites connected with the CECW. The organizational structure of this partnership is detailed in the figure 11.1. Planning began in April 2001, and the First Nations Research Site became fully operational in November of the same year. The site is managed by a full-time research coordinator, who draws upon the academic expertise within the University of Manitoba's Faculty of Social Work.

The Caring Society provides overall direction to the First Nations Research Site, and reserved site staff work in partnership with the Society. The role of CECW is to assist the Site staff with training and access to research and other resources. CECW provides direction in conducting analyses of the data from the Research Site's studies.

The First Nations Research Site will provide a national research forum for First Nations child welfare agencies, researchers, policy makers, and others interested in the development of child welfare research that incorporates and respects Indigenous knowledge and the cultural world views of First Nations in Canada. The goals of the First Nations Research Site are as follows:

- to assist the Centre of Excellence for Child Welfare in analyzing and reporting on Canadian child welfare data, specifically data within the First Nations child welfare context
- to share innovations and issues in practice, policy, knowledge,

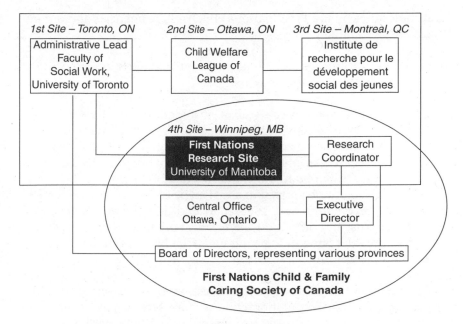

Figure 11.1: Centre of Excellence for Child Welfare

research, skill development, and administration in First Nations child welfare
- to stimulate discussion among local, regional, provincial, and national child welfare agencies on current research, policies, and/or practices that affect or benefit First Nations children, youth, families, and/or communities
- to promote networking and the exchange of ideas among First Nations practitioners, academic researchers, policy makers, and advocates who work in the First Nations child and family services field
- to assist in building and strengthening research capacity among First Nations individuals, agencies, and organizations engaged in child welfare research, policy, and/or practice
- to build a pool of resources and networks with academic and private First Nations researchers
- to promote the training of professional staff, researchers, caregivers, and volunteers
- to promote the development of techniques for evaluating the programs and services delivered to First Nations children, families, and

communities by the First Nations child welfare agencies and organizations in Canada.

Some of the objectives established by the First Nations Research Site to meet its goals are as follows:

- to develop and maintain a database that identifies the First Nations researchers (both academically and privately) and the types of child welfare research being conducted by First Nations or Indigenous agencies, researchers, and/or nongovernment organizations in Canada, the United States, and internationally
- to develop an online journal to assist in the collection and dissemination of information and research to all child welfare agencies, organizations, and other non-government organizations that work with or are interested in working with First Nations children, families, and communities in Canada.

As a national organization that seeks to provide services to the approximately 120 First Nation child welfare agencies in Canada, the Caring Society recognizes the importance of building partnerships in which Indigenous knowledge is not only respected but allowed to flourish. The Caring Society's collaboration with other Aboriginal organizations through research conducted by the First Nations Research Site will be an important step in supporting Aboriginal child welfare organizations. The research will help to showcase the best Aboriginal child welfare practices for Canada and the world. Indeed, there are many innovative initiatives in Aboriginal communities, which promise to make the fields of social work and child welfare more congruent with the needs of Aboriginal peoples.

Conclusion

The First Nations Research Site provides a foundation for affirming Indigenous knowledge as an essential component in redressing the effects of colonization and in supporting our children, youth, and families as they meet contemporary and future challenges. The Research Site highlights the importance of partnerships between First Nation organizations and other research centres to bridge gaps in meeting community needs and delivering contemporary social work education.

We start from the premise that First Nations have their own knowledge systems that must survive for the benefit of future generations. We must begin the process of conducting our own research to contribute to Indigenous knowledge, which will undoubtedly grow with future generations. We hope that our written words fuel discussions that will help shape individual, community, and government action to decolonize all systems, including those that touch upon the construction, validation, and preservation of knowledge. We hope that this process ultimately leads to paths of respect, freedom, and equal opportunity for First Nations peoples in Canada. In First Nations communities prior to colonization, positive systems of child and family welfare were predicated on Indigenous values and ways of knowing, doing, and being. The challenge for us is to ensure that these positive systems continue and that the best practices they foster are brought to the forefront, shared, and adequately expressed through our own Indigenous research frameworks.

NOTES

1 Portions of this chapter were previously published in 2002 in the Child Welfare League of Canada's journal, *Canada's Children*, 9.3, 27–33.
2 Within Canada, Aboriginal peoples are compromised of various groups, who are recognized constitutionally as the Inuit, Métis, and First Nations (or Indian) people. Readers will note that words such as 'Aboriginal,' 'First Nations,' 'Native,' and/or 'Indigenous' have been capitalized throughout this paper. Many Aboriginal peoples and Indigenous researchers in Canada and internationally have argued that such words should be capitalized when referring to a specific people, in much the same manner that words like 'English' and 'French' are capitalized (Issac, 1999). The authors of this report agree with this perspective and hence the capitalization of those words is found throughout.

PART FIVE

Conclusion

12 Learning from International Comparisons of Child Protection, Family Service, and Community Caring Systems of Child and Family Welfare

NANCY FREYMOND and GARY CAMERON

Creating systems of child and family welfare that respond effectively to children and families is a daunting undertaking in all developed nations. For the purpose of understanding these challenges, systems of child and family welfare in different countries can be grouped in terms of their understanding of family difficulties, ideas about helping others, and beliefs about partnerships among families, communities, and the state in caring for children. In this volume, three broad generic approaches to child and family welfare have been examined – family service, community care, and child protection.

These systems of child and family welfare reflect deeply held and intensely debated societal values and priorities. It is also clear that the variations among these systems have important consequences for children and parents, for service providers, and for relationships among families, community, and the state. Notwithstanding the constraints of particular histories and institutional arrangements, all systems of child and family welfare have space for change (Cooper, Hetherington, & Katz, 2003). Understanding similarities and differences across international jurisdictions opens opportunities for clarifying and rethinking choices within a given system. Such comparisons enrich considerations of niches for innovations, as well as visions of more positive orientations to child and family welfare.

This chapter examines selected patterns in family service, community caring, and child protection orientations to child and family welfare. In doing so, our analyses are inevitably shaped by our greater familiarity with Anglo-American child protection models, particularly in Canada. The discussion in this chapter is organized around four topics: (1) conceptions of children and families, (2) everyday living realities, (3) congruence, and (4) authority and collaboration. It concludes with some general reflections about the lessons learned from these international comparisons.

Some caveats are required about comparing community caring approaches developed by Indigenous peoples with family service and child protection models predominating in Europe and North America. Community caring models are much newer, less elaborated, and more fragile. In important aspects, they are in-between systems, reflecting ongoing tensions between First Nations' aspirations and the exigencies of surrounding, more powerful Anglo-American child protection systems. Consequently, less can be said about the operations of community caring policy or practice, or what the eventual compromises with the larger systems might be. Nonetheless, it is essential in understanding international child and family welfare to acknowledge the distinct nature of Aboriginal peoples' community caring aspirations. It also is important for those of us within child protection and family service systems to remain open to learning from these community caring traditions.

Conceptions of Children and Families

The ease with which the words children and family are used in everyday conversation requires that their core meanings and nuances be widely shared. However, across countries and cultures, the words childhood and family do not have fixed associations. In addition, childhood and family ideals and realities evolve and, in some jurisdictions, are changing rapidly. Across community caring, family service, and child protection systems of child and family welfare, conceptions of children and families are associated with contextually specific values, assumptions about everyday living, and priorities for helping.

Within First Nation communities, family is understood as a network or web of relationships where identity is anchored. Aboriginal philosophies stress interconnections and interdependence among all of creation. A balanced coexistence is seen as essential to the survival of First Nations, and central to the health and well-being of their people (Maidman & Connors, 2001). This ideal requires that families and communities function as cooperative, interdependent units. Identity is defined through tribal groups, formed over many generations, that share language and customs. Ideally, caring for children is a shared responsibility among immediate family, extended family, and community. Kin and community networks are central in teaching children; elders share stories and legends to instil values, beliefs, and understanding of identity (Mandell, Carlson, Fine, & Blackstock, 2003, chapter 9).

For the Maori, as discussed in chapter 10, individual identity does not centre on distinctions between self and other. The self is indivisible from *whanau* (extended family), *hapu* (subtribal groups of extended family who share common genealogy), and *iwi* (tribes composed of hapu groups with an eponymous ancestor). These relationships are foundational to Maori conceptions of childhood and family, and repairing and enhancing this web of relationships is central to their conception of child and family welfare. The separation of the welfare of children from the welfare of family and community has no meaning within this world view. Likewise, the severing of children's connections with family and community to protect them, or to enhance their well-being, contradicts the fundamental understandings of Aboriginal peoples.

A family services orientation assumes that the interests of families and the state are indivisible. The family is the foundation of society, essential to the proper education and development of children (future citizens). Within these systems, to various degrees, there is an emphasis on the social inclusion of children and families, and on maintaining family connections.

Chapter 6 describes the relationship between the French family and the state as an alliance, having a shared responsibility for the care and education of children. There is a dual emphasis on children as members of a family and as citizens. As Alain Grevot (2001) explains, a decision in the late 1980s to decentralize child and family welfare responsibility from the central state to local authorities, considered to be the weakest level of French democracy, was seen as altering the national social contract, and removing legitimacy for child and family welfare interventions, leading to greater reliance on the authority of the legal system.

Unlike Anglo-American jurisdictions, however, there has been a more recent countermovement towards the principles of enhancing coeducation (constructive partnerships) between service providers and users, and providing supportive services to families. Also, for the first time in forty years, there has been a reduction in reliance on the authority of Children's Judges, a pivotal figure in the French family service model. Grevot says 'there is general consensus about the legitimacy of co-education, a shared State-parent responsibility for child-rearing' (26).

In chapter 8, A.W.M. Veldkamp explains that, in the Netherlands, voluntary assistance through securing parental cooperation is seen as preferable to the use of coercive legal measures. As a consequence of recent reforms, there is more restraint in issuing care orders, greater importance attached to maintaining parents-children bonds, providing assistance to children along with improving parents-children relationships, and preventing the separation of children from parents. Providing assistance to children and families is seen as the main purpose of the Dutch family service system.

Bruno Palier (2004) locates both France and the Netherlands, along with Germany, France, Austria, and the other Benelux countries, within a conservative-corporatist system of social protection in mid-continental Europe. He argues that this social protection policy system 'is often highly fragmented, is administered by agencies and funds that are more or less independent of the state, and managed by representatives of employers and workers. Individuals not covered or no longer covered by social insurance have recourse to a "social safety net" consisting of minimum benefits, in the form of income support, that are financed through tax revenues' (p. 32). He argues that these social protection systems 'seek much less to reduce inequalities than to preserve social stratification and status' (p. 32). He also illustrates that these conservative European systems have had greater difficulties modifying their relatively generous social insurance protection environments, for certain segments of society, to the realities of globally integrated economies, than either liberal or social democratic systems of social protection. Consequently they are facing continuing problems of competitiveness and sustaining current levels and formats of social protection provisions.

Sweden, along with the Nordic countries of Denmark, Finland, Norway, and Iceland, follow a social democratic model of social protection where the core concept is equality (Palier, 2004). 'Social rights are associated primarily with citizenship, and benefits provided by the public sector are delivered in the form of free services or all-inclusive benefits' (p. 31). Gunvor Andersson (chapter 7) illustrates this social democratic social protection environment by describing the generous social provisions available to children, parents, and families in Sweden, and emphasizing that child welfare services are not separate from other social services in Sweden. In addition, no separation is made between protecting children and supporting families in Sweden. She states that the 'collaborative model [between family and state is] ... most fully developed in Sweden and Norway' (208). A strong emphasis is placed upon securing children's and parents' voluntary cooperation in services, and in providing assistance to children, parents, and families. Andersson points out that 75% of all out-of-home care in Sweden takes place with parental consent, and every effort is made to maintain parent-children connections while children are in care, with a view to their return home. In marked contrast to Anglo-American child protection systems, in France and Sweden, there are no legal provisions for the permanent severing of children's connection with their biological families.

England, Canada, Australia, Ireland, New Zealand, and the United States have a liberal tradition of social protection, where greater emphasis is given to the market than to the state in allocating resources (Palier, 2004). 'The state must, above all, maintain a residual role: welfare benefits must be very low and minimum incomes and income support must constitute the main form of state intervention ... They promote a pronounced dualism in society between the haves and have-nots ...' (p. 31). Children and families in countries with child protection systems are understood through the prism of individualism. Baker and Phipps (1997) note that liberal social protection laws and policies 'have incorporated the values of self-reliance, individualism, and family privacy' (p. 105).

The legal doctrine of *parens patriae* gives the state authority to intervene in families, but only where parents have not fulfilled their minimum responsibilities for caring for their children (Swift & Callahan, chapter 5). Services should be withdrawn when these minimum responsibilities are met, lest they erode the principles of family responsibility and self reliance (Baistow, Hetherington, Spriggs, & Yelloly, 1996; Djao, 1983). Child protection systems make clear distinctions between protecting children and supporting families, with the lowest emphasis on the latter of the three generic orientations to child and family welfare. The practices of protecting children by separating them from deficient parents (and thus from extended family and community networks), having stand-alone residual child protection authorities, and relying extensively on legal authority to intervene in violating families, are consistent with these conceptions of individual identities, family, community, and the state.

Conceptions of family are not static. As new conceptions of family emerge within countries and cultures, shifts within systems of child and family welfare are inevitable. For example, in Aboriginal communities, colonization and the effects of pervasive disruptions of family and community relationships over generations have eroded traditional conceptions of the family. There is a tension between degrees of mainstream acculturation within some families and communities, and adherence to traditional conceptions in others (Mandell, Carlson, Fine, & Blackstock, 2003, chapter 9). It is unclear how these changes will be reflected in community caring systems over time.

In continental Europe, the United Nations Convention on the Rights of the Child (CRC), which acknowledges children as independent bearers of provision, protection, and participation rights, is modifying traditional conceptions of family. There is increased recognition of the autonomous rights of children. For instance, in the Netherlands, the basis for the parent-child relationship reportedly is shifting, with more emphasis being placed on mutual affection rather than on parental authority:

> The authority pattern within the normal Dutch family is characterized by limited negotiation: 75% of young people (12–18 years) state that they can make decisions themselves, but that they also have to take into account the views of their parents. Father and mother are ultimately responsible for the family regime, but their authority is no longer a matter of course. (*Fact Sheet: Parenting Support*, 2002, p. 1)

The CRC has increased the profile of youth policy issues in the Netherlands. Veldkamp (chapter 6) argues that this has created an increased emphasis on the law in the safeguarding of children's rights.

The CRC also has influenced youth policies in Sweden. The Swedish Children's Ombudsman is a national authority that, in accordance with the values of the CRC, seeks to represent the interests of children. The yearly report to the Swedish government includes recommendations for constitutional changes in order to realize the intentions of the Convention (Andersson, chapter 7). Grevot (chapter 6) talks about how influences such as the CRC, social policy expectations within the European Union, changing statuses of women and women's lobby organizations, and the realities of increasing numbers of immigrant families have modified traditional French reliance on paternalistic authority, and led to shifts towards concepts of coeducation and a renewal of the social contract between the state and families to care for children.

Evolving family structures and norms often differ substantially from the assumptions about families upon which interventions in Anglo-American child protection systems are predicated. For example, in the chapters on Aboriginal child and family welfare (chapters 9, 10, 11), the devastation of traditional Indigenous families and extended kin networks is well documented. Another illustration of divergence from official prescriptions comes from the Partnerships for Children and Families Project program of research in Ontario, Canada. In this research, it was common for children in families involved with child protection services to have different fathers, for extended families to include varieties of blended families, and for community expectations of family life to differ substantially from those of middle-class communities (Cameron & Hoy, 2003; Freymond, 2003; Maiter, Palmer, & Manji, 2003). Child protection organizations in this research, with their relatively standardized interventions, had limited capacity to adapt to these variations in everyday living realities and community expectations.

Everyday Lives[1]

From its earliest days until the present, Anglo-American child protection systems have focused their attention on the most impoverished segments of the population, as well as on immigrant and other marginalized groupings. Over the years, the rationales for the disproportionate involvement of these disadvantaged groups have included maintaining economic productivity, public safety, and proper moral standards, as well as rescuing children from 'dangerous and unwholesome' environments (Cameron, Freymond, Cornfield, & Palmer, 2001).

Findings from the Partnerships for Children and Families Project's program of research with families involved with child protection authorities in Ontario, Canada, are used below to illustrate some of these common daily living realities. It is impossible to read the stories about these families without confronting dramatic evidence of the ongoing pressures of living with lesser privilege,[2] and the extraordinary efforts required to survive and to overcome such obstacles. The story of Elizabeth is typical.

Elizabeth

Elizabeth currently lives with her daughter and a girlfriend in the back of a house, in a noisy neighbourhood that has a lot of drug dealing and prostitution. Elizabeth survives on the funds she receives from Workers Compensation and from the orphan's benefits which she receives because Steven (the father of her oldest child) died. These sources of income provide her with $900 (CDN) a month. Elizabeth also should receive child support from Ben, her ex-partner; however, she claims that he recently quit his job to avoid the monthly payments.

Elizabeth survives by taking advantage of any means available to her. She describes herself:

> I'm really resourceful ... I find out a lot about the community, the things that the community has to offer, um, so I go that way resourceful. I've survived a lot. Not as much as others but to me it's a lot. Um, you have to because if you're sitting there with no money and no food you have to find a means for it you know. There's different ways, umpteen ways you can get food and you just gotta figure out a way to do it ...

Three broad interpretive themes related to lives of lesser privilege emerged from the analyses in the Partnerships for Children and Families research. First, child protection services involve communities and generations of individuals and families with ways of living reflecting their own ideals, norms, and exigencies of childhood, parenting, and family. Such patterns of living cannot be understood solely in terms of individual characteristics and responsibilities. This program of research also identified a gap between the lives of families and child protection service providers – emotional, intellectual, social, and practical – that is hard to bridge in helping these families and communities.

Second, lesser privilege brings with it lives characterized by high levels of adversity, daily stress, and periodic crises. Coping with adversity and crisis is a pattern that often is ongoing from childhood into adult life. The challenges confronted by these families are well known to service professionals: conflict and violence, addictions, unstable homes, job and income insecurity, emotional challenges, and poor physical health. Here is Amber's story.

Amber

During Amber's childhood, her father went to jail for several years for drug trafficking. After her parents' separation, Amber, a First Nation woman, 'bounced around a lot' between family members and foster homes. When Amber was fourteen, she was living on the street, sleeping on park benches. She would sneak into bars and drink and use drugs. Amber recalls that she was close to the sex trade, but she couldn't bring herself to become a prostitute. At age sixteen, Amber was living at home with her mother again, but left because of the sexual advances of her mom's partner. She moved to Alberta to live with her stepfather.

Most of the women in the Partnerships for Children and Families research at some point have been single mothers and typically this coincided with a substantial drop in their income. Most have been on social assistance at least once. About half of these women had not finished high school; very few had attended college. Long hours of work, shift work, low pay, and limited benefits were common for women working outside the home and for their partners. Living space typically was rented and modest, sometimes in neighbourhoods considered harmful by the mothers. Almost all of these women described financial and living circumstances that left their families very vulnerable to disruptions.

Particularly striking was the level of daily living stress described by some of these women, as they invested so much of themselves into working to pay the bills, caring for their children, keeping their families together, and maintaining a home. For example, Karen, after leaving her adoptive home and moving through several foster homes when she was fourteen, was living on her own at a young age. She and her partner work overlapping shifts six days a week, trading off care of the children. Between getting her two boys off to school in the morning and doing housework late at night after work, Karen does not get many hours of sleep. She describes their efforts as 'running really hard just to live on the margins.'

A third subtheme that is less frequently acknowledged by child protection service providers is the efforts by parents, and mothers in particular, to manage this adversity over many years and their personal victories along the way. Readers of these stories frequently comment on the endurance and persistence of these women and marvel at how many of them manage to keep hope alive in their lives.

Annette

Growing up, Annette was the target of her father's abuse. Annette performed very well in school, but the stress from her home life eventually caught up with her. In grade eight, her grades plummeted. Despite difficulties at home, Annette worked hard to finish high school; she planned to leave home when she received her diploma. Annette recalls her graduation from high school:

That was one of the happiest days of life, to get that diploma in my hands. I carried that everywhere. I didn't care how wrinkly it got, but that was my ticket to freedom. And I graduated in June and I hitchhiked up here in

October. And that was an experience in itself. The best thing I ever done.
Because my mom says, you get on that highway, and you don't look back.
You look back, you're going to come back. And I didn't look back once,
only to see if there was more traffic coming, but that's about it. And I've
been a survivor since.

After graduating from high school, Annette hitchhiked from her home
province to Ontario. Along the way, a friendly truck driver gave her
fifty dollars. Once she reached her destination, she used this fifty dollars to stay in a hotel. Immediately, Annette went job hunting.

The literature about child protection focuses a great deal on the
struggles within families: inadequate or harmful parenting, hurtful
childhoods of parents, conflict and violence between partners, and
unstable relationships and homes for children (Freymond, 2003). The
Partnerships for Children and Families program of research certainly
illustrates the dramatic nature of these types of struggles for many
families. Yet there is another story fundamental to understanding and
helping these families. It is a tale about the continuity and central
importance of family in the lives of these parents and their children,
and their persistent desire and effort to have a family and a home.
These contrasting stories coexist and need to be understood in relation
to each other as we hear about ways of living that may be very different
from our own.

Most of these women tell of a series of relationships with different
men over time. Most of them, at some time, have been involved in a
physically and emotionally abusive relationship with a live-in male
partner, some in several. Many of their children are not living with their
biological fathers and many have minimal if any contact with their
dads. Siblings have different biological fathers in quite a few families.
Yet there is another dimension to this image of partnerships. These
stories tell of a strong motivation to partner, to try again, coupled with a
strong desire for a normal family and home. In addition, in most of their
current partnerships, the women feel that they are doing better than
with past partners and, in many if not all tales, there are descriptions
suggesting that their perceptions of improvements may be accurate.

In the Partnerships for Children and Families program of research,
these families remained central to parents and children being well, and
feeling that they belong and that someone cares. A critical point is that,
in many of these stories, mothers generally provide the only continuity
of parenting and family for their children over time. In many of these

stories, becoming and being a mom is central in these women's lives. A commonality in many of these stories, particularly surprising in circumstances of very abusive childhoods, is the central role that relations with parents, especially with their mothers, and other family members have for many of these women and their families.

There is an endurance and continuity of family in these stories which is central to understanding the lives of many of these women and their children. For perhaps half of these parents and children, families of origin and extended family were the most common sources of emotional and tangible support. Many of these families did most of their socializing with their extended families. There are strengths in these family networks which often went unrecognized in service providers' focus on past and ongoing troubles. These families will be around for most of these women and their children long after child protection authorities have gone away.

Mothers were almost always the primary caregivers of the children in this research. The well-being of these women is central to these families. Yet many of these mothers tell truly horrendous stories of what they have had to overcome in their own childhoods and how this has impacted on their adult lives. Sandy is an example.

Sandy

Sandy's mom and dad were both alcoholics and her dad was abusive to her mom. Sandy described in detail a particular instance when her mom was seriously hurt. Her parents were divorced by the time she was four years old. Her mom was poor and, Sandy suspects, worked as a prostitute until she married Sandy's stepfather. Sandy was sexually abused by her oldest brother. He was responsible for caring for the family, with her mom and stepdad being out most of the time. Sandy's mom and stepdad also drank together and both would become quite violent.

In the Partnerships for Children and Families program of research, approximately 40% of families with a child placed in the care of child protection authorities were struggling with the challenging behaviour of a child. In addition, most of the families with a child placed in residential mental heath care had prior involvement with child protection organizations. Three themes from the research with these families are germane to understanding everyday living in these families.

First, families with such a 'difficult' child live 'under a state of siege,' experiencing an intensity of ongoing pressure and disruption unlike any other families in the Partnerships for Children and Families program of research:

> He'd break the furniture, put holes in the walls, hurting my animals ... he used to try and hurt the young one ... he once took her head and banged it against the table and she lost all her teeth ... he was going to kill me because he had threatened me many times ... (Cameron, de Boer, Frensch, & Adams, 2003)

Second, mothers, in particular, make extraordinary sacrifices to help these children, often with substantial costs to their physical and emotional health, to their relationships with partners, and to their social and work involvements. Third, parents' efforts to find someone to believe what is happening in their homes and to find help for their 'challenging child' typically go on for years.

Within the Canadian child protection system, Swift & Callahan (chapter 5) concur that the focus has been primarily on poor mothers. They state that many families in these systems are headed by lone female parents, usually mothers, receiving low levels of social assistance or are among the ranks of the working poor. Patricia Schene (chapter 4) talks about building community partnerships in various American demonstration projects, as an antidote to the increasing dissatisfaction with the performance of their child protection systems. Consistent with the above descriptions of lives of lesser privilege, she provides a profile of two disadvantaged communities hosting such demonstration projects. One community in Florida is comprised of five public housing developments, where all household live at or near the poverty line. The other community in Missouri has high rates of child abuse and neglect, poverty, and transience. As another illustration of the realities of lives of lesser privilege, in reference to the English child protection system, Parton, Thorpe, and Wattam (1997) comment:

> What the DoH research shows is that we have a very ineffective system for those who are legitimately entitled to use it. Rather than question this legitimacy of use and suggest that other issues might be lurking in the background which could be more usefully used to address the problems created by poverty, long-term unemployment, relationship difficulties and even domestic violence, the social worker is remonstrated for being too focused on finding those children who have harms and injuries and

not focused enough on responding to a wealth of social problems largely beyond their, or any individual agents' control. (p. 231)

The First Nation stories in the Partnerships for Children and Families program of research have unique themes requiring attention. Besides being about very difficult personal journeys, these are also tales of collapsed communities. The parents of the mothers in this research often were themselves products of foster homes and residential schools. These stories illustrate the pervasive challenges facing many First Nation communities, including the negative impacts of colonialism, systemic racism, and persistent poverty.

First Nations and Maori populations fare poorly across a range of social indicators and are overrepresented in child protection systems. Mandell and her colleagues (chapter 9) show that poverty, unemployment, substance use, child abuse and neglect, violence against women, youth suicide, and community disintegration are widespread in many First Nation Communities in Canada. Love (chapter 10) states that Maori, compared with non-Maori populations in Aotearoa/New Zealand, have shorter lives, are more likely to be incarcerated, to die prematurely by suicide or accident, to be unemployed, to have children at a young age, to have large families, and to live in overcrowded situations on low incomes.

Sweden, along with other Nordic countries, has relatively generous and broadly accessible social protection provisions for all children and families. Nonetheless, Andersson (chapter 7) states that social workers are concerned about the erosion of the Swedish welfare model, and the increasing income gaps among social classes. She highlights that Sweden is rapidly becoming a multiethnic society, where immigrant and refugee populations confront higher levels of unemployment, discrimination, and overcrowded living conditions. She indicates that the child and family welfare system in Sweden focuses disproportionately on single mothers, particularly those without jobs and with limited education, and tends to hold mothers more accountable than fathers.

In arguing for more integration of law and assistance orientations within the child and family welfare system in the Netherlands, Veldkamp (chapter 8) identifies concerns about multi-problem families that he describes as 'steeped in misery and ... often in a serious state of social incapacitation' (242) along with concerns about the capacity of the Dutch system to respond to the needs of these families. In France, official reports that have been pivotal in bringing reform to their family service system recognize the increased economic and social precarious-ness of families (chapter 6). These reports also illustrate broader social concerns including perceived dramatic increases in adolescent violence and growing concerns about disparity in the world views of immigrant families and French social workers.

Nancy Freymond (2003), based on her research with mothers in-volved with the child protection system in Ontario, Canada, makes an argument central to this discussion:

> Mothers do not merely absorb and comply with the advice of profession-als. They attempt to interpret and to incorporate that advice into their daily living contexts. When child welfare expectations contradict what is 'common sense' in the world of biological mothers, the expectations are met with frustrations and resistance. (p. 1)

Building a balanced and flexible child and family welfare system requires establishing congruency with the lives of involved children, parents, families, and communities. Lack of access to adequate re-sources and opportunities for enhancing child, parent, and family well-being; high vulnerability to disruption in existing supports; high levels of daily living stress; tremendous personal challenges of parents in their childhood and adult lives; and conflicts within families and painful disruptions of family continuity are common themes among these popu-lations. Equally important to recognize is the resolve, endurance, and capacity for action and mutual aid evident in these communities. The challenge of congruence involves, in addition to endeavouring to safe-guard children from physical, sexual, and emotional harm, bringing relevant tangible, educational, and healing resources to children, par-ents, families, and communities; and engaging people in ways that are acceptable and make sense to them.

Congruence

Within all systems of child and family welfare, there is a danger that services will become self referential, intervening in ways that are con-gruent with policy, administrative, and professional requirements, but not necessarily with the everyday lives and expectations of service users. For service providers to provide appropriate and acceptable assistance, there must be a minimal understanding and compassion for the trials as well as the strengths of their clientele. There need to be opportunities to create mutually acceptable relationships between service providers and individuals, families, and communities. Finally, the capacity to provide congruent assistance is heavily dependent upon the types and levels of social protection provisions available, and the willingness and capacity of the child and family welfare system to involve members of extended family and community networks, along with other service organizations, in implementing its mandate.

From this volume, it is clear that the concepts of child maltreatment and the prevention of specific types of harm to children (physical, sexual, emotional) do not have to be the only, or even the dominant, organizing ideas for a healthy system of child and family welfare. It is also clear that all systems of child and family welfare struggle with finding a balance between sustaining child and family well-being and protecting children from harm.

This ongoing tension between social service and legal enforcement priorities, and ways of working, was evident in the discussions of family service systems, particularly in the Netherlands and France. Nonetheless, in contrast with Anglo-American child protection systems, to a greater or lesser extent, family service systems in Sweden, France, and the Netherlands all place a heavy emphasis upon providing services and supports to maintain and to repair child and family well-being. Indeed, in many settings, enhancing child and family well-being is the dominant emphasis philosophically, as evidenced by high investments of resources in supportive rather than justice-driven interventions.

In many Anglo-American child protection jurisdictions, particularly over the past decade, this ongoing struggle to balance well-being and protection orientations has been managed essentially by eliminating concerns about child and family well-being from official child protection policy and practice deliberations. This shift has been heavily influenced by the neoconservative or neoliberal ideologies dominating public policy over the past two decades, coupled with continued and increasing emphases upon residual or minimalist provisions for social protection.

Within community caring orientations, tensions have centred on deeply rooted philosophical differences between child protection priorities, and the world views of Aboriginals. There have been attempts to respond in ways that are more congruent with the values and traditions of Aboriginal populations. For example, in Aotearoa/New Zealand, more Maori social workers have been recruited into child welfare, with mixed results. While Indigenous social workers are more apt to comprehend the realities of Maori populations, they are heavily constrained in how they work with children and families by official child protection requirements. There also have been attempts to incorporate Maori values and procedures into the larger child protection system; one well-known effort has been implemented through family group conferencing. In chapter 10, Catherine Love is critical of how the mainstream child protection system dilutes and distorts family group conferencing practices by transforming and removing key elements. She also laments what she sees as an insidious encroachment in Maori *whanau* (extended family) life and domains of authority.

In First Nations in Canada, delegated models of child protection have been created where either full or partial authority to provide service is assigned to Aboriginal communities. As Mandell and her colleagues describe in chapter 9, these initiatives are evolving and have not led so far to the creation of community caring models of child and family welfare consistent with the traditions and aspirations of First Nations. Also, indicated in the previous section, First Nation and Maori populations have much higher instances of individual, family, and community distress than most mainstream groupings, while having substantially less access to social protection provisions. When added to the less generous social protection provisions in Anglo-American settings compared to many Nordic and central European jurisdictions, it is evident that severe limitations exist on these community caring systems' capacity to respond effectively and acceptably to the challenges facing Indigenous children, families, and communities.

In family service systems, the ability to tailor relevant assistance to particular children, parents, families, communities, and populations would vary depending on the levels and types of social protection provisions available, and the discretion allowed in negotiating and providing assistance. The chapters in this volume indicate that there is substantial variation among family service on these attributes. In particular, there may be patterned differences between Nordic countries, such as Sweden, with its more generous levels of social provision and perhaps the highest emphasis on providing voluntary assistance to families, and the more socially conservative policy environments of central Europe, including France and the Netherlands. The ease of access to protective and remedial resources such as daycare, public health services, educational supports, child care employment leave, social and recreational opportunities, mental health treatment and counselling, adequate housing and family income, and supportive peers will fundamentally determine child and family welfare systems' capacities to develop congruent and acceptable responses to families.

One of the congruence challenges facing family service and child protection systems is accommodating different ideals and ways of living presented by various immigrant populations, particularly those coming from traditions differing substantially from European or Anglo-American cultures. All three family service chapters (on Sweden, the Netherlands, and France) emphasize the difficulties that adapting to these new communities present for their family service systems. Nonetheless, in theory, with their emphases on providing services and supports and, in some settings, on local community and service provider discretion, these family service systems may be better situated to adapt to changed expectations than child protection systems.

The child protection settings in this volume (England, Canada, and the United States) focus on children within nuclear families, and seek out particular types of proscribed behaviours to which a set of mandated remedies are applied. Within this tightly controlled paradigm, there is little questioning of how these child protection proscriptions or prescriptions might be required to adapt to other conceptions of self, childhood, family, and community, or to divergent ideas of how to care for children and to remedy harmful family situations. The most evident example of this rigidity in this volume is the gap between child protection norms and Indigenous populations' community caring ideals.

Waldfogel (1998, 2001) criticizes child protection systems in the United States for their failure to account for the varied needs of families and children. She proposes a differential response paradigm emphasizing coordinated services, and involving helpers from extended family and community networks in supporting families and preventing child maltreatment. Differential response models use an investigative response in emergency and high risk situations and, ideally, offer services and supports to the majority of families not falling into this category (Schene, chapter 4). Differential response models have been developed in several jurisdictions in the United States, Australia, and, more recently, in Alberta, Canada.

Unfortunately, the experience with North American differential response systems has been less than encouraging in many cases (English, Fluke, & Ying-Ying, 2003). A practical motivation for public officials in many jurisdictions to initiate differential response systems has been to reduce escalating costs from legal investigations of so many families, and the increasing numbers of children entering state care (Meeting of Ministers of Social Services, 2003). In many jurisdictions, the service and support sectors of differential response systems have provided families with minimal levels of assistance. It is also true that the levels of social provisions available to help children and families in child protection jurisdictions are minimal compared to most family service jurisdictions. Finally, outside of the types of special demonstration projects described by Schene (chapter 4), collaborations across service organizations in North America have proved to be very slow and difficult to create (Cameron, Karabanow, Laurendeau, & Chamberland, 2001). While the ambitions of bringing more helpful resources to families, and reducing the use of coercive investigations are laudable, there is little evidence to date of any deep impacts of these differential response experiments on the dominant focuses and procedures of mainstream child protection systems in North America.

Authority and Collaboration

All systems of child and family welfare in developed (relatively affluent) nations use some combination of communal norms for assistance with child caring and family life, and the coercive power of the law to justify interventions into families and to gain family compliance. For example, despite their emphasis on voluntary assistance, family service and community caring systems use the authority of police and the courts to remove children from dangerous circumstances, particularly when parents reject offers of assistance. It is also true that, despite an emphasis on legal enforcement, a portion of parents involved with child protection authorities are desirous of receiving help and enter into voluntary service agreements. However, the relative emphasis upon evoking communal norms for helping and enforced legal compliance differs strikingly across various child and family welfare orientations.

For Aboriginal communities, the struggle to assume responsibility for the well-being of their children and families is an important part of nation building and revitalizing Indigenous heritages. Residential school and child welfare intrusions are considered central agents of the devastating effects conquest and colonialism have had on Indigenous populations (Love, chapter 10; Mandell et al., chapter 9). Consequently, more than any of the three generic child and family welfare orientations, community caring ideals for child and family welfare envision the active collaboration of all elements of community life, including agencies of Aboriginal self government, tribal elders, extended families, and community members, as well as available educational, mental health, and community justice resources. Whenever possible, it is traditional values and community expectations that provide the justification for involvement with children and families, and establish guidelines for patterns of engagement. When court involvement cannot be avoided, as seen in the illustrations in chapter 1, efforts have been made to use concepts of restorative justice, involving extended family and community members in the deliberations and solutions. The principles of restoring relationships, consensus, and cooperation are central to ideals of community and the use of authority in First Nations (Maidman & Connors, 2001; Morrissette, McKenzie, & Morrissette, 1993).

There is substantial variance among the family service orientations discussed in this volume. Despite these differences, and notwithstanding periodic shifts towards greater legal child protection emphases in some settings (see the discussion of France in chapter 6), all three of these family service systems primarily rely upon the normality of receiving assistance with the care and education of children to approach families, with concerns about child maltreatment and with offers of assistance. Sweden (see chapter 7) and other Nordic countries (see the illustrations in chapter 1), in particular, do not distinguish between services to general populations and those for maltreating families, and emphasize the use of a broad range of social protection provisions in both enterprises. Sweden also uses lay contact families/persons in its most popular child and family welfare program. Other family service systems involve civil society through the use of elected bodies overseeing selected services or through the use of lay mediators (see the illustrations in chapter 1).

Hetherington, Cooper, Smith, and Wilford (1997) provide evidence that a unique characteristic of many family service systems is the creation of 'intermediary spaces' (Freymond, 2003) in between voluntary assent and legally enforced compliance. These are places where efforts to mediate differences between child and family welfare service providers and families, and to establish mutually acceptable service plans, can occur. Ideally, both family members and service providers can request access to mediation by an impartial third party, whose only authority is to endeavour to broker an agreement. If such efforts fail, recourse to formal court applications is available. A corollary process is that most family service systems rely extensively, except in emergencies or with particularly severe abuse, on relationships between front-line service providers and families, and on service provider judgment and discretion, to negotiate service agreements. Compared to child protection systems, these service providers typically have more time and encouragement to build collaborative relationships with children and parents, and opportunities to use their skills to try to resolve service disagreements.

For example, in the French child and family welfare system, historically, there has been considerable reliance on the office of the Children's Judge to negotiate agreements. Children's judges are supposed to solicit the consent of families to any court-ordered measures, to help to reestablish parents' authority, and to mobilize resources in order to facilitate these outcomes (King & Piper, 1995; Luckock, Vogler, & Keating, 1996).

Andersson (chapter 7) describes the child and family welfare system in the district of Rosengaard in Sweden, where 84% of the inhabitants are immigrants or the children of immigrants. The entry point is where 'an administrative social worker responds if you wish to report suspected child abuse, apply for social assistance (supplementary benefits) or social support, or ask for help in handling your child's drug abuse problem or your husband's violence' (p. 221). Referrals can be made to the Child and Family Welfare Centre, which 'acts on the principle that the needs of families, children, and young people direct their work. No one should be turned away, but neither should anyone be forced to receive help from the centre ... The centre's social workers cooperate with ... voluntary organizations in the district, such as immigrant and women's organizations' (p. 222). Partnerships with families are emphasized, including seeking parental consent for out-of-home care, although compulsory care can be court ordered. Discretion for social workers in their jobs is valued; 'the relation between the client and the social worker is seen as important and flexible enough to accommodate different solutions to problems' (p. 226).

Hetherington and Nurse (chapter 3) state that, within child protection systems, language and thinking are dominated by legal discourse. Attending to legal rights and the requirements of gathering evidence to prove malfeasance in possible court action are central. Courts are focused on formal procedures to guarantee due process, and adversarial in nature with lawyers for all involved parties arguing their position in front of a judge. Court involvements often are intimidating for social workers and family members (Swift & Callahan, chapter 5). Increasingly, legal mandates provide the primary authority to intervene in families, and judicial orders become a basic method of protecting children and enforcing family compliance. When voluntary service agreements are negotiated, all the parties are aware of the frequency and ease of making a formal court application.

Front-line service providers in child protection systems manage their concerns about child safety, and protect themselves against retribution for possible errors by relying on judicial authority and conformance to formal service guidelines and documentary requirements. For example, in the Partnerships for Children and Families program of research in Ontario, Canada, at a local child protection agency, 70% of open child protection cases involved a formal court order. Also related to these emphases on investigation and legally mandated supervision of families is the lower proportion of time available to connect families with helpful resources, or to develop trusting helping relationships (Cameron & Hoy, 2003; Freymond, 2003; Maiter, Palmer, & Manji, 2003).

In North America, recently, there has been increased discussion of the value of partnerships in implementing child protection and family support mandates. Partnerships are presented as central to more efficient and constructive child and family welfare systems. Schene (chapter 4) discusses in substantial detail American experiences with creating formal and informal community partnerships for child protection and family support. These experiments are motivated, in addition to concerns about escalating costs and system effectiveness and fairness, by an interest in interventions that build on family and community strengths, respond to more families positively, and share the responsibilities for caring and safety. There has been an effort to increase formal service alliances within communities, and to involve extended family and community networks, voluntary associations, and faith organizations to help individual children and families, and to develop community capacity for constructive action. Data on the impacts of these experiences with partnerships on children, families, and communities, as well as on child protection systems, are not yet available.

Conclusions

A reality shared by all of the child protection, family service, and community caring exemplars discussed in this book is that the majority of the children, parents, families, and communities that come to their attention are relatively impoverished, and characterized by high levels of ongoing adversity. These three generic child and family welfare orientations differ significantly in their official acknowledgments of the realities and consequences of lives of lesser privilege, and in their capacities to respond in useful ways, and with help that is appreciated by children and families.

While Indigenous community caring orientations place the highest emphasis upon these oppressive conditions and their reversal, the previous chapters show that community caring systems are heavily constrained by the expectations of more powerful surrounding child protection systems, and very low comparative access to supportive services and resources. Family service systems, in particular those in the social democratic Nordic countries, seem better positioned to acknowledge and to provide useful resources to disadvantaged children, parents, families and communities. Finally, while service providers and policy developers are very aware of poverty and adversity in the lives of children, families, and communities, Anglo-American child protection systems, because of their mandated focus on specific types of maltreatment in the home, and policy environments increasingly less open to generous social protection provisions, are not well positioned to recognize or to adapt to conditions of lesser privilege.

The capacities of child and family welfare systems for congruent responses to children and families are heavily shaped by the social protection policy environments in which they function. It matters a great deal whether families and service providers have relatively easy or difficult access to resources such as adequate housing, adequate income supports, public health services, daycare and early childhood education, employment and retraining supports, mental health services, after school and educational supports, nutritional education and supports, parenting education and supports, and social and recreational opportunities. As Rachael Hetherington illustrates in chapter two, in reference to the English child protection system, if service providers have no capacity to respond to difficulties (such as improper child nutrition or school difficulties), such concerns quickly drop from their considerations of family circumstances and how to respond. The social protection policy environments for all of these child and family welfare systems have been affected by the realities of competing in increasingly integrated global economies. In all instances, these new realities have led to reductions in some social benefits, and to closer linkages of policies with the needs of employment markets (Palier, 2004). However, the differences in the magnitude and nature of social protection policy adjustments across international settings are striking.

The basic provisions and principles of the social protection welfare model in Nordic countries, despite necessary adjustments, have been maintained and continue to receive broad public support (Anderson, chapter 7; Palier, 2004). Bruno Palier states that the social protection policy environments in socially conservative European countries such as France, Germany, and the Netherlands have proven more difficult to adjust, and remain the subject of considerable public controversy. The European family service systems in this volume have all been influenced by the United Nations Charter of the Rights of Children, and in the future are likely to be affected by the efforts to establish common social protection principles for the European Union (Palier, 2004).

Anglo-American child protection systems have been constrained by very substantial reductions in the levels of social protection provisions over the past decade, and an increased preference to rely on the resources available to children and families through the market. Palier (2004) comments that these reductions have created substantially greater divides between the haves and have nots in liberal democratic policy regimes, such as England, Canada, and the United States. The community caring chapters in this volume stress that, within such relatively impoverished liberal social protection regimes, Indigenous populations fare far worse than other groupings on access to social protection resources, and on most indicators of child, adult, family, and community well-being.

An increasing challenge facing child protection and family service systems is adapting to families emigrating from countries with different conceptions of childhood and family, and contrasting perspectives about appropriate interventions. For example, in one of our local child protection agencies in southern Ontario, Canada, about 25% of children in state care are from non-European or non-Anglo-American cultures (personal communication, 16 April 2004). Both child protection and family service systems evolved from specific historic conceptions of childhood and family. Their capacities to accommodate more inclusive conceptions of family, divergent norms of child care and behaviours, and individual identities defined by extended family, community, and religious connections are unknown.

If the official response to such differences is a blanket insistence upon conformance to mainstream expectations, then tensions and resistance from various communities should be anticipated. The Aboriginal community caring chapters in this volume all provide dramatic testimony about the destructive consequences of host child protection systems' inabilities to acknowledge and enhance First Nation family and community values and traditions. Catherine Love (chapter 10) talks about the active political resistance and civil disobedience of Maori communities in Aotearea/New Zealand in response to the intrusions of child protection authorities.

There is agreement across all of the chapters in this volume that child and family welfare cannot be reduced to a technical or objective exercise. Whatever the contributions of technical risk assessment or formally structured investigations, the analyses in the preceding chapters concur that effective child and family welfare ultimately must be grounded in relationships between families and service providers, and in cooperation among child and family welfare agencies, other service and community organizations, and extended family and community networks. It is no coincidence that the three child protection chapters in this volume (Canada, England, the United States) make the strongest arguments for improving helping relationships, and expanding collaborations in child and family welfare.

There is also consensus that child and family welfare must be both a care and protection endeavour. Ongoing tensions in all of the systems of child and family welfare discussed here include creating an acceptable balance between care and protection requirements, and, as is highlighted in the recent reforms in the Netherlands, maintaining productive cooperation between care and protection orientations that have different priorities and ways of working. The family service systems analyzed, as well as the visions for culturally appropriate community caring systems, all have principled and practical reasons for prioritizing caring services and offers of assistance, with stated intentions of avoiding involvement with legal child protection systems whenever feasible. In sharp contrast, child protection systems have increasingly become legal investigation and enforcement systems, with their already relatively modest concerns with care provisions of earlier eras greatly reduced, if not eliminated. All three child protection chapters in this volume (England, the United States, Canada) argue for the urgency of finding a more appropriate and acceptable balance between care provisions and protection enforcement. There is a consensus among the authors in this book that formal, legal child protection enforcement should not be the primary influence shaping child and family welfare systems, dominating everyday work requirements, as is presently the case in most English, American, and Canadian jurisdictions.

An ongoing debate in American child and family welfare is whether child protection and family care (support) functions should be housed separately. There has been ongoing concern about the increasing number of families being drawn into 'one-size-fits-all' child protection investigations, and the realization that most of these families end up receiving very little assistance from these involvements (see the discussion in Cameron et al., 2001). Such organizational divisions between family care and legal protection already exist in most European family service jurisdictions. Pivotal considerations in such arrangements are how families enter each system, and whether families in one system have access to the resources of the other. Families under investigation, including most families with a child in state care, can profit from the types of services and supports envisioned for family care (Freymond, 2003). It is equally imperative that families receiving supportive services be connected quickly with legal protection enforcement services should dangers be detected. It is critical to avoid rigid barriers between care and protection divisions, and to create possibilities for children and parents not only to move between both sectors, but to be involved with both simultaneously, if appropriate.

In North American differential response/dual track child and family welfare reforms, the tendency has been to rely upon formal child protection assessments, including reliance on technical assessment instruments, to decide which track is appropriate for families (Alberta Children's Services, 2003). There has been some consideration given to expanding technical assessments to include a more complete emphasis on family strengths and resources, as well as risks of child maltreatment (Ontario Ministry of Children's Services, 2003). European family service systems have relied more on relationships between service providers and families for assessments, and offers of assistance to families as usual first responses, unless otherwise indicated. In addition, common points of entry are general service organizations or specialized child and family welfare organizations, rather than legal child protection units. There are reasons to believe that some of these family service configurations have advantages both in terms of flexibility of responses and acceptability to families, compared to North American differential response/dual track models. However, the relative paucity of social protection provisions, the historical obstacles to shared child welfare mandates, and the specialized focuses of child protection authorities are substantial impediments to emulating such organizational arrangements in North America. Nonetheless, the creation of formal and informal partnerships to enhance North American child protection and family support efforts, and to increase systems' capacities for flexible responses, have been identified as priorities in the preceding chapters. It is too early to assess the depth and scope of the impacts that these reform efforts will have on North American child and family welfare.

The child protection and family service systems examined in this book reflect the dominant political and cultural expectations of the settings within which they have evolved. Whether they are experienced as harsh or supportive by families, whether they are appreciated or difficult places to work, whether they produce desirable outcomes or not, each of these Anglo-American and European systems is congruent with central values and ways of living endorsed by its host environment. As realities and expectations in these host environments change, these child protection and family service systems adjust to remain congruent and supported.

Such patterns of historical evolution and congruence, being grounded in broadly shared principles and ambitions, are not true for the community caring systems of Indigenous peoples. The land inhabited by Aboriginal populations has been occupied by foreign powers, and the traditional ways of living of First Nations has been the focus of eradication and assimilation projects for over a century. All three of the First Nation chapters paint distressing portraits of the devastating effects of these processes on traditional ways of living, and on the well-being of Aboriginal children, adults, families, communities, and nations. All three chapters identify mainstream child protection systems as among the most pernicious agents of colonization.

Community caring systems cannot be adequately understood by focusing solely upon how they operate and might evolve. They are fundamental to First Nation resistance and nation building. Gaining control over the treatment of children and families, rebuilding damaged communities and ways of living, and creating child and family welfare and justice procedures congruent with Aboriginal values and procedures are integral to Indigenous liberation and self-government projects. Community caring systems represent the aspirations of less powerful groups struggling to create a congruent space for themselves within dominant child protection systems. Earlier, community caring systems were described as 'in-between' systems, trying to modify delegated mandates from larger child protection systems that fit uneasily with their preferred ways of life. Consequently, community caring systems are less operationally articulated than child protection or family service systems. They also face the challenge of creating congruent services for First Nation peoples who themselves are living in two worlds. Many Indigenous people in North America and Aotearoa/New Zealand now live in urban environments, while others continue to live in relatively homogeneous Aboriginal communities. This creates unique challenges for the design and orientation of First Nation community caring systems.

About four years ago, as we began the investigations of the Partnerships for Children and Families Project into the child protection system in Ontario, Canada, we asked ourselves the question: 'Does anyone elsewhere do this work differently?' Somewhat shockingly, neither we nor any of our colleagues had any clear idea of the answer to this question. We see this as a rather sad testimony to the insularity of our deliberations into child and family welfare at that time. However, we believe that this insularity is typical of child protection systems, in North America at least, where inspiration is seldom sought from environments different than our own.

International comparisons of systems of child and family welfare broaden our understanding of the nature of the enterprise and the range of what can be done. They question our convictions about the inevitability and the superiority of specific approaches to child and family welfare. As Hetherington argued in chapter 2, international comparisons allow us to understand our own systems with greater clarity, helping us to locate niches where innovation is possible, and to identify principles and procedures that we think are important to maintain. International comparisons also open possibilities for informed dialogues across jurisdictions about principles and procedures characteristic of positive systems of child and family welfare, and how such ideals might be adapted to the cultures and institutional arrangements of particular settings.

Regrettably, there is very little international comparative research upon which to base comparisons of systems of child and family welfare. Most comparisons are based upon the analyses and impressions of knowledgeable informants within particular systems, as are the discussions in this volume (for example, see the comparisons in Callahan, Hessle, & Strega, 2000; Gilbert, 1997; Pires, 1993). An exception is the work of Hetherington and her colleagues (see Baistow, Hetherington, Spriggs, & Yelloly, 1996; Cooper, Hetherington, Baistow, Pitts, & Spriggs, 1995; Hetherington et al., 1997; Wilford, Hetherington, & Piquardt,

1997). For the most part, this work concentrates on comparisons between English child protection and selected family service systems in continental Europe.

The Partnership for Children and Families Project is seeking funding for a program of research comparing child protection (England, Ontario and Quebec in Canada), family service (Sweden, France, Germany), and community caring (Manitoba and British Columbia in Canada, Maori in Aotearoa/New Zealand) systems of child and family welfare.

To the best of our knowledge, no similar in-depth cross-national comparisons of systems of child and family welfare have been attempted, certainly none which includes Indigenous community caring systems. There are certainly many topics worthy of cross-national explorations. For example, we know little about the procedures and experiences of having a child placed in out-of-home care under these various systems. We do not know what differences exist in how specific populations are approached (e.g., children with a mentally ill mother, addicted parents, various visible minority populations, young mothers, etc.), and the effects of these differences. We do not know what it is like to be a service provider in these different models. We can only surmise how children and parents experience their involvement. We have no bases for understanding the relative merits of different methods of general system organization, or specific aspects of system organization (e.g., legal services, residential placements, mediation services, assessment services), other than general speculations. There is much that we do not understand.

In the final analysis, this book is an argument against continuing our insular discussions of systems of child and family welfare, and an argument for opening ourselves to the possibilities of learning from others and to alternative ways of understanding. Certainly, within the European Union, there will be an increasing emphasis upon comparative social policy analyses, including child and family welfare policy, and upon discussions of common principles to guide action within individual member countries. Our contention is that it is time to expand these investigations and discussions to include the three generic models presented in this volume. It is also critical to try to understand the variety of arrangements in the less affluent world, rather than continuing to assume that such countries should or could simply emulate what we have done. Our experiences with cross-national comparisons and dialogues, despite the substantial challenges involved, is that they are much needed tonics for imagining innovations, and for renewing beliefs in the possibilities of building positive systems of child and family welfare.

NOTES

1 The information from the Partnerships for Children and Families program of research is selected from Cameron, G., *Finding a Fit: Family Realities and Service Responses* (in press). In G. Cameron, N. Coady, & G. Adams (eds.), *Towards Positive Systems of Child and Family Welfare: Current Issues and Future Directions*. Waterloo, ON: Wilfrid Laurier University Press.
2 Privilege refers to access to valued educational and employment opportunities and to the sufficiency of financial resources to provide adequate access to daily living resources. Lesser is in comparison to the educational, employment, and financial circumstances of those who study and write about these families, and of many child protection personnel in contact with them. Both concepts refer to living conditions during childhood as well as adult life.

Appendix A: Partners in Child Protection and Well-Being

Formal Partners

- CPS – intake, assessment, ongoing services
- Mandated and nonmandated reporters
- Law enforcement
- Courts
- Parents and caregivers
- Health care providers, emergency care
- Foster care, emergency shelters, group homes, and residential treatment facilities
- Formal, in-home services provided through or by CPS
- Schools
- Childrens' Advocacy Centres for interviewing child victims
- Substance abuse evaluation and treatment agencies
- Family preservation services
- Domestic violence shelters and programs
- Developmental screening resources
- Public agencies providing services to families involved with CPS – such as mental health programs, family counseling
- Wrap-around service programs

Non-Formal Partners

- Extended family, close friends, neighbors, concerned citizens
- Public housing community staff and residents
- Child care centres
- After-school programs

- Nutrition programs
- Welfare agencies – including 'welfare to work' programs
- Faith communities
- Home visiting programs for new parents
- YM/YWCA, YM/YWHA, 4-H
- Recreational organizations, parks, sports programs
- Big Brothers/Big Sisters or other mentoring programs
- County extension services
- Family resource centres

Appendix B: Guiding Principles for Building Partnerships

- The safety of children is the paramount purpose and goal of the partnership. Partnerships have to share responsibility for the protection of children.
- Partnerships have to focus on specific communities or neighbour-hoods. Even if a broader array of services is utilized, they are accessible through local points of contact.
- Everyone living or working in the community can have a role in the partnership; a basic objective is to increase the propensity to offer help as well as to accept help.
- Governance of the partnership has to be formalized; decision making must reflect the thinking of formal agencies and institutions, but also parents, local residents, involved communities of faith, and other nonformal supports to families.
- A continuum of supports and services should be offered by the partnership, including primary prevention, early intervention, careful assessment of reports of child abuse and neglect, concrete services to protect children and stabilize families, and aftercare as well as sustainable supports for parents and children.
- Approaches to families are consistently respectful, recognize the strengths of even the most troubled families, and endeavour to preserve family ties whenever possible.
- Comprehensive assessments using common tools across the part-nership will facilitate the identification of needs and strengths and the responsiveness of the partnership to children and parents. This will lead to more effective engagement of families in services and supports and better outcomes for children.

- When a case is opened to any service or support from the partnership, intervention will be coordinated across all those involved in the work with the family.
- The partnership will organize itself to identify the major gaps in services and supports and work together to address those needs, including active advocacy efforts to obtain resources.

Appendix C: Timeline of the Evolution of the French Child Protection System

1638	Foundation of the 'lost children hospital' in Paris	First institution for abandoned children
1789	French revolution	First breach in the Roman civil paternal absolute power on children.
1810	Imperial Napoleonic civil code	Restored paternal power but introduced penalty for extreme abuse of children
1889	Republican civil code	Introduction of new items in the civil code opening a father to the forfeit of his parental rights
1892	Dr Tardieu's forensic works	Study on child physical abuse syndrome
1912	Creation of Children's Judge function	A professional and specialized judge in charge of juvenile delinquency cases
1933	Legal evolution	Law on neglected and abandoned children
1945	Legal evolution: Ordonnance de 1945 sur les mineurs delinquents	Law about juvenile delinquency. Firmly centred on the priority for 'éducative' answers to juvenile delinquency (until age 21), this law established the Children's Judge as the moral authority of the child welfare system

1958	Legal evolution (*ordonnance*): the concept of judicial protection: *Assistance educative*	The Children's Judge got power to protect children in danger and kept their role for young delinquency.
1959	Legal evolution (*ordonnance*): The concept of administrative protection: *Protection administrative*, implemented by Aide Social à l'Enfance, a department of the DDASS, a state local administration.	The Family and Social Action code included a duty for state social services, to bring help, support, and counselling to families 'facing social difficulties endangering their well-being.' These interventions included voluntary or negotiated care for children, and are based on the concept of risk of danger.
1984/5	Decentralization of administrative protection *ASE* from state to local authorities (*Départements*)	All the DDASS administration workforces (social services, PMI and ASE) were removed from state to *Départements*, equivalent to counties in many English-speaking countries.
1989	Legal evolution: July 1989, the Prevention of Abuse of Children Act.	Gave to the local authorities (ASE department) the duty to set up a permanent plan of action to collect information about abused children and to investigate all suspected cases in connection with Justice, to train all practitioners on the subject of maltreatment, and to collect data about the incidence and prevalence of abuse.
1991	Creation of the national observatory of children in danger.	The priority action of ODAS was to elaborate a glossary to enable professionals to speak about the same things.

1998	17 July 1998 Act on per-petrators and victims of sexual abuse	Improved the support offered to child victims of sexual abuse in criminal proceedings: video recordings, development of child advocate (*administrateur ad hoc*), therapeutic support.
2000/1	5 official reports scrutinize the French system at work	• Recommend to reduce the gap between professionals and service users • Promote negotiations between professionals and users before calling for Children's Judges' intervention • Tend to clarify the confusion between Children's Judges (judicial protection) and ASE (administrative protection) jurisdictions
2002	March 2002 law on the evolution of judicial protection *Assistance educative* proceeding	• Allows children and their parents to read their judicial files • Aims to reduce traumas produced by the impact of discretionary decision

Glossary

Administrative protection: Interventions based on voluntary or negotiated intervention and implemented (directly or by nonprofit organizations ordered and funded by local authorities) by the administration of the local authority (Département). This administration is composed of three different departments:

1 Aide Sociale à l'enfance (ASE): Child Welfare department which works not only with their own teams (social workers, psychologists) based in local units, but also with the network of children's homes and foster care services from the nonprofit sector by means of conventions and agreements producing a very close financial and technical control over it.
2 PMI department: the Mother and Infant Health protection department that implements primary and secondary free social and medical actions for children under the age of 6. Their professionals (nurses, nursery nurses, pediatricians) are firmly linked with hospitals and Ecole maternelle' – a French free/public preschool for 3–6-year-old children.
3 Service Social: generic social work implemented by *assistante sociale de secteur*.
   Professionals of these three departments are based in the same local unit named Circonscription d'action sanitaires et socials – an average of 25,000 inhabitants per unit.

Children's Judges (*Juges des enfants*) (*JE*): professional and specialized judges trained in a three-year program in the Ecole Nationale de la Magistrature in Bordeaux and Paris. The JE's jurisdiction includes:

• Juvenile delinquency. He/She judges both in office hearings and court hearings. He/she leads investigation (except crimes), and follows up the implementation of decisions.

- Children in danger. He/She judges in office hearings, leads various kinds of investigations, and follows up the evolution of the case by means of planned or emergency hearings.
- Since 1974 (change of the minority age from 21 to 18) young adults (18/21) in trouble.
- Control of the use of family allowances.
- In the 'assistance educative' field (Children in danger), he/she has to know about children's cases if the health, safety, or morality of the child is threatened or if educative conditions are seriously endangered. The threat has to be determined as being significant and the child has to live in France, whatever his/her nationality.

Cases come to the JE through several channels:

1 Procureur de la République (Procurator) / He/She receives all kinds of referrals about children in danger (for example, in Département de Seine-Saint-Denis 52% of all referrals came from local authorities SSD, 7% from schools, 5% from hospitals and private doctors; 11% from police and gendarmerie, 19% from parents and children, 6% from relatives and neighbours). The Procureur can decide whether or not to refer cases to JE, to prosecute parents for confirmed incidents of abuse or neglect, to ask for police investigations, and to prosecute perpetrators of abuses.
2 Parents
3 Child her/himself (5% of all referrals)
4 Judge her/himself, for example, when he/she has come to know of a child's situation through his/her knowledge of another case.

- Children's Judges (JE) are only involved in the child's life on the basis of suspected danger. Divorce and parental conflicts, based on a child's upbringing and education, belong to the Juge des affaires familiales' jurisdiction (JAF). The JE can have knowledge of a child's case, in divorce or parental conflict situations, only if elements of danger influence the implementation of the JAF's decision, and generate the need of a modification.
- Children's Judges have to summon up educational, social, psychological, and material resources to restore failing or vacant parental authority. They can order the following:

1 Investigative orders named IOE (Investigation et orientation éducative) implemented by multidisciplinary teams.

2 Family supervision and treatment orders, named Action éducative en milieu ouvert (AEMO) implemented by social work teams including also psychologists and psychiatrists.

- IOE and AEMO are mostly implemented by teams form the nonprofit sector. IOE are funded by the Ministry of Justice and AEMO by the ASE department. Care orders are implemented by the ASE department which widely contracted with the nonprofit sector for that purpose. Care orders only restricted parental rights. Children's Judges do not have any power to definitively separate parents and children. These orders are reviewed every year.

Judicial protection: Group of interventions ordered by the Children's Judges to protect children in danger.

References

Aboriginal Justice Inquiry (AJI). (1991). *The justice system and Aboriginal people: Public inquiry into the administration of justice and Aboriginal people* (Vol. 1). Winnipeg: Province of Manitoba.

Aboriginal Justice Inquiry – Child Welfare Initiative (AJI-CWI). (2001). *Promise of hope: Commitment to change.* Winnipeg: The Assembly of Manitoba Chiefs, The Manitoba Metis Federation, Manitoba Keewatinowi Okimakanak, and the Government of Manitoba. Retrieved 8 January 2002 from www.aji-cwi.mb.ca/pdfs/promiseofhope.pdf.

Aboriginal Justice Inquiry – Child Welfare Initiative (AJI-CWI). (2002). *Summary report on the AJI-CWI phase 3: Public feedback process.* Winnipeg: The Assembly of Manitoba Chiefs, The Manitoba Metis Federation, Manitoba Keewatinowi Okimakanak, and the Government of Manitoba. Retrieved 30 May 2002 from www.aji-cwi.mb.ca/pdfs/feedbacksummaryreport.pdf.

Adams, P., & Nelson, K. (1995). *Reinventing human services: Community and family-centered practice.* New York: Aldine de Gruyter.

Alberta Children's Services. (2003). *Alberta adopts a new direction: A brief history of strategic policy shifts and change management.* In 4th National Child Welfare Symposium: Community Collaboration on Differential Response. Alberta Response Model: Transforming Outcomes for Children Youth and Families. Banff.

Aldgate, J. (1993). Respite care for children – an old remedy in a new package. In P. Marsh & J. Triseliotis (Eds.), *Prevention and reunification in child care.* (pp. 43–78) London: Batsford in association with British Agencies for Adoption and Fostering.

Aldgate, J., & Bradley, M. (1999). *Supporting families through short-term fostering.* London: HMSO.

Ammerman, R.T., & Hersen, M. (Eds.). (1990). *Children at risk: An evaluation of factors contributing to child abuse and neglect.* New York: Plenum Press.

Andersson, G. (1992). Social workers and child welfare. *British Journal of Social Work, 22(3)*, 253–69.

Andersson, G. (1993). Support and relief: The Swedish contact person and contact family program. *Scandinavian Journal of Social Welfare, 2*, 54–62.

Andersson, G. (1999a). Involving key stakeholders in evaluation – a Swedish perspective. *Social Work in Europe, 6(1)*, 1–7.

Andersson, G. (1999b). Children in permanent foster care in Sweden. *Child and Family Social Work, 4*, 175–86.

Andersson, G. (1999c). Children in residential and foster care – a Swedish example. *International Journal of Social Welfare, 8*, 253–66.

Andersson, G. (2003). Evaluation of the contact family service in Sweden. In I. Katz and J. Pinkerton (Eds.), *Evaluating family support: Thinking internationally, thinking critically* (pp. 291–306). Chichester: Wiley.

Andersson G., & Bangura Arvidsson, M. (2001). *Vad vet vi om insatsen kontaktperson/familj?* [What do we know about the measure contact person/family?] Lunds universitet, Finland: Meddelanden från socialhögskolan, nr 1.

Antler, J., & Antler, S. (1979). From child rescue to family protection. *Child and Youth Services Review, 1*, 177–204.

Armitage, A. (1993). Family and child welfare in First Nation communities. In B. Wharf (Ed.), *Rethinking child welfare in Canada* (pp. 131–71). Toronto, ON: Oxford University Press.

Armitage, A., Callahan, M., & Lewis, C. (2001). Social work education and child protection: The B.C. experience. *Canadian Social Work Review, 18(1)*, 9–24.

Armstrong, L. (1995). *Of sluts and bastards: A feminist decodes the child welfare debate.* Monroe, ME: Common Courage Press.

Arnup, K. (1995). *Lesbian parenting: Living with pride & prejudice.* Charlottetown, PEI: Gynergy Books.

Assembly of First Nations and Department of Indian Affairs and Northern Development. (2000). *First Nations child and family services joint national policy review.* Ottawa, ON: Assembly of First Nations.

Association of Native Child and Family Services Agencies of Ontario (ANCFSAO). (2001). *Child welfare reform initiatives: Issues and recommendations.* (Final draft).

Audit Commission. (1994). *Seen but not heard: Co-ordinating community child health and social services for children in need.* London: HMSO.

Auger, D. (1997). Empowerment through First Nation control of education: A Sakaw Cree philosophy of education. In R.J. Ponting (Ed.), *First Nations in Canada: Perspectives on opportunity, empowerment, and self-determination* (pp. 326–51). Toronto, ON: McGraw-Hill Ryerson.

Awasis Agency of Northern Manitoba. (1997). *First Nations family justice: Mee-noo-stah-tan Mi-ni-si-win*. Thompson, MA: Awasis Agency of Northern Manitoba.

Baartman, H.E.M. (1997). Over legitimering en noodzaak van primaire preventie. N*ederlands Tijdschrift voor Opvoeding, Vorming en Onderwijs, 13(5)*, 300–7.

Badgely, R.F. (1984). *Sexual offences against children* (Vols. 1–2). Ottawa, ON: Canadian Government Publishing Centre.

Bailey, B. (2000). A white paper on aboriginal education in universities. *Canadian Ethnic Studies, 32(1)*, 126–35.

Baistow, K. (2000). Cross-national research: What can we learn from inter-country comparisons. *Social Work in Europe, 7(3)*, 8–13.

Baistow, K., & Hetherington, R. (1998). Parents' views of child welfare interventions: An Anglo-French comparison. *Children and Society, 12*, 124–33.

Baistow, K., Hetherington, R., Spriggs, A., & Yelloly, M. (1996). *Parents speaking: Anglo-French perceptions of child welfare interventions, a preliminary report.* London: Brunel University.

Baistow, K., & Wilford, G. (2000). Helping parents, protecting children: Ideas from Germany. *Children and Society, 14*, 343–354.

Baker, M., & Phipps, S. (1997). Family change and family policies: Canada. In S.B. Kamerman & A. Kahn (Eds.), *Family change and family policies in Great Britain, Canada, New Zealand and the United States* (pp. 103–206). Oxford: Clarendon Press.

Barsky, A. (1999). Community involvement through child protection mediation. *Child Welfare 78(4)*, 481–502.

Barth, R. (1992). Child welfare services in United States and Sweden: Different assumptions, laws and outcomes. *Scandinavian Journal of Social Welfare, 5*, 159–64.

Battiste, M., & Barman, J. (1995). *First Nations education in Canada: The circle unfolds*. Vancouver, BC: University of British Columbia Press.

Battiste, M., & Youngblood Henderson, J. (2000). *Protecting Indigenous knowledge and heritage: A global challenge.* Saskatoon, SK: Purich Publishing.

Battle, K. (2001). *Ottawa should expand the Canada Child Tax Benefit.* Presentation to the Commons Subcommittee on Children and Youth at Risk. Ottawa, ON: Caledon Institute of Social Policy.

Battle, K., & Mendelson, M. (2001). *Benefits for children: A four country study.* Ottawa, ON: Caledon Institute of Social Policy.

Beaufort-Caspers, J., & Veldkamp, A.W.M. (Eds.). (1991). *Kinderbescherming Maak het Waar!!!* Breda: VVS.

Bennett, M. (2002). *Aboriginal youth and racism: A review of the literature.* Unpublished paper prepared for the Department of Canadian Heritage, Winnipeg, MB.

Bennett, M., & Blackstock, C. (2002). *A literature review and annotated bibliography on aspects of Aboriginal child welfare in Canada.* Retrieved 7 January 2003 from First Nations Child and Family Caring Society of Canada web site: http://www.fncfcs.com/.

Berge, I.J. ten. (1998). *Besluitvorming in de kinderbescherming.* Delft: Eburon.

Bering Pruzan, V.L. (1997). Denmark: Voluntary placements as a family support. In N. Gilbert (Ed.), *Combatting child abuse: International perspectives and trends* (pp. 125–42). New York: Oxford University Press.

Bianco, J.L., & Lamy, P. (1980). *L'aide à l'enfance demain.* Paris: Ministère de la Santé et de la Sécurité Sociale.

Bisschops, L. (1998). Kinderbescherming: Tussen bescherming en emancipatie! *Tijdschrift voor de Rechten van het Kind, 8(2),* 2–6.

Blackstock, C. (2001). Restoring peace and harmony in First Nations communities. In K. Kufeldt & B. McKenzie (Eds.), *Child welfare: Connecting research policy and practice* (pp. 331–41). Waterloo, ON: Wilfred Laurier University Press.

BO Barnombudsmannen [The Children's Ombudsman]. (2001). *Upp till 18. Fakta om barn och ungdom* [Up to 18. Facts about children and young people]. Stockholm: BO och SCB.

Bodley, J.H. (1990). *Victims of progress* (3rd ed.). Mountain View, CA: Mayfield.

Bowlby, J. (1969). *Attachment and loss.* Vol. 1, *Attachment.* London: Hogarth.

Bradley, J. (1995a). The resolve to devolve: Maori and social services. *Social Work Now, 1,* 29–35.

Bradley, J. (1995b). Before you tango with our whanau you better know what makes us tick: An indigenous approach to social work. *Te Komako: Social Work Review, 7,* 1.

Bradley, J. (1995c). Totara Tree Without Roots. *Te Komako: Social Work Review, 7,* 1.

Brown, L., Haddock, L., & Kovach, M. (2002). Watching over our families and children: Lahum'utul'Smun'eem child and family services. In B. Wharf (Ed.), *Community work approaches to child welfare* (pp. 131–51). Toronto, ON: Broadview Press.

Burik, A. van, & de Savornin Lohman, P. (1994). *Tussenevaluatie projecten verbetering samenwerking kindermishandeling.* Amsterdam: Van Dijk, Van Soomeren, & Partners B.V.

Cajete, G. (2000). *Native science: Natural laws of interdependence.* Sante Fe, NM: Clear Light Publishers.

Callahan, M. (1993). Feminist approaches: Women recreate child welfare. In B. Wharf (Ed.), *Rethinking child welfare in Canada* (pp. 172–209). Toronto, ON: Oxford University Press.

Callahan, M., Field, B., Hubberstey, C., & Wharf, B. (1998). *Best practice in child welfare.* A report to the Ministry of Children and Families. British Columbia.

Callahan, M., Hessle, S., & Strega, S. (Eds.). (2000). *Valuing the field: Child welfare in an international context.* Aldershot, UK: Ashgate Press.

Cameron, G. (1995). The nature and effectiveness of parent mutual aid organizations in child welfare. In J. Hudson & B. Galaway (Eds.), *Child welfare in Canada: Research and policy implications* (pp. 66–81). Toronto, ON: Thompson Educational Publishing.

Cameron, G., de Boer, C., Frensch, K.M., & Adams, G. (2003). *Siege and response: Families' everyday realities and experiences with children's residential mental health services.* Waterloo, ON: Wilfrid Laurier University, Partnerships for Children and Families Project.

Cameron, G., Freymond, N., Cornfield, D., & Palmer, S. (2001). *Positive possibilities for child and family welfare: Options for expanding the Anglo-American child protection paradigm.* Waterloo, ON: Wilfrid Laurier University, Partnerships for Child and Families Project.

Cameron, G., & Hoy, S. (2003). *Stories of mothers and child welfare.* Waterloo, ON: Wilfrid Laurier University, Partnerships for Children and Families Project.

Cameron, G., Karabanow, J., Laurendeau, M.-C., & Chamberland, C. (2001). Program implementation and diffusion. In I. Prilleltensky, G. Nelson, & L. Peirson (Eds.), *Promoting family wellness and preventing child maltreatment: Fundamentals for thinking and action* (pp. 339–74). Toronto, ON: University of Toronto Press.

Cameron, G., O'Reilly, J., Laurendeau, M.-C., & Chamberland, C. (2001). Programming for distressed and disadvantaged adolescents. In I. Prilleltensky, G. Nelson, & L. Peirson (Eds.), *Promoting family wellness and preventing child maltreatment: Fundamentals for thinking and action* (pp. 289–338). Toronto, ON: University of Toronto Press.

Cameron, G., Vanderwoerd, J., & Peirson, L. (1997). *Protecting children and supporting families: Promising programs and organisational realities.* New York: Aldine de Gruyter.

Campaign 2000. (2001). *Child poverty in Canada. Family security in insecure times: Tackling Canada's social deficit. November 2001 Bulletin.* Retrieved 30 December 2001 from www.campaign2000.ca.

Canadian Broadcasting Corporation. 2000, June. *Ideas: To hurt or to heal.* Toronto, ON: Canadian Broadcasting Corporation.

Caring for First Nations Children Society. (2002). *Aboriginal social worker training program curriculum CORE-15.* For more information see the Caring for First Nations Children Society web site: www.cfncs.com.

Carlson, J. (1994). *Journey from Fisher River: A celebration of the spirituality of a people through the life of Stan McKay*. Toronto, ON: United Church Publishing House.

Carlson, J. (1995). *Dancing the dream: The First Nations and the church in partnership*. Toronto, ON: Anglican Book Centre.

Castellano, M.B., Stalwick, H., & Wien, F. (1986). Native social work in Canada: Issues and adaptations. *Canadian Social Work Review, 4*, 167–84.

Center for the Study of Social Policy. (1997). *Community partnerships for protecting children: Documentation of the first year*. New York: Edna McConnell Clark Foundation.

Chandler, M. (2002, November). *Stabilizing cultural identity as a hedge against suicide in Canada's First Nations*. Unpublished paper presented at the Aboriginal Research and Policy Conference, Ottawa, Ontario.

Chen, X. (2001). *Tending the gardens of citizenship: Child protection in Toronto, 1880s-1920s*. Unpublished doctoral dissertation, School of Social Work, University of Toronto.

Child Ombudsman's Annual Report. (2001). *Rapport annuel du Défenseur des Enfants au Président de la République et au Parlement*. Retrieved 6 February 2002 from http://www.defenseurdesenfants.fr /pdf/rapport2001.

Children, Young Persons and Their Families Service (1993). Brief to the Minister of Social Welfare. *Trapski's Family Law, 1/8/96,* A-25.

Churchill, W. (1996). *From a native son: Selected essays on Indigenism, 1985/1995*. Boston: South End Press.

Clasen, J. (Ed.). (1999). *Comparative social policy: Concepts, theories and methods*. Oxford: Blackwells.

Colapinto, J.A. (1995). Dilution of family process in social services: Implications for treatment of neglectful families. *Family Process, 34,* 59–74.

Colclough, L., Parton, N., & Anslow, M. (1999). Family support. In C. Wattam & N. Parton (Eds.), *Child sexual abuse* (pp. 159–80). New York: Wiley.

Colorado, P. (1988). Bridging Native and Western science. *Convergence, 21,* 49–72.

Committee on Child Protection Law. [Commissie voor de herziening van het Kinderbeschermingsrecht]. (1971). *Jeugdbeschermingsrecht's*. Gravenhage: Staatsuitgeverij.

Connors, E., & Maidman, F. (2001). A circle of healing: Family wellness in Aboriginal communities. In I. Prellitensky, G. Nelson, & L. Peirson (Eds.), *Promoting family wellness and preventing child maltreatment: Fundamentals for thinking and action* (pp. 349–416). Toronto, ON: University of Toronto Press.

Convention on the rights of the child. (1990). Stockholm: Government publication.

Cook, G., & Carlson, J. (1997). Gladys Taylor Cook. In J. Carlson & A. Dumont

(Eds.), *Bridges in spirituality: First Nation Christian women tell their stories* (pp. 102–44). Toronto, ON: Anglican Book Centre and United Church Publishing House.

Cooper, A., Hetherington, R., Baistow, K., Pitts, J., & Spriggs, A. (1995). *Positive child protection: A view from abroad.* Lyme Regis: Russell House Publishing.

Cooper, A., Hetherington, R., & Katz, I. (2003). *The risk factor: Making the child protection system work for children.* London: Demos.

Cornell, S., & Kalt, J. (2002). Reloading the dice: Improving the chances for economic development on American Indian reservations. Retrieved 13 January 2003 from Harvard Project on American Indian Economic Development web site: http://www.ksg.harvard.edu/hpaied/res_main.htm.

Costin, L.B. (1985). The historical context of child welfare. In J. Laird & A. Hartman (Eds.), *A handbook of child welfare* (pp. 34–60). New York: The Free Press.

Costin, L.B., Karger, H.J., & Stoesz, D. (1996). *The politics of child abuse in America.* New York: Oxford University Press.

Courtney, M.E. (1998). The costs of child protection in the context of welfare reform. *Future of Children, 8(1),* 88–103.

Courtney, M.E, Barth, R.P., Duerr-Berrick, J., Brooks, D., Needell, B., & Park, L. (1996). Race and child welfare services: Past research and future directions. *Child Welfare, 75(2),* 99–137.

Daly, K., & Sobol, M. (1993). *Adoption in Canada: Final report.* Ottawa, ON: Health and Welfare Canada.

Davies, L., Fox, K., Krane, J., & Schragge, E. (2002). Community child welfare: Examples from Quebec. In B. Wharf (Ed.), *Community work approaches to child welfare* (pp. 63–81). Toronto, ON: Broadview Press.

Deboutte, D. (1989). *Jeugd en hulp: een psychiatrisch-epidemiologische verkenning.* Leuven/Amersfoort: Acco.

Department of Health. (1989). *An introduction to the Children Act 1989.* London: HMSO.

Department of Health. (1991–92). *Guidelines to the Children Act 1989* (Vols. 1–8). London: HMSO.

Department of Health. (1995). *Protecting children: Messages from research.* London: HMSO.

Department of Health. (1999). *Working together to safeguard children.* London: HMSO.

Department of Health. (2000). *The framework for the assessment of children in need and their families.* London: HMSO.

Department of Health. (2001). *The Children Act 1989 report.* London: HMSO.

Department of Indian Affairs and Northern Development. (2002). *Basic departmental data – 2001*. First Nations and Northern Statistics Section, Corporate Information Management Directorate, Information Management Branch. Ottawa, ON: Canada. Retrieved 30 May 2002 from http://www.ainc-inac.gc.ca/pr/sts/bdd01/bdd01_e.html.

Deschamps, J-P. (2001). *Rapports 'Deschamps' au Garde des Sceaux sur 'le contradictoire et la communication des dossiers en assistance educative.'* Rapport du groupe de travail présidé par Jean-Pierre Deschamps, Président du tribunal pour enfants de Marseille. Paris: Ministère de la Justice.

Djao, A.W. (1983). *Inequality and social policy*. Toronto, ON: Wiley.

Doek, J.E. (1991). De Wet jeugdhulpverlening en het isolement van de justitiële hulpverlening. *Tijdschrift voor Familie- en Jeugdrecht, 13(7/8)*, 166–72.

Dominelli, L. (1999). *Community approaches to child welfare: International perspectives*. Aldershot, UK: Ashgate Press.

Doreleijers, Th.A.H. (1995). *Diagnostiek tussen jeugdstrafrecht en hulpverlening*. Arnhem: Gouda Quint.

DPJJ/ADF. (2001). *Evaluation et diagnostic des dispositifs de protection de l'enfance*. Rapport final du comité national de suivi et d'évaluation Ministère de la Justice DPJJ & Assemblée des Départements de France.

Durie Hall, D., & Metge, J. (1992). Kua tutu te puehu, kia mau – Maori aspirations in family law. In M. Henaghan & B. Atkin (Eds.), *Family law & policy in New Zealand* (pp. 54–63). Auckland, NZ: Oxford University Press.

Durst, D. (1999). *Canada's national child benefit: Phoenix or fizzle?* Halifax, NS: Fernwood Publishing.

English, D. (1998). The extent and consequences of child maltreatment. *Future of Children, 8(1)*, 39–53.

English, D., Fluke, J.D., & Yuan, Y.Y.T. (2003). Alternative response to child protective services investigations in the United States. In N. Trocmé, D. Knoke, & C. Roy (Eds.), *Community collaboration and differential response: Canadian and international research and emerging models of practice* (pp. 64–74). Ottawa, ON: Centre of Excellence for Child Welfare.

English, D., Wingard, M., Orme, D., & Orme, P. (n.d.). *Alternative responses to child protective services: Emerging issues and concerns*. Olympia, WA: Office of Children's Administration Research, Department of Social and Health Services, State of Washington.

Esping-Andersen, G. (1990). *The three worlds of welfare capitalism*. London: Polity Press.

Esping-Andersen, G. (1999). *Social foundations of postindustrial economies*. Oxford: Oxford University Press.

Faas, M. (1991). De Tweede Kamer en de kinderbescherming. *Tijdschrift voor Orthopedagogiek, 30(6),* 294–304.

Fact sheet: Parenting support [Internationaal Tolkagentschap b.v.]. (2002, May). Utrecht: International Centre of the Netherlands Institute for Care and Welfare.

Family Preservation and Family Support Initiative. (1993). *Public Law 103–66 (amended 1997).* Washington, DC: United States Government.

Farmer, E., & Owen, M. (1995). *Child protection practice: Private risks and public remedies.* London: HMSO.

Farmer, E. & Owen, M. (1998). Gender and the child protection process. *British Journal of Social Work, 28,* 545–64.

Farrow, F., & Executive Session. (1997). *Child protection: Building community partnerships.* Boston: John F. Kennedy School of Government, Harvard University.

Federal/Provincial Working Group on Child and Family Services Information. (2001). *Child and family services statistical report, 1996–67 to 1998–99.* Ottawa, ON.

First Nations Child and Family Caring Society of Canada. (2002). *History and background.* Retrieved 25 May 2002 from www.fncfcs.com.

Fitznor, L. (1998). The circle of life: Affirming aboriginal philosophies in everyday living. In D.C. McCance (Ed.), *Life ethics in world religions: University of Manitoba studies in religion* (pp. 21–40). Atlanta, GA: Scholars Press.

Fournier, S., & Crey, E. (1997). *Stolen from our embrace: The abduction of First Nations children and families and the restoration of Aboriginal communities.* Vancouver, BC: Douglas and McIntyre.

Fox Harding, L. (1991). *Perspectives in child care policy.* London: Longmans.

Freiler, C., Stairs, F., & Kitchen, B. with Judy Cerny. (2001). *Mothers as earners, mothers as carers: Responsibility for children, social policy and the tax system.* Ottawa: Status of Women Canada.

Freymond, N. (2003). *Child placement and mothering ideologies: Images of mothers in child welfare.* Unpublished doctoral comprehensive paper, Wilfrid Laurier University, Waterloo, ON.

Freymond, N. (2003). *Mothers' everyday realities and child placement experiences.* Waterloo, ON: Wilfrid Laurier University, Partnerships for Children and Families Project.

Fuchs, D. (1995). Preserving and strengthening families and protecting children: Social network intervention, a balanced approach to the prevention of child maltreatment. In J. Hudson & B. Galaway (Eds.), *Child welfare in Canada: Research and policy implications* (pp. 113–22). Toronto, ON: Thompson Educational Publishing.

Furstenberg, F. (1997). State-family alliances and children's welfare. *Childhood, 4(2)*, 183–92.

Ghesquière, P. (1993). Multi-problem gezinnen met ernstige opvoedings-problemen: een strijd om perspectief. *Tijdschrift voor Orthopedagogiek, 32(12)*, 536–50.

Gibbons, J., Conroy, S., & Bell, C. (1995). *Operating the child protection system: A study of child protection practices in English Local Authorities.* London: HMSO.

Gilbert, N. (Ed.). (1997). *Combatting child abuse: International perspectives and trends.* New York: Oxford University Press.

Gilchrist, L. (1997). Aboriginal communities and social science research: Voyeurism in transition. *Native Social Work Journal, 1(1)*, 69–85.

GIPEM. (2000). Ministère déléguée à la famille et à l'enfance. *L'enfance maltraitée.* Rapport au Parlement Loi du 10 Juillet 1989. Paris: Groupe inter-ministériel pour l'enfance maltraitée.

Gove Enquiry into Child Protection. (1995). Victoria: Ministry of Social Services, British Columbia.

Grevot, A. (2001). *Voyage en protection de l'enfance: Une comparaison européenne.* Centre National de Formation et d'etudes de la Protection Judiciaire de la Jeunene. Paris: Ministère de la Justice.

Grinde, T. (1996). Developmental trends in child welfare: British and Nordic views and priorities. In E.K.M. Tisdall (Ed.), *Child welfare: Reviewing the framework.* Edinburgh: HMSO, Children in Scotland.

Haanappel, P.P.C., & Mackaay, E., (Eds.), Warendorf, H., & Thomas R. (Trans.). (2002). *The civil code of the Netherlands Antilles and Aruba* (Series of Legislation in Translation, 17). New York: Kluwer Law International.

Hampton, E. (1995). Towards a redefining of Indian education. In M. Battiste & J. Barman (Eds.), *First Nations education in Canada: The circle unfolds* (pp. 5–46). Vancouver: University of British Columbia Press.

Hantrais, L., & Mangen, S. (Eds.). (1996). *Cross-national research methods in the social sciences.* London: Sage.

Harris, J., & Melichercik, J. (1986). Age and stage-related programs. In J. Turner & R. Turner (Eds.), *Canadian social welfare* (2nd ed., pp. 154–81). Toronto, ON: Collier Macmillan.

Hellinckx, W., Colton, M., & Williams, M. (Eds.). (1997). *International perspectives on family support.* Aldershot, UK: Ashgate Press.

Hepworth, H.P. (1980). *Foster care and adoption in Canada.* Ottawa, ON: Canadian Council on Social Development.

Hessle, S., & Vinnerljung, B. (1999). *Child welfare in Sweden – an overview.* (Stockholm Studies of Social Work, no 15.) Stockholm: Stockholm University, Department of Social Work.

Hetherington, R. (1996). The educational opportunities of cross-national comparison. *Social Work in Europe, 3(1)*, 26–30.

Hetherington, R. (1998). Issues in European child protection research. *European Journal of Social Work, 1(1)*, 71–82.

Hetherington, R., Baistow, K., Katz, I., Mesie, J., & Trowell, J. (2002). *The welfare of children with mentally ill parents: Learning from inter-country comparisons*. Chichester: Wiley.

Hetherington, R., Cooper, A., Smith, P., & Wilford, G. (1997). *Protecting children: Messages from Europe*. Lyme Regis: Russell House.

Hetherington R., & Piquardt, R. (2001). Strategies for survival: Users' experience of child welfare in three welfare regimes. *Child and Family Social Work, 6(3)*, 239–49.

Hirini, P. (1997). He whakawhitiwhiti nga whakaaro: Counselling Maori clients. *New Zealand Journal of Psychology, 27*, 13–18.

Hodgson, M. (2002). Rebuilding community after residential schools. In J. Bird, L. Land, & M. MacAdam (Eds.), *Nation to nation: Aboriginal sovereignty and the future of Canada* (pp. 92–108). Toronto, ON: Irwin.

Hudson, J., Morris, A., Maxwell, G., & Galaway, B. (1996). *Family group conferences: Perspectives on policy and practice*. Monsey, NY: The Willow Tree Press.

Hughes, C. (1995). Child poverty, campaign 2000, and child welfare practice: Working to end child poverty in Canada. *Child Welfare, 74(3)*, 779–94.

Hutchinson, Y., et al. (1992). *Profile of clients in the Anglophone youth network: Examining the situation of the black child*. Montreal, QC: Joint report of Ville Marie Social Service Centre and McGill University School of Social Work.

Ife, J. (1998). *Rethinking social work*. Melbourne, AU: Longmans.

Indian Residential School Survivors Society Newsletter. (2002). *The survivor's journey: The newsletter of the Indian Residential School Survivor's Society*. West Vancouver: Indian Residential School Survivor's Society.

Innocenti Research Centre (2003, September). League table of child maltreatment deaths in rich nations. *Innocenti Report Card, Issue 5*. Retrieved 19 November 2003 from http://www.unicef-icdc.org/publications/.

Issac, T. (1999). *Aboriginal law: Cases, materials and commentary*. Saskatoon, SK: Purich.

Jackson, M. (1988). *Maori and the criminal justice system: He Whaipaanga Hou: A new Perspective* (Parts I & II). Wellington, NZ: Department of Justice.

Jackson, M. (1992). *The Treaty of Waitangi*. Wellington, NZ: Nga Kaiwhaka-marama I Nga Ture: Wellington Maori Legal Service.

Jackson, M. (1995). Cultural justice: A colonial contradiction or a rangatiratanga reality? In F. McElrea (Ed.), *Rethinking criminal justice: Justice in the community* (Vol. 1). Auckland, NZ: Legal Research Foundation.

Johnston, P. (1983). *Native children and the child welfare system.* Toronto, ON: Canadian Council on Social Development.

Jones, C. (1985). *Patterns of social policy: An introduction to comparative analysis.* London: Tavistock.

Junger-Tas, J. (1997). Jeugd en Gezin II. *Naar een effectief preventiebeleid.* The Hague: Ministerie van Justitie, Directoraat-Generaal Preventie, Jeugd en Sancties.

Kalverboer, M.E. (1996). *Onderzoek naar de wijze van rapporteren over opvoedings-en verzorgingsproblematiek bij de Raad voor de Kinderbescherming Direktie Noord.* Groningen: Stichting Kinderstudies.

Katz, I., & Pinkerton, J. (Eds.). (2003). *Evaluating family support: Thinking internationally, thinking critically.* Chichester: Wiley.

Kimelman, E.C. (1985). *No quiet place: Review committee on Indian and Métis adoptions and placements.* Winnipeg: Manitoba Department of Community Services.

King, M. (Ed.). (1992). *Te ao hurihuri: Aspects of Maoritanga.* Auckland, NZ: Reed.

King, M., & Piper, C. (1990). *How the law thinks about children* (1st ed.). Aldershot, UK: Gower.

King, M., & Piper, C. (1995). *How the law thinks about children* (2nd ed.). Aldershot, UK: Ashgate Press.

Kirby, S., & McKenna, K. (1989). *Experience, research, social change: Methods from the margins.* Toronto, ON: Garamond Press.

Koens, M.J.C. (1992). Op de goede weg naar een nieuwe jeugdbescherming? *Tijdschrift voor Familie- en Jeugdrecht, 14(11),* 251–5.

Korbin, J. (1994). Sociocultural factors in child maltreatment. In G. Melton & F. Barry (Eds.), *Protecting children from abuse and neglect: Foundations for a new national strategy* (pp.182–223). New York: Guilford Press.

Koster, A. (2001, June). *Child welfare philosophy paper.* Unpublished discussion paper prepared for Ontario Association of Children's Aid Societies. Ontario: OACAS.

Koster, A., Morrissette, V., & Roulette, R. (2000, May). *Aboriginal child welfare review: Comprehensive report.* Ontario: Ministry of Community and Social Services.

Kufeldt, K., Simard, M., & Vachon, J. (2000, October). *The looking after children in Canada project: Educational outcomes.* Unpublished paper presented at Child Welfare 2000: The state of the art and direction for the future. Cornwall, ON.

Kyle, I., & Kellerman, M. (1998). *Case studies of Canadian Family Resource Programs: Supporting families, children and communities.* Ottawa, ON: Canadian Association of Family Resource Programs.

Laird, J. (1993). Gay and lesbian families. In F. Walsh (Ed.), *Normal family processes* (pp. 282–328). New York: Guilford Press.

Landrine, H. (1992). Clinical implications of cultural differences, the referential versus the indexical self. *Clinical Psychology Review, 12,* 401–15.

La Rocque, E. (1997). Re-examining culturally appropriate models in criminal justice applications. In M. Asch (Ed.), *Aboriginal and treaty rights in Canada: Essays on law, equity, and respect for difference* (pp. 75–96). Vancouver, BC: University of British Columbia Press.

Lawrence-Karski, R. (1997). United States: California's reporting system. In N. Gilbert (Ed.), *Combatting child abuse: International perspectives and trends* (pp. 9–37). New York: Oxford University Press.

Lee, B., & Richards, S. (2002). Child protection through strengthening communities: The Toronto Children's Aid Society. In B. Wharf (Ed.), *Community work approaches to child welfare* (pp. 93–115). Toronto, ON: Broadview Press.

Levin, C. (1998). *Uppfostringsanstalten. Om tvång i föräldrars ställe.* [The Reformatory. Coercion in loco parentis]. Unpublished doctoral dissertation, Lund University, Lund: Arkiv.

Linden, A.P. van der. (1992). Om wie het gaat in het jeugdbeschermingsrecht. *Tijdschrift voor Familie- en Jeugdrecht, 14(8),* 174–9.

Linden, A.P. van der, & Hendrickx, J.J.P. (1991). Met of zonder maatregel. Justitiële jeugdbeschermingsmaatregelen en geestelijke jeugdgezondheidszorg. *Tijdschrift voor Familie- en Jeugdrecht, 13(7/8),* 161–5.

Lobmeyer, P., & Wilkinson, R. (2000). Income, inequality and mortality in 14 developed countries. *Sociology of Health and Illness, 22(4),* 410–14.

London Borough of Brent. (1985). *A child in trust: The report of the panel of inquiry into the circumstances surrounding the death of Jasmine Beckford.* London: London Borough of Brent.

London Borough of Greenwich. (1987). *A child in mind: Protection of children in a responsible society. Report of the commission of inquiry into the circumstances surrounding the death of Kimberley Carlile.* London: London Borough of Greenwich.

Love, C. (1999). *Maori voices in the construction of indigenous models of counselling theory and practice.* Unpublished doctoral dissertation, Massey University, Palmerston North, NZ.

Love, C. (2000). Family group conferencing: Cultural origins, sharing and appropriation – a Maori reflection. In G. Burford & J. Hudson (Eds.), *Family group conferencing: New directions in child and family practice.* New York: Walter de Gruyter.

Luckock, B., Vogler, R., & Keating, H. (1996). Child protection in France and

England – authority, legalism and social work practice. *Child and Family Law Quarterly, 8(4),* 297–311.

Luckock, B., Vogler, R., & Keating, H. (1997). The Belgian Flemish child protection system – confidentiality, voluntarism, and coercion. *Child and Family Law Quarterly, 9(2),* 101–13.

Lundström, T., & Wijkström, F. (1997). *The nonprofit sector in Sweden.* Manchester and New York: Manchester University Press.

Mabbett, D., & Bolderson, H. (1999). Theories and methods in comparative social policy. In J. Clasen (Ed.), *Comparative social policy: Concepts, theories and methods* (pp. 34–56). Oxford: Blackwells.

MacAulay, J. (2002). Searching for common ground: Family resource programs and child welfare. In B. Wharf (Ed.), *Community work approaches to child welfare* (pp. 163–80). Toronto, ON: Broadview Press.

MacDonald, K. (2002). *Missing voices: Aboriginal mothers who have been at risk or who have had their children removed from their care.* Vancouver, BC: National Action Committee on the Status of Women, British Columbia Region.

Maidman, F., & Connors, E. (2001). A circle of healing: Family wellness in Aboriginal communities. In I. Prilleltensky, G. Nelson, & L. Peirson (Eds.), *Promoting family and wellness and preventing child maltreatment: Fundamentals for thinking and action* (pp. 375–466). Toronto, ON: University of Toronto Press.

Maiter, S., Palmer, S., & Manji, S. (2003). *Invisible Lives: The experiences of parents receiving child protective services.* Waterloo, ON: Wilfrid Laurier University, Partnerships for Child and Families Project.

Malorek, V. (2000, April 19). Red tape, bungling and broken bodies of tragic children 'ignored to death.' *Globe and Mail,* A11.

Mandell, D., Clouston Carlson, J., Fine, M., & Blackstock, C. (in press). Aboriginal child welfare. In G. Cameron, N. Coady, & G. Adams (Eds.), *Towards positive systems of child and family welfare: Current issues and future directions.* Waterloo, ON: Wilfrid Laurier University Press.

Marneffe, C., & Broos, P. (1997). Belgium: An alternative approach to child abuse reporting and treatment. In N. Gilbert (Ed.), *Combatting child abuse: International perspectives and trends* (pp. 167–91). New York: Oxford University Press.

Martin, F., & Palmer, T. (1997). *Transition to adulthood: A youth perspective.* Ottawa, ON: Child Welfare League of Canada.

Martin, K. (2001). *Ways of knowing, ways of being and ways of doing: Developing a theoretical framework and methods for Indigenous research and Indigenist research.* Retrieved 5 January 2002 from www.aiatsis.gov.au/rsrch/conf2001/abstracts/B1_Abstracts.pdf.

Martin, M. (1985). Poverty and child welfare. In K.L. Levitt & B. Wharf (Eds.), *The challenge of child welfare* (pp. 53–65). Vancouver: University of British Columbia Press.

McDonald, R.J., & Ladd, P. (2000). *First Nations child and family services joint national policy review: Final report, June 2000.* Ottawa, ON: The Assembly of First Nations and Department of Indian and Northern Development.

McKay, S. & Clouston Carlson, J. (2003). Stanley McKay: Growing up in family and community the traditional way. In J. Clouston Carlson & A. Dumont (Eds.), *Bridges in understanding: Aboriginal Christian men tell their stories* (pp. 73–122). Toronto, ON: Anglican Book Centre.

McKeen, W. (2001). Shifting policy and politics of federal child benefits in Canada. *Social Politics, Summer,* 186–90.

McKenzie, B. (1989). Child welfare: New models of service delivery in Canada's Native communities. *Human Services in the Rural Environment, 12(3),* 6–11.

McKenzie, B., Seidle, E., & Bone, N. (1995). Child and family service standards in First Nations: An action research project. *Child Welfare League of America, (3),* 633–53.

McKenzie, B. (1997). Developing First Nations child welfare standards: Using evaluation research within a participatory framework. *The Canadian Journal of Program Evaluation, 12(1),* 133–48.

McKenzie, B., & Flette, E. (2001). Community building through block funding in Aboriginal child and family services. In K. Kufeldt & B. McKenzie (Eds.), *Child welfare: Connecting research, policy and practice* (pp. 343–53). Waterloo, ON: Wilfrid Laurier University Press.

McKenzie, B., & Morrissette, V. (2002). Social work practice with Canadians of Aboriginal background: Guidelines for respectful social work. In A. Al-Krenawi & J. Graham (Eds.), *Multi-cultural social work practice in Canada* (pp. 251–82). Toronto, ON: Oxford University Press.

Mead, A. (1996, September). *Cultural and intellectual property rights of Indigenous peoples of the Pacific.* Unpublished paper presented at a regional meeting on the United Nations Draft Declaration on the Rights of Indigenous Peoples, Fiji.

Meeting of Ministers of Social Services. (2003). *New directions in child welfare: Background discussion document.* In 4th National Child Welfare Symposium: Community Collaboration on Differential Response. Alberta Response Model: Transforming Outcomes for Children Youth and Families. Banff, Alberta.

Mertens, N.M. (1996). *Gezinsvoogden aan het werk.* Arnhem: Gouda Quint.

Metzger, B. (1997). Mediation in child protection in British Columbia. *Family and Conciliation Courts Review, 35(4),* 418–23.

Michigan Family Independence Agency (2001). Various state reports and interviews by author on the five-category disposition system and the Multi-Purpose Collaborative Bodies.

Mikaere, A. (1999). *Colonisation and the imposition of patriarchy: A Ngati Raukawa woman's perspective.* Otaki, NZ: Te Wananga O Raukawa.

Millar, J., & Warman, A. (1996). *Family obligations in Europe.* London: Family Policy Studies Centre.

Ministerial Advisory Committee. (1986). *Puao-te-Atatu: The report of the Ministerial Advisory Committee on a Maori perspective for the Department of Social Welfare.* Wellington, NZ: Department of Social Welfare.

Montfoort, A.J. van. (1993). In onmacht en teleurstelling: over het ontstaan van de justitiële kinderbescherming: 1870–1905. In A. Groen & A.J. van Montfoort (Eds.), *Kinderen beschermen en jeugd hulpverlenen* (pp. 13–35). Arnhem: Gouda Quint.

Montfoort, A.J. van. (1994). *Het topje van de ijsberg. Kinderbescherming en de bestrijding van kindermishandeling in sociaal juridisch perspectief.* Utrecht: SWP.

Montfoort, A.J. van, & Nijnatten, C.H.C.J. van. (1991). Jeugd, zorg en dwang: de kinderbescherming ter discussie. *Maandblad Geestelijke volksgezondheid, 26(11),* 1179–1192.

Morrissette, V., McKenzie, B., & Morrissette, L. (1993). Towards an Aboriginal model of social work practice: Cultural knowledge and traditional practices. *Canadian Social Work Review, 10(1),* 91–108.

Morse, B. (1984). Native Indian and Métis children in Canada: Victims of the Child Welfare System. In G.K. Verna & C. Bagley (Eds.), *Race relations and cultural differences: Educational and interpersonal perspectives* (pp. 259–77). New York: St Martin's Press.

National Research Council. (1993). *Losing generations: Adolescents in high-risk settings.* Washington, DC: National Academy Press.

National Youth-in-Care Network. (1998). *About us.* Retrieved 3 February 2001 from NYICN web site: http://www.youthincare.ca.

Naves, P., & Cathala, B. (2000). Rapport 'Naves-Cathala' d'inspection sur 'l'accueil provisoire et placements d'enfants.' IGAS. Retrieved 8 February 2001 from http://www.sante.gouv.fr.

Nelson, G., Laurendeau, M.-C., Chamberland, C., & Peirson, L. (2001). A review and analysis of programs to promote family wellness and prevent the maltreatment of pre-school and elementary school-aged children. In I. Prilleltensky, G. Nelson, & L. Peirson (Eds.), *Promoting family wellness and preventing child maltreatment: Fundamentals for thinking and action* (pp. 221–88). Toronto, ON: University of Toronto Press.

New Zealand Children and Young Persons Service (NZCYPS). (1996, July).

National protocol agreed by the Ministry of Education, the New Zealand School Trustees Association and NZCYPS: Breaking the cycle. Wellington, NZ: Ministry of Education.

Nijnatten, C.H.C.J. (1995). *Het gezicht van gezag.* Amsterdam/Meppel: Boom.

Nijnatten, C.H.C.J. van, & Montfoort, A.J. van. (1992). Van kinderbescherming naar publieke jeugdzorg. *Maandblad Geestelijke volksgezondheid, 47(3),* 259–70.

O'Hara, K. (1998). *Comparative family policy: Eight countries' stories* (CPRN Study No. F/04). Ottawa, ON: Canadian Policy Research Networks.

Olsson Hort, S.E. (1997). Sweden: Toward a deresidualization of Swedish child welfare policy and practice. In N. Gilbert (Ed.), *Combatting child abuse: International perspectives and trends* (pp. 105–24). New York: Oxford University Press.

O'Meara, S., & West, D.A. (1996). Introduction. In S. O'Meara & D.A. West (Eds.), *From our eyes: Learning from Indigenous peoples.* Toronto, ON: Garamond Press.

Ontario Association of Children's Aid Societies. (2001). *Workload measurement project report.* Toronto, ON.

Ontario Ministry of Children's Services. (2003, November). *Child welfare program evaluation.* Toronto, ON.

Owen, M., & Farmer, E. (1996). Child protection in a multi-racial context. *Policy and Politics, 24,* 299–313.

Øyen, E. (Ed.). (1990). *Comparative methodology, theory and practice in international social research.* London: Sage.

Ozment, S. (1983). *When father ruled: Family life in reformation Europe.* Cambridge, MA: Harvard University Press.

Palier, B. (2004). *Social protection reforms in Europe: Strategies for a new social model.* Ottawa, ON: Canadian Policy Research Networks.

Parton, N. (1991). *Governing the family: Child care, child protection and the state.* Basingstoke: Macmillan.

Parton, N. (Ed.). (1997). *Child protection and family support: Tensions, contradictions and possibilities.* London: Routledge.

Parton, N., Thorpe, D., & Wattam, C. (1997). *Child protection: Risk and the moral order.* Basingstoke: Macmillan.

Pecora, P.J., Whittaker, J.K., & Maluccio, A.N. (1992). *The child welfare challenge: Policy, practice, and research.* New York: Aldine de Gruyter.

Peirson, L., Laurendeau, M.-C., & Chamberland, C. (2001). Context, contributing factors, and consequences. In I. Prilleltensky, G. Nelson, & L. Peirson (Eds.), *Promoting family wellness and preventing child maltreatment: Fundamentals for thinking and action* (pp. 39–122). Toronto, ON: University of Toronto Press.

Pennell, J., & Burford, G. (1996). Attending to context: Family group decision making in Canada. In J. Hudson, A. Morris, G. Maxwell, & B. Galaway (Eds.), *Family group conferences: Perspectives on policy and practice*. Monsey, NY: The Willow Tree Press.

Pere, R.R. (1988). Te Wheke: Whaia te maramatanga me te aroha. In S. Middleton (Ed.), *Women in education in Aotearoa*. Wellington, NZ: Allen Unwin/Port Nicholson Press.

Pere, R.R. (1991). *Te wheke: A celebration of infinite wisdom*. Gisborne, NZ: Ao Ako Global Learning.

Pires, S.A. (1993). *International child welfare systems: Report of a workshop*. Washington, DC: National Academy Press.

Pool, I. (1991). *Te Iwi Maori*. Auckland, NZ: Auckland University Press.

Poso, T. (1997). Finland: Child abuse as a family problem. In N. Gilbert (Ed.), *Combatting child abuse: International perspectives and trends* (pp. 143–66). New York: Oxford University Press.

Prilleltensky, I., Nelson, G., & Peirson, L. (1999). *Promoting family wellness and preventing child maltreatment: Fundamentals for thinking and action*. Toronto, ON: University of Toronto Press.

Pringle, K. (1998). *Children and social welfare in Europe*. Buckingham: Open University Press.

Rangihau, J. (1992). Being Maori. In M. King (Ed.), *Te ao hurihuri: Aspects of Maoritanga*. Auckland, NZ: Reed.

Redhorse, J., Martinez, C., Day, P., Day, D., Pouport, J., & Scharnberg, D. (2000). *Family preservation: Concepts in American Indian communities*. Seattle, WA: Casey Family Programs.

Reitsma Street, M., & Neysmith, S. (2000). Restructuring and community work: The case of community resource centres for families in poor urban neighbourhoods. In S. Neysmith (Ed.), *Restructuring caring labour: Discourse, state practice and everyday life* (pp. 142–63). Toronto, ON: Oxford University Press.

Roelofs, M.A., & Baartman, H.E. (1997). The Netherlands: Responding to abuse – compassion or control? In N. Gilbert (Ed.), *Combatting child abuse: International perspectives and trends* (pp. 192–211). New York: Oxford University Press.

Roméo, C. (2001). *Rapport: Roméo sur 'l'évolution des relations parents-enfants-professionnels dans le cadre de la protection de l'enfance.'* Ministère délégué à la famille, à l'enfance et aux personnes handicapées. Paris.

Rooney, R.H., & Bibus, A.A. (1996). Multiple lenses: Ethnically sensitive practice with involuntary clients who are having difficulties with drugs or alcohol. *Journal of Multicultural Social Work, 4(2)*, 59–73.

Rosenbluth, D. (1995). Moving in and out of Foster Care. In J. Hudson & B. Galaway (Eds.), *Child welfare in Canada: Research and policy implications* (pp. 233–44). Toronto, ON: Thompson Educational Publishing.

Royal Commission on Aboriginal Peoples (RCAP). (1995). *Choosing life: Special report on suicide of Aboriginal people.* Ottawa, ON: Canada Communication Group.

Royal Commission on Aboriginal Peoples (RCAP). (1996a). *People to people, nation to nation: Highlights of the Royal Commission on Aboriginal Peoples.* Ottawa, ON: Canada Communication Group.

Royal Commission on Aboriginal Peoples (RCAP). (1996b). *Looking forward, looking back* (Vol. 1). Ottawa, ON: Canada Communication Group.

Royal Commission on Aboriginal Peoples (RCAP). (1996c). *Gathering strength* (Vol. 3). Ottawa, ON: Canada Communication Group.

Royal Commission on Aboriginal Peoples (RCAP). (1996d). *For seven generations: An information legacy of the Royal Commission on Aboriginal Peoples* (CD-Rom). Ottawa, ON: Libraxus.

Royal Commission on Social Policy. (1988). *The April report: Future directions.* Wellington, NZ: Government Publication.

Rutman, D., Callahan, M., Lundquist A., Jackson, S., & Field, B. (1999). *Substance use and pregnancy: Conceiving women in the policy process.* Ottawa, ON: Status of Women Canada.

Sallnäs, M. (2000). *Barnavårdens institutioner – framväxt, ideologi och struktur* [Residential care for children and young people – history, ideology and present-day structure]. Unpublished doctoral thesis, University of Stockholm.

Sampson, E.E. (1988). The debate on individualism: Indigenous psychologies of the self and their role in personal and societal functioning. *American Psychologist, 43(1)*, 15–22.

Sampson, E.E. (1993a). *Celebrating the other: A dialogic account of human nature.* New York: Harvester Wheatsheaf.

Sampson, E.E. (1993b). Identity politics. *American Psychologist, 48(12)*, 1219–1230.

Schäfer, H. (1995). Legal notebook: The principle of subsidiarity. *Social Work in Europe, 2(3)*, 52–3.

Schene, P. (1998). Past, present, and future roles of child protective services. *The Future of Children, 8(1)*, 23–39.

Schene, P. (2000). *Community child protection in St. Louis, Missouri.* Unpublished internal report to Edna McConnell Clark Foundation, New York City.

Schene, P. (2001). *Differential response. Best Practice/Next Practice.* Washington, DC: The National Resource Center on Family-Centered Practice.

Shields, C. (1995). Improving the life prospects of children: A community systems approach. *Child Welfare, 124(3)*, 37–51.

Scholte, E.M. (1997). Diagnostiek door de Raad voor de Kinderbescherming en de Gezinsvoogdij. In J.D. v.d. Ploeg, J.M.A.M. Janssens, & E.E.J. De Bruyn (Eds.), *Diagnostiek in de jeugdzorg* (pp. 11–32). Groningen: Wolters-Noordhoff.

Secretary of State for Social Services. (1988). *Report of the inquiry into child abuse in Cleveland.* Cmnd. 412. London: HMSO.

Secure institutional treatment for young offenders – instead of prison. (1999). Stockholm: National Board of Institutional Care and Sis [booklet in English].

Six Nations of the Grand River. (2002, May). *Customary care policy and procedures* [draft]. Under review for passage by Band Council of the Six Nations.

Slot, N.W., Theunissen, A., Esmeijer, F.J., & Duivenvoorden, Y. (2001). *Een onderzoek naar de doelmatigheid van de ondertoezichtstelling.* Amsterdam: Vrije Universiteit.

Sluker, G. (1995). *Endangered cultures.* Palmerston North, NZ: Massey University, Department of Social Anthropology.

Smale, G. (1995). Integrating community and individual practice: A new paradigm for practice. In P. Adams & K. Nelson (Eds.), *Reinventing human service: Community and family centered practice* (pp. 59–86). New York: Aldine de Gruyrer.

Smith, L.T. (1999). *Decolonising methodologies: Notes from Down Under.* London: Zed Books.

Snider, J. (1996). Scholarship, morality and apologies for empire. In S. O'Meara & D.A. West (Eds.), *From our eyes: Learning from Indigenous peoples.* Toronto, ON: Garamond Press.

Social Planning Council of Winnipeg. (2003). *The Manitoba child poverty report card: An agenda for action.* Retrieved 5 January 2004 from http://www.spcw.mb.ca/reference/report%20card%202.pdf.

Social services act and care of young persons (special provisions): Act and care of abusers (special provisions act). (1999). Stockholm: Ministry of Health and Social Affairs.

Social Services Inspectorate (SSI). (2001). *Redeveloping quality to protect children: Report of the inspection of local council children's services.* London: Department of Health.

Socialtjänst (Social Services). (2001:8). *Barn och unga – insatser år 2000.* [Children and young persons subjected to measures 2000. Measures under the Social Services Act and the Care of Young Persons Act]. Stockholm:

Socialstyrelsen [National Board of Health and Welfare]. Summary in English.

Soetenhorst-de Savornin Lohman, J. (1993). De armslag van de uitvoerend werker op het raakvlak tussen hulp en recht. In A. Groen & A.J. van Montfoort (Eds.), *Kinderen beschermen en jeugd hulpverlenen* (pp. 127–45). Arnhem: Gouda Quint.

Soetenhorst-de Savornin Lohman, J. (1998). Kind in het geding: Kinderbescherming tussen traditie en vernieuwing. In Th. N.M. Schuyt & M. Steketee (Eds.), *Zorgethiek: ruimte binnen regels* (pp. 21–39). Utrecht: SWP.

SOU Statens Offentliga Utredningar. (2000:3). *Välfärd vid vägskäl: Utvecklingen under 1990–talet.* [Welfare at a cross-road: The development during the 1990s]. Stockholm: Socialdepartementet [Ministry of Health and Welfare].

SOU Statens Offentliga Utredningar. (2000:77). *Omhändertagen: Samhällets ansvar för utsatta barn och unga.* [A review of the Care of Young Persons Act, on mandate from the government, with a summary in English]. Stockholm: Socialdepartementet, Betänkande av LVU-utredningen.

Soydan, H. (1996). Using the vignette method in cross-cultural comparisons. In L. Hantrais & S. Mangen (Eds.), *Cross-national research methods in the social sciences* (pp. 120–8). London: Sage.

Soydan, H., & Stål, R. (1994). How to use the vignette technique in cross-cultural research. *Scandinavian Journal of Social Welfare, 3,* 75–80.

Stalker, K. (1996). Principles, policy and practice in short-term care. In K. Stalker (Ed.), *Developments in short-term care: Breaks and opportunities.* London: Jessica Kingsley.

Statistics New Zealand (2002). Retrieved 13 December 2002 from www.statistics.govt.nz.

Strega, S. (2000). Efforts at empowering youth: Youth-in-care and the youth-in-care networks in Ontario and Canada. In M. Callahan, S. Hessle, & S. Strega (Eds.), *Valuing the field: Child welfare in an international context.* Aldershot, UK: Ashgate Press.

Swift, K. (1995a). *Manufacturing 'bad mothers': A critical perspective on child neglect.* Toronto, ON: University of Toronto Press.

Swift, K. (1995b). 'An outrage to common decency': Historical perspectives on child neglect. *Child Welfare, 74(1),* 71–91.

Swift, K. (1995c). 'Missing persons': Women in child welfare. *Child Welfare, 74(3),* 486–502.

Swift, K. (1997). Canada: Trends and issues in child welfare. In N. Gilbert (Ed.), *Combatting child abuse: International perspectives and trends* (pp. 38–71). New York: Oxford University Press.

Swift, K. (1998). Contradictions in child welfare: Neglect and responsibility. In C.T. Baines, P.M. Evans, & S. Neysmith (Eds.), *Women's caring: Feminist perspectives on social welfare* (pp. 160–90). Toronto, ON: Oxford University Press.

Swift, K. (2001). The case for opposition: Challenging contemporary child welfare policy directions. *Canadian Review of Social Policy, 47*, 59–76.

Swift, K., & Birmingham, M. (2000). Location, location, location: Restructuring and the everyday lives of 'welfare moms.' In S. Neysmith (Ed.), *Restructuring caring labour: Discourse, state practice and everyday life* (pp. 93–115). Toronto, ON: Oxford University Press.

Taylor-Henley, S., & Hudson, P. (1992). Aboriginal self-government and social services: First Nations – provincial relationships. *Canadian Public Policy, 18(1)*, 13–26.

Tesh, S.N. (1988). *Hidden arguments: Political ideology and disease prevention.* New Brunswick, NJ: Rutgers University Press.

Thoburn, J., Lewis, A., & Shemmings, D. (1995). *Paternalism or partnership? Family involvement in the child protection process.* London: HMSO.

Thomas, N. (1994). *Colonialism's culture: Anthropology, travel and government.* Princeton, NJ: Princeton University Press.

Thorpe, D. (1994). *Evaluating child protection.* Buckingham, UK: Open University Press.

Timpson, J. (1993). *Four decades of child welfare services to Native Indians in Ontario: A contemporary attempt to understand the 'sixties scoop' in historical, socio-economic and political perspective.* Unpublished doctoral dissertation, Wilfrid Laurier University, Waterloo, ON.

Timpson, J. (1995). Four decades of literature on Native Canadian child welfare. *Child Welfare League of America, 74(3)*, 525–46.

Toughill, K. (2001, February 3). Judge Jim: An Inuk's compassion and understanding transform his people's view of the justice system. *The Toronto Star*, pp. K1, K3.

Trocmé, N., MacLaurin, B., Fallon, B., Daciuk, J., Billingsley, D., Tourigny, et al. (2001). *Canadian incidences study of reported child abuse and neglect: Final report.* Ottawa, ON: Minister of Public Works and Government Services Canada.

Tunstill, J. (1997). Family support clauses of the 1989 Children Act: Legislative, professional, and organisational obstacles. In N. Parton (Ed.), *Child protection and family support: Tensions, contradictions, and possibilities* (pp. 39–58). London: Routledge.

Tuomisto, R., & Vuori-Karvia, E. (1997). Child protection in Finland. In M. Harder & K. Pringle (Eds.), *Protecting children in Europe: Towards a new millennium* (pp. 77–100). Aalborg, Denmark: Aalborg University Press.

Union of British Columbia Indian Chiefs. (2002). *Calling forth our future: Options for the exercise of Indigenous people's authority in child welfare*. Retrieved 14 December 2002 from Union of British Colombia Indian Chiefs web site: http://www.ubcic.bc.ca/welcome.htm.

United States Advisory Board on Child Abuse and Neglect. (1993). *Neighbors helping neighbors: A new national strategy for the protection of children*. Washington, DC: U.S. Government Printing Office.

United States Department of Health and Human Services, Administration of Children, Youth and Families, Children's Bureau. (1999). *Child maltreatment 1997: Reports from the states to the National Child Abuse and Neglect Data System*. Washington, DC: U.S. Government Printing Office.

United States Department of Health and Human Services, Administration for Children and Families, Children's Bureau. (2001). *Child maltreatment, 1999*. Washington, DC: US Government Printing Office.

Veldkamp, A.W.M. (1993). De toekomst van de kinderbescherming. In A. Groen & A.J. van Montfoort (Eds.), *Kinderen beschermen en jeugd hulp verlenen* (pp. 93–113). Arnhem: Gouda Quint.

Veldkamp, A.W.M. (Ed.). (1995a). *Werkwijze en Organisatie Primair Proces Beschermingszaken*. Utrecht: Raad voor de Kinderbescherming.

Veldkamp, A.W.M. (1995b). Het gezicht van gezag besproken. *Tijdschrift voor de Sociale Sector, 49(12)*, 42–3.

Veldkamp, A.W.M. (1997a). Het kind van de rekening. In A. Remy (Ed.), *Tussen te kort komen en te kort doen* (pp. 17–35). Horn, the Netherlands: Jeugddorp Bethanië.

Veldkamp, A.W.M. (1997b). De Raad voor de Kinderbescherming en de toepassing van kinderbeschermingsmaatregelen: Beschermen tégen of opkomen vóór? In I.E.A.M. Beljaars (Ed.), *OTS en ontheffing* (pp. 1–14). Lelystad, the Netherlands: Vermande Studiedagen.

Veldkamp, A.W.M. (1997c). Nog te vroeg voor een feestje! De doorwerking van het Internationaal Verdrag inzake de Rechten van het Kind in de jeugdbescherming. *Tijdschrift voor de Rechten van het Kind, 7(4)*, 4–6.

Veldkamp, A.W.M. (2001). *Over grenzen! Internationaal vergelijkende verkenning van de rol van de overheid bij de opvoeding en bescherming van kinderen*. The Hague: Ministerie van Justitie.

Vinnerljung, B., Langlet, P., Zaar, A.-K., & Gunnarsson, T. (2000). Prevalens av långa årdtider m.m. bland barn som placerats i dygnsvård – en kohort-studie. [Prevalence of long-term care, etc., among children in out-of-home placements – a cohort study]. In SOU Statens Offentliga Utredningar (2000:77), bilaga 3. Stockholm: Socialdepartementet, Betänkande av LVU-utredningen.

Vinnerljung, B., Sallnäs, M., & Kyhle Westermark, P. (2001). *Sammanbrott vid onårsplaceringar – om ungdomar i fosterhem och på institution*. [Breakdown in out-of-home placements for teenagers – about young people in foster and residential care]. Stockholm: Socialstyrelsen, Centrum för utvärdering av socialt rbete. Summary in English.

Vogl, R., & Bala, N. (2001). *Testifying on behalf of children: A handbook for Canadian professionals*. Toronto: Thompson Educational Publishing.

Waitangi Tribunal (1996). *The Taranaki report: Kaupapa tuatahi*. Wellington, NZ: GP Publications.

Waitere-Ang, H., & Johnson, P.M. (1999). *If all inclusion in research means is the addition of researchers that look different, have you really included me at all?* Te Uru Maraurau: Palmerston North, NZ: The Department of Maori and Multicultural Education, Massey University.

Waldfogel, J. (1998a). *The future of child protection*. Cambridge, MA: Harvard University Press.

Waldfogel, J. (1998b). Rethinking the paradigm for child protection. *Future of Children, 8(1)*, 104–19.

Waldfogel, J. (2001). *The future of child protection: How to break the cycle of abuse and neglect*. Cambridge, MA: Harvard University Press.

Walker, R. (1987). *Nga tau tohetohe: Years of anger*. Auckland, NZ: Penguin Books.

Walker, R. (1996). *Nga pepa a Ranginui: The Walker papers*. Auckland, NZ: Penguin Books.

Walker, S. (2002). Family support and the role of social work: Renaissance or retrenchment? *European Journal of Social Work, 5(1)*, 43–54.

Ward, H. (Ed.). (1995). *Looking after children: Research into Practice: The second report to the Department of Health on assessing outcomes in child care*. London: HMSO.

Weightman, K., & Weightman, A. (1995). 'Never right, never wrong': Child welfare and social work in England and Sweden. *Scandinavian Journal of Social Welfare, 4*, 75–84.

Wells, M. (1990). *Canada's law on child sexual abuse*. Ottawa, ON: Ministry of Justice.

Wharf, B. (1992). *Communities and social policy in Canada*. Toronto: McClelland and Stewart.

Wharf, B. (2002). *Community work approaches to child welfare*. Toronto, ON: Broadview Press.

White, A. (n.d.). *Community partnerships for protection of children – Jacksonville, Florida*. New York: Edna McConnell Clark Foundation.

Wilford, G., Hetherington, R., & Piquardt, R. (1997). *Families ask for help: Parental perceptions of child welfare and child protection services – an Anglo-German study.* London: Brunel University.

Wolff, R. (1997). Germany: A nonpunitive model. In N. Gilbert (Ed.), *Combatting child abuse: International perspectives and trends* (pp. 212–31). New York: Oxford University Press.

Yazzie, R. (2000). Indigenous peoples and postcolonial colonialism. In M. Battiste (Ed.), *Reclaiming indigenous voice and vision* (pp. 39–49). Vancouver: University of British Columbia Press.

Zlotkin, N. (1994). Aboriginal control over child welfare: Canadian and American approaches. In R. Gosse, J. Youngblood Henderson, & R. Carter (Eds.), *Continuing Poundmaker and Riel's quest: Presentations made at a conference on Aboriginal Peoples and Justice* (pp. 185–91). Saskatoon, SA: Purich.

Contributors

Gunvor Andersson obtained her PhD in psychology and is a professor in social work at the School of Social Work, Lund University, Sweden. She participates in the social worker education and the PhD program, is involved in child welfare research, and is the author of several publications in the field.

Marlyn Bennett is Research Coordinator, First Nations Research Site, First Nations Child and Family Caring Society of Canada, Manitoba.

Cindy Blackstock is the executive director of the First Nations Child and Family Caring Society of Canada, Manitoba. In addition, Cindy supervised the design, development, and delivery of the first comprehensive provincial professional development program designed for First Nations Child and Family Service social workers in Canada.

Marilyn Callahan is a professor emeritus from the University of Victoria, School of Social Work in Victoria, British Columbia. She has conducted extensive research on the experiences of mothers, teens, and workers in child welfare. Recently she was head of a Canada–Europe project that exchanged students, faculty, and practitioners in child welfare between three Canadian provinces and the United Kingdom, Sweden, and the Netherlands.

Gary Cameron is a professor in the Faculty of Social Work at Wilfrid Laurier University and has been the principal investigator for a variety of major research and demonstration projects focusing on interventions with vulnerable children and families and project/program development. Currently, he is the Project Director for the Partnerships for Children and Families Project, a Community University Research Alliance, and the Lyle S. Hallman Chair in Child and Family Welfare. His recent research includes the study of family support programs, mutual aid organizations, prevention programming for disadvantaged children and families, effective program development, and the implications of this research for the evolution of service organizations and delivery systems.

Joyce Clouston Carlson is a PhD student in the Faculty of Social Work, Wilfrid Laurier University. She is a social worker who has worked with Aboriginal leaders to assist in publication of several volumes of oral cultural stories.

Marshall Fine is a professor in the Faculty of Social Work, Wilfrid Laurier University, and has published numerous journal articles and book chapters about couple and family therapy. A specific interest is therapeutic relationships and issues of power and collaboration. His research includes a study of the experiences of participants and therapists in couple therapy. His scholarship is grounded in ongoing direct practice with couples and families.

Nancy Freymond is a PhD candidate at Wilfrid Laurier University, a research associate with the Partnerships for Children and Families Project, and a former front-line child welfare worker. Her research interest is in the area of child placement, focusing on the experience of placement from the mother's perspective. Her writing is centered on topics that include positive possibilities for child and family welfare, international comparisons of practice in child protection, worker experiences in making placement decisions, child placement history, and mothers' experience of child placement.

Alain Grevot is the director of a social work agency working with a children's court in northern France. He works for Jeunesse, Culture, Loisirs, Techniques, a voluntary agency working with children and young people, and has developed their research activities with a particular interest in comparative social work practice. He has written numerous publications on child protection and comparative child protection.

Rachael Hetherington, a former associate research fellow at Brunel University College in London, England, is currently an independent social work researcher and consultant. She has previously worked as a lecturer, a psychiatric social worker, and a Guardian ad Litem. As the former director of the Centre for Comparative Social Work Studies, Rachael has done extensive internationally comparative research and produced numerous publications in the field.

Catherine Love is a member of Te Atiawa, Taranaki, and Ngati Ruanui tribes of Aotearoa/New Zealand. She is active in community and tribal affairs, a member of the New Zealand Psychologists Board, and Director of Indigenous Research and Development in the School of Psychology, Victoria University of Wellington.

Deena Mandell is an associate professor of Social Work at Wilfrid Laurier University. Her research and writing have focused on divorced fathers and non-payment of child support, families coping with chronic health problems, Family Group Conferencing, the experiences of families and workers in the child welfare and mental health systems, and a review of the literature on the child welfare system and Aboriginal peoples of Canada. Dr Mandell's experience as a practitioner in the community includes family services, outpatient mental health, inpatient hospital services, direct service with individuals, families and groups, program development, and professional development education.

Tracey Nurse is a child protection coordinator at Nottingham City Social Services, Nottingham, England.

Patricia Schene has been working in the field of children and family services for twenty-five years as a state administrator, private agency director, researcher, writer, and educator. Since 1995, she has been working independently as a consultant in children and family services as well as writing articles and presenting in national forums. Patricia has had a leadership role in defining and implementing policy changes at the state level, definition and measurement outcomes in child welfare, risk assessment, national data system development, curriculum development, building community collaboratives to protect children, and helping jurisdictions design and implement systems of differential response to reports of child maltreatment.

Karen Swift received her PhD in social work from University of Toronto, and is currently an associate professor at the School of Social Work, York University. She has written extensively about the history and structure of Canadian child welfare. She has also participated in an international roundtable with European and North American scholars to explore and compare child welfare approaches and systems. Her most recent research project addresses the implications of risk assessment procedures for front-line social workers, for families who are investigated, and for the Canadian child welfare system.

A.W.M. Veldkamp is a family therapist and lawyer specializing in the field of child (sexual) abuse and neglect. For four years he has managed his own training and consultancy firm, carrying out research, training professionals, and providing consultation for professional agencies, as well as local, regional, and state authorities. Ton has authored numerous publications in the Netherlands and his current research is focused on state interference in families from an international perspective.